Pro Apache XML

Poornachandra Sarang, Ph.D.

Apress®

Lead Editor: Jason Gilmore
Technical Reviewer: Lalitha Sanatkumar
Editorial Board: Steve Anglin, Ewan Buckingham, Gary Cornell, Jason Gilmore, Jonathan Gennick,
    Jonathan Hassell, James Huddleston, Chris Mills, Matthew Moodie, Dominic Shakeshaft,
    Jim Sumser, Keir Thomas, Matt Wade
Project Manager: Richard Dal Porto
Copy Edit Manager: Nicole LeClerc
Copy Editor: Sharon Wilkey
Assistant Production Director: Kari Brooks-Copony
Production Editor: Janet Vail
Compositor: Linda Weidemann, Wolf Creek Press
Proofreader: April Eddy
Indexer: Valerie Perry
Artist: April Milne
Cover Designer: Kurt Krames
Manufacturing Director: Tom Debolski

For information on translations, please contact Apress directly at 2560 Ninth Street, Suite 219, Berkeley, CA 94710. Phone 510-549-5930, fax 510-549-5939, e-mail info@apress.com, or visit http://www.apress.com.

The source code for this book is available to readers at http://www.apress.com in the Source Code section.

To my mother, Shobha

Contents at a Glance

Contents

About the Author

DR. POORNACHANDRA SARANG, one of the leading software architects in the industry, has more than 20 years of IT experience and provides consulting on the architecture and design of IT solutions to worldwide clients. He has taught at the University of Notre Dame and is currently an adjunct professor in the Department of Computer Science at the University of Mumbai in India. Fond of open source technologies and Java, Dr. Sarang has successfully completed several industry projects on these and other platforms. He is a regular speaker at many international events. Dr. Sarang has several journal articles and research papers to his credit and has also coauthored several books, including *Professional Apache 2.0* and *Professional Open Source Web Services* (Wrox Press, 2002).

About the Technical Reviewer

MS. LALITHA SANATKUMAR has been in the field of Information Technology for over three decades and has worked in a variety of environments, from mainframes to desktop systems, assembly languages to Java. She holds a master's degree in operations research and is also a Certified Information Systems Security Professional (CISSP). She has worked on technology applications in the fields of financial markets, banking, e-governance, health-care systems, textiles, and the chemical industry. She has also conducted training programs and seminars on a variety of topics. She is currently working on a web multimedia presentation of classical works in the Sanskrit language.

Acknowledgments

I would like to acknowledge the efforts of Pradeep Shinde in helping me test all applications in this book on both Windows and Linux platforms. I thank Vijay Jadhav, who provided valuable assistance in formatting the manuscript. I am indebted to the technical reviewer, Lalitha Sanatkumar, who constantly provided valuable suggestions for improving the technical content and who performed rigorous testing of all code examples. My sincere thanks to the entire Apress editorial team, without whose efforts this book would not have been possible. I would like to mention a few names of those on the editorial team with whom I had direct interactions throughout the writing of this book. I thank Jason Gilmore for providing valuable tips during the entire editing process; this helped improve the quality of the book. I thank Sharon Wilkey, from whom I learned several English grammar tips during the copyediting process. I would like to thank Janet Vail for her support during the book's production stage. Finally, I am grateful to Richard Dal Porto for providing excellent coordination and management during the entire project life cycle.

Introduction

In recent years, open source technologies have gained wide acceptance in the industry, as has XML. If you want to create XML-based applications by using powerful and tested open source technologies, this book is for you.

The Apache Software Foundation (http://www.apache.org/) has played a particularly important role in spearheading the adoption of these XML-focused open source technologies due to its oversight of several key projects. This book provides comprehensive coverage of many of these projects.

The book begins with an introduction to XML—defining XML syntax, its structure, and several fundamental concepts such as the Document Type Definition (DTD) and XML schema.

Chapter 2 covers various XML parsing techniques. It covers both SAX and DOM APIs and Apache's implementation of them in the Xerces project. Apache also provides XML data binding techniques in their XMLBeans project, and this chapter covers the XMLBeans implementation.

Chapter 3 introduces you to today's widely accepted and most popular web application architecture: web services. Here you will learn the web services architecture and its three important components, SOAP, WSDL, and UDDI.

Chapter 4 introduces you to Apache's implementation of the SOAP API. You will learn to create web services by using this implementation. The chapter discusses the creation of both RPC- and Document-style web services. You will learn to develop client applications for these web services. You will also study the structure of SOAP request and response messages.

Chapter 5 introduces you to yet another important feature of XML: XSL transformations. XSL allows you to transform an XML document from one format to another. XSL is a language that defines such transformations. You will learn how to use XSL to transform XML documents via both command-line utilities and Java applications.

Chapter 6 takes you a step further in XSL transformations by covering the Apache XSL-FO project, which defines a way to transform XML documents into a device-specific format for rendering content on a specific output device. You will learn the use of command-line tools and a programmatic approach for performing such transformations.

Chapter 7 discusses the popular web development framework: Apache Cocoon. Cocoon uses an easily configurable pipeline architecture for processing web clients' requests. The pipeline uses pluggable components for the various stages of processing. This chapter provides thorough coverage of this architecture and teaches you to define processing pipelines for your web applications.

Being text-based, XML can be a cause for concern among developers interested in transferring XML-based data over otherwise unsecure networks. Chapter 8 covers security principles and Apache's XML-Security project to teach you how to implement security in your XML applications.

XML-dependent organizations soon amass a large number of XML documents that need to be organized for quick and easy access. The Apache Xindice project defines a way to organize XML documents. Chapter 9 introduces this project.

Finally, any software project needs documentation. The Apache Forrest project provides a framework for creating documentation for your software projects. Forrest is also used for creating extensible websites. Chapter 10 shows you how to use Forrest to create a website containing dynamic content.

This book uses a brokerage case study to illustrate the usefulness of the various Apache projects. The code examples in each chapter are based on this brokerage theme.

This book can help you master the development of XML-based web applications by using several open source projects.

Preface

Recent years have seen tremendous acceptance of both XML and open source technologies in the IT industry. Apache developed several projects that use XML extensively. However, most of the Apache projects are documented primarily for programmers and carry very little documentation for novices. It becomes extremely difficult for a beginner or an intermediate user to use these projects in their applications without the availability of adequate code examples. This book tries to bridge this gap by bringing together important Apache projects that are useful for developing XML applications along with documentation and ample code examples on each project.

The general impression in the industry is that Apache projects necessarily require use of the Linux operating system. Thus, most books on Apache are written around Linux. However, Apache projects support the Windows operating system and run equally well on Windows. Although all of the examples in this book are developed on Windows, the applications are Java based. Because Java is a platform-neutral language, all the applications could run on both operating systems without any code modifications; what differs is only the software installation for each project. These differences are minor and typically involve only setting the path and other environment variables. For those who use Linux, I have included an appendix that describes the software installation for each chapter.

The book uses a stock brokerage theme to describe the XML-based application development. This gives you a near real-life application development perspective.

CHAPTER 1

■■■

XML

In today's world, electronic data transfer has become an important aspect of our everyday life. When you withdraw money from an ATM, make credit card purchases, pay your utility bills on the Web, look up a news channel for current world happenings, look up an online map for driving directions, and so on, the data flows in electronic format between various applications. These applications have been developed by different vendors at different times without any prior agreement on the format of data transfers.

Many companies have set up their own standards for communication with business partners. These are generally binary based, not human-readable, and require extra effort to implement. These communication protocols never became world standards because of their complexities. What people really wanted was a standard that everybody across the globe would accept as a common protocol for data transport. That's where Extensible Markup Language (XML) was born. XML solves most of the problems faced in the existing protocols of data transport.

XML is rapidly becoming the de facto industry standard for data transport. Nowadays XML is used everywhere: for setting your application configurations, transporting data across machines, storing data in databases, invoking business methods on remote servers, and so on. These days you will hardly find any recently developed application that does not use XML.

Thus, with the widespread use of XML in software applications, you need to learn how to create, process, and successfully use XML documents for data interchange. This chapter gives you a brief overview of XML, its syntax, and namespaces. You'll also be introduced to the Document Type Definition (DTD) and XML Schema standards, which play a key role in creating valid XML documents. You'll begin by first understanding the need for XML.

Why Use XML?

The Web is heavily based on the use of HyperText Markup Language (HTML). HTML defines several tags—for example, <h1>, <h2>, and <body>—that describe how to render the document's contents on the browser. However, these tag elements do not usually convey any meaning about the data embedded in the document but instead just describe how the data should be presented. XML solves this problem by allowing the document creator to devise meaningful tag names that express the purpose of the embedded data rather than how it should be presented.

XML offers several benefits to the user:

- *XML simplifies data interchange*: A readily-available third-party tool can be used to transform an XML document into any other standard format. This makes it easy to exchange data between various organizations or within several departments in an organization.

- *XML is extensible*: Because new tags can be created by anybody, the language itself is easily extensible and is not restricted to the use of limited tags (as in the case of HTML). There is no restriction on the number of tags you create. Such tags can be defined in a document definition against which the documents can be validated. The document definition can be reused to create multiple documents having the same structure.

- *XML is text based*: This makes XML documents easily human-readable.

- *XML tags are meaningful*: Because there is no restriction on the length of the tag name, the designer can create tags that convey to other users the meaning of the encapsulated data. For example, you can create tags called Heading1 and Heading2 in place of the standard HTML tags h1 and h2. Similarly, you can create tags called catalog, bookAuthor, zipcode, and more. These tag names are generally self-explanatory to human readers.

- *XML can penetrate firewalls*: Because XML is text based and corporate firewalls are usually opened for text-based HTML documents, XML documents can penetrate corporate firewalls. An XML document can encapsulate a remote procedure call, making it possible to invoke remote methods on servers. This makes it easy to integrate applications deployed on diverse platforms and technologies.

- *XML enables smart searches*: Because XML documents can be structured to identify every piece of information that they represent, you can create smart searches on XML documents. For example, an XML document that stores an inventory of computer parts can be easily searched for the presence or the quantity of a particular part because the document tags typically refer to fields such as part name or part quantity.

What Is XML?

Extensible Markup Language (XML) is a specification created and maintained by the World Wide Web Consortium (W3C, http://www.w3c.org), an organization focused on the promotion of interoperability standards for the Web. Derived from its more complicated predecessor, Standard Generalized Markup Language (SGML), XML is optimized for the definition, exchange, validation, and interpretation of data used for a variety of applications.

Like HTML, XML relies on a set of tags in order to describe a document. However, whereas HTML is constrained to a fixed set of tags, XML is extensible and allows document creators to devise their own tags to describe the information contained therein. For instance, consider the XML document shown in Listing 1-1.

Listing 1-1. *A Sample XML Document*

```xml
<?xml version="1.0" encoding="UTF-8"?>
<catalog>
  <product>
    <name>
      Shampoo
    </name>
    <price>
      $5.50
    </price>
  </product>
  <product>
    <name>
      HairTonic
    </name>
    <price>
      $10.25
    </price>
  </product>
</catalog>
```

All statements in this listing use nonstandard tags—except the first statement, which is common to all XML documents. For example, catalog, product, name, and price are nonstandard tags.

As seen in Listing 1-1, an XML document consists of the following two components:

- *Data that makes up the content:* For example, Shampoo and HairTonic are the data items that describe the product names, and $5.50 and $10.25 represent the corresponding product prices.

- *Meta information about data:* The meta information is also called *markup*. This markup describes the document structure. The catalog, product, name, and price specify the meta information in Listing 1-1.

The meaningful names used for this markup make it easier for the human reader to interpret the document contents. Looking at Listing 1-1, a person can easily deduce that this document refers to a product catalog listing two products, Shampoo and HairTonic. You can easily deduce the price of each item by looking up the data enclosed in the price tag.

XML Syntax

Although XML allows you to create your own tags, it follows stricter rules of document formatting than HTML. The syntax rules for XML documents are discussed in this section.

XML Documents Are Text Based

XML documents contain only human-readable text characters. This gives the benefit of easy interpretation by humans and also the advantage of penetrating corporate firewalls. The disadvantage of being text based is that such documents could turn out to be much longer than corresponding documents based on binary standards. Typically, an XML document may be four to five times larger than its corresponding binary version. This results in larger bandwidth requirements during transmission and more storage space on your hard drive and databases.

XML Is Case Sensitive

The markup, or metadata, in XML is case sensitive. Thus, the tag names Catalog and catalog are considered distinct. Similarly, productPrice and ProductPrice would be considered distinct. Because the data embedded within elements is not interpreted by XML parsers,[1] this need not be case sensitive.

XML Restricts the Use of Certain Characters

XML tags use angle brackets (> and < symbols) for enclosing tag names. Thus, these characters cannot appear in the element data. If you want to include these symbols in your data, you must use replacement character sequences. Table 1-1 lists all special characters and their corresponding replacement character sequences in XML.

Table 1-1. *XML Representation of Special Characters*

Special Character	Replacement
&	&amp;
'	&apos;
"	&quot;
<	&lt;
>	&gt;

Because these special characters are used in meta information, if you include them in your text contents, the parser will try to interpret them as a part of the markup, resulting in an error. Say you would like to include the following string in your data:

```
This is <servlet> tag
```

This string must be written as follows in your XML document:

```
This is &lt;servlet&gt; tag
```

The parser will now interpret this correctly and produce the desired output.

Likewise, if you decide to include the string Tom&Jerry in your contents, you will need to specify it as Tom&Jerry. When the document is rendered or interpreted, it will convert this string to Tom&Jerry as desired.

---

1. XML parsers are discussed in Chapter 2.

XML Documents Begin with an XML Declaration

An XML document typically begins with the following line of code, although (as per the XML specification) it is not mandatory:

```
<?xml version="1.0" encoding="UTF-8"?>
```

This indicates that the current document is an XML document, and is formally referred to as the *XML declaration*. The xml element uses optional attributes that indicate the version and the encoding used by the document contents.

XML Documents Are Marked by Using Elements

An entire XML document consists of markups specified by several elements. The element in an XML document is specified by using the following syntax:

```
<elementName attribute=value … >
```

The markup starts with an opening angle bracket (<) and closes with a closing angle bracket (>). Within the bracket, elementName appears first. This is mandatory. This is followed by one or more optional attribute/value pairs. The following line defines an element called article with one attribute named type. The value assigned to type is journal:

```
<article type="journal">
```

Every Element Has a Start and an End Tag

An element declaration begins with <elementName>. Each element declaration must end with a corresponding end tag.

The end tag for an element is specified by prefixing the element name with a forward slash. The following code fragment declares an element called article that is properly closed with the corresponding end tag </article>:

```
<article type="journal">
    Indigo Architecture - an overview
</article>
```

Between the start and end tags, you write the content (data) that the element represents.

Every XML Document Must Start with a Root Element

The first element in an XML document is treated as its root element. The remaining elements of the document are arranged in a tree structure under this root.

Elements in an XML Document Can Be Nested

An XML document typically consists of several element declarations. The document starts with a root element, and all other elements appear under this root. The element declarations can be nested; however, you must observe proper scoping while nesting the elements. A partial overlap during nesting is not permitted.

The following example shows a properly nested XML document:

```
<article>
  <articleData>
    <title>
      Introduction to EJB 3.0
    </title>
    <author>
      John Dhvorak
    </author>
  </articleData>
</article>
```

The following example depicts an improper nesting of elements:

```
<article>
  <articleData>
    <title>
      Introduction to EJB 3.0
    <author>
    </title>
      John Dhvorak
    </author>
  </articleData>
</article>
```

Note the start of the author element; it starts before the title element is closed. The XML parsers[2] and validators recognize the nesting errors and will flag such documents as invalid when they process it.

An Element Can Be Empty

An empty element does not contain any data. The following example declares an empty element called br. In your XML document, you will declare an empty element as follows:

```
<br> </br>
```

An empty element can also be specified as follows:

```
<br/>
```

An XML Document Can Contain User-Written Comments

A comment starts with the character sequence <!-- and closes with the character sequence -->. The text between these character sequences is ignored by XML parsers and is generally useful only to human readers. The following example shows a comment declaration:

```
<!-- This is a Comment -->
```

---

2. XML parsers are discussed in Chapter 2.

CDATA Encloses Data That Should Not Be Interpreted by Parsers

Sometimes you may want to include data containing valid XML elements in your XML documents. However, you may not want the parser to interpret this data. This is achieved by using the CDATA element, as illustrated in Listing 1-2.

Listing 1-2. *Use of the* CDATA *Element in an XML Document*

```
<?xml version="1.0" encoding="UTF-8"?>
<articles>
  <article>
    <articleData>
    <![CDATA[
      <title>EJB Programming</title>
      <author>Dr. John</author>
    ]]>
    </articleData>
  </article>
</articles>
```

In this example, title and author elements enclosed in the CDATA section will not be interpreted by parsers.

XML Namespaces

As seen in the previous paragraphs, XML allows you to create your own tags. To represent a customer address, you could create elements such as customer, street, zipcode, and so forth. Because these are generic names, many other programmers in the world could use the same element names in their documents. However, these programmers could assign different meanings to these elements in their documents. Then, when the documents were exchanged, it would be difficult to deduce the correct meanings, especially given the likelihood that these documents would be interpreted by machines and not humans. To resolve this ambiguity in naming elements in an XML document, the concept of a namespace is introduced.

What Is a Namespace?

Your local machine can have more than one file with the same name. As long as these identically named files are stored in a distinct directory, there is no conflict, and the operating system will manage files with duplicate names by examining their full path. Thus, by adding a qualifying path string, the filenames are resolved without any ambiguity. The same concept is applied in XML by using a namespace.

A *namespace* is essentially a qualifying path for the element that you use in your documents. A namespace is declared by using an attribute/value pair as shown here:

```
xmlns:xmlbook="http://www.apress.com/2005/apache"
```

The namespace declaration uses the xmlns prefix. The xmlns is a prefix used only to declare namespace bindings and is by definition bound to the namespace name http://www.w3.org/2000/xmlns/.

The xmlns prefix is followed by a colon (:) and a name to be used as a short name for the Uniform Resource Identifier (URI) on the right-hand side of the expression. In the preceding example, the prefix name is xmlbook.

Note An XML namespace is identified by an Internationalized Resource Identifier (IRI) reference. IRIs contain URIs and certain additional characters (most Unicode characters from #xA0 onward). However, because work is currently in progress to define RFCs for IRIs, only URI references are used in the declarations.

The namespace name should be unique. After a namespace is declared as shown in the preceding example, you use it to qualify the elements in your document.

Note The prefix xml is by definition bound to the namespace name http://www.w3.org/XML/1998/namespace. All other prefixes beginning with the three-letter sequence x, m, l, in any case combination, are reserved.

Creating Fully Qualified Elements

Consider the following code fragment that declares a namespace called xmlbook. We use the xmlbook prefix to qualify the different elements belonging to this namespace:

```
<book xmlns:xmlbook="http://www.apress.com/2005/apache">
   ...
    <xmlbook:title>Pro Apache XML</xmlbook:title>
    <xmlbook:author>Poornachandra Sarang</xmlbook:author>
    <xmlbook:isbn>1-59059-641-2</xmlbook:isbn>
   ...
</book>
```

Now, even if another document uses element names such as title, author, or isbn, the elements in our document will be resolved correctly because they belong to a unique namespace prefixed by the short name xmlbook. Each element in the preceding document should be prefixed with the name xmlbook to resolve any naming ambiguities.

Creating Multiple Namespaces

Your organization could have several projects under development at the same time. If you create a single namespace to reference the elements required by all the projects, the list could become too long. In such a case, you could create a project namespace or even create multiple namespaces within a large project. This is equivalent to creating a directory hierarchy on your hard drive for organizing various files. How to create multiple namespaces is discussed in this section.

Just as you can create multiple folders on your hard drive to create several qualifying pathnames for your files, in XML you can create multiple namespaces. You declare multiple namespaces in your document as follows:

```
<book
  xmlns:mlbook="http://www.apress.com/2005/apache"
  xmlns:javabook="http://www.apress.com/2005/java"
  xmlns:netbook="http://www.apress.com/2005/net" >
```

The preceding example creates three namespaces called mlbook, javabook, and netbook. You can now include the following declarations in your document:

```
<mlbook:title>
  Apache XML Programmer's Guide
</mlbook:title>
<mlbook:author>
  Poornachandra Sarang
</mlbook:author>
<javabook:title>
  Java Programmer's Guide
</javabook:title>
<javabook:author>
  James Gosling
</javabook:author>
<netbook:title>
  Programmer's heaven to .NET
</netbook:title>
<netbook:author>
  Bill Gates
</netbook:author>
```

Although in the preceding example title and author elements in all three namespaces contain similar data and have the same constraints, nothing prevents you from assigning an altogether different data type for each of these elements. Thus, the meaning of each element will differ depending on the namespace it belongs to.

A namespace can contain any element names. For example, the namespace javabook can contain a definition for an element called BookAuthor in addition to the definition for an author element. The use of namespaces just ensures that even if anybody else in the world uses the same name while defining an element, your element will be resolved properly by the parser because the parser would use a fully qualified name for each element.

Consider another example using multiple namespaces:

```
<Limousine
  xmlns:midsize="http://www.toyota.com/car/2005/midsize"
  xmlns:luxury="http://www.toyota.com/car/2005/luxury">
<midsize:seats>
  Leather
</midsize:seats>
```

```
<luxury:stereo>
  Blapunkt
</luxury:stereo>
</Limousine>
```

This example declares two namespaces denoted by midsize and luxury prefixes. The midsize namespace contains an element called seats, and the luxury namespace contains an element called stereo. Because the luxury cars have extra fittings as compared to the midsize cars, we create a separate set of elements to specify these extra fittings. This additional set of elements can be organized in a separate luxury namespace.

The use of namespaces mandates you to prefix each element that is used in the document. Sometimes, this can be too much to type, if you are not a good typist. That is where the concept of a default namespace is introduced.

Using a Default Namespace

When you declare a namespace without a prefix, it is treated as the *default namespace* for the current document. The following statement declares a default namespace:

```
xmlns="http://java.sun.com/xml/ns/j2ee"
```

An element declared in the document without the use of a prefix will be treated as belonging to the default namespace. Consider the following code fragment that uses the preceding declared namespace:

```
<servlet>
  <name>
    MyServlet
  </name>
</servlet>
```

Both servlet and name elements are assumed to belong to the default namespace identified by the URI http://java.sun.com/xml/ns/j2ee.

Listing 1-3 provides another example of a default namespace, used by a web service.

Listing 1-3. *A Sample XML Document Using a Default Namespace*

```
<?xml version="1.0" encoding="utf-8" ?>
<configuration xmlns="http://schemas.microsoft.com/.NetConfiguration/v2.0">
  <system.serviceModel>
    <services>
      <service
          serviceType="abcom.BrokerageCalculatorService"
          behaviorConfiguration="BrokerageCalculatorServiceBehavior">
          <!-- use base address provided by host -->
          <endpoint address=""
              bindingSectionName="wsProfileBinding"
              bindingConfiguration="CalcBinding"
```

```
                    contractType="abcom.ICalculator, service"/>
        </service>
    </services>

    <bindings>
        <wsProfileBinding>
            <binding configurationName="CalcBinding" soapVersion="Soap12" />
        </wsProfileBinding>
    </bindings>

    <behaviors>
        <behavior
            configurationName="BrokerageCalculatorServiceBehavior"
            returnUnknownExceptionsAsFaults="True" >
        </behavior>
    </behaviors>

</system.serviceModel>

<system.web>
    <compilation debug="true" />
</system.web>

</configuration>
```

In the preceding document, configuration is the root element. The default namespace is specified by the URI http://schemas.microsoft.com/.NetConfiguration/v2.0. All the elements used in the document, such as service, bindings, behaviors, behavior, and so on, belong to this default namespace.

Using Both Default and Prefixed Namespaces

You can use both default and prefixed namespaces in the same document. The following example illustrates this:

```
<?xml version="1.0" encoding="UTF-8"?>
<web-app xmlns="http://java.sun.com/xml/ns/j2ee" version="2.4"
             xmlns:xsi="http://www.w3.org/2001/XMLSchema-instance"
             xsi:schemaLocation="http://java.sun.com/xml/ns/j2ee ➥
                  http://java.sun.com/xml/ns/j2ee/web-app_2_4.xsd">
    <display-name>books</display-name>
    <listener>
        <listener-class>listeners.ContextListener</listener-class>
    </listener>
```

```
<servlet>
  <display-name>books</display-name>
  <servlet-name>books</servlet-name>
  <jsp-file>/books.jspx</jsp-file>
</servlet>
...
</web-app>
```

Here the default namespace is specified by the URL http://java.sun.com/xml/ns/j2ee. The second namespace is named xsi and is specified by the URI http://www.w3.org/2001/XMLSchema-instance. The elements belonging to this namespace are prefixed with xsi. The schemaLocation attribute belongs to the xsi namespace, while the rest of the elements in the document do not use any prefix. Thus, all these elements belong to the default namespace.

Now that you have seen how to resolve the name conflict, your next task is to understand how to define different element types and the structure for the document. This is done with the help of DTDs and XML schemas. Both are explained in the following sections.

Document Type Definition

The *Document Type Definition (DTD)* consists of formalized definitions of all data elements found in an XML document. Given a DTD and corresponding XML document, it's possible to validate an XML document for correctness.

The following example shows a sample DTD specified as a part of an XML document:

```
<?xml version="1.0" encoding="us-ascii"?>
<!--
DTD for a simple "slide show".
-->
<!ELEMENT slideshow (slide+)>
<!ELEMENT slide (title, item*)>
<!ELEMENT title (#PCDATA)>
<!ELEMENT item (#PCDATA | item)* >
```

The DTD defines elements called slideshow, slide, title, and item. The definition also shows the subelements, the number of allowed occurrences of these subelements, the data type, and other characteristics for each element. In this section, you will learn how to create a DTD and then how to include one in your documents. You will also see some of the drawbacks of DTDs.

Writing a DTD

An XML document consists of a collection of elements, with each element containing zero or more attribute/value pairs. The DTD defines the structure of these elements and attributes.

Writing Elements

To define an element, we use the following syntax:

```
<!ELEMENT element_name (child_element)>
```

The keyword ELEMENT marks the beginning of the element definition, and element_name specifies the name of the element. This name has to be unique within the given scope. An element can contain other elements (nesting of elements). These are called *child elements* of the current element. The child elements are specified in parentheses following the element name. Consider the code fragment from the earlier example:

```
<!ELEMENT slideshow (slide+)>
```

This statement declares an element called slideshow. The slideshow element contains a slide element. The plus sign (+) indicates that the subelement slide must appear at least one time within the slideshow element.

The child element containment is specified by an element content model. The containment rules of this model are listed next.

An Element Can Contain a Single Child Element

This rule indicates that there can be only one child element within the specified element. For example, the following declaration specifies that the slideshow element can contain only one child element, called slide:

```
<!ELEMENT slideshow (slide)>
```

An Element Can Contain More Than One Child Element

If an element contains more than one child element, a comma-delimited list of such child elements is specified in parentheses. Consider the following code fragment from our previous example:

```
<!ELEMENT slide (title, item)>
```

In this example, the slide element contains two elements, called title and item. The list also specifies the order in which the elements should appear within the slide element. Changing this order will make the document invalid. An element can be omitted in the document if it is declared optional in the definition. You will see how to create an optional element in the subsequent section.

An Element Can Be Empty

An element can be empty; this means that it does not contain any child elements.

The use of the keyword EMPTY indicates that the given element does not contain any child elements. Consider the following declaration:

```
<!ELEMENT slide (EMPTY)>
```

The statement indicates that the slide element should not contain any child elements, and an error will result if child elements are declared within the slide element.

You will declare a slide element based on the preceding definition in your XML document as follows:

```
<slide/>
```

or

```
<slide></slide>
```

An Element Can Contain Text Data

You may want to include character data in the element that should not be parsed by the parser. You do so by using the keyword (#PCDATA). The following statement declares an element called slide that contains character data that should not be parsed by the parser:

```
<!ELEMENT slide (#PCDATA)>
```

You can now declare the slide element in your XML document as follows:

```
<slide>
  This can contain any character data including valid XML statements
</slide>
```

An Element Can Contain Any Combination of Subelements

The ANY keyword specifies that the element can contain any combination of subelements. Listing 1-4 illustrates the use of the ANY keyword.

Listing 1-4. *Use of the* ANY *Keyword*

```
<?xml version="1.0" encoding="utf-8" ?>
<!DOCTYPE slideshow [
  <!ELEMENT slideshow (slide+)>
  <!ELEMENT slide ANY>
  <!ELEMENT subslide (#PCDATA)>
]>

<slideshow>
  <slide>
    This is slide data.
    <subslide>
      This is subslide data.
    </subslide>
  </slide>
</slideshow>
```

The XML document in Listing 1-4 includes a DTD at the beginning. The root element of the document is slideshow, as specified by the DOCTYPE keyword. The slideshow element contains one or more slide elements. A slide element can contain any combination of subelements, as indicated by the ANY keyword. In the current situation, the slide element can contain a subelement called subslide that contains any character data. Additionally, the slide element itself can contain any character data. In this case, the character data is specified by the string This is slide data.

As you have seen under the first containment rule, if you want to include the child element subslide within an element slide, you would write the following declaration:

```
<!ELEMENT slide (subslide)>
```

If you want to include only character data in the `slide` element, you would write the following declaration (refer to the earlier rule, "An Element Can Contain Text Data"):

```
<!ELEMENT slide (#PCDATA)>
```

If you want to include both child element and character data, you would use the ANY keyword as in the following declaration:

```
<!ELEMENT slide ANY>
```

An Element Can Contain Only Subelements Specified in a Choice List

To restrict the subelements within an element, you specify the list of desired subelements, each separated from the other with a pipe (|) character. Consider the following code fragment:

```
<!ELEMENT slide (subslideA|subslideB)>
```

The `slide` element can contain either a `subslideA` or `subslideB` element. The use of both elements within a single instance of the `slide` element will result in an error. Consider another example:

```
<!ELEMENT slide (#PCDATA|subslideA|subslideB)*>
```

In this case, the `slide` element can contain any character data or the child element `subslideA` or `subslideB`. The asterisk (*) indicates that the subelement can occur zero or many times, as discussed next.

Specifying Instance Quantities

The number of occurrences of each subelement can be specified in the definition of an element. By default the subelement must occur one and only one time. Table 1-2 lists the available options.

Table 1-2. *Instance Quantity Specifiers*

Symbol	Meaning
+	At least one time
*	Any number of times
?	At most one time

Quantity Specifier +

The quantity specifier + indicates that the subelement must occur at least one time.

Consider the following declaration:

```
<!ELEMENT slideshow (slide+)>
```

The statement declares an element called `slideshow` that contains at least one occurrence of the `slide` element. The `slideshow` element can contain multiple `slide` elements. Listing 1-5 illustrates the use of the quantity specifier +.

Listing 1-5. *A Sample XML File Using the Quantity Specifier +*

```
<?xml version="1.0" encoding="utf-8" ?>
<!DOCTYPE slideshow [
  <!ELEMENT slideshow (slide+)>
  <!ELEMENT slide (#PCDATA)>
]>

<slideshow>
  <slide>
    First Slide
  </slide>
  <slide>
    Second Slide
  </slide>
</slideshow>
```

Here slideshow must contain at least one slide. The example document in Listing 1-5 creates two instances of the slide element within the slideshow element.

Quantity Specifier *

In the following example, the element slide contains a subelement called item:

```
<!ELEMENT slide (item*)>
```

The element item can occur within the slide element multiple times or may not occur at all.

Quantity Specifier ?

In the following example, the subelement slide can occur at most one time within the slideshow element:

```
<!ELEMENT slideshow (slide?)>
```

An error will result if slide is included more than once in slideshow.

Writing Attributes

Instead of individually defining each attribute of a particular element, we specify them together in the attribute list for that element. For this we use the ATTLIST keyword.

The attributes are specified by using the following syntax:

```
<!ATTLIST elementname attrname attrtype defaultvalue>
```

The elementname represents the tag for which we are defining the attribute. The name of the attribute is specified by attrname. The attrtype can be any one of the values specified in Table 1-3.

Table 1-3. *List of Attribute Types*

Attribute Type	Meaning
CDATA	Character data with no markup
ID and IDREFID	A unique value that cannot be repeated anywhere in the document
NMTOKEN	Name token, the value of the attribute is intended to act as a name for the element
(choice1 | choice 2 | ...... | choice n)	Choice list

The defaultvalue specifies the additional characteristics of the attribute and can be one of the following:

- #Fixed default_value: Here the value specified by default_value is the only acceptable value for this attribute. Consider the following statement:

```
<!ATTLIST address country #PCDATA  #Fixed USA>
```

This statement declares a country attribute for the element address. The country attribute has the fixed value USA assigned to it. Assigning any other value results in an error.

- #Required: The use of the additional specifier #Required indicates that the value for this attribute must always be specified. Not specifying the attribute value will result in an error in this case.

- #Implied: The #Implied specifier indicates that the use of this attribute is implicit in the definition and thus the attribute need not be explicitly declared in the element instance.

Writing Entities

Entities allow you to create shorter names for long fragments of contents. For example, say that the word California occurs in your document several times. You can create a shorter name such as CA for this word by creating an entity as shown here:

```
<!ENTITY CA  "California">
```

Any occurrence of CA in your document will be replaced by the word California before the document is validated. The following code illustrates how to define and use an entity in your XML documents:

```
<!DOCTYPE travel [
  <!ELEMENT travel (word)>
  <!ELEMENT word ANY>
  <!ENTITY CA  "California">
]>
<travel>
  <word>
  &CA;
  </word>
</travel>
```

All the entities are resolved before the validation takes place. If you open the preceding document in Microsoft Internet Explorer, you will see the following output:

```
<?xml version="1.0" encoding="utf-8" ?>
<!DOCTYPE travel (View Source for full doctype...)>
<travel>
  <word>California</word>
</travel>
```

Including a DTD in a Document

Now you know how to create a DTD, the next task is to learn how to include it in your document. You include the DTD in your document so that your document structure can be validated against the structure defined in the DTD. There are two ways to include the DTD in your XML document: internal or external.

Internal

In an internal DTD, the DTD is placed directly in the XML document itself. Listing 1-6 illustrates an internal DTD.

Listing 1-6. *An XML Document Using an Internal DTD*

```
<?xml version="1.0"?>
<!DOCTYPE note [
  <!ELEMENT note (to,from,heading,body)>
  <!ELEMENT to (#PCDATA)>
  <!ELEMENT from (#PCDATA)>
  <!ELEMENT heading (#PCDATA)>
  <!ELEMENT body (#PCDATA)>
]>
<note>
  <to>Tove</to>
  <from>Jani</from>
  <heading>Reminder</heading>
  <body>Don't forget me this weekend!</body>
</note>
```

The code shown in bold contains the DTD, which starts with the character sequence <!DOCTYPE and ends with the character sequence]>. The rest of the XML document uses the element names defined in this DTD. The structure of the XML document will be validated against this DTD by validating parsers.[3]

---

3. Parsers are discussed in Chapter 2.

External

An external DTD is external to the XML document and resides in a separate file on the local or remote file system. A sample external DTD is shown in the following code:

```
<?xml version="1.0"?>
<!ELEMENT note (to,from,heading,body)>
<!ELEMENT to (#PCDATA)>
<!ELEMENT from (#PCDATA)>
<!ELEMENT heading (#PCDATA)>
<!ELEMENT body (#PCDATA)>
```

This is stored in a physical file called note.dtd. DTD files generally have the extension .dtd.

Referencing a Local DTD

If the preceding DTD file is available on a local system disk, you will create an XML document that uses this file as follows:

```
<?xml version="1.0"?>
<!DOCTYPE note SYSTEM "note.dtd">
<note>
  <to>Tove</to>
  <from>Jani</from>
  <heading>Reminder</heading>
  <body>Don't forget me this weekend!</body>
</note>
```

The line in bold shows the inclusion of note.dtd in the current document. We use the SYSTEM keyword to indicate that the DTD is available on the current system. If you do not specify the full path for the file, it is assumed to be present in the current folder. If the file exists in some other folder, you can specify either the relative or the full path of the file.

Referencing a Remote DTD

If the DTD is not available on the current system, it can be included in the XML document by using the URL reference, as illustrated in Listing 1-7.

Listing 1-7. *An XML Document Referencing a Remote DTD*

```
<?xml version="1.0"?>
<!DOCTYPE note PUBLIC "http://www.mydomain.com/dtd/booklist.dtd">
<note>
  <to>Tove</to>
  <from>Jani</from>
  <heading>Reminder</heading>
  <body>Don't forget me this weekend!</body>
</note>
```

We use the PUBLIC keyword to designate the URI reference to the external DTD.

Understanding DTD Drawbacks

As seen in the preceding examples, DTDs use Extended Backus-Naur Form (EBNF) notation for defining elements and attributes. This notation is somewhat cryptic and may not be easily interpreted by many people.

■**Note** The Backus-Naur Form (BNF) is a notation for writing the grammar of a context-free language. The Extended Backus-Naur Form (EBNF) adds the regular expression syntax of regular languages to the BNF notation. The documentation on this may be obtained from the International Organization for Standardization (http://www.iso.org).

DTDs have another major drawback: they do not provide any data validation and provide only the structure validation for the document.

The XML schemas discussed in the next section provide both structure and data validations.

XML Schema

An XML schema provides an alternative to a DTD for describing the document structure. Unlike a DTD, the schema itself is written in XML and is thus easily interpreted by humans. The schema is defined by using the format shown in Listing 1-8.

Listing 1-8. *Format for Defining XML Schemas*

```
<? xml version="1.0" encoding="UTF-8"?>
<xsd:schema xmlns:xsd="http://www.w3.org/2001/XMLSchema"
                elementFormDefault="qualified"
                attributeFormDefault="unqualified">
  <xsd:element name="ROOT_ELEMENT_OF_THE_XML_DOCUMENT">
  .
  .
    Element definition etc
  .
  .
  </xsd:element>
</xsd:schema>
```

The root element for this document is schema. This is prefixed by the xsd namespace. The xsd namespace designates the URI http://www.w3.org/2001/XMLSchema. Within the schema element, all its child elements are defined, starting with the definition of the root element.

In the preceding document, the root element is specified by the value of the ROOT_ELEMENT_ OF_THE_XML_DOCUMENT variable. All other element definitions follow the root element declaration.

Defining Elements

You define the elements in an XML schema by using following notation:

```
<xsd:element
  name="element_name"
  type="element_type"
/>
```

You use the element tag to begin the definition of an element. The name attribute specifies the name of the element, and the type attribute specifies its data type. The following statement illustrates how to define an element:

```
<xsd:element name="author" type="xsd:string"/>
```

The element that is defined in the preceding statement is called author. The data type for this element is of type string. Like string, there are several other primitive data types defined in the xsd namespace. If you do not specify the type, the default is taken as xsd:string type.

■**Note** A complete list of built-in data types can be found at http://www.w3.org/TR/2001/REC-xml➡ schema-2-20010502/#built-in-datatypes.

Defining Attributes

You define element attributes by using the following notation:

```
<xsd:attribute
  name="attribute_name"
  type="attribute_type"
/>
```

The attribute name is specified by the name attribute, and its data type is specified by the type attribute. Consider the following attribute definition:

```
<xsd:attribute name="first" type="xsd:string"/>
```

In this example, we define an attribute called first having the data type string.

Using Additional Specifiers

There are several additional specifiers that can be used while defining attributes. These are discussed here.

The optional Specifier

The optional specifier indicates that the inclusion of this attribute in an XML document is optional. Consider the following code fragment:

```
<xsd:element name= "competition" type="xsd:string">
<xsd:attribute name="race" type="xsd:string" use="optional"/>
</xsd:element>
```

Here, the element competition is declared to have one attribute called race. The data type for the attribute is string, and its use is optional. Thus, the following statements in an XML document based on the preceding definition would be valid:

```
<competition>
  2005 World Championship
</competition>
<competition race= "horse">
  2005 Horse Race Championship
</competition>
```

Note the second instance of competition declares the attribute race and assigns the value horse to it.

The required Specifier

The required specifier indicates that the corresponding attribute must be defined in the XML document wherever the concerned element is instantiated. The following code segment defines a race attribute for the competition element with the required specifier:

```
<xsd:element name= "competition" type="xsd:string">
<xsd:attribute name="race" type="xsd:string" use="required"/>
</xsd:element>
```

The value for race must be specified in the instance of the competition element; otherwise, the parser or the document validator will flag this as an error.

The default Specifier

You use the default specifier to specify the default value for the attribute. The following statement defines an attribute called domain of type string that has a default value of com:

```
<xsd:element name= "URL" type= "xsd:string">
<xsd:attribute name="domain" type="xsd:string" default="com"/>
</xsd:element>
```

Consider the following XML declaration based on the preceding definition:

```
<URL domain= "org">
  http://www.appress.com
</URL>
```

The element URL defines an attribute called domain with the value org. Note that in this case we do not assign a default value to the domain attribute. Now, consider the following code fragment:

```
<URL>
  http://www.appress.com
</URL>
```

In this case, we do not explicitly declare the domain attribute in the URL element. The implicitly created domain attribute would take the default value of com.

The fixed Specifier

The fixed attribute is used for specifying a fixed value for the attribute. Assigning any other value to the attribute results in an error. You declare the fixed value as follows:

```
<xsd:attribute name="country" type="xsd:string" fixed="US"/>
```

In this example, the country attribute has a fixed value of US. Assigning any other value to this attribute would result in making the document invalid.

The minOccurs and maxOccurs Specifiers

The minOccurs and maxOccurs specifiers specify the minimum and maximum occurrences of the attribute. Consider the following definition for the element articleList:

```
<xs:element name="articleList">
    <xs:complexType>
      <xs:sequence>
        <xs:element name="articleTitle" type="xs:string" minOccurs="1"➥
                                                         maxOccurs="10" />
      </xs:sequence>
    </xs:complexType>
  </xs:element>
```

The following XML code can be created based on the preceding definition:

```
<articleList ... >
  <articleTitle>Indigo - Architecture and Overview</articleTitle>
  <articleTitle>J2EE Web Services Architecture</articleTitle>
  <articleTitle>Open Source implementation of Web Services</articleTitle>
 </articleList>
```

This is a valid XML code fragment. It uses the attribute articleTitle three times in the definition of the articleList element. The minimum number of occurrences for articleTitle is one and the maximum is ten. Thus, three occurrences are within the specified range.

Annotating XML Schemas

Though XML documents are easily read by humans, sometimes you may want to add some annotation to the document. Such annotation is added by using annotation and documentation tags. You can annotate the entire schema and/or an individual element.

Annotating Schema

To annotate the entire schema, you add the annotation tag immediately after the
<xsd:schema> element as shown here:

```
<xsd:schema
     targetNamespace="http://www.appress.com/xml/book/apache"
     xmlns:xsd="http://www.w3.org/2001/XMLSchema"
     ... >
  <xsd:annotation>
    <xsd:documentation>
      Copyright Apress L.P. All rights reserved.
    </xsd:documentation>
  </xsd:annotation>
     ...
</xsd:schema>
```

You can add your comments under the documentation tag. These comments would per-
tain to the entire schema definition.

Annotating Elements

To annotate an element defined in the schema, you add the annotation tag immediately after
the element definition tag, as shown in the following example:

```
<xsd:element name="PersonalComputer">
  <xsd:complexType name="Memory">
    <xsd:annotation>
      <xsd:documentation>
          Specifies the type of memory
      </xsd:documentation>
    </xsd:annotation>
  </xsd:complexType>
</xsd:element>
```

Thus, each element defined in the schema can include its own comments.

Using Simple Data Types in XML Schemas

A schema definition supports two types of data: simple and complex. In this section, you'll
look at simple types. A discussion of complex types will follow.

A *simple type* of element contains only unstructured data. This is equivalent to primitive
data types in programming language grammar. An XML schema provides a rich set of simple
types. Some of the common predefined simple types are listed in Table 1-4.

Table 1-4. *Built-in Data Types*

Type	Description
xsd:string	Character string
xsd:date	Calendar date
xsd:time	Instance of time
xsd:decimal	Decimal number
xsd:Boolean	Boolean type

■**Note** The complete list of all simple types can be found at its source: http://www.w3.org/TR/2001/
REC-xmlschema-2-20010502/#built-in-datatypes.

The following XML code fragment illustrates the use of simple types:

```
<xsd:element name="publicationDate" type="xsd:date"/>
<xsd:element name="author" type="xsd:string"/>
```

Here the publicationDate element has a data type of date, and author has a data type of
string. You will create elements of this type in your XML document as follows:

```
<publicationDate>2006-01-01</publicationDate>
<author>"Poornachandra Sarang"</author>
```

Derived Types

You may also derive new data types from simple types. *Derived types* provide for type extensibility. The general syntax for derived types is given here:

```
<xsd:simpleType name="typeName">
  <xsd:restriction base="someSimpleType">
    Deriving Rule
  </xsd:restriction>
</xsd:simpleType>
```

Deriving Rule can be a string pattern, range of values, enumeration, and so on. The following examples illustrate the use of some of the deriving rules.

Using Patterns

You may want to restrict the user to a predefined format while entering element data. This is
achieved by extending the simple data types to create a derived type. For example, a telephone
number must be specified, say, in the format ###-#######, where # denotes a decimal number
between 0 and 9. You could then define an element called phone as follows:

```
<xsd:element name="phone">
  <xsd:simpleType>
    <xsd:restriction base="xsd:string">
      <xsd:pattern value="\d{3}-\d{7}"/>
    </xsd:restriction>
  </xsd:simpleType>
</xsd:element>
```

The data type for phone is a string type. The string value follows a pattern definition specified by the string "\d{3}-\d{7}". This indicates that the phone number must consist of three decimal digits followed by a hyphen that is then followed by seven decimal digits. If this pattern is not followed while entering the values for the phone number, the document is treated as invalid.

Note The complete list of patterns can be found at http://www.w3.org/TR/2001/REC-xml➥ schema-2-20010502/#built-in-datatypes.

Limiting String Length

State codes in the United States are restricted to a two-character length. This can be specified in the document definition as follows:

```
<xsd:element name="stateCode">
  <xsd:simpleType>
    <xsd:restriction base="xsd:string">
      <xsd:length value="2"/>
    </xsd:restriction>
  </xsd:simpleType>
</xsd:element>
```

Here we define an element called stateCode that is of string data type. The length of this string is restricted to two characters. Thus, IL, IN, CA, and VA will be valid stateCodes, whereas ILL, CAL, and so on will be invalid codes.

Restricting Numbers

You may want to restrict the number input to a certain width and precision. For example, weight measurements may be restricted to five digits, with two digits assigned for the precision. This can be achieved by creating a weight element defined as follows:

```
<xsd:element name="weight">
  <xsd:simpleType>
    <xsd:restriction base="xsd:decimal">
      <xsd:precision value="5"/>
      <xsd:scale value="2"/>
    </xsd:restriction>
  </xsd:simpleType>
</xsd:element>
```

Valid values for the weight would be 140.50, 50.35, and 20, whereas invalid values would be 100.125 and 1000.50.

Specifying Lists

You may sometimes want to specify a list of values to the element such as top gainers or losers in the stock market. The following code fragment illustrates how to specify the list of values for an element:

```
<xsd:element name="topGainers">
  <xsd:simpleType>
    <xsd:list base="xsd:string"/>
    <xsd:length value="5">
  </xsd:simpleType>
</xsd:element>
```

The topGainers element in the preceding definition can contain a list of five strings. The following XML declaration based on this definition is valid:

```
<topGainers>
  "IBM" "Microsoft" "GE" "ACCENTURE" "INFOSYS"
</topGainers>
```

Note The complete list of deriving rules can be found at http://www.w3.org/TR/2001/REC-xml➡ schema-2-20010502/#built-in-datatypes.

Named vs. Anonymous Types

You assign a name to a simpleType by adding the name attribute to its definition as shown here:

```
<xsd:simpleType name="USPhone">
```

If the data type is named, it can be used while defining other elements within the scope of such a definition. To extend the definition scope, we create such named data types outside the scope of any other element. Thus, the definition can be applied to all subsequent element definitions. This is illustrated in the following example:

```
<xsd:simpleType name="value">
  <xsd:restriction base="xsd:integer">
    <xsd:minInclusive value="15"/>
    <xsd:maxExclusive value="40"/>
  </xsd:restriction>
</xsd:simpleType>

<xsd:element name="PlayerAge" type="value"/>
<xsd:element name="RefereeAge" type="value"/>
```

The preceding example creates a simple type called value. The value is of integer type, and the minimum value that can be assigned to it is 15 and the maximum is 40. Because this simple type is named, its definition can be used while defining subsequent elements. The example creates two elements called PlayerAge and RefereeAge that use the value simple type as their data type.

Using Complex Types in XML Schemas

If you want to create empty elements, or elements having subelements, or elements having attributes, you will need to define them by using complexType.

The hierarchy for a complex type can be represented as follows:

- An empty element or
- Nonempty element
  - With text only
  - With elements only
  - Mixed (with text and elements)

Empty Complex Types

You have already seen the use of an empty element in our earlier examples—the <br/> element is an empty element. To define such an element in the XML schema, you use the following definition:

```
<xsd:complexType name = "br" >
  <xsd:complexContent>
  </xsd:complexContent>
</xsd:complexType>
```

The tag complexType defines the complex type element. The name for the complex type in this example is br. The complexContent tag defines the contents for the complex type, which in this case are not defined. To use the br element in your XML document, you would use one of the following declarations:

**
 </br>**

or

</br>

Nonempty Complex Types

As stated, a nonempty complex type can be a text-only element, or an element containing only subelements, or a mixture of both.

Text-Only Elements

The following example illustrates how to create a complex type element that can contain only text:

```
<xsd:complexType name="player">
  <xsd:simpleContent>
    <xsd:extension base="xsd:string">
      <xsd:attribute name="weight" type="xsd:string"/>
    </xsd:extension>
  </xsd:simpleContent>
</xsd:complexType>
```

Here we define a complex type called player. It contains a single attribute called weight of type string. We use simpleContent and extension tags to define this attribute. You use this element in your XML document as follows:

```
<player weight = "80" />
```

Here, we define the player element as having a weight attribute value of 80.

Elements-Only Complex Types

A complex type can contain other subelements. The order of occurrence of these subelements, whether they are mandatory, whether they have a fixed set of values, and so on, are controlled by the use of the following tags:

- sequence
- all
- choice
- group

The sequence Tag

You use sequences whenever you want to create a complex type that contains subelements in a certain strict order. Listing 1-9 illustrates the use of sequencing.

Listing 1-9. *Sequence of Subelements*

```
<xsd:element name="personinfo">
  <xsd:complexType>
    <xsd:sequence>
    <xsd:element name="name"/>
    <xsd:element name="address">
      <xsd:complexType>
        <xsd:sequence>
          <xsd:element name="street"/>
          <xsd:element name="city"/>
          <xsd:element name="zipcode"/>
        </xsd:sequence>
      </xsd:complexType>
    </xsd:element>
```

```
      <xsd:element name="phone"/>
      <xsd:element name="email"/>
      </xsd:sequence>
    </xsd:complexType>
</xsd:element>
```

Here, we define an element called personinfo. The personinfo element contains four subelements: name, address, phone, and email. Out of these four elements, the address element itself is a complex type element. The address element consists of street, city, and zipcode subelements. The order of each subelement is important and must be honored while using this personinfo element in your XML document. You declare a personinfo element in your XML document as follows:

```
<personinfo>
  <name>Samson Abel</name>
  <address>
    <street> "Carlson st" </street>
    <city> "Chicago" </city>
    <zipcode> "45655" </zipcode>
  </address>
  <phone> "312-444-5555" </phone>
  <email> "Samson@gmail.com" </email>
</personinfo>
```

Note Sequences can be nested or can contain choices or groups.

The xsd:all Tag

If you want to define a complex type that can contain subelements declared in any order, you use the all tag. Listing 1-10 shows the use of the all tag in the definition of the element called playerdetails.

Listing 1-10. *An XML Document Using the* all *Tag*

```
<xsd:element name="playerdetails">
<xsd:complexType>
  <xsd:all>
    <xsd:element name="name"/>
    <xsd:element name="age" type=xsd:decimal/>
    <xsd:element name="weight" type=xsd:decimal />
    <xsd:element name="height" type=xsd:decimal />
  </xsd:all>
</xsd:complexType>
</xsd:element>
```

The playerdetails element contains subelements called name, age, weight, and height. These subelements can be specified in any order while declaring the playerdetails element in your XML document. This is illustrated in the following code fragment:

```
<playerdetails>
  <name>"John Michell"</name>
  <weight>80</weight>
  <age>24</age>
  <height>145</height>
</playerdetails>

<playerdetails>
  <height>155</height>
  <name>"Michael Johnson"</name>
  <age>22</age>
  <weight>120</weight>
</playerdetails>
```

Note that the two instances use a different order for nested elements. In each case, the order in which the subelements occur also differs from the original order specified in the definition of the playerdetails element.

Note The subelements declared under the all tag can be only elements—and not sequences, choices, or groups.

The xsd:choice Tag

You use choice whenever you want to define a complex element that contains more than one subelement and allows the user to specify any one of them in its declaration. The following example illustrates the use of the choice tag:

```
<xsd:element name="student">
  <xsd:complexType>
    <xsd:choice>
      <xsd:element name="name"/>
      <xsd:element name="id" type=xsd:decimal />
    </xsd:choice>
  </xsd:complexType>
</xsd:element>
```

Here, the student element can be specified with the subelement value name or id. You declare student in your XML document as follows:

```
<student>
  name = "Sam Johnathan"
</student>
<student>
  id = 15
</student>
```

Note The choice element can consist of a group of elements defined by using another complex type within.

The xsd:group Tag

Sometimes you may want to group together a set of related elements and use this group in definitions of other elements. In this case, you use a group tag as illustrated in Listing 1-11.

Listing 1-11. *Using the group Tag*

```
<xsd:group name="PAN">
  <xsd:all>
    <xsd:element name="number"/>
    <xsd:element name="dateOfIssue">
  </xsd:all>
</xsd:group>

<xsd:element name="individual">
  <xsd:complexType>
    <xsd:sequence>
      <xsd:element name="name"/>
      <xsd:group ref="PAN"/>
    </xsd:sequence>
  </xsd:complexType>
</xsd:element>

<xsd:element name="corporation">
  <xsd:complexType>
    <xsd:sequence>
      <xsd:element name="name"/>
      <xsd:element name="dateOfIncorporation"/>
      <xsd:group ref="PAN"/>
    </xsd:sequence>
  </xsd:complexType>
</xsd:element>
```

Here we define a group by using the xsd:group tag. The group name is PAN. In India, the government issues a unique number called the Permanent Account Number (PAN) to taxpayers—both individuals and corporations. The PAN consists of a decimal number and the date of issue and may contain additional elements such as details of the issuing authority. Because this set of information is applicable to both individual and corporate taxpayers, we create a group and apply it to individual and corporate elements. The definitions of individual and corporate elements differ from each other in terms of the elements they contain, as seen in Listing 1-11.

The following code fragment shows the use of the group defined in Listing 1-11.

```
<individual>
  <name>Smita Desai</name>
  <number>123-456-7890</number>
  <dateOfIssue>"1/1/2000"</dateOfIssue>
</individual>
<corporation>
  <name>Tata Consultancy Services</name>
  < dateOfIncorporation >"2/5/1990"</ dateOfIncorporation >
  <number>987-654-3210</number>
  <dateOfIssue>"5/8/1995"</dateOfIssue>
</corporation>
```

Note the use of group elements in both individual and corporation element declarations.

Mixed Elements

The use of the mixed attribute allows you to define a complex type that can contain text as well as the subelements within it. The following example illustrates the use of the mixed attribute in the definition of the complex type called text:

```
<xsd:complexType name="text" mixed="true">
  <xsd:all>
    <xsd:element name="bold"/>
    <xsd:element name="italic"/>
    <xsd:element name="underscore"/>
    <xsd:element name="strikethrough"/>
  </xsd:all>
</xsd:complexType>
```

The text element contains bold, italic, underscore, and strikethrough elements. The text can also contain any text (character string) in its declaration. The following code fragment illustrates the use of the text element in an XML document:

```
<text>
  The text may contain
  <bold>bold </bold>
  <italic>italic</italic>
  <underscore>underscored</underscore>
```

```
and
<strikethrough>strikethrough</strikethrough>
words.
</text>
```

A document formatter could render the following output after appropriately interpreting the tags in the preceding declaration:

The text may contain **bold,** *italic,* <u>underscored,</u> and ~~strikethrough~~ words.

Named and Anonymous Complex Types

Just as you created named and anonymous simple types, you can create named and anonymous complex types. If you want to use the complex type definition in other definitions, you name the complex type. If you want to use the definition immediately within its scope and not use it elsewhere, you create an anonymous type.

Named Complex Type

The following example illustrates how to create a named complex type:

```
<xsd:complexType name="height">
  <xsd:sequence>
    <xsd:element name="unit"/>
    <xsd:element name="value" type=xsd:decimal/>
  </xsd:sequence>
</xsd:complexType>
```

The name assigned to complexType is height and it contains two elements: unit and value. The element height now can be included in other definitions as illustrated here:

```
<xsd:element name="person">
<xsd:complexType>
  <xsd:sequence>
    <xsd:element name="name"/>
    <xsd:element name="personHeight" type=height/>
  </xsd:sequence>
</xsd:complexType>
</xsd:element>

<xsd:element name="building">
<xsd:complexType>
  <xsd:sequence>
    <xsd:element name="name"/>
    <xsd:element name="street"/>
    <xsd:element name="buildingHeight" type=height/>
  </xsd:sequence>
</xsd:complexType>
</xsd:element>
```

In the preceding example, both person and building elements use the complex type height. You can now create instances of person and building in your XML document as follows:

```
<person>
  <name>Lisa Ray</name>
  <personHeight>
    <unit>cms</unit>
    <value>136</value>
  </personHeight>
</person>

<building>
  <name>Washington Plaza</name>
  <street>"Washington St"</street>
  <buildingHeight>
    <unit>feet</unit>
    <value>50</value>
  </buildingHeight >
</building>
```

Anonymous Complex Type

In the preceding example, we created a height data type and used its definition in the person and building elements. However, if you do not want to reuse the height definition in multiple elements, you do not name it, thereby creating an anonymous data type. The following code snippet shows the definition of the person data type that uses the definition of the height data type from the previous example, but without naming it. The code marked in bold shows the definition of an anonymous complex type:

```
<xsd:element name="person">
  <xsd:complexType>
  <xsd:sequence>
    <xsd:element name="name"/>
    <xsd:complexType>
      <xsd:sequence>
        <xsd:element name="unit"/>
        <xsd:element name="value" type=xsd:decimal/>
      </xsd:sequence>
    </xsd:complexType>
  </xsd:sequence>
  </xsd:complexType>
</xsd:element>
```

You can now instantiate a person in your XML document as follows:

```
<person>
  <name>Lisa Ray</name>
  <unit>cms</unit>
  <value>136</value>
</person>
```

Including XML Schemas

After defining the schema, you need to add its reference to an XML document during its creation so that the validating parsers can validate your document against the definitions in the schema. You add a reference to the schema after the first line of the XML document and before the actual document content.

The schema definition can be specified by a file on the local system or as a URI reference.

Local System File Reference

The schema file can be stored on your local drive. Listing 1-12 illustrates how to reference a schema stored on the local file system.

Listing 1-12. *Referencing Schema from a Local File System*

```
<?xml version="1.0" encoding="UTF-8"?>
<articleList
        xmlns:xsi="http://www.w3.org/2001/XMLSchema-instance"
        xsi:noNamespaceSchemaLocation="C:\ArticleList.xsd">
  <article>
    ...
  </article>
</articleList>
```

This schema definition is stored in the file called ArticleList.xsd that is located in the root folder of drive C. The document structure is now validated against the structure defined in this schema by validating parsers.

URI Reference

A reference to the external schema file can also be specified by using a URI as shown in the following example:

```
<?xml version="1.0" encoding="UTF-8"?>
<web-app
        xmlns:xsi="http://www.w3.org/2001/XMLSchema-instance"
        xsi:schemaLocation=
        "http://java.sun.com/xml/ns/j2ee/web-app_2_4.xsd">
  <servlet>
    ...
  </servlet>
</web-app>
```

Here the schemaLocation attribute specifies the URI for the external schema. The current document will be validated against this schema definition by validating parsers.

Summary

XML has become a de facto industry standard for data interchange. XML is derived from SGML and offers several benefits over HTML. XML is human-readable, extensible, and allows smart searches. In this chapter, you studied the basic structure of an XML document.

In XML, tags are user defined. This can give rise to a conflict in tag names when the same tag names meaning different things are created by different users across the globe. Such name conflicts can be problematic, especially when the documents are interpreted by machines. The name conflicts in XML documents are resolved by introducing the concept of a namespace. Each tag name is associated with a namespace. The namespace itself is guaranteed to be unique because it is based on URI definitions. This chapter has discussed the importance and use of namespaces in XML documents.

The XML document follows certain document-formatting rules. We use DTDs to define the structure of an XML document. The structure of an XML document is validated against the structure defined in the DTD by validating parsers. You studied how to create DTDs in this chapter. DTDs carry a few drawbacks: they are not easily understood by humans because of their cryptic syntax and also do not provide any data validations.

The new standard for defining XML document structure is called an XML schema. The schemas are written in XML and thus are easily interpreted by humans. The schema provides both structure validations and data validations.

The schema allows the definition of simple and complex types. The simple types are useful for creating only unstructured data, whereas complex types allow you to create elements that contain structured data and empty elements. Both simple and complex types can be named or anonymous. You use named types if you want to reuse the definition in other element definitions. You can derive new types from both simple and complex types to extend their functionalities. After defining a schema, you can include it in the XML document by using a local file reference or a remote reference. This chapter has covered the schema definitions and its use to a sufficient depth.

In the next chapter, you will learn how to parse XML documents. You will see the various parsing techniques and their use in practical situations.

CHAPTER 2

■ ■ ■

XML Processing

As you learned in Chapter 1, XML offers an efficient and standardized mode for data transport. Accordingly, you can find XML support for many tasks, including managing configuration files, communicating customer data, and archiving data. Given such diversity, it is important that applications are able to properly interpret and manipulate XML files. That is where XML parsing techniques come into play. An XML parser accepts an XML document as its input and processes it to interpret the data that it contains. The parser may even manipulate the data and re-create yet another XML document for further use by another application.

In this chapter, you will learn about the need for XML parsing. You'll review a few practical applications where such techniques are used and then see the details of the three main XML parsing techniques.

Need for XML Parsing

When considering XML parsing, the following questions need to be answered:

- Why do I need to parse an XML document?

- Do I need a parser to extract data from an XML document?

- What parsing techniques are available to me?

- Are there any ready-to-use parsers available, and if so how do I get them?

- After parsing the document, can I convert it to some other form?

We will consider answers to all these questions in this section.

Understanding the Need for Parsing

As you learned in the previous chapter, XML documents are used in practically every application in the world today. Although these documents are often easily interpreted by humans, their true use lies in electronic processing and manipulation. This is accomplished with a *parser*, which is responsible for scanning the document, identifying the various elements in it, and making these elements and the data they contain available for further electronic processing.

Extracting Data by Using Parsers

An XML document consists of elements, attributes, and data. A typical XML document that describes a purchase order may contain elements such as PersonalComputer, Scanner, Printer, and so on. Each of these may contain subelements such as Quantity and Price. Listing 2-1 presents such a purchase order.

Listing 2-1. *A Sample Purchase Order*

```
<?xml version="1.0" encoding="utf-8" ?>
<PurchaseOrder>
  <PersonalComputer Type="Desktop">
    <Price>
      $995
    </Price>
    <Quantity>
      10
    </Quantity>
  </PersonalComputer>
  <PersonalComputer Type="Portable">
    <Price>
      $1295
    </Price>
    <Quantity>
      5
    </Quantity>
  </PersonalComputer>
  <Scanner Type="Desktop">
    <Price>
      $165
    </Price>
    <Quantity>
      2
    </Quantity>
  </Scanner>
  <Printer Type="Inkjet">
    <Price>
      $85
    </Price>
    <Quantity>
      4
    </Quantity>
  </Printer>
  <Printer Type="LaserPrinter">
    <Price>
      $485
    </Price>
```

```
    <Quantity>
      1
    </Quantity>
  </Printer>
</PurchaseOrder>
```

You may like to process the purchase order document to gather information about the number of personal computers, scanners, and printers ordered; their net purchase price; and the total purchase value of the order.

The XML document parser scans the purchase order to locate each of the aforementioned elements in the purchase document. It extracts the Quantity and Price element data for each of the ordered items and does the arithmetic to derive the net order value of each item and the gross value of the order. Thus, the XML parsers help in extracting data from XML documents for further processing.

Using Parsing Techniques

There are three major techniques available for XML parsing:

- *Simple API for XML (SAX)*: This is an event-based parsing. The parser generates an application event whenever it encounters an element or data in the document being parsed.

- *Document Object Model (DOM)*: In this model, the parser builds an in-memory structure for the entire document that is parsed. You can then traverse the memory tree structure to visit various nodes, examine their contents, modify their contents, and more.

- *XMLBeans*: In this technique, the document is mapped to Java classes that represent the document structure. The entire document instance can be created in memory by using this technique while retaining the original document structure in the image created in memory.

All three techniques are discussed in depth later in this chapter.

Obtaining Ready-to-Use Parsers

Based on the various techniques listed in the previous section, there are both commercial and open-source noncommercial parsers available for your use. Some of the popular parsers are listed here:

- The Apache Xerces project: http://xml.apache.org/dist/xerces-j/

- Microsoft XML parser: http://msdn.microsoft.com/xml

- The Expat XML parser: http://sourceforge.net/projects/expat/

Because this book is on Apache XML APIs, we will use the Apache Xerces parser in this chapter and all subsequent chapters.

Using XML Transformations

After parsing an XML document, it is possible to convert it to some other format. For example, to render an XML document on a browser, you will need to first convert it to HTML. This process is known as *XML transformation.* We use stylesheets to perform these conversions. Such transformations are called Extensible Stylesheet Language Transformations (XSLT).[1]

Practical Applications of XML Parsing

Before learning the details of the parsing techniques, you will explore a few applications where such techniques are practically used. This section describes a few practical scenarios in which XML parsing techniques are useful: a stock brokerage, a market survey application, and application configurations.

Stock Brokerage

Consider a stock brokerage that has many brokers as affiliates. In turn, each broker works with many clients. Figure 2-1 shows an infrastructure architectural diagram for our brokerage.

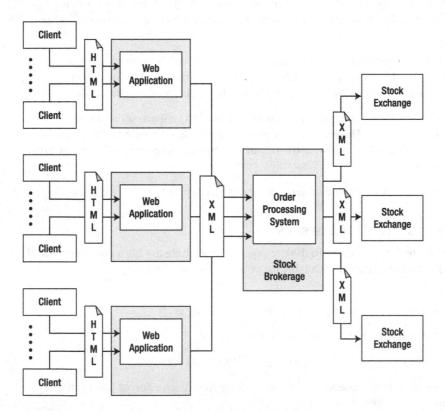

Figure 2-1. *Stock brokerage order application architecture*

---

1. XSLT is covered in depth in Chapter 5.

As Figure 2-1 illustrates, a client places an order with a broker by using a web-based interface. Such orders are typically placed by using HTML forms. The orders are placed over a secured channel using HTTPS.[2] Each broker web application validates the order and converts it to an XML format for further processing by our stock brokerage. Our stock brokerage is registered with stock exchanges—for example, the NYSE, NASDAQ, or AMEX.

The XML-based order is then dispatched over a channel that may be a public Internet channel or a secured proprietary channel. Upon receiving orders from the broker, an application controlled by the brokerage processes them for placement on various stock exchanges. For instance, prior to placement, each order must be validated for correctness. Furthermore, several orders possessing the same trade value may be consolidated in order to facilitate order placement. We might also consider validating the net value of orders from each broker against that broker's current credit limit.

Likewise, a considerable amount of processing may be performed on these XML documents in the order processing system at our stock brokerage. After processing the orders, the same order processing system may generate XML documents containing orders to be placed on a stock exchange such as the NYSE. Finally, these newly created XML order documents will be dispatched to the NYSE, which in turn would require internal processing to execute the order that may result in a trade.

As you can see, XML processing is required at various tiers. Some of the applications in this architecture simply parse the XML document to extract the data, and some applications generate new XML documents based on the parsed data.

Market Survey Application

Imagine an application that enables you to conduct a market survey for a particular company. You might design a multiple-choice questionnaire, with each question having a fixed set of answers. After collecting all the survey forms, you want to consolidate the results to find out how many participants answered A to the first question, how many answered C to the third question, and so on. A general architecture for implementing this solution is proposed in Figure 2-2.

In this application, each survey participant completes an HTML form presented within a web browser. After the required validations are completed, the data is converted into an XML document before being dispatched to the central processing application on a remote machine. The survey processing application processes each received document, consolidates the results, and generates a report by using its reporting tool. The report may be another XML document. The report can then be dispatched to a printer or local storage or another remote application for warehousing or further processing.

Again, you will notice that XML processing is required at each participating node in the entire architecture.

---

2. HyperText Transfer Protocol over SSL, or Secured HyperText Transport Protocol

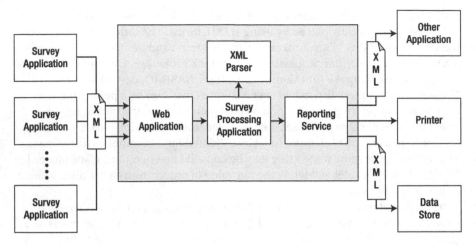

Figure 2-2. *Market survey system architecture*

Application Configurations

When developing and deploying a Java web or J2EE[3] application, the application configuration information is stored in an XML document. The application configuration may consist of the name of the servlet, its class name, initialization parameters, security access information, and other items. Similarly, an Enterprise JavaBeans (EJB) container's configuration information may consist of the name of the EJB object, its local and remote interfaces, home interface, implementation class, and so forth. A typical EJB configuration file is presented in Listing 2-2.

Listing 2-2. *A Typical EJB Deployment Configuration File*

```
<?xml version = "1.0" encoding = "UTF-8"?>

<ejb-jar xmlns = "http://java.sun.com/xml/ns/j2ee" version = "2.1"
         xmlns:xsi = "http://www.w3.org/2001/XMLSchema-instance"
         xsi:schemaLocation = "http://java.sun.com/xml/ns/j2ee
                               http://java.sun.com/xml/ns/j2ee/ejb-jar_2_1.xsd">
  <display-name>Car Rental</display-name>
  <enterprise-beans>
    <session>
      <display-name>ReservationAgentBean</display-name>
      <ejb-name>ReservationAgent</ejb-name>
      <home>samples.ejb.stateless.simple.ejb.CarRental</home>
      <remote>samples.ejb.stateless.simple.ejb.Reservation</remote>
      <ejb-class>samples.ejb.stateless.simple.ejb.ReservationAgent</ejb-class>
      <session-type>Stateless</session-type>
```

---

3. J2EE's latest version is now known as Java EE 5.

```
        <transaction-type>Bean</transaction-type>
        <security-identity>
          <use-caller-identity/>
        </security-identity>
      </session>
    </enterprise-beans>
</ejb-jar>
```

As you can see in Listing 2-2, the configuration file also contains information about transaction control, access permissions to various methods, and so on.

At the application level, another XML configuration file contains information about the application roles, mapping users to roles, references to resources required by the application at deployment time, and more. Thus, both web and EJB containers require a module for XML processing to understand the required application configuration before the application is deployed on the container.

Other Applications

I have listed only a few cases that illustrate the usefulness of XML processing. You will find many more applications in which XML processing is used. Thus, it is important for an application programmer to study the various XML processing techniques, which are covered in subsequent sections. First, however, you need to take a moment to examine how these techniques fit into the larger system architecture.

System Architecture for XML Processing

A typical client/server application exchanges data by using XML documents. The XML processing takes place at both client and server tiers. I will discuss the XML processing architecture with the help of the diagram in Figure 2-3.

A client sends a request, consisting of an XML document, to the business application server. The request may consist of invoking a method on the remote server or may contain some data for the server application's use. The request is encapsulated in an XML document as in the case of web services architecture.[4] For this, the business application must be exposed as a web service; the client sends a SOAP request (which is an XML document) to the business application server. The SOAP request contains information about the method to be invoked on the remote server and contains a message type that tells the server the format of the response expected by the client. The SOAP request may also encapsulate data to be processed by the remote application.

The messaging between the client and server is achieved with the help of Java APIs for XML Messaging (JAXM). The web services standard does not restrict you to use JAXM; you may use a messaging standard of your choice.

After the XML document is received by the server, the server will process the document by using any one or all three of the processing techniques, as depicted in Figure 2-3. After processing the document, the server may create a new XML document as a way of response. The response is dispatched back to the client with the help of JAXM. In web services architecture, such a response will be a SOAP response, which is once again an XML document.

---

4. Web services architecture is covered in Chapter 3.

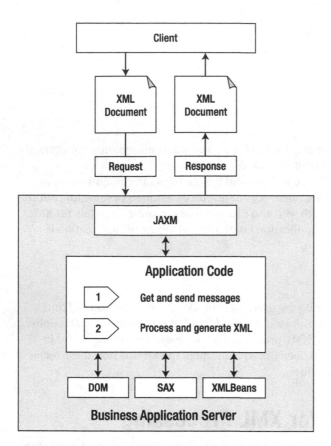

Figure 2-3. *XML processing system architecture*

Installing Software

To execute the applications in the following sections, you will need XML parsing libraries developed as a part of the Apache Xerces project. You can download Apache Xerces project code from the following URL: `http://xml.apache.org/xerces2-j/` or `http://archive.apache.org/dist/xml/xerces-j/`. After downloading the archive file, unzip it to the desired folder and follow the instructions to set up your environment.

Set the `XERCES_HOME` environment variable to the directory where you have installed Xerces and add `%XERCES_HOME%\bin` to your `PATH` variable. Also include the `xerces-api.jar` file in your classpath.

Note For those of you installing on Linux, Appendix A provides detailed installation instructions for all the chapters in this book.

Parsing with SAX

Simple API for XML (SAX) processing was developed by the members of the XML-DEV mailing list and does not have an official standards body. It is not maintained by the W3C or any other official body. However, SAX has become a de facto standard in the industry and is widely used by developers interested in XML parsing.

As its name indicates, SAX really is a simple API for processing XML documents. SAX is event based; as the document is processed, SAX generates events for the use of the processing application. Such events indicate the beginning of the document, the end of the document, each element occurrence, and so on. For example, referring to Listing 2-2, when the EJB configuration file is parsed, an event will be generated whenever the parser encounters an element such as <session> or <home>. Because the events are generated while the document is being parsed, you do not have to wait for the entire document to be read before processing occurs.

SAX Processing Model

Consider the sample XML program first presented in Chapter 1, reproduced here as Listing 2-3 for your convenience.

Listing 2-3. *A Sample XML Document*

```
<?xml version="1.0" encoding="UTF-8"?>
<catalog>
  <product>
    <name>
      Shampoo
    </name>
    <price>
      $5.50
    </price>
  </product>
  <product>
    <name>
      HairTonic
    </name>
    <price>
      $10.25
    </price>
  </product>
</catalog>
```

When this document is processed by a SAX parser, the following events will be generated:

■**Note** For brevity, all Characters events are not shown in the following output.

```
Start document
Start element (catalog)
Characters (white space)
Start element (product)
Start element (name)
Characters (Shampoo)
End element (name)
Start element (price)
Characters ($5.50)
End element (price)
End element (product)
Start element (product)
...
End element (product)
Characters (white space)
End element (catalog)
End document
```

In the beginning, a Start document event is generated, which indicates to the processing application that processing of the XML document has begun. Next, a Start element event is generated with the parameter value equal to catalog. This indicates to the processing application that the parser has encountered an element called catalog during its processing. Moving on, a Characters event is generated with a parameter value equal to white space, indicating that some white space was found in the document. In fact, whenever the parser encounters a white space in the document, it generates a Characters event. This may be too disturbing for the processing application. You can set the parser to ignore all white spaces. How to do this is discussed later. After the catalog element, the parser encounters the product element and once again generates a Start element event. This is followed by another Start element event for the name element. The name element contains character data. Thus, the parser generates the Characters event with the value Shampoo; these are the data contents of the name element. After this data, the parser encounters the end tag for the name element. Thus, it generates the End element event.

After the name element, the document contains the price element. The parser again generates the appropriate start and end element events and Characters event for the price element data. After the price element ends, the product element ends. This is indicated by the End element event with the product value.

After this, another product element starts. The sequence of events will be the same as the earlier product event. At the end of the product element, the parser encounters the end of the catalog element. It generates an End element to indicate this to the processing application.

At the end of the document, the End document event is generated, indicating to the application that the document processing is over.

As you can see, the SAX parser generates an event for each element or data encountered in the processed document.

Pros and Cons of SAX Processing

Being event based, SAX offers several benefits to its user. At the same time, it also comes with certain disadvantages. Both sides of this coin are presented in this section.

SAX presents four particularly compelling advantages, each of which is presented here:

- *Immediate analysis*: SAX generates the events continually while processing a document. The document analysis can begin immediately, and you need not wait to do the analysis until the entire document is processed. This is equivalent to streaming media, where the media contents are rendered immediately and you need not wait until the entire media is read.

- *Fewer constraints on memory requirements*: SAX examines the document contents as it reads the document and immediately generates events on the processing application. Thus, it need not store the data that it has already processed. This puts fewer constraints on the application memory requirements.

- *Easier processing of large documents*: Because the document's contents are not stored in memory, it is easier to process very large documents as compared to other processing techniques discussed later. Other techniques that require the entire document to be read into memory before processing can sometimes place severe constraints on system resources.

- *Faster processing*: The application need not process the entire document if it is interested in a certain criterion. After that criterion is met, further processing can be abandoned. Other techniques (discussed later in this chapter) require the document to be parsed fully before any processing can be done.

SAX does come with certain disadvantages:

- *No backward navigation*: SAX is akin to a one-pass compiler. After it reads part of the document, it cannot navigate backward to reread the data it has processed, unless you start all over again. Backward navigation is required while processing a purchase order such as the one in Listing 2-1. To get the gross purchase value for each type of item (printer or scanner, for example), you need to navigate the document back and forth several times. Backward navigation may also be required while processing the purchase order placed on our stock brokerage application, illustrated in Figure 2-1.

- *No data manipulation*: Because SAX does not store the data that it has processed, you cannot modify this data and store it back in the original document. In our stock brokerage example, a broker may modify the order placed by the customer before forwarding it to the stock brokerage. The broker may also add identity information along with the time of processing of the order. This is required for postauditing of orders. SAX will not be useful in such applications.

- *No document creation*: Because SAX does not create an in-memory document structure, you cannot build an XML document by using a SAX parser. In our stock brokerage example, I mentioned that the stock brokerage may create a consolidated order to place it on the NYSE. Thus, the processing application should be able to build an XML document dynamically from scratch. Again, SAX cannot be used in such cases.

SAX Processing Model Architecture

The SAX implementation provides several classes for flexible, extensible processing based on the SAX model. Figure 2-4 presents the SAX processing model architecture.

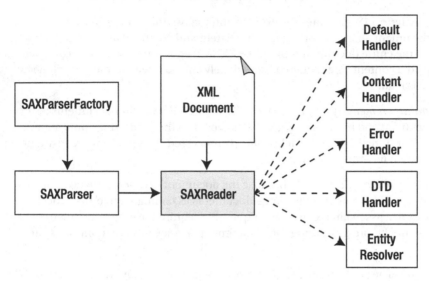

Figure 2-4. *SAX processing model architecture*

At the heart of the architecture, the SAXReader class is responsible for processing a given XML document. SAXReader obtains its input for parsing from the specified XML document. We associate an instance of the SAXParser class to SAXReader. The SAXParser object is created by using the SAXParserFactory instance. SAXParser is pluggable, and you can easily choose from several parsers, maybe from different vendors.

The SAXReader class also has many pluggable event handlers associated with it, several of which are available by default. For example, ErrorHandler is responsible for error processing, and DTDHandler handles DTD processing. DefaultHandler includes the implementations of both ContentHandler and ErrorHandler methods and also others. You can extend DefaultHandler to override the existing functionality or to provide additional functionality. You can write your own custom handler for handling events. The handlers are pluggable, and the SAXReader can use any such custom handlers.

During processing, SAXReader will generate events in your application to be handled by your event handlers. You are responsible for providing any desired business processing in these handlers.

Document Processing Using SAX

Now that you understand the SAX processing model and the pros and cons of SAX, you are ready to look at the steps used in processing a document and how to code these steps.

SAX processing incorporates the following steps:

1. Create an event handler.

2. Create the SAX parser.

3. Parse the document.

4. Process the document data.

To illustrate these steps, we'll create an application. Consider the stock brokerage application presented earlier in the chapter. Our stock brokerage receives orders from various brokers. Such orders are created as XML documents. We will write a console application to process the order documents. To begin, we'll determine the number of customers who have placed their orders through an order document. Next, we will determine the number of trade requests for the specified stock, and last we will determine the gross trade quantity for all buy/sell trades requested for the specified stock.

We will first consider the structure of this purchase order.

Sample Document Structure

Listing 2-4 shows the sample purchase order document.

Listing 2-4. `Orders.xml` *Stock Purchase Order* (Ch02\src\Orders.xml)

```xml
<?xml version="1.0" encoding="utf-8" ?>
<Orders>
  <Customer ID="C001">
    <StockSymbol>
      MSFT
      <Quantity>
      200
      </Quantity>
      <TradeType>
      B
      </TradeType>
    </StockSymbol>
  </Customer>
      ...
  <Customer ID="C004">
    <StockSymbol>
      MSFT
      <Quantity>
      150
      </Quantity>
      <TradeType>
      B
      </TradeType>
    </StockSymbol>
```

```
    <StockSymbol>
      IBM
      <Quantity>
        150
      </Quantity>
      <TradeType>
        S
      </TradeType>
    </StockSymbol>
  </Customer>
      ...
</Orders>
```

Note Listing 2-4 gives only the partial purchase order document. The complete listing of `Orders.xml` (`Ch02\src\Orders.xml`) is available from the Source Code area of the Apress website (`http://www.apress.com`).

Each broker uses this format to place orders with the stock brokerage. The `Orders` element is the root element of our purchase document. The document contains orders from several customers. Each customer is identified by an `ID` attribute and can place orders for one or more buy/sell trades. Each trade is identified by the `StockSymbol` element, which contains text data indicating the stock symbol on which the trade is desired. The `StockSymbol` element contains `Quantity` and `TradeType` subelements. The `Quantity` element indicates the trade quantity, and `TradeType` specifies buy or sell.

Note In reality, such a purchase order document would consist of many more fields. For example, each trade should also contain an indicative price at which trade is desired. I have excluded such additional elements to keep the document simple and facilitate your understanding of how to process an XML document by using SAX.

Application for Processing Purchase Order

We will write a console-based Java application to process the purchase order given in Listing 2-4. The application uses the SAX parsing technique. The full application code is given in Listing 2-5.

Listing 2-5. *Java Application for Processing Purchase Order* (Ch02\src\SAXExample1.java)

```
package apress.apacheXML.ch02;

import java.io.*;
import org.xml.sax.*;
import org.xml.sax.helpers.DefaultHandler;
import javax.xml.parsers.SAXParserFactory;
import javax.xml.parsers.ParserConfigurationException;
import javax.xml.parsers.SAXParser;

/**
  *This class implements SAX Parser
  */
public class SAXExample1 extends DefaultHandler {
  private int count=0;

  public static void main(String[] argv) {
    if (argv.length != 1) {
      System.err.println("Usage: SAXExample1 Filename");
      System.exit(1);
    }

    // Create an Object of the SAXExample1 class for SAX event handler
    SAXExample1 saxObject = new SAXExample1();

    // Create an object of SAXParserFactory for validating purpose.
    SAXParserFactory spfactory = SAXParserFactory.newInstance();

    try {
      // Parse the specified ".xml" file
      SAXParser saxParse = spfactory.newSAXParser();
      saxParse.parse(new File(argv[0]), saxObject);
    } catch (SAXParseException spExcept) {
      // Error generated while parsing
      System.out.println("\n** Error occurred while parsing **" + ", line " +
              spExcept.getLineNumber());
      System.out.println("   " + spExcept.getMessage());
    } catch (SAXException sExcept) {
      // Error generated while initializing the parser.
      Exception Except = sExcept;
        if (sExcept.getException() != null) {
          Except = sExcept.getException();
        }
        Except.printStackTrace();
      } catch (ParserConfigurationException pcExcept) {
```

```
      // Parser with specified options cannot be built
      pcExcept.printStackTrace();
    } catch (IOException ioExcept) {
      // I/O error
      ioExcept.printStackTrace();
    } catch (Throwable t) {
      t.printStackTrace();
    }
  System.exit(0);
}

/**
 * The parser calls this method whenever it encounters END of document
 */
public void endDocument() throws SAXException {
  System.out.println("\nNumber of Customers: "+ count);
}

/**
 * The parser calls this method whenever it encounters START of element
 */
public void startElement(String namespaceURI, String simpleName,
        String qualifiedName, Attributes attributeList) throws SAXException {
  if (qualifiedName.equals("Customer"))
    count++;
}

/**
 * This overrides the default Error Handler.
 */
public void error(SAXParseException spExcept) throws SAXParseException {
  throw spExcept;
}
}
```

The various classes required for SAX parsing are defined in the org.xml.sax, org.xml.sax. helpers, and javax.xml.parsers packages. You need to import these packages in your code to use the SAX parser.

Creating a SAX Parser

We create a SAX parser instance by first instantiating the SAXParserFactory class. This class cannot be directly instantiated because the class does not provide a public constructor. We obtain its instance by calling its newInstance static method:

```
SAXParserFactory spfactory = SAXParserFactory.newInstance();
```

Next, we call the newSAXParser method on the created factory instance to create an instance of the parser:

```
SAXParser saxParse = spfactory.newSAXParser();
```

At this stage, we will have an instance of the parser available and referred by the saxParse variable. The property org.xml.sax.driver in our environment decides the parser class to be used for instantiation. While running the application, we can specify this property on the command line as follows:

```
java -Dorg.xml.sax.driver=org.apache.xerces.jaxp.SAXParserFactoryImpl SAXExample1
```

Extending the Event Handler

As you learned earlier in this section, SAX provides default implementations for several event handlers. The built-in DefaultHandler provides implementations for both ContentHandler and ErrorHandler. Thus, we simply need to extend our class from DefaultHandler to provide event handling code in our application:

```
public class SAXExample1 extends DefaultHandler
```

The class SAXExample1 extends from DefaultHandler. This is going to be our main application class. We will create a console application to process the document file given in Listing 2-4. As the DefaultHandler class implements all the event handling methods with a null implementation body, we need to override only those event handling methods in which we are interested.

To determine the number of customers who have placed orders in the current order document, we simply count the number of occurrences of the Customer element. For this, we override the startElement method as shown here:

```
/* The parser calls this method whenever it encounters an element in the
   parsed document. The method receives the namespace, simple name,
   qualified name and list of attributes as parameters.
*/
public void startElement(String namespaceURI, String simpleName,
        String qualifiedName, Attributes attributeList) throws SAXException {
    if (qualifiedName.equals("Customer"))
        count++;
}
```

The startElement method receives four parameters and throws SAXException. All the event handling methods are required to throw SAXException.

We compare the qualifiedName parameter value to the Customer string. If this matches, we increment a class variable called count. Thus, every time the parser encounters the Customer element, the event handler will increment the count variable. At the document end, the count variable will hold the count for the total number of occurrences of the Customer element.

To print the total count at the end of processing, we need to override the endDocument method as follows:

```
/* The parser calls this method when it encounters an end of document being
    processed */
public void endDocument() throws SAXException
{
  // Print the count value on the user console
  System.out.println("\nNumber of Customers: "+ count);
}
```

The endDocument method simply prints the count value on the user console.

We do not need to override other event handling methods to accomplish our task of counting the total number of customers who have placed orders in the current document.

Parsing a Document

After we create an event handler and an instance of the parser, we can start parsing the XML document by calling the parse method on the parser:

```
SAXExample1 saxObject = new SAXExample1();
saxParse.parse(new File(argv[0]), saxObject);
```

The parse method takes two arguments. The first argument specifies the name of the file to be parsed. In our application, the name of the file to be parsed is specified as the first parameter on the command line. The second parameter to the parse method specifies the instance of the event handler. Remember, we extended SAXExample1 from the DefaultHandler class. Thus, we instantiate the SAXExample1 class and pass its instance as the second parameter to the parse method.

Processing Document Data

After the parsing begins with the invocation of the parse method, the parser keeps calling the event handler for each occurrence of a node in your document. For instance, in our example, the startElement method of the ContentHandler is overridden. The parser calls this method whenever it encounters a new element in the document:

```
/* The parser calls this method whenever it encounters an element in the
    parsed document. The method receives the namespace, simple name,
    qualified name and list of attributes as parameters.
*/
public void startElement(String namespaceURI, String simpleName,
        String qualifiedName, Attributes attributeList) throws SAXException {
  if (qualifiedName.equals("Customer"))
     count++;
}
```

The startElement event handler method keeps incrementing the count for every occurrence of the Customer element.

When the file is fully parsed, the endDocument event handler is called, in which we print the count value on the user console:

```java
public void endDocument() throws SAXException
{
    System.out.println("\nNumber of Customers: "+ count);
}
```

The events that are not overridden by our application code will use the default handler that does nothing.

Providing Error Handling

Our program must catch several parsing errors while parsing the document. This is illustrated in the following code snippet:

```java
try
{
    SAXParser saxParse = spfactory.newSAXParser();
    saxParse.parse(new File(argv[0]), saxObject);
}
catch (SAXParseException spExcept) {...}
catch (SAXException sExcept) {...}
catch (ParserConfigurationException pcExcept) {...}
catch (IOException ioExcept) {...}
catch (Throwable t) {...}
```

Note that the actual event handling code in the catch block is not shown here. SAXParseException encapsulates an XML parse error or warning, and contains information for locating the error in the original XML document. SAXParseException inherits from SAXException. SAXException contains basic error or warning information from either the XML parser or the application. ParserConfigurationException details the configuration errors.

Running the Application

Compile the source SAXExample1.java by using the following command line:

```
C:\<working folder>\ch02\src>javac -d . SAXExample1.java
```

Run the application by using the following command line:

```
C:\<working folder>\ch02\src>java apress.apacheXML.ch02.SAXExample1 Orders.xml
```

When you run this application on the sample XML document that is provided in the download folder, you will see the following output:

```
Number of Customers: 6
```

Note The full source code for this application (Ch02\src\SAXExample1.java) can be downloaded from the Source Code area of the Apress website (http://www.apress.com).

Extending Application Functionality

We will now extend the functionality of our application to determine the number of trade orders and the total trade quantity for the specified stock.

We'll begin by copying SAXExample1.java to SAXExample2.java and adding more functionality to the existing code. The complete code for SAXExample2 is given in Listing 2-6.

Listing 2-6. *Application That Counts Number of Trades and Total Trade Quantity* (Ch02\src\SAXExample2.java)

```java
package apress.apacheXML.ch02;

import java.io.*;
import org.xml.sax.*;
import org.xml.sax.helpers.DefaultHandler;
import javax.xml.parsers.SAXParserFactory;
import javax.xml.parsers.ParserConfigurationException;
import javax.xml.parsers.SAXParser;

/**
 *This class implements SAX Parser
 */
public class SAXExample2 extends DefaultHandler {
  private int count=0;
  private int stockCount=0;
  private String stockSymbol;
  private boolean countQuantity;
  private boolean countSymbol;
  private long Quantity=0;

  public static void main(String[] argv) {
    if (argv.length != 2) {
      System.err.println("Usage: SAXExample2 Filename StockSymbol");
      System.exit(1);
    }

    // Create an Object of the SAXExample2 class for SAX event handler
    SAXExample2 saxObject = new SAXExample2();
    saxObject.stockSymbol = argv[1];

    // Create an object of SAXParserFactory for validationg purpose.
    SAXParserFactory spfactory = SAXParserFactory.newInstance();
```

```java
    try {
      // Parse the specified ".xml" file
      SAXParser saxParse = spfactory.newSAXParser();
      saxParse.parse(new File(argv[0]), saxObject);
      } catch (SAXParseException spExcept) {
        // Error generated while parsing
        System.out.println("\n** Error occurred while parsing **" + ", line " +
          spExcept.getLineNumber());
        System.out.println("   " + spExcept.getMessage());
      } catch (SAXException sExcept) {
        // Error generated while initializing the parser.
          Exception Except = sExcept;

          if (sExcept.getException() != null) {
            Except = sExcept.getException();
          }

          Except.printStackTrace();
      } catch (ParserConfigurationException pcExcept) {
        // Parser with specified options can't be built
        pcExcept.printStackTrace();
      } catch (IOException ioExcept) {
        // I/O error
        ioExcept.printStackTrace();
      } catch (Throwable t) {
        t.printStackTrace();
      }
      System.exit(0);
  }

/**
 * The parser calls this method whenever it encounters END of document
 */
public void endDocument() throws SAXException {
  // Print the desired information on the user console
  System.out.println("\nNumber of Customers: "+ count);
  System.out.println("Number of " + stockSymbol + " Orders: " + stockCount);
  System.out.println("Total Trade Quantity: " + Quantity);
}

/**
 * The parser calls this method whenever it encounters START of element
 */
```

```java
public void startElement
        (String namespaceURI, String simpleName, String  qualifiedName,
                Attributes attributeList) throws SAXException {
  if (qualifiedName.equals("Customer"))
    count++;
    // if the qualified name of the current element is Quantity set
    //counting true.
      if (qualifiedName.equals("Quantity"))
        countQuantity = true;
}

/**
 * The parser calls this method whenever it encounters the END of element
 */
public void endElement
  (String namespaceURI, String simpleName, String qualifiedName)
          throws SAXException {
  // if the current element is Quantity, reset both counting flags
  if (qualifiedName.equals("Quantity")) {
    countQuantity = false;
    countSymbol = false;
  }
}

/**
 * The parser calls this method whenever it encounters a character data
 * in the document being processed
 */
public void characters(char[] buff, int offset, int len) throws SAXException
{
  // retrieve the string
  String str = new String(buff, offset, len);
  str = str.trim();
  // check if character string matches the desired symbol string
  if (str.equals(stockSymbol)) {
    // set counting true
    countSymbol = true;
    // increment stock count
    stockCount++;
  }
  // if counting for quantity and symbol both are set true, add count
  // for quantity
  if (countQuantity && countSymbol) {
    Quantity += Integer.parseInt(str.trim());
    countQuantity = false;
  }
}
```

```
/**
 * This overrides the default Error Handler.
 */
public void error(SAXParseException spExcept) throws SAXParseException {
  throw spExcept;
}
}
```

We extend SAXExample2 from DefaultHandler as in the earlier case:

```
public class SAXExample2 extends DefaultHandler
```

The SAXExample2 application accepts two command-line parameters instead of one. The first parameter specifies the name of the XML file to be processed. The second parameter specifies the stock code on which the information is sought. We will print the number of trade orders and the total trade quantity for this stock code. The program copies the stock code from the second argument into a class variable called stockSymbol:

```
SAXExample2 saxObject = new SAXExample2();
saxObject.stockSymbol = argv[1];
```

We modify the startElement event handler to add the following code:

```
public void startElement(String namespaceURI, String simpleName,
        String qualifiedName, Attributes attributeList) throws SAXException
{
  if (qualifiedName.equals("Customer"))
    count++;
  // if the qualified name of the current element is Quantity set counting true.
  if (qualifiedName.equals("Quantity"))
    countQuantity = true;
}
```

We now check for the Quantity element. If it is found, we set the countQuantity Boolean variable to true. The true value on this variable indicates that the quantity value found as data under the Quantity element should be accumulated in the grand total variable.

We now override the characters method as follows:

```
/* The parser calls this method whenever it encounters character data
   in the document being processed
*/
 public void characters(char[] buff, int offset, int len)
        throws SAXException
{
    // retrieve the string
    String str = new String(buff, offset, len);
    str = str.trim();
```

```
      // check if character string matches the desired symbol string
      if (str.equals(stockSymbol))
        {
          // set counting true
          countSymbol = true;
          // increment stock count
          stockCount++;
        }
      // if counting for quantity and symbol both are set true, add count
      // for quantity
      if (countQuantity && countSymbol)
        {
          Quantity += Integer.parseInt(str.trim());
          countQuantity = false;
        }
  }
```

The characters method is an event handler that is called by the parser whenever it encounters the element data. Because the element data is always available in text format, the event handling method receives the character buffer, offset, and length as its parameters. Using these parameters, we construct a new String object str. We now compare the value of this str variable with the stock symbol that was received as the second command-line argument. If a match is found, we set the countSymbol Boolean variable to true to begin a quantity count on this symbol. We also increment the stockCount variable. The stockCount variable will track the number of trade orders for the specified stock.

The characters event handler is called for each and every element in the document that contains some data. Thus, for both StockSymbol and Quantity elements, the parser calls this method. In this method, we check whether both countQuantity and countSymbol variables are set to true. If so, we accumulate the current element data in the gross Quantity variable and reset the countQuantity flag.

We will also need to override the endElement method as follows:

```
/* The parser calls this method whenever it encounters the end of element */
public void endElement(String namespaceURI, String simpleName,
        String qualifiedName) throws SAXException
{
  // if the current element is Quantity, reset both counting flags
  if (qualifiedName.equals("Quantity"))
  {
    countQuantity = false;
    countSymbol = false;
  }
}
```

In this method, we look for the occurrence of the Quantity element. If it is found, we reset both the flags countQuantity and countSymbol.

Finally, we will modify our endDocument method as follows:

```
/* The parser calls this method whenever it encounters end of document */
public void endDocument() throws SAXException
{
    // Print the desired information on the user console
    System.out.println("\nNumber of Customers: "+ count);
    System.out.println("Number of " + stockSymbol + " Orders: " + stockCount);
    System.out.println("Total Trade Quantity: " + Quantity);
}
```

In this event handler, we print the stockCount variable that indicates the number of trade orders found for the specified stock. Note that such trade orders consist of both buy and sell orders. We also print the total trade quantity. Again, this includes quantities for both buy and sell orders.

When you run this application on the sample XML document that is provided in the download folder, you will see the following output:

```
Number of Customers: 6
Number of MSFT Orders: 5
Total Trade Quantity: 600
```

Note The full source for this application (Ch02\src\SAXExample2.java) can be downloaded from the Source Code area of the Apress website (http://www.apress.com).

SAX API

The previous section presented several examples of SAX processing. In this section, you will study some of the important SAX classes and interfaces.

The SAXParserFactory Class

This class provides a factory API that allows you to configure a SAX-based parser for your applications. Some of the important methods of this class are as follows:

- newInstance: This is the static method that returns a new instance of SAXParserFactory. You cannot instantiate the factory class directly by using the new operator because the class does not provide any public constructor. You need to call the newInstance method to obtain the factory object.

- newSAXParser: This method creates a new instance of the SAX parser by using the parameters in your installation's configuration file.

- setValidating: This method accepts one parameter and if set to true, it sets the validating parser for your application. The validating parser validates your input document against the specified schema to ensure that it conforms to the structure defined in the schema.

- setSchema: This method sets the XML schema to be used during parsing. The method is used for setting the XML schema dynamically in your application code. The document that is parsed after this method call will be validated against the schema set by this method call.

The SAXParser Class

This is an abstract class that wraps an XMLReader implementation class. You obtain a reference to this class by calling the newSAXParser method on the factory class.

The input to the parser can come from a variety of sources, such as InputStreams, Files, URLs, and SAX InputSources. You can open an InputStream on the document to be parsed and send the reference to it as an argument to the parse method of the parser. Instead of InputStream, you can pass an instance of the File class or a URL reference or a SAX InputSource as an argument to the parse method. The InputSource class defined in the org.xml.sax package provides a single input source for an XML entity. A single input source may be a byte stream and/or a character stream. It may also be a public or system identifier.

As this parser object parses the document, the handler methods will be called. Some of the important methods of the SAXParser class are as follows:

- parse: This is the most important method of this class. There are several overloaded parse methods that take different parameters, such as File, InputSource, InputStream, and uri. For each of the different input types, you also specify the handler to be used during parsing.

- getXMLReader: This method returns the XMLReader that is encapsulated by the implementation of this class.

- get/setProperty: These methods allow you to get and set the parser properties, such as the validating parser.

The XMLReader Interface

Implemented by the parser's driver, this interface is used for reading an XML document. The interface allows you to register an event handler for document processing. Some of the important methods of this interface follow:

- parse: There are two overloaded parse methods that take input from either an InputSource object or a String URI. The method parses the input source document and generates events in your handler. The method call is synchronous and does not return until the entire document is parsed or an exception occurs during parsing.

- setContentHandler: This method registers a content event handler. If the content event handler is not registered, all the content events during parsing will be ignored. It is possible to change the content handler in the middle of parsing. If a new content handler is registered during parsing, the parser will immediately use the new handler while processing the rest of the document.

- setDTDHandler: Like a content handler in the previous paragraph, this method registers a DTD handler. You use DTDHandler to report notation and unparsed entity declarations to the application. If the DTD handler is not registered, all DTD events are ignored. As with the content handler, it is possible to change the DTD handler during parsing. Because DTDs are supported only for maintaining backward compatibility (the new standard being XML schemas[5]), you may not be using this handler frequently in your applications.

- setEntityResolver: Like the previous two methods, setEntityResolver allows you to define an EntityResolver that can be changed during processing.

The DefaultHandler Class

This class provides a default implementation for all the callback methods defined in the following interfaces:

- ContentHandler: The class implementing this interface receives notifications on basic document-related events such as the start and end of elements and character data.

- ErrorHandler: This provides the basic interface for SAX error handlers. The SAX application implements this interface to provide customized error handling.

- DTDHandler: The class implementing this interface receives notification of basic DTD-related events.

- EntityResolver: This provides a basic interface for resolving entities. The SAX application implements this interface to provide customized handling for external entities.

You can use only the DefaultHandler in your application and override the desired methods from the four handler interfaces.

Some of the important methods of the DefaultHandler class are as follows:

- startDocument/endDocument: These are callback methods called by the parser whenever it encounters a start and end of a parsed document.

- startElement/endElement: These are callback methods called by the parser whenever it encounters a start and end of an element during parsing. The method receives the parameters that indicate the local and qualified name of the element.

- characters: This method receives notification of character data inside an element during parsing.

- processingInstruction: This method receives notification of a processing instruction during parsing.

DOM

In Chapter 1, you learned that a well-formed XML document consists of a hierarchy of nodes. The entire document can be arranged in a tree-like structure. *Document Object Model (DOM)* creates a tree representation of an XML document, describing the nodes and the relationship between them.

---

5. XML schemas are discussed in Chapter 1.

DOM is maintained by the W3C. The W3C recommendation, which is currently at Level 3, is an API that defines objects in an XML document. The API also defines methods and properties to access and manipulate these objects.

DOM Processing Model

When you process a document by using the DOM API, it builds an in-memory tree structure of nodes representing your document. A node can be an element, text, attribute, and so on. Consider the example document in Listing 2-3. If you process this by using the DOM API, you will have the in-memory structure shown in Figure 2-5 representing the document.

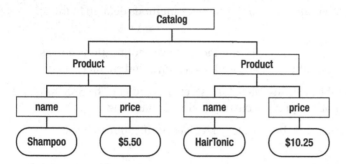

Figure 2-5. *DOM representation in memory*

Note For brevity, the diagram does not show all the document nodes.

At the root of the tree appears the catalog node. A catalog contains two child nodes of product type. Each product node, in turn, contains two nodes of name and price type. Each name and price node has a text node.

Because the entire document tree is available in memory, you can use the DOM API to navigate the tree, modify the document contents, and store the modified document into another XML file. You can also add nodes, delete nodes, add and delete attributes, and perform other tasks to the in-memory tree before you save the document tree to an external file.

Pros and Cons of DOM

Just as you have seen the pros and cons of using SAX, you will look at the advantages and disadvantages of DOM.

DOM offers the following advantages:

- *Bidirectional navigation*: Because the entire document is loaded in memory and arranged in a tree structure, it is possible to navigate the document tree in both backward and forward directions. Note that this was not possible with SAX, in which case you could move only forward. Bidirectional navigation is useful when you want to process XML documents such as the purchase order in Listing 2-1. While computing the gross purchase value of each of the items listed in the purchase order, you will need to move back and forth in the document several times.

- *Data manipulation*: As you visit each node in the built-in memory structure, you can easily modify the element data. The data you modify will be the in-memory copy of the document data. You can later serialize the modified data to an XML file. Once again, note that this was not possible with SAX. The purchase order of Listing 2-1 may require modifications of the quantity element during its approval by the senior management. In such cases, the DOM API will be useful in modifying the in-memory copy of the document and writing these changes back to a new XML document.

- *Structure creation and modification*: It is possible to add/delete nodes containing elements, attributes, and so on to the in-memory tree. You can even create a new independent tree structure. After a tree is built in memory, it can be saved to an external file as an XML document. Again, this is not possible with SAX. Considering again our purchase order example of Listing 2-1, the approving authority may like to add a few comments to the document before returning it to the originator. Using the DOM API, you can add nodes to the document. The approving authority may disapprove purchases of certain items listed in the purchase order. This can be done by deleting nodes in the in-memory document.

- *XML document creation*: After manipulating data in an existing tree or after creating an altogether new tree structure, the memory contents can be easily serialized to an XML document. Thus, your application can programmatically create an XML document.

- *Manipulation of partial trees*: You may manipulate only a part of the entire tree and serialize it to an external XML file, thus creating a subset of a large XML document.

Like SAX, DOM also comes with certain disadvantages:

- *Resource intensive*: DOM is resource-hungry. Because the entire document is read into memory, it can take up a huge amount of memory resources, especially when large documents are parsed using the DOM API. Therefore, using DOM on large documents is not recommended. What is "large" is determined by your system resources.

- *Increased processing time and power*: Building the in-memory tree for the entire document may require substantial processing time and CPU power. SAX is faster because it keeps processing the document while reading it. When using DOM, you cannot process the document until the entire tree structure is built in the memory.

- *Not suited for large documents*: Because of the aforementioned disadvantages, DOM is not suitable for processing large documents. For processing large documents, SAX provides a better alternative.

Document Processing Using DOM

Now you are ready to look at the steps for processing a document when using DOM and how to code those steps. DOM processing uses the following steps:

1. Create the instance of the DocumentBuilderFactory class.

2. Create the instance of the DocumentBuilder class.

3. Parse the document.

Creating the DocumentBuilderFactory Class Instance

You obtain an instance of DocumentBuilderFactory by calling its static newInstance method:

```
DocumentBuilderFactory dbf = DocumentBuilderFactory.newInstance();
```

Before you create a parser by using the created factory, you can set a few parameters for customizing parser operations. For example, the following line of code will make the parser ignore the white space within the element contents:

```
dbf.setIgnoringElementContentWhitespace(true);
```

You might also request that the parser validate the document by calling the setValidating method on the factory object, as shown here:

```
dbf.setValidating(true);
```

The default value for validation is false, so you need to set this to true by using the preceding call, if you want the parser to validate your document.

For setting the parser properties, the factory class provides four other methods: setIgnoringComments, setCoalescing, setExpandEntityReferences, and setNamespaceAware. They provide the functionality suggested by their names. For example, calling setIgnoringComments instructs the parser to ignore comments in the input document. The setCoalescing method determines whether the parser turns CDATA nodes into text, and merges them with surrounding text nodes. You can refer to the API documentation[6] for an explanation of the remaining methods.

Creating the DocumentBuilder Class Instance

You obtain the instance of the DocumentBuilder class by calling the newDocumentBuilder method on the factory object:

```
DocumentBuilder db = dbf.newDocumentBuilder();
```

You use the document builder for parsing the document.

---

6. http://java.sun.com/j2se/1.5.0/docs/api/javax/xml/parsers/DocumentBuilderFactory.html

Parsing the Document

You parse the document by calling the parse method on the DocumentBuilder object. The method takes a File object as a parameter:

```
Document doc = db.parse(new File (fileName));
```

The method returns a Document object. This refers to the document root and is used as a starting reference to traverse the entire document tree.

To better illustrate these steps, we will write an application. We will use the Orders.xml file from Listing 2-4 and process it by using the DOM API. First, we will write an application that counts the total number of customers who have placed an order in the current order document. Next, we will modify this application so that it allows us to change a sell order to a buy order for a specified customer.

Application for Counting Number of Customers

We will write an application that counts the total number of customers in our Orders.xml document. The full application code is given in Listing 2-7.

Listing 2-7. *Application That Uses DOM Parsing Technique* (Ch02\src\DOMExample1.java)

```java
package apress.apacheXML.ch02;

import java.io.*;
import org.w3c.dom.*;
import org.xml.sax.*;     // DOM parser uses SAX methods

import javax.xml.parsers.DocumentBuilderFactory;
import javax.xml.parsers.DocumentBuilder;

public class DOMExample1 {
  static private int count=0;
  public static void main(String[] args) {
    if (args.length != 1) {
      System.err.println("Usage: DOMExample1 Filename");
      System.exit(1);
    }

    Document doc = BuildTree(args[0]);
      if (doc != null)
        getElement(doc);
        System.out.println("Number of Customers: " + count);
  }

  /**
  * The BuildTree method parses the received document and creates an
  in-memory instance.
  */
```

```java
public static Document BuildTree(String fileName) {
    Document doc;
      try {
        // Obtain Factory instance
        DocumentBuilderFactory dbf = DocumentBuilderFactory.newInstance();
        // Request parser to ignore white space in the document
        dbf.setIgnoringElementContentWhitespace(true);
        // Obtain DocumentBuilder instance from the factory object
        DocumentBuilder db = dbf.newDocumentBuilder();
        // Parse the input file
        doc = db.parse(new File(fileName));
        // return reference to the root node
        return doc;
      } catch (Exception ex) {
        ex.printStackTrace();
      }
    return null;
}

/**
* The getElement method receives a node reference as an argument and traverses
* the tree recursively taking this reference as the tree root.
*/
public static void getElement(Node node) {
    // the null value indicates that you have reached a leaf node
    if (node == null) { return; }
      // Increment the count if the node is of type Customer.
      if(node.getNodeName().equals("Customer"))
        count++;
      // Look for children of the current node
      NodeList children = node.getChildNodes();
      // for each child call the function recursively to visit nodes of each child.
        for (int i = 0; i < children.getLength(); i++)
          getElement(children.item(i));
    }
}
```

The required classes for DOM processing are defined in the org.w3c.dom package. The DOM internally uses SAX, and thus you need to include the org.xml.sax package:

```java
import org.w3c.dom.*;
import org.xml.sax.*;    // DOM parser uses SAX methods
```

The main function receives a command-line parameter that identifies the order document to be processed. It calls the BuildTree method to parse and build an in-memory DOM. On successfully building the tree, it calls the getElement method that counts the number of occurrences of the Customer element in the memory tree.

Building DOM in Memory

The BuildTree method builds the in-memory tree structure representing the input document and returns a reference to the root node of the document. It first creates the factory object, then obtains a DocumentBuilder, and finally uses this builder to construct an in-memory DOM:

```
/* The BuildTree method parses the received document and creates an
   in-memory instance.
*/
public static Document BuildTree(String fileName) {
  Document doc;
  try {
    // Obtain Factory instance
    DocumentBuilderFactory dbf = DocumentBuilderFactory.newInstance();
    // Request parser to ignore white space in the document
    dbf.setIgnoringElementContentWhitespace(true);
    // Obtain DocumentBuilder instance from the factory object
    DocumentBuilder db = dbf.newDocumentBuilder();
    // Parse the input file
    doc = db.parse(new File(fileName));
    // return reference to the root node
    return doc;
    } catch (Exception ex) {
    ex.printStackTrace();
  }
  return null;
}
```

Processing Data

In our application, we want to determine the number of customers who have placed their orders in the current order document. For this, we will write a method called getElement that traverses the tree recursively to count the number of times the Customer element is encountered. The method definition is shown here:

```
/*
The getElement method receives a node reference as an argument and traverses
the tree recursively taking this reference as the tree root.
*/
public static void getElement(Node node)
{
    // the null value indicates that you have reached a leaf node
    if (node == null) { return; }
    // Increment the count if the node is of type Customer.
    if(node.getNodeName().equals("Customer"))
      count++;
    // Look for children of the current node
    NodeList children = node.getChildNodes();
```

```
// for each child call the function recursively to visit nodes of each child.
   for (int i = 0; i < children.getLength(); i++)
       getElement(children.item(i));
}
```

The method visits each node in the document until there are no more nodes, as indicated by a null reference. The node name is retrieved by calling the getNodeName method on the node object. We compare this with the name Customer, and if a match is found, we increment our counter. The program retrieves the child nodes of a given node by calling the getChildNodes method on it. It then iterates through all the child nodes and its children recursively by calling the getElement method with the new node value.

The main function now simply calls the preceding getElement method by passing the document reference to it:

```
getElement(doc);
```

Note that doc refers to the root element. When the method completes, the count will contain the number of occurrences of the Customer element in the entire document. We print this number on the user console:

```
System.out.println ("Number of Customers: " + count);
```

Providing Error Handling

While processing the document, you will need to catch several exceptions that may occur due to errors during processing. You can catch the exceptions as illustrated in the following code snippet:

```
try
{
  DocumentBuilderFactory dbf = DocumentBuilderFactory.newInstance();
  DocumentBuilder db = dbf.newDocumentBuilder();
  doc = db.parse(File);
}
catch (javax.xml.parsers.ParserConfigurationException pce) {...}
catch (java.io.IOException ie) {...}
catch (org.xml.sax.SAXException se) {...}
catch (java.lang.IllegalArgumentException ae) {...}
  ...
```

As in the SAX example, the implementation of exception handlers is not shown here. The exception handlers are similar to the SAX exception handlers discussed earlier.

■Note The full source for this application (Ch02\src\DOMExample1.java) can be downloaded from the Source Code area of the Apress website (http://www.apress.com).

Updating a Document by Using DOM

In the previous example (DOMExample1.java), we parsed the Orders.xml document to count the number of customers who placed an order. Earlier we concluded that SAX is a better API than DOM for this kind of application, and this can be easily verified by examining the coding involved in the two program examples. However, the real usefulness of DOM is that it can be used for modifying document contents.

In this section, we will write an application that parses the Orders.xml file, locates a specified customer, and modifies its trade order to sell. The program that updates the orders document is shown in Listing 2-8.

Listing 2-8. *Application That Updates Purchase Order Using DOM API* (Ch02\src\DOMExample2. java)

```
package apress.apacheXML.ch02;

import java.io.*;
import org.w3c.dom.*;
import org.xml.sax.*; // DOM parser uses SAX methods

import javax.xml.parsers.DocumentBuilderFactory;
import javax.xml.parsers.DocumentBuilder;

public class DOMExample2 {
    static String CustomerID;

    // application main method
  public static void main(String[] args) {
    if (args.length != 2) {
      System.err.println("Usage: DOMExample2 Filename CustomerID");
      System.exit(1);
    }

    // Store the received customer ID in a local variable
    CustomerID = args[1];
    // Construct an in-memory document instance
    Document doc = BuildTree(args[0]);
    // Locate and modify the order for the specified customer
    updateOrder(doc);
  }

  /**
  * The BuildTree method parses the received document and creates an
  * in-memory instance.
  */
```

```java
public static Document BuildTree(String fileName) {
  Document doc;
  try {
    // Obtain Factory instance
    DocumentBuilderFactory dbf = DocumentBuilderFactory.newInstance();
    // Request parser to ignore white space in the document
    dbf.setIgnoringElementContentWhitespace(true);
    // Obtain DocumentBuilder instance from the factory object
    DocumentBuilder db = dbf.newDocumentBuilder();
    // Parse the input file
    doc = db.parse(new File(fileName));
    // return reference to the root node
    return doc;
  } catch (Exception ex) {
    ex.printStackTrace();
  }
  return null;
}

/* The LocateAndUpdateTrade method receives the node containing the
 * desired customer. It searches this node recursively for TradeType
 * element. Once located it modifies its contents.
 */
public static void LocateAndUpdateTrade(Node node) {
  Node nn = null;
  // Get list of child nodes
  NodeList nl = node.getChildNodes();
  for (int i = 0; i < nl.getLength(); i++) {
    nn = nl.item(i);
    // Check if node name matches TradeType node
    if (nn.getNodeName().equals("TradeType")) {
      // The first child of this node contains the trade type
      Node nd = nn.getFirstChild();
      System.out.println("Current Trade Type: " + nd.getNodeValue());
      // Set the trade type to sell
      nd.setNodeValue("S");
      System.out.println("New Trade Type: " + nd.getNodeValue());
    }
    // recursively traverse the tree
    LocateAndUpdateTrade(nn);
  }
}

/* The searchCustomer receives a node as an argument. The method obtains the
 * attributes of the current node and checks if it matches the desired
 * customer.
 */
```

```java
public static void searchCustomer(Node node) {
    // check if element contains the attributes
    if (node.getAttributes() != null) {
        // Get the list of attributes
        NamedNodeMap nmdrp = node.getAttributes();
        if ((nmdrp.item(0) != null))
            // Check if the attribute is CustomerID
            if (nmdrp.item(0).getNodeValue().equals(CustomerID)) {
                // Print its value on user console
                System.out.println("Customer: "
                    + nmdrp.item(0).getNodeValue() + " found");
                // Pass the node to next method for updation
                LocateAndUpdateTrade(node);
            }
    }
}

/* The UpdateOrder method recursively traveses the tree and passes each
 * located Node to searchCustomer method for further processing
 */
public static void updateOrder(Node node) {
    // Return on presence of leaf node
    if (node == null) {
        return;
    }
    // Pass the current node to searchCustomer method for searching the
    // desired customer.
    searchCustomer(node);
    // Get children of current node
    NodeList children = node.getChildNodes();
    // Iterate through all children nodes recursively
    for (int i = 0; i < children.getLength(); i++)
        updateOrder(children.item(i));
}
```

The Orders.xml file identifies each customer by its ID specified as an attribute to the Customer tag. The trade type is saved as either B or S depending on whether it is a buy or sell order, respectively. The trade type is stored as TradeType element data. We will send the customer ID as a command-line argument to our application.

Application Class

In the application class file DOMExample2, we create a class variable called CustomerID for storing the parameter obtained from the command line:

```java
public class DOMExample2 {
    static String CustomerID;
```

The `main` Method

In the `main` method, we store the second command-line argument and call the `BuildTree` method to parse the document specified by the first command-line argument:

```
// application main method
public static void main(String[] args) {
 // Store the received customer ID in a local variable
 CustomerID = args[1];
 // Construct an in-memory document instance
 Document doc = BuildTree(args[0]);
 // Locate and modify the order for the specified customer
 UpdateOrder(doc);
}
```

After the DOM tree is constructed, the `main` method calls `UpdateOrder` by passing the reference to the document instance. The `UpdateOrder` method will locate the desired customer, and if found will update its trade order.

The `UpdateOrder` Method

The `UpdateOrder` method receives the root node as its parameter, traverses the memory tree recursively, and passes each located node to the `searchCustomer` method:

```
/* The UpdateOrder method recursively traveses the tree and passes each
   located Node to searchCustomer method for further processing
*/
public static void updateOrder(Node node) {
  // Return on presence of leaf node
  if (node == null) {
    return;
  }
  // Pass the current node to searchCustomer method for searching the
  // desired customer.
  searchCustomer(node);
  // Get children of current node
  NodeList children = node.getChildNodes();
  // Iterate through all children nodes recursively
  for (int i = 0; i < children.getLength(); i++)
    updateOrder(children.item(i));
}
```

The `searchCustomer` Method

The `searchCustomer` method receives a node as an argument. It calls the `getAttributes` method on the node to obtain its attributes. The `getAttributes` method returns a `NamedNodeMap` object that contains the map list of all the available attributes to the specified element. The function iterates through each attribute and compares its value with the `CustomerID` variable. If a match is found, the method prints a message on the user console and calls the `LocateAndUpdateTrade` method to update the trade type for the located customer:

```
/* The searchCustomer receives a node as an argument. The method obtains the
   attributes of the current node and checks if it matches the desired
   customer.
*/
public static void searchCustomer(Node node) {
  // check if element contains the attributes
  if (node.getAttributes() != null) {
    // Get the list of attributes
    NamedNodeMap nmdrp = node.getAttributes();
    if ((nmdrp.item(0) != null))
      // Check if the attribute is CustomerID
      if (nmdrp.item(0).getNodeValue().equals(CustomerID)) {
        // Print its value on user console
        System.out.println("Customer: "
            + nmdrp.item(0).getNodeValue() + " found");
        // Pass the node to next method for updation
        LocateAndUpdateTrade(node);
      }
  }
}
```

The LocateAndUpdateTrade Method

The LocateAndUpdateTrade method receives a node object as an argument. This method is
again recursive and traverses down the tree until it locates the TradeType element:

```
/* The LocateAndUpdateTrade method receives the node containing the desired
   customer. It searches this node recursively for TradeType element. Once
   located it modifies its contents.
*/
public static void LocateAndUpdateTrade(Node node) {
  Node nn = null;
  // Get list of child nodes
  NodeList nl = node.getChildNodes();
  for (int i = 0; i < nl.getLength(); i++) {
    nn = nl.item(i);
    // Check if node name matches TradeType node
    if (nn.getNodeName().equals("TradeType"))
    {
      // The first child of this node contains the trade type
      Node nd = nn.getFirstChild();
      System.out.println("Current Trade Type: "
          + nd.getNodeValue());
      // Set the trade type to sell
      nd.setNodeValue("S");
      System.out.println("New Trade Type: "
          + nd.getNodeValue());
    }
```

```
      // recursively traverse the tree
      LocateAndUpdateTrade (nn);
    }
  }
```

When the TradeType element is located, the method finds its first child element. As we understand from the Orders.xml document, the TradeType element contains only one child of the character data type that holds the trade type value. We obtain the node value of the child element and print it on the user console. The program then sets the node value to S by calling the setNodeValue method on the node object. The program finally prints the new value on the user console.

Program Output

If you run the preceding program with the second command-line argument equal to C003, the program will locate the customer with ID C003 and modify its trade order type to S. You will see the following program output:

```
Customer: C003 found
Current Trade Type:
      B

New Trade Type: S
```

If you run the program with the customer ID C004 as the second argument, you will see the following output:

```
Customer: C004 found
Current Trade Type:
      B

New Trade Type: S
Current Trade Type:
      S

New Trade Type: S
```

Note that for the located customer, each order is modified to the sell type, irrespective of its earlier order type.

You could modify this application further to accept the stock code as one of the command-line arguments and modify the order for only the specified stock.

■**Note** The full source for this application (ch02\src\DOMExample2.java) can be downloaded from the Source Code area of the Apress website (http://www.apress.com).

DOM API

Now that you have seen a few examples of DOM processing, you will study some of the important classes and interfaces in the DOM API.

The DocumentBuilderFactory Class

As seen in our programming examples, we use this class to obtain a reference to the factory object. The factory object enables us to obtain a parser for parsing XML documents and producing DOM trees from them. The following are the important methods of this class:

- newInstance: The DocumentBuilderFactory provides a newInstance static method to obtain a reference to itself. After a factory object is obtained, you can call different methods on it to set the parser features. Note that the class does not define any public constructor and thus the reference to the class object is obtained by calling the newInstance static method.

- setValidating: This method is used to turn on/off the document validation. If you need to validate the document against the schema, you will need to turn on the validations by using this method.

- setNamespaceAware: This method specifies whether the parser should support XML namespaces.[7] By default the value of this method is set to false. Thus, the parser by default will not support the namespaces if your document contains the namespaces.

- setIgnoringComments: This method instructs the parser to ignore the comments in the document. Your document may contain many comments. The processing application often will not be interested in the events generated on the occurrence of comments in your document. You will use these methods to enable/disable those events. By default the value of this is set to false, indicating that the events would be generated on the occurrence of comments.

- setCoalescing: This method instructs the parser to convert the CDATA nodes to Text nodes and append each to an adjacent text node, if it exists. As you learned in Chapter 1, the CDATA element may contain an XML code fragment that is not processed by the parser. By calling this method, you instruct the parser to convert such CDATA nodes to Text nodes.

- setSchema: This method sets the schema to be used by parsers created from this factory. The XML schema is used for validating documents. The schema can be changed dynamically so that different document instances can be validated against different schemas.

The DocumentBuilder Class

An instance of the DocumentBuilder class parses the XML documents. The source for an XML document can be InputStreams, Files, URLs, and SAX InputSources. You obtain an instance of this class by calling the newDocumentBuilder method on the factory object. The class is useful

---

7. XML namespaces are covered in Chapter 1.

for obtaining a DOM `Document` instance. Some of the important methods of this class are as follows:

- `parse`: This is the most important method of this class. The class provides five overloaded versions of this method. The different versions take different parameters such as `File`, `InputSource`, `InputStream`, and `uri`. After the document is parsed, a `Document` object is returned to the caller.

- `newDocument`: This method returns a new instance of a DOM `Document` object that may be used to build a DOM tree.

- `setEntityResolver`: This specifies the `EntityResolver` that should be used for resolving entities. The `EntityResolver` is basically an interface. The `DefaultHandler` class that we saw earlier implements this interface. This method can be used for setting your custom handlers.

The Interfaces

The DOM API defines several interfaces that help you in navigating the DOM tree, accessing/modifying its contents, creating new document instances, and more. We will discuss a few of the important interfaces here:

- `Document`: This interface represents the entire XML document. It refers to the document root and provides methods for creating subelements, text nodes, comments, processing instructions, and more. It provides several create methods (such as `createElement`, `createComment`, and `createAttribute`) to create such nodes. It also provides several getter methods for accessing document nodes. The `getElementById` method returns the element with the `ID` attribute matching the specified value. The `getElementsByTagName` returns a list of nodes with a matching tag name.

- `Element`: This represents an element in the XML document. The elements may have attributes and thus this interface provides accessor/mutator methods for manipulating these attributes. It also provides methods for adding/removing attributes.

- `Node`: This is the primary data type for the entire DOM. The `Element` interface inherits from the `Node` interface, and so do several other interfaces including `Attr`, `CharacterData`, `Comment`, `Document`, and `Entity`. This provides several getter methods, such as `getFirstChild`, `getLastChild`, and `getNextSibling` with which you can navigate the entire DOM tree. It also provides setter methods for setting the node value, text contents, and more.

XMLBeans

So far you've examined the SAX and DOM parsers, both of which require the user to know XML. However, most Java developers would like to forego such knowledge and take advantage of the document without intimate knowledge of its content and structure. *XMLBeans* provides this capability by allowing you to access and manipulate XML documents in Java.

XMLBeans Processing Model

In XMLBeans, the starting point is the XML schema. As you learned in Chapter 1, the XML schema defines rules for an XML document. A well-formed valid XML document conforms to this schema.

XMLBeans maps this schema to a set of Java interfaces. It provides a compiler called scomp to do this. Figure 2-6 illustrates the result of the schema compilation.

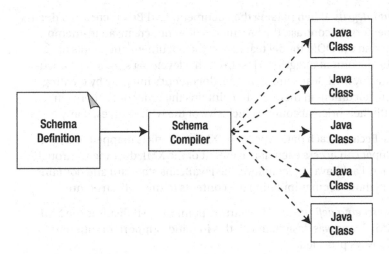

Figure 2-6. *Schema compilation*

When you run the schema compiler on a schema definition, it generates a set of Java classes. Each Java class is mapped to a particular data type (simple or complex) in the schema definition. The compiler creates a Java ARchive (JAR) file containing these classes. It also provides Java interfaces for these classes. By default, you get only the compiled Java classes in your JAR file; however, if you want to look up the generated source, you can request that the compiler keep the source files by adding appropriate command-line switches during compilation.

After you obtain the Java interfaces and the JAR file containing the Java classes, you can instantiate them in your Java application. The generated classes contain a Factory class with a parse method. You use this parse method to parse the desired XML document. If the document is successfully parsed, an in-memory document instance will be created. You can access this instance, both data and structure, by using the generated interfaces and classes. You will study this process very shortly in the following sections.

Pros and Cons of XMLBeans

As compared to other XML processing techniques discussed so far, XMLBeans offers several benefits:

- *Object-based view of XML data*: As XMLBeans creates Java classes that map to an XML document instance, you get an object-based view of an XML document. Developers are generally more comfortable with object-based views than text-based views, especially when they are required to access and manipulate the document through their program code. A text-based view of the document requires lots of string processing code, as seen in the SAX and DOM models examples. The object-based view preserves the original, native structure of the XML document.

- *No loss in document integrity*: When parsing the document, XMLBeans creates a document instance in memory. In contrast, the SAX model does not create an in-memory document instance, and the DOM model tears apart the document and works on it piecemeal. Thus, the document integrity is lost from the developer's sight. The document instance created by XMLBeans preserves the document's integrity by creating an instance of the entire document in memory. It maintains the order of elements in the document along with their original contents inclusive of the white spaces, if any.

- *JavaBeanlike access*: Because each data type of the XML schema is mapped to a Java interface, the developer can access each data element of the XML document through a Java object interface. Each Java object follows the JavaBeans standard and contains accessor/mutator methods for manipulating the contents of the XML structure.

- *Support for different schema definitions*: The starting point for XMLBeans is the XML schema. Because XMLBeans was designed with this in mind, support for different schema versions is always provided.

- *Faster access to document contents*: Because the entire document instance is created in memory while retaining its structure, you have fast access to its structure and contents. In the SAX model, the entire document is not available in memory, so even though SAX also provides fast access to document contents, you cannot go backward in the document and therefore will have to parse the document again if you need to access previously visited data. In DOM, the entire document is loaded in memory and is arranged in a tree structure. Thus, accessing the document contents may require recursive travel on the tree.

The major disadvantage of XMLBeans is the need for additional compilation. If the schema changes, you will need to perform compilation again and make modifications to your Java code to incorporate the new classes. With SAX and DOM, the schema changes need not require major changes in the application code.

Installing the XMLBeans Software

Before you try out the programs described in the next section, you will need to download and install XMLBeans software on your machine. You can download the archive file from http://xmlbeans.apache.org/. Unzip the downloaded file and follow the setup instructions.

Set the XMLBEANS_HOME environment variable to the directory where you installed XMLBeans and add %XMLBEANS_HOME%\bin to your PATH.

Note For those of you installing on Linux, Appendix A provides detailed installation instructions for all the chapters in this book.

You can test the installation by trying the scomp command at your command prompt. It should display the usage message on your console. The installation comes with several sample examples installed under the samples folder. We will create our applications in this samples folder and follow the folder structure used by sample applications.

Create a subfolder called XMLBeans-Example under the samples folder. Under the XMLBeans-Example folder, create three subfolders: schemas, src, and xml. We will save our schema definition that is to be processed under the schemas folder. The src folder will contain our application source, and the xml folder contains the XML document to be parsed and processed.

The samples use Apache Ant to build and run the applications. We will also use Ant to build and run our applications, so you will need to follow the suggested folder structure.

Note If you decide not to use the Ant tool, you will need to study the build.xml file used by Ant to understand how it builds the source and runs the generated application by using the predefined libraries.

Document Processing Using XMLBeans

In this section, you will learn how to use XMLBeans to process an XML document. We will use the Orders.xml document from our earlier examples. As in the earlier cases, we will first write an application that counts the number of customers who have placed an order in the current document. Next, we will write an application that modifies an existing order for a specified customer and changes its trade type to sell. We will then write an application that deletes a record for the specified customer in the document instance and writes the modified document instance to a new XML file for forwarding to further business logic. Finally, we will write an application that builds a new orders document by using the generated classes.

XMLBeans requires a schema definition. So, we'll first discuss the schema definition for our Orders.xml document file.

Schema Definition

All the applications in this section will process the Orders.xml file. The schema definition to which Orders.xml conforms is given in Listing 2-9.

Listing 2-9. `Orders.xsd` *Schema Definition*

```
<?xml version="1.0" encoding="utf-8"?>
<xs:schema targetNamespace = "http://www.apress.com/apacheXML"
  xmlns:xsi="http://www.w3.org/2001/XMLSchema-instance"
  attributeFormDefault="unqualified"
  elementFormDefault="qualified"
  xmlns:xs="http://www.w3.org/2001/XMLSchema">
  <xs:element name="Orders">
    <xs:complexType>
      <xs:sequence>
        <xs:element maxOccurs="unbounded" name="Customer">
          <xs:complexType>
            <xs:sequence>
              <xs:element maxOccurs="unbounded" name="StockSymbol">
                <xs:complexType mixed="true">
                  <xs:sequence>
                    <xs:element name="Quantity" type="xs:unsignedByte" />
                    <xs:element name="TradeType" type="xs:string" />
                  </xs:sequence>
                </xs:complexType>
              </xs:element>
            </xs:sequence>
            <xs:attribute name="ID" type="xs:string" use="required" />
          </xs:complexType>
        </xs:element>
      </xs:sequence>
    </xs:complexType>
  </xs:element>
</xs:schema>
```

Note that `Orders` is the root element that can contain multiple occurrences of `Customer` elements. Each `Customer` element can contain any number of `StockSymbol` elements. The `StockSymbol` is a mixed `complexType` and contains `Quantity` and `TradeType` elements. The `Quantity` element is of `unsignedByte` type, and the `TradeType` element is of `string` type. Each `Customer` also has a required attribute called `ID` of type `string`.

Using the Ant Tool

We will be using Apache Ant to compile all the applications in this section. You can refer to the Ant build script (`C:\<working folder>\Ch02\src\XMLBeans-examples\build.xml`) provided at the Source Code area of the Apress website. When you run the Ant build tool, the preceding schema definition from the `schema` folder will be mapped to Java interfaces and classes. All the generated classes and interfaces are stored under the `build` folder created by the Ant tool. We will be interested in the `OrdersDocument.java` file that contains the interfaces required by our application.

Generated Code

The schema compiler generates the interfaces for all the elements in your schema file. The interfaces follow the same structure as the structure defined in the schema file. Thus, for each subelement defined in the schema, you will find an inner (nested) interface created within the outer interface. The entire Java code is packaged in a Java package.

The Java Package

If you open the OrdersDocument.java file, you will notice that it defines a package called com.apress.apacheXML. The schema compiler uses the targetNamespace string defined in the schema to create a package name. The package name follows the hierarchy defined by the target namespace. If you do not create the targetNamespace in your schema definition, the compiler creates a default package called noNamespace.

Java Interfaces

The root element of our Orders.xsd schema is Orders. The compiler creates an interface called OrdersDocument that will represent an instance of the XML document conforming to our schema definition:

```
public interface OrdersDocument extends org.apache.xmlbeans.XmlObject
```

The interface declares methods for getting/setting Orders and adding new Orders:

```
com.apress.apacheXML.OrdersDocument.Orders getOrders();
void setOrders(com.apress.apacheXML.OrdersDocument.Orders orders);
com.apress.apacheXML.OrdersDocument.Orders addNewOrders();
```

Within the OrdersDocument interface, the Orders interface is declared:

```
public interface Orders extends org.apache.xmlbeans.XmlObject
```

The Orders interface declares methods such as the following:

```
com.apress.apacheXML.OrdersDocument.Orders.Customer[] getCustomerArray();
com.apress.apacheXML.OrdersDocument.Orders.Customer getCustomerArray(int i);
int sizeOfCustomerArray();
void setCustomerArray
    (com.apress.apacheXML.OrdersDocument.Orders.Customer[] customerArray);
void setCustomerArray
    (int i, com.apress.apacheXML.OrdersDocument.Orders.Customer customer);
com.apress.apacheXML.OrdersDocument.Orders.Customer insertNewCustomer(int i);
com.apress.apacheXML.OrdersDocument.Orders.Customer addNewCustomer();
void removeCustomer(int i);
```

Our Orders element can contain multiple occurrences of the Customer element. The schema compiler creates a Customer array to represent multiple occurrences of the Customer element in the document. It provides methods for accessing and manipulating this array. The compiler also provides methods for inserting a new Customer element at a desired index in the array and provides methods for adding/deleting a specified customer. With these add/new/insert methods, you will be able to modify the document instance in memory easily. Thus, you will be able to add new customer orders to an existing order document. Changes made to the document instance can then be serialized to another XML document file. This is illustrated later, in Listing 2-12.

Within the Orders interface, the compiler creates an inner interface called Customer:

```
public interface Customer extends org.apache.xmlbeans.XmlObject
```

Note that the Customer is a subelement of the Orders element. Thus, the compiler generates an inner interface for Customer within the Orders interface. The Customer interface defines several methods for accessing/manipulating StockSymbol element instances. The StockSymbol element is contained within the Customer element.

Each interface also contains an inner Factory class to create instances that map to these interfaces. The Factory class defined within the StockSymbol interface is shown here:

```
public static final class Factory
  {
    public static com.apress.apacheXML.OrdersDocument.Orders.
                        Customer.StockSymbol newInstance()
    {
      return (com.apress.apacheXML.OrdersDocument.Orders.
                        Customer.StockSymbol)
      org.apache.xmlbeans.XmlBeans.getContextTypeLoader().
                        newInstance( type, null );
    }

    public static com.apress.apacheXML.OrdersDocument.Orders.
                        Customer.StockSymbol
    newInstance(org.apache.xmlbeans.XmlOptions options)
    {
      return (com.apress.apacheXML.OrdersDocument.Orders.
                        Customer.StockSymbol)
      org.apache.xmlbeans.XmlBeans.getContextTypeLoader().newInstance
                        ( type, options ); }

    private Factory() { } // No instance of this class allowed
    }
  }
```

The Factory class is final and cannot be extended. It also defines a no-argument constructor that is declared private. Thus, the class cannot be instantiated. The class declares two overloaded newInstance methods. By using these methods, you will be able to create new document instances of the StockSymbol type and add them to the outer Customer array.

Likewise, the compiler generates the interfaces for all the subelements and provides methods to manipulate various XML data instances. You can refer to the generated Java file to study the various generated interfaces and accessor/mutator methods on various Java objects that map to XML instances. Also, note the declaration of the Factory class within each interface.

Now, we will develop console applications by using the classes we have discussed to access the contents of an XML document based on the Orders.xsd schema.

As in the earlier cases of SAX and DOM, our first application will simply count the number of occurrences of Customer elements in the given document and print this information on the user console.

Application for Counting Customers

The console application that counts the number of customers in a given purchase order is given in Listing 2-10.

Listing 2-10. *XMLBeans-Based Application for Counting Customers* (Ch02\src\ XMLBeans-Example\src\XMLBeansExample1.java)

```java
/**
 * This example uses Schema-Compiler generated classes to count
 * the number of customers whose orders are present in the
 * specified Orders.xml document.
 */

package apress.apacheXML.ch02;

import org.apache.xmlbeans.*;
import com.apress.apacheXML.*;
import com.apress.apacheXML.OrdersDocument.*;
import com.apress.apacheXML.OrdersDocument.Orders.*;

import java.io.File;
import java.util.ArrayList;
import java.util.Iterator;

public class XMLBeansExample1 {
  static OrdersDocument doc;
  /**
   * The main method parses and validates the document specified
   * in the parameter and on success counts the number of occurences of
   * Customer element.
   */
  public static void main(String[] args)
        throws org.apache.xmlbeans.XmlException, java.io.IOException {
    if (validate(args[0]))
      countCustomers();
  }

  /**
   * Build and validate the specified document
   */
```

```
    public static boolean validate(String filename)
        throws org.apache.xmlbeans.XmlException, java.io.IOException {
      System.out.println("parsing document: " + filename);
      // Use the generated classes' parse method to parse input document
      doc = OrdersDocument.Factory.parse(new File(filename));
      // Create an array list
      ArrayList errors = new ArrayList();
      // Set up an error listener
      XmlOptions opts = new XmlOptions();
      opts.setErrorListener(errors);
      // Validate the document
      if (doc.validate(opts)) {
        System.out.println("document is valid.");
      } else // Print the error list
      {
        System.out.println("document is invalid!");
        Iterator iter = errors.iterator();
        while (iter.hasNext()) {
          System.out.println(">> " + iter.next());
        }
        return false;
      }
      return true;
    }


    // Counts the total number of customers
    public static void countCustomers() {
      // get a reference to Orders instance
      Orders orders = doc.getOrders();
      // Determine the customer count from the array size
      System.out.println("Customer count: " + orders.sizeOfCustomerArray());
    }
}
```

We declare a class called XMLBeansExample1 and create a class variable called OrdersDocument:

```
public class XMLBeansExample1
{
  static OrdersDocument doc;
```

Note that the schema-compiler (scomp) generated classes contain the OrdersDocument class, which represents the root of our document instance.

In the main method of the application, we first validate the input document for conformance and then call the countCustomers method to obtain the number of customers:

```
        if (validate(args[0]))
          countCustomers();
```

The XML file to be processed is passed to the application as the command-line parameter.

The validate method parses the input file by calling the factory parse method:

```
// Use the generated classes' parse method to parse input document
doc = OrdersDocument.Factory.parse (new File(filename));
```

The program may generate errors during parsing. To catch exceptions, we instantiate the XmlOptions class provided in the XMLBeans library and set the error listener on it to the errors array list:

```
// Create an array list
ArrayList errors = new ArrayList();

// Set up an error listener
XmlOptions opts = new XmlOptions();
opts.setErrorListener(errors);
```

When we parse the input file, the errors, if any, will be accumulated in the errors list. The document itself is parsed with the following command:

```
// Validate the document
if (doc.validate(opts))
```

If the function returns true, the input file is valid. If not, we iterate through the errors list and print out the errors on the user console.

After the document is validated, we call the countCustomers method to compute the total number of customers. The countCustomers method calls the getOrders method on the root element of the document instance to obtain a reference to the Orders instance. Calling the sizeOfCustomerArray method on this instance returns the number of customers in the current document; this is printed on the user console:

```
// get a reference to Orders instance
Orders orders = doc.getOrders();
// Determine the customer count from the array size
System.out.println ("Customer count: " + orders.sizeOfCustomerArray());
```

You can run this application with the Ant tool by using the provided build file. Run the application by running the Ant task run-1 as shown in the following command:

```
C:\<working folder>\ch02\src\XMLBeans-examples>ant run-1
```

You will see the following output:

```
run-1:
    [echo] ============================== running XMLBeansExample1
    [java] parsing document: xml/Orders.xml
    [java] document is valid.

    [java] Customer count: 6

BUILD SUCCESSFUL
```

Note The main program does not check for the presence of command-line parameters. The Ant build script ensures that proper parameters are passed on the command line. This is the case for all the subsequent examples in this section. If you decide not to use the Ant tool and provided build.xml file, you may want to provide the error handling code for checking the presence of appropriate command-line parameters.

Compare this code with the SAX and DOM application code written for counting customers. XMLBeans gives us more compact code that is more intuitive to Java programmers. The programmers do not have to work with a text-based file; instead they work with an object view of the document instance.

Note The full source for this application (Ch02\src\XMLBeans-Example\src\XMLBeansExample1. java) can be downloaded from the Source Code area of the Apress website (http://www.apress.com).

Application for Modifying Trade Order

We will now write our next application that modifies the trade order type for a specified customer. This application accepts the name of the XML file to be processed as the first parameter, and the customer ID for which the trade type is to be modified as the second parameter. The complete program source is given in Listing 2-11.

Listing 2-11. *Application for Modifying Trade Order* (Ch02\src\XMLBeans-Example\src\ XMLBeansExample2.java)

```
/**
 * This example uses Schema-Compiler generated classes to
 * update the specified customer's order from buy to sell
 * specified Orders.xml document.
 */
package apress.apacheXML.ch02;

import org.apache.xmlbeans.*;
import com.apress.apacheXML.*;
import com.apress.apacheXML.OrdersDocument.*;
import com.apress.apacheXML.OrdersDocument.Orders.*;
import com.apress.apacheXML.OrdersDocument.Orders.Customer.*;

import java.io.File;
import java.util.ArrayList;
import java.util.Iterator;
```

```java
public class XMLBeansExample2 {
  static OrdersDocument doc;
  static String customerID = null;

  /**
   * The main method parses and validates the document specified
   * in the parameter and on success updates the specified
   * customer's order.
   */
  public static void main(String[] args)
      throws org.apache.xmlbeans.XmlException, java.io.IOException {
    customerID = args[1];
    if (validate(args[0]))
      updateCustomerTrade();
  }

  /**
   * Build and validate the specified document
   */
  public static boolean validate(String filename)
      throws org.apache.xmlbeans.XmlException, java.io.IOException {
    System.out.println("parsing document: " + filename);
    // Use the generated classes' parse method to parse input document
    doc = OrdersDocument.Factory.parse(new File(filename));
    // Create an array list
    ArrayList errors = new ArrayList();
    // Set up an error listener
    XmlOptions opts = new XmlOptions();
    opts.setErrorListener(errors);
    // Validate the document
    if (doc.validate(opts)) {
      System.out.println("document is valid.");
    } else // Print the error list
    {
      System.out.println("document is invalid!");
      Iterator iter = errors.iterator();
      while (iter.hasNext()) {
        System.out.println(">> " + iter.next());
      }
      return false;
    }
    return true;
  }

  /**
   * This method updates the customer's order from buy to sell type
   */
```

```
public static void updateCustomerTrade() {
  // get a reference to Orders instance
  Orders orders = doc.getOrders();
  // Get a list of customers from orders instance
  Customer[] customers = orders.getCustomerArray();
  // Iterate through the list of customers
  for (int i=0; i<customers.length; i++) {
    // Check for the desired customer ID
    if (customers[i].getID().equals(customerID)) {
      System.out.println("Customer " + customerID + " Found");
      // Retrieve the list of orders placed by the customer
      StockSymbol[] stocks = customers[i].getStockSymbolArray();
      // For each ordered stock, change the trade type to sell
      for (int j=0; j<stocks.length; j++) {
        System.out.println("Current Trade Type: " +
            stocks[j].getTradeType());
        stocks[j].setTradeType("S");
        System.out.println("New Trade Type: " +
            stocks[j].getTradeType());
      }
    }
  }
}
```

We declare a class called XMLBeansExample2 and create two class variables:

```
public class XMLBeansExample2
{
  static OrdersDocument doc;
  static String customerID = null;
```

The customerID variable stores the value of the second command-line argument. As in the previous application, the main function calls the validate method to ensure that the input document conforms to our schema:

```
if (validate(args[0]))
  updateCustomerTrade();
```

In the updateCustomerTrade method, we first obtain an instance of the Orders class by calling the getOrders method on the document instance:

```
// get a reference to Orders instance
Orders orders = doc.getOrders();
```

We now obtain the customer array by calling the getCustomerArray method on the orders object. This returns the list of customers in the current orders document instance in the customers array:

```
// Get a list of customers from orders instance
Customer[] customers = orders.getCustomerArray();
```

The program then iterates through the entire array to locate the customer with the ID matching customerID:

```
// Iterate through the list of customers
for (int i=0; i<customers.length; i++)
{
    // Check for the desired customer ID
    if (customers[i].getID().equals (customerID))
```

After the desired customer is located, we call the getStockSymbolArray method on it to retrieve all the stocks for which the customer has placed the order:

```
// Retrieve the list of orders placed by the customer
StockSymbol[] stocks = customers[i].getStockSymbolArray();
```

We now iterate through the stocks array and obtain the trade type for each stock by calling its getTradeType method. We print the value of TradeType for each stock on the user console. The program also modifies the trade type to sell, and prints the modified value on the user console:

```
// For each ordered stock, change the trade type to sell
for (int j=0; j<stocks.length; j++)
{
  System.out.println ("Current Trade Type: " + stocks[j].getTradeType());
  stocks[j].setTradeType ("S");
  System.out.println ("New Trade Type: " + stocks[j].getTradeType());
}
```

You can run this application by using the provided Ant build file. Use the run-2 argument on the ant command to run the application as shown:

```
C:\<working folder>\ch02\src\XMLBeans-examples>ant run-2
```

You can change the customer ID parameter in the build file to any desired value. If you run the application with the customer ID value set to C003, you will see the following output:

```
run-2:
    [echo] ============================== running XMLBeansExample2
    [java] parsing document: xml/Orders.xml
    [java] document is valid.

    [java] Customer C003 Found
    [java] Current Trade Type:
    [java]          B
    [java]
    [java] New Trade Type: S

BUILD SUCCESSFUL
```

Note that the current trade type for customer C003 is modified from buy to sell.

If you run the application for customer C004, you will see the following output:

```
run-2:
    [echo] ============================= running XMLBeansExample2
    [java] parsing document: xml/Orders.xml
    [java] document is valid.

    [java] Customer C004 Found
    [java] Current Trade Type:
    [java]         B
    [java]
    [java] New Trade Type: S
    [java] Current Trade Type:
    [java]         S
    [java]
    [java] New Trade Type: S

BUILD SUCCESSFUL
```

In this case, both orders for the C004 customer are changed to the sell type. The order that is originally of sell type remains of the same type.

■**Note** The full source for this application (Ch02\src\XMLBeans-Example\src\XMLBeansExample2. java) can be downloaded from the Source Code area of the Apress website (http://www.apress.com).

Application for Deleting Order

Now we will develop an application that deletes the entire order placed by a specified customer and writes the modified document instance to a new XML document for further processing. The program source is given in Listing 2-12.

Listing 2-12. *XMLBeans-Based Application for Deleting Customer Order* (Ch02\src\ XMLBeans-Example\src\XMLBeansExample3.java)

```
/**
 * This example uses Schema-Compiler generated classes to
 * delete all orders placed by a specified customer and
 * generate a new orders document.
 */
package apress.apacheXML.ch02;
```

```java
import org.apache.xmlbeans.*;
import com.apress.apacheXML.*;
import com.apress.apacheXML.OrdersDocument.*;
import com.apress.apacheXML.OrdersDocument.Orders.*;
import com.apress.apacheXML.OrdersDocument.Orders.Customer.*;

import java.io.File;
import java.util.ArrayList;
import java.util.Iterator;

public class XMLBeansExample3 {
  static OrdersDocument doc;
  static String customerID = null;
  /**
   * The main method parses and validates the document specified
   * in the parameter and on success deletes the specified
   * customer's orders. It then generates a new orders document.
   */
  public static void main(String[] args)
      throws org.apache.xmlbeans.XmlException, java.io.IOException {
    // store the command line argument
    customerID = args[1];
    // Validate the input XML document
    if (validate(args[0])) {
      // Delete customer order
      deleteCustomerOrder();
      // Save the contents to new XML document
      saveXML();
    }
  }

  /**
   * Build and validate the specified document
   */
  public static boolean validate(String filename)
        throws org.apache.xmlbeans.XmlException, java.io.IOException {
    System.out.println("parsing document: " + filename);
    // Use the generated classes' parse method to parse input document
    doc = OrdersDocument.Factory.parse(new File(filename));
    / Create an array list
    ArrayList errors = new ArrayList();
    // Set up an error listener
    XmlOptions opts = new XmlOptions();
    opts.setErrorListener(errors);
```

```java
  // Validate the document
  if (doc.validate(opts)) {
    System.out.println("document is valid.");
  } else // Print the error list
  {
    System.out.println("document is invalid!");
    Iterator iter = errors.iterator();
    while (iter.hasNext()) {
      System.out.println(">> " + iter.next());
    }
    return false;
  }
  return true;
}


/**
 * This method locates and deletes the customer record from the
 * list of orders loaded in memory structure
 */
public static void deleteCustomerOrder() {
  // get a reference to Orders instance
  Orders orders = doc.getOrders();
  // Get a list of customers from Orders instance
  Customer[] customers = orders.getCustomerArray();
  // iterate through customer list
  for (int i=0; i<customers.length; i++) {
    // Check for the desired customer ID
    if (customers[i].getID().equals(customerID)) {
      System.out.println("Customer " + customerID + " Found");
      // Remove the customer record from the orders list
      orders.removeCustomer(i);
    }
  }
}


/**
 * This method saves the modified in-memory document to a physical file
 */
public static void saveXML() {
  // Set options for saving the document
  XmlOptions xmlOptions = new XmlOptions();
  xmlOptions.setSavePrettyPrint();
  // Create a new file for outputting memory document
  File f = new File("test.xml");
  try{
```

```
    // Save the document
    doc.save(f,xmlOptions);
    } catch(java.io.IOException e){
        e.printStackTrace();
    }
  System.out.println("\nXML Instance Document saved at : " + f.getPath());
  }
}
```

As in the previous application, we will accept the customer ID as a command-line parameter. The main function saves this argument in a local variable and validates the input file. If the file is valid, it calls the deleteCustomerOrder method to delete the customer record. It then calls the saveXML method to save the modified document instance to a physical file:

```
/* The program accepts the customer ID as a command line parameter and
   deletes the order placed by the customer from the XML document.
*/
public static void main(String[] args)
 throws org.apache.xmlbeans.XmlException, java.io.IOException
 {
    // store the command line argument
    customerID = args[1];
    // Validate the input XML document
    if (validate(args[0]))
    {
        // Delete customer order
        deleteCustomerOrder();
        // Save the contents to new XML document
        saveXML();
    }
 }
```

As in the previous example, the deleteCustomerOrder method first obtains a reference to the Orders instance and gets a list of customers in the Customer array. The method iterates through this array to locate the desired customer. After a desired customer is located, the program calls the removeCustomer method to delete the customer instance from the document. Note that this results in removing all the orders placed by the specified customer:

```
/**
* This method locates and deletes the customer record from the
* list of orders loaded in memory structure
*/
public static void deleteCustomerOrder()
{
    // get a reference to Orders instance
    Orders orders = doc.getOrders();
    // get a list of customers from Orders instance
    Customer[] customers = orders.getCustomerArray();
```

```
      // iterate through customer list
      for (int i=0; i<customers.length; i++)
      {
         // Check the current customer ID with the desired one
         if (customers[i].getID().equals (customerID))
          {
             // Desired Customer located
             System.out.println ("Customer " + customerID + " Found");
             // Remove customer record from Orders
             orders.removeCustomer(i);
          }
      }
   }
```

Next, we save the document instance to a physical XML file by calling the saveXML method.
The saveXML method creates an instance of XmlOptions and calls its setSavePrettyPrint method
to provide us with a nicely formatted document file:

```
// Set options for saving the document
XmlOptions xmlOptions = new XmlOptions();
xmlOptions.setSavePrettyPrint();
```

Next, we create a File object to store our document instance:

```
// Create a new file for outputting memory document
File f = new File("test.xml");
```

We save the document instance to this physical file by calling the save method on the
document object:

```
// Save the document
doc.save(f,xmlOptions);
```

The program then prints an appropriate message to the user:

```
System.out.println("\nXML Instance Document saved at : " + f.getPath());
```

Use the run-3 task on the Ant tool to run this application:

```
C:\<working folder>\ch02\src\XMLBeans-examples>ant run-3
```

When you run this application by using the customer ID of C003, you will see the following
output:

```
run-3:
    [echo] =============================== running XMLBeansExample3
    [java] parsing document: xml/Orders.xml
    [java] document is valid.

    [java] Customer C003 Found
```

```
    [java] XML Instance Document saved at : C:\xmlbeans-2.0.0\samples\XMLBeans-
Example\test.xml

BUILD SUCCESSFUL
```

Examine the generated test.xml file to verify that the order for customer C003 has been deleted.

Note The full source for this application (Ch02\src\XMLBeans-Example\src\XMLBeansExample3. java) can be downloaded from the Source Code area of the Apress website (http://www.apress.com).

Application for Creating Order Document

XMLBeans-generated classes allow you not only to parse and manipulate an existing document, but also to create a new XML document easily. We will develop an application that creates a new purchase order conforming to the Orders schema definition. Create a console application called XMLBeansExample4 as given in Listing 2-13.

Listing 2-13. *XMLBeans-Based Application for Creating XML-Based Order Document* (Ch02\src\ XMLBeans-Example\src\XMLBeansExample4.java)

```java
/**
 * This examples uses the schema-compiler generated classes to dynamically create
 * a new orders document.
 */
package apress.apacheXML.ch02;

import org.apache.xmlbeans.*;
import com.apress.apacheXML.*;
import com.apress.apacheXML.OrdersDocument.*;
import com.apress.apacheXML.OrdersDocument.Orders.*;
import com.apress.apacheXML.OrdersDocument.Orders.Customer.*;

import java.io.File;
import java.util.ArrayList;
import java.util.Iterator;

public class XMLBeansExample4 {
  static OrdersDocument doc;
  /**
   * The main method builds an in-memory document using
   * schema-compiler generated classes and saves it to
   * an XML file.
   */
```

```
public static void main(String[] args)
    throws org.apache.xmlbeans.XmlException, java.io.IOException {
  // Create an in-memory instance of XML document
  createOrderDocument();
  // Save the memory instance to a physical file
  saveXML();
}

public static void createOrderDocument() {
  // Create a document instance
. doc = com.apress.apacheXML.OrdersDocument.Factory.newInstance();
  // Add Orders element to the created document
  com.apress.apacheXML.OrdersDocument.Orders orders = doc.addNewOrders();
  // Add a Customer element with ID equal to C005
  com.apress.apacheXML.OrdersDocument.Orders.Customer customer =
      orders.addNewCustomer();
  customer.setID("C005");
  // Add an order for GE
com.apress.apacheXML.OrdersDocument.Orders.Customer.StockSymbol stockSymbol =
      customer.addNewStockSymbol();
  XmlString xmlStr = XmlString.Factory.newValue("GE");
  stockSymbol.set(xmlStr);
  stockSymbol.setQuantity((short)200);
  stockSymbol.setTradeType("B");
}

/**
 * This method saves the modified in-memory document to a physical file
 */
public static void saveXML() {
  // Set options for saving the document
  XmlOptions xmlOptions = new XmlOptions();
  xmlOptions.setSavePrettyPrint();
  // Create a new file for outputting memory document
  File f = new File("NewOrder.xml");
  try{
    // Save the document
    doc.save(f,xmlOptions);
    } catch(java.io.IOException e){
      e.printStackTrace();
    }
  System.out.println("\nXML Instance Document saved at : " + f.getPath());
  }
}
```

The main method calls the createOrderDocument method to create a new document. The saveXML method (that is the same as in the earlier example) saves the created document to a physical file:

```
/**
 * The main method builds an in-memory document using
 * schema-compiler generated classes and saves it to
 * an XML file.
 */
  public static void main(String[] args)
      throws org.apache.xmlbeans.XmlException, java.io.IOException
  {
    // Create an in-memory instance of XML document
    createOrderDocument();
    // Save the memory instance to a physical file
    saveXML();
  }
```

The createOrderDocument method creates a document instance by using the Factory class and calling the newInstance method on it:

```
// Create a document instance
doc = com.apress.apacheXML.OrdersDocument.Factory.newInstance();
```

After a document object is created, we add an Orders element to it by calling the addNewOrders method on the instance of the document:

```
// Add Orders element to the created document
com.apress.apacheXML.OrdersDocument.Orders orders = doc.addNewOrders();
```

The program now adds a Customer element to it by calling the addNewCustomer method on the orders object. Note that Customer is a subelement of the Orders element:

```
// Add a Customer element with ID equal to C005
com.apress.apacheXML.OrdersDocument.Orders.Customer customer =
                        orders.addNewCustomer();
```

We set the customer ID by calling the setID method on the customer object:

```
customer.setID ("C005");
```

Next, we create a StockSymbol element within the Customer element:

```
// Add an order for GE
com.apress.apacheXML.OrdersDocument.Orders.Customer.
      StockSymbol stockSymbol =?customer.addNewStockSymbol();
```

For the stock symbol, we need to set the stock name as a text element and its quantity and trade type. We do this by using the following code snippet:

```
XmlString xmlStr = XmlString.Factory.newValue("GE");
stockSymbol.set (xmlStr);
stockSymbol.setQuantity ((short)200);
stockSymbol.setTradeType ("B");
```

Note that we create an instance of XmlString by using the available Factory class and then set this as text content for the stock symbol. We add the quantity and trade type to the stock symbol by calling setQuantity and setTradeType methods on it.

At this stage, the addition of customer C005 is completed. For this application, we will add only one customer to our order document. The main function now calls saveXML to save the document contents to a physical file.

When you run the application by using the run-4 task in the Ant tool, you will see the NewOrder.xml file created on your disk:

```
C:\<working folder>\ch02\src\XMLBeans-examples>ant run-4
```

The contents of the generated XML document are as follows:

```
<?xml version="1.0" encoding="UTF-8"?>
<apac:Orders xmlns:apac="http://www.apress.com/apacheXML">
  <apac:Customer ID="C005">
    <apac:StockSymbol>
      GE
        <apac:Quantity>200</apac:Quantity>
        <apac:TradeType>B</apac:TradeType>
    </apac:StockSymbol>
  </apac:Customer>
</apac:Orders>
```

SAX, DOM, XMLBeans—Which One to Use?

This chapter has covered three techniques of XML parsing. All three techniques have their own merits. Which one you select depends on the needs of the application.

SAX is useful for quickly searching for a particular element and discarding the rest of the processing after the element or the desired data is found. SAX is also preferred for parsing large document files because it puts less strain on resources.

DOM is used if you want to navigate bidirectionally in the parsed document. DOM builds an in-memory structure of the parsed document and thus allows you to navigate in either direction after the document is parsed. DOM is also useful if you want to modify the contents of an existing document and save it to a physical XML file, or if you want to create a new XML document from scratch. DOM comes with the disadvantage of requiring heavy resources and longer processing time. The initial response time or the time required before you start manipulating your document could be extremely long, especially in the case of very large documents. For these reasons, avoid using DOM for large documents.

If you are not good at XML or prefer working with an object-based view of data rather than a text-based view, use the XMLBeans technique of parsing. XMLBeans provides an object view of the document, enabling easier manipulation by programmers.

There is another way of creating an object view of the XML document, although I did not mention this anywhere so far. This is provided by the Java Architecture for XML Binding

(JAXB)[8] API developed by the Java Community Process (JCP). Like XMLBeans, JAXB creates several classes that map to document data types. It provides methods for marshalling and unmarshalling data between Java objects and the parsed document. Because such Java objects exist in isolation and are independent of each other, the entire document structure is not retained in memory.

XMLBeans maintains the document structure in memory and thus reduces the overhead of marshalling and unmarshalling. This makes even the navigation easier as compared to JAXB techniques, which require understanding the complete object model. JAXB follows the DOM-oriented model to represent the document instance in memory.

■**Note** Apache provides an implementation of JAXB in their JAXMe 2 project (`http://ws.apache.org/jaxme/`).

Summary

This chapter started by explaining the need for and importance of XML parsing. Because XML documents are manipulated electronically, we need to parse them electronically. You learned about several parsing techniques supported by Apache and considered several practical situations in which XML parsing techniques are applied.

The chapter covered three main techniques of parsing XML documents: SAX, DOM, and XMLBeans. For each technique, the processing model was explained. We considered the pros and cons of each technique. The chapter discussed several programming examples to illustrate the processing models. Finally, the chapter covered the merits and demerits of each technique, comparing and contrasting their use in practical applications.

You will now move on to study an important and very wide use of XML in today's applications. XML is the foundation for data transport in web services architecture, which you will learn about in the next chapter. Subsequent chapters will cover the in-depth use of XML in this new and widely accepted architecture.

---

8. Refer to http://java.sun.com/webservices/jaxb/index.jsp for information on JAXB architecture.

CHAPTER 3

■ ■ ■

Web Services Architecture

In the previous two chapters, you learned about XML and XML processing techniques. In this chapter, you will study an important application architecture that is based on XML technologies: web services architecture.

Over the last few years, the web services wave has caught the IT industry by storm. No longer solely a subject of marketing hype, web services are already achieving tremendous acceptance in the marketplace. Several new applications have been developed by using web services technology. Also, several existing applications have been rewritten or modified to expose their otherwise closed interfaces as web services.

Several companies (Google, Yahoo!, and Microsoft, for example) are providing access to their traditionally website-specific services by way of a web service interface. For example, Internet juggernaut Google provides a *web API service* (http://www.google.com/apis/) that can be used by your application to query more than 8 billion of its indexed web pages. Yahoo! also exposes several of its services as web services (http://developer.yahoo.net/), which allow you to interact with services such as a travel trip planner, photo-sharing website Flickr, and its indexed page repository. XMethods (http://services.xmethods.net/) provides several stock-related web services that allow you to easily retrieve a delayed quote for any stock listed on the NYSE or obtain fundamentals and technical charts for any corporation listed on the stock exchange. Additionally, Microsoft, IBM, Sun Microsystems, SAP, and others provide a lot of developer support for creating your own web services.

So what is a web service? In this chapter, you will learn about web services, the web service architecture, and its various components.

What Is a Web Service?

Simply put, a *web service* can be defined as any application component that exposes its functionality by using standard web protocols.

Gartner (http://www.gartner.com) offers the following web services definition:

Web services are loosely coupled software components that interact with one another dynamically via standard Internet technologies.

Forrester Research (http://www.forrester.com) defines web services as follows:

Web services are automated connections between people, systems, and applications that expose elements of business functionality as a software service and create new business value.

IBM (http://www.ibm.com) offers a somewhat more technical definition:

A software system designed to support interoperable machine-to-machine interaction over a network. It has an interface described in a machine-processable format.

Finally, the W3C (http://www.w3c.com) offers the most elaborate definition, describing a web service as follows:

A service that is accessible by means of messages sent using standard web protocols, notations, and naming conventions, including XML protocol (or until XML protocol is standardized, SOAP). Web service may also imply the use of ancillary mechanisms, such as WSDL and UDDI for defining web services interfaces.

Though multiple definitions exist, ultimately each conveys the same meaning—that a web service is an application component that exposes its functionality by using standard web protocols. The standard web protocols are SOAP[1] and Web Services Description Language (WSDL). Both are XML based. SOAP is typically used for invoking a method on a remote server, and WSDL describes the service interface for a remote service. SOAP can also be used for exchanging data between two applications, for example, returning response data from the server to the client in a format both sides can understand.

Web services help integrate heterogeneous applications that were developed using different languages, run on different platforms, and use different technologies. In this chapter, you will learn how this is achieved. First, I describe the web services integration model, which explains how the two applications connect to each other.

Web Services Integration Model

Web services technology connects two applications by using XML-based protocols. An application requests a service from another cooperating application by sending an XML-based message to it. This message is called a *SOAP request*. The requestor embeds a method call for the remote application within the message. In addition, this message contains the parameters required by the remote method. The remote application executes the requested method and may send another XML-based message in response to the requestor. Like the requesting message, the response is also in SOAP format and contains the return value of the remote procedure call. This request/response messaging model is illustrated in Figure 3-1.

---

1. SOAP was originally an acronym for Simple Object Access Protocol, but the full name has been dropped.

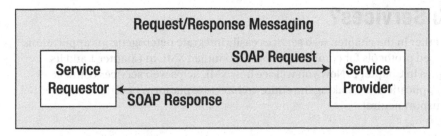

Figure 3-1. *Request/response messaging model*

In some situations, a client may not be interested in receiving any response from the server. In this case, we use one-way messaging, as illustrated in Figure 3-2.

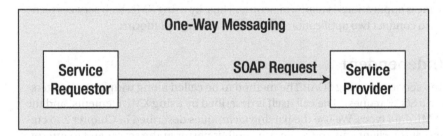

Figure 3-2. *One-way messaging model*

In both situations, SOAP is the protocol of choice for transporting data between the applications. In both models, a SOAP request encapsulates a call to a method exposed on the remote machine. In the first model, when a SOAP response is returned to the client, it contains the data for the service requestor. Thus, SOAP does not always have to embed a method call. It can simply be used for data transport between two applications. SOAP is a high-level protocol that rides over another network protocol such as HyperText Transport Protocol (HTTP), Simple Mail Transfer Protocol (SMTP), or Transmission Control Protocol/Internet Protocol (TCP/IP).

■**Tip** There is another model available for web services construction: Representational State Transfer (REST). [2] It is based on transaction-oriented services, rather than publishing-oriented services. REST is a term coined by Roy Fielding in his PhD dissertation (http://www.ics.uci.edu/~fielding/pubs/dissertation/top.htm).

Before learning about web services architecture and components in detail, take a look at why you should use web services.

---

2. The topic of REST is beyond the scope of this book. For further information, refer to the article "Building Web Services the REST Way" by Roger L. Costello (http://www.xfront.com/REST-Web-Services.html).

Why Web Services?

As mentioned earlier in the chapter, web services easily integrate heterogeneous applications and use XML-based protocols for communication. You studied XML in Chapter 1 and its parsing techniques in Chapter 2. Now you will see how XML helps web services connect heterogeneous applications by making the entire architecture platform neutral, language neutral, and transport neutral.

Platform Independent

As you learned in previous chapters, XML is platform independent. Not a binary protocol, XML's text-based implementation does not depend on a particular hardware or software platform. XML-based web services use SOAP and WSDL. Because both are XML based, the applications that you write by using web services technology also become platform neutral. Note that the business application at either end is platform dependent; however, the software component that connects two business applications is platform neutral. Thus, by using XML, web services technology allows you to connect two applications that run on different platforms.

Language Independent

A client calls a web service by using SOAP. The method to be called along with its parameters is encapsulated in a SOAP request. The call itself is described by using XML elements, and the parameters use XML data types. We use the parsing techniques described in Chapter 2 to create a SOAP request at the client end and again use another parser at the server end to interpret the call into a binary method call required by the server. Because the SOAP calls use XML data types, the calls are language neutral. Thus, even if the client and server applications are written in different languages, the data type mismatch on the method parameters and method return types does not occur.

Transport Independent

SOAP is a high-level protocol that rides on top of HTTP. Though the current SOAP implementations support only HTTP, nothing prevents us from using other transport protocols. This makes the web services architecture transport neutral.

In addition to having a platform-, language-, and transport-neutral architecture, web services derive additional benefits from the use of XML and HTTP.

XML's Extensibility

XML is *extensible*, meaning you can add your own tags to an XML document. You simply need to follow a few formatting rules described in Chapter 1. When SOAP was originally designed, it came with several limitations. Most notably, transporting a binary security context or a transaction context in a SOAP request was not possible because it was a text-based protocol. However, XML's extensibility made it possible to add new features to SOAP. For instance, now a SOAP request can have binary attachments containing security and transaction context. In the future, even more features may be easily added to SOAP because of XML's extensible nature.

HTTP Tunneling

HTTP tunneling is defined as the process of hiding another protocol inside HTTP messages. This is important because even tightly controlled corporate firewalls are generally open to HTTP traffic. Because the SOAP protocol rides on top of HTTP, SOAP requests and responses can penetrate the firewall as if they were HTTP messages.

Web Services Architecture

The web services architecture consists of three major components:

- Service provider
- Service requestor
- Universal Description, Discovery, and Integration (UDDI) registry

The first two components are mandatory. Use of the UDDI registry is optional. The *service provider* creates a service and publishes it for the use of others. The *service requestor* requests the service from the service provider and consumes it. The *UDDI registry* makes available a list of services for service consumers to find. If a service requestor is aware of an existing service, it does not need to use the registry to locate the service. The service registry stores the references to service descriptions, namely WSDL documents. WSDL is discussed later in this chapter.

Let's now consider the purpose of each component by walking through the sequence of operations as illustrated in Figure 3-3.

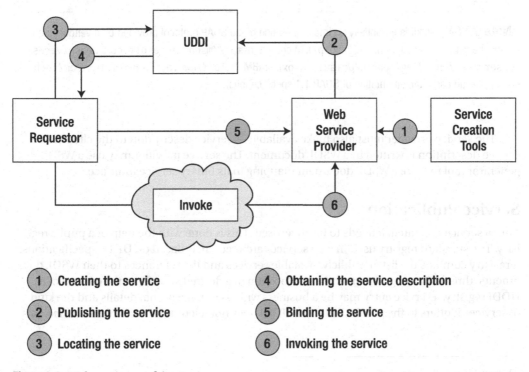

Figure 3-3. *Web services architecture*

The following operations take place in the specified sequence throughout the life cycle of a web service, from creation to consumption:

1. Creating the service

2. Publishing the service

3. Locating the service

4. Obtaining the service description

5. Binding the service

6. Invoking the service

Each of these operations is explained in detail next.

Service Creation

The service provider creates a service in much the same way as a standard application has been built over the years, because a service is essentially a software component written in any desired language. The difference is that the service exposes a certain part of its functionality to the public. The service requestor invokes these public methods by sending a SOAP request. The server may send a SOAP response to the requestor. The service provider must contain an XML parser to interpret SOAP requests and to generate a SOAP response to the consumer. The service provider may use a SOAP toolkit to facilitate this development.

Note A SOAP toolkit is essentially an implementation of the SOAP protocol provided by a vendor, such as Apache (http://ws.apache.org/soap/), Microsoft (http://msdn.microsoft.com/webservices/webservices/building/soaptk/default.aspx), or IBM (http://www.alphaworks.ibm.com/tech/soap4j/—an early implementation of SOAP 1.1 specifications).

The service provider must also make available its service description to the clients. The service description is written in a WSDL document. The service provider may use a WSDL generator tool to write a WSDL document mapping to its binary service interface.

Service Publication

After a service is created, it needs to be advertised. This is done with the help of a public registry. The standard registry used in web services architecture is based on UDDI specifications.[3] A registry contains the list of publicly available services and the references to their WSDL documents, thus facilitating the search for the location of a desired service. In the context of a UDDI registry, a service entry may be a business with its organizational details and the kind of services it offers to the public. Note that UDDI does not tell us how to invoke a service; this

---

3. http://www.uddi.org

is accomplished in a WSDL document. UDDI simply holds the reference URL from which the WSDL document can be obtained. Note that the registry itself can be private or public; this matter is discussed in further detail later in the chapter.

Service Location

A client searches for a desired service on the UDDI registry. UDDI itself is exposed as a web service and thus the search uses XML-based protocols. The client specifies a search criterion while searching the UDDI registry. The UDDI API provides methods for publishing information in the registry and searching the registry for desired information. UDDI uses the request/response messaging model for the search. Thus, the client sends a SOAP request for searching UDDI and receives a SOAP response containing search results. A typical search result may return a collection of services that match the given search criterion.

Service Description

After selecting a service from the list of services obtained from the registry, the client obtains the service description from the URL specified in the registry. The service description is contained in a WSDL document, which describes the message structures for both the SOAP request and response. To give you a feel for what a WSDL document looks like, I have included a sample in Listing 3-1. The structure of this document is fully explained later, in the "WSDL" section.

Listing 3-1. *A Sample WSDL Document*

```
<?xml version="1.0" encoding="UTF-8"?>
<definitions xmlns="http://schemas.xmlsoap.org/wsdl/" xmlns:tns="urn:Foo"
            xmlns:xsd="http://www.w3.org/2001/XMLSchema"
            xmlns:soap="http://schemas.xmlsoap.org/wsdl/soap/"
                name="MyHelloService" targetNamespace="urn:Foo">
<types/>
  <message name="HelloIF_sayHello">
    <part name="String_1" type="xsd:string"/>
  </message>
  <message name="HelloIF_sayHelloResponse">
    <part name="result" type="xsd:string"/>
  </message>
  <portType name="HelloIF">
    <operation name="sayHello" parameterOrder="String_1">
      <input message="tns:HelloIF_sayHello"/>
      <output message="tns:HelloIF_sayHelloResponse"/>
    </operation>
  </portType>
  <binding name="HelloIFBinding" type="tns:HelloIF">
    <soap:binding transport=
          "http://schemas.xmlsoap.org/soap/http" style="rpc"/>
      <operation name="sayHello">
        <soap:operation soapAction=""/>
          <input>
```

```
          <soap:body
                encodingStyle=http://schemas.xmlsoap.org/soap/encoding/
                use="encoded" namespace="urn:Foo"/>
        </input>
        <output>
          <soap:body
                encodingStyle=http://schemas.xmlsoap.org/soap/encoding/
                        xmlns:wsdl="http://schemas.xmlsoap.org/wsdl/"/>
        </output>
      </port>
    </service>
</definitions>
```

The client and server must both adhere to the structures defined within the WSDL while interacting with the service. For instance, the request may require a few input parameters to be passed to the service. The type of parameters and their restrictions are listed in the message structure given in the WSDL document. Similarly, the data type of the response is described in the output message structure. Note that in both cases the data types used are XML data types.[4]

Service Binding

The WSDL document obtained from the service provider also provides information on how to bind to the service. The binding information consists of the network IP at which the service is running, the port at which it is listening, and the network protocol that the service understands. The client uses this information to connect to the service provider. When the client connects successfully to the service, we say that it is *bound* to the service.

Service Invocation

At this stage, the client is connected to the service provider. From there, the client consumes the service by invoking various methods exposed by the provider (see Figure 3-4).

For each method call, the client has to construct a SOAP request. You can use DOM or XMLBeans models described in Chapter 2 to construct an XML-based SOAP request document. Alternatively, you can use other APIs such as SOAP with Attachments API for Java (SAAJ)[5] for constructing SOAP request documents using Java. The request document is dispatched to the server by using messaging infrastructure.

On the server side, the message request document is parsed by using some of the parsing techniques described in Chapter 2. A binary method call is constructed that maps to the requested operation. The server runs this method and returns a binary result. The result is then encapsulated in a SOAP document and dispatched to the client by using a messaging infrastructure. The client interprets this message and extracts the return value of the method call for its use.

This completes our discussion of the complete life cycle of a web service operation. Now you will study the web service components: SOAP, WSDL, and UDDI.

---

4. XML data types are discussed in Chapter 1.

5. http://java.sun.com/webservices/saaj/index.jsp

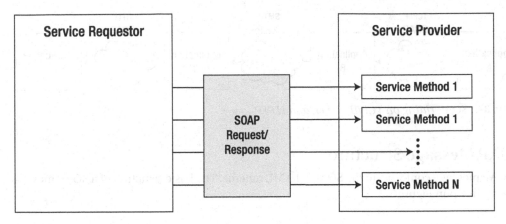

Figure 3-4. *Invocation of multiple services*

SOAP

SOAP is a widely accepted standard messaging protocol that facilitates the exchange of data between network-enabled applications. Supported by Microsoft, IBM, Sun Microsystems, HP, Oracle, SAP, BEA Systems, and many others, and endorsed by the W3C in May 2000 as the standard protocol for application-to-application messaging, SOAP is enjoying strong support in all areas of the web services camp. SOAP is also endorsed by other major standards organizations including the Web Services Interoperability Organization (WS-I)[6] and the Organization for the Advancement of Structured Information Standards.[7] At the time of this writing, the current version of SOAP is 1.2.

What Is SOAP?

SOAP encapsulates and encodes XML-based data, readying it for transmission as a payload of some other network protocol such as HTTP, although protocols such as File Transfer Protocol (FTP), SMTP, and TCP/IP are all perfectly acceptable network vehicles.

Figure 3-5 illustrates how SOAP messages can be communicated among several protocols throughout the course of transmission. The communication protocol between Application A and Application B is raw TCP/IP. Between Application B and Application C, SOAP messages are sent as part of e-mail that uses SMTP for transport. Applications C and D connect by using HTTP, and SOAP rides on HTTP in this case. Thus, SOAP is a top-level protocol that can ride on any of the existing network protocols.

An XML-based protocol, SOAP also facilitates interoperability between applications written in different programming languages and running on different operating systems.

---

6. http://www.ws-i.org/

7. http://www.oasis-open.org

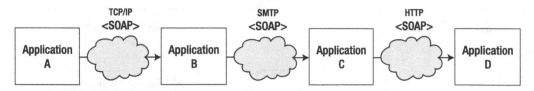

Figure 3-5. *SOAP riding on TCP/IP, SMTP, and HTTP*

SOAP Message Structure

A SOAP message conforms to the SOAP 1.1 XML schema. The basic structure of a SOAP message is shown in Figure 3-6.

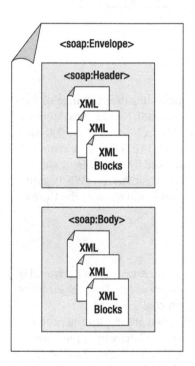

Figure 3-6. *SOAP message structure*

A SOAP message consists of an outer Envelope element. This becomes the root element of a SOAP document. Within the Envelope, you have an optional Header and a mandatory Body element.

The header provides for extensibility and can be used for passing information that is not part of the application payload. The application payload contains the data that one application wants to share with the other application, whereas the header may contain contextual information related to the processing of the current message. Additionally, the header may contain instructions to the receiving node on how to process the payload. Thus, the header effectively extends the SOAP message in an application-specific manner.

A typical SOAP message is shown in Listing 3-2. This message is fully explained in Chapter 4.

Listing 3-2. *A Typical SOAP Message*

```
<?xml version="1.0" encoding="UTF-8" ?>

<SOAP-ENV:Envelope
  xmlns:xsi="http://www.w3.org/2001/XMLSchema-instance"
  xmlns:xsd="http://www.w3.org/2001/XMLSchema"
  xmlns:SOAP-ENV="http://schemas.xmlsoap.org/soap/envelope/">
  <SOAP-ENV:Body>
    <ns1:getStockQuote
      xmlns:ns1="urn:QuoteService"
      SOAP-ENV:encodingStyle="http://schemas.xmlsoap.org/soap/encoding/">
      <symbol xsi:type="xsd:string">
        MSFT
      </symbol>
    </ns1:getStockQuote>
  </SOAP-ENV:Body>
</SOAP-ENV:Envelope>
```

The first statement in Listing 3-2 declares the current document as an XML document instance. The root element Envelope on the second line indicates that this is a SOAP document. The Envelope element declares the SOAP-ENV namespace. The Body element belongs to this SOAP-ENV namespace. Similarly, the Header and Fault elements belong to the SOAP-ENV namespace. The Fault element may occur in a response message generated by the server.

You can declare other namespaces in the Envelope element or in any other element, such as Header or Body. Such declarations will obviously have the scope of the corresponding element. Thus, if you declare a namespace in the Body element, it will be visible within the scope of that element. The namespaces and their declaration scopes were discussed in Chapter 1.

The optional Header element can contain application-specific data, if it is present. This information might be added by an application after processing the information in the message body. For instance, in our stock brokerage application in Chapter 2, an intermediary can add the "processed by" information in the header. Because such information is independent of the document contents (for example a purchase order), it should not be added in the SOAP body. Thus, it is added in the SOAP header. The subsequent recipients can examine the header to check the approvals. This scenario is explained further in the upcoming section "Application of Header Blocks."

The Body element contains the application payload. This might include a call to the remote server method. If a call results in some exception, the SOAP document describes it by using the Fault element. For a request message, the Body element encapsulates the method call and its parameters. For a response message, the Body element encapsulates the method result or an exception object.

I will now describe these three elements (Envelope, Header, Body) in more detail.

The Envelope Element

Envelope is the SOAP message's root element and is mandatory in all messages. It identifies the current XML document as a SOAP message. Envelope consists of an optional Header element and a mandatory Body element and can contain an attribute called encodingStyle. This attribute indicates the serialization rules used in a SOAP message. You declare the encoding style as shown in the following code fragment:

```
<?xml version="1.0"?>
<soap:Envelope xmlns:soap=http://schemas.xmlsoap.org/soap/envelope/
    soap:encodingStyle=http://www.w3.org/2001/12/soapencoding>
    ...
</soap:Envelope>
```

The encodingStyle attribute is global and can be used on other elements in the SOAP document. The following declaration shows the application of encodingStyle in other elements:

```
<soap:body use="encoded" namespace="http://example.com/stockquote"
encodingStyle="http://schemas.xmlsoap.org/soap/encoding/"/>
```

Thus, the different elements in the document can use different encoding styles.

The Header Element

Header is an optional element. If present, it must be the first child of the Envelope element. The Header must be fully qualified, and all its child elements must also be fully namespace qualified. As seen in Chapter 1, a fully qualified element consists of a namespace URI and a local name.

The header provides a mechanism for extending the SOAP message in a decentralized and modular way because it can consist of zero or more SOAP header blocks. A SOAP message may pass through several nodes before it reaches its ultimate destination. A header block can be used for storing processing information for the intermediate nodes.

The Header element can possess the following attributes:

- actor

- mustUnderstand

- encodingStyle

The actor Attribute

This actor attribute is used to address the Header element to a particular endpoint. A URI is used to specify the attribute value. Omitting this attribute indicates that the recipient is the ultimate destination of the SOAP message. The following code fragment illustrates the use of the actor attribute:

```
<soap:Header>
  <book:Order
    xmlns:book="http://www.apress.com/book/"
    soap:actor="http://www.amazon.com/xml/">
      Java XML book
  </book:Order>
</soap:Header>
```

In this document, the actor www.amazon.com operates on the order before forwarding the request to the next node, which may be www.apress.com.

The mustUnderstand Attribute

The mustUnderstand attribute indicates to the message receiver whether processing the received message is mandatory or optional. A value of 1 for this attribute indicates that the receiving node must process the message. A value of 0 indicates that processing is optional. This is an optional attribute, and its absence is semantically equivalent to its presence with the value 0. Note that the message recipient is defined by the corresponding SOAP actor attribute in the header block. The following code fragment illustrates the use of this attribute:

```
<soap:Header>
  <book:Order
    xmlns:book="http://www.apress.com/book/"
    soap:actor="http://www.amazon.com/xml/"
    soap:mustUnderstand="1">
      Java XML book
  </book:Order>
</soap:Header>
```

In this case, the receiving node, www.amazon.com, must process the current order before forwarding it to the next node.

The encodingStyle Attribute

The purpose of the encodingStyle attribute is the same as discussed earlier in the context of the Envelope element. It defines the serialization rules used in the XML document.

Application of Header Blocks

The application of header blocks can be illustrated with the use of a typical processed-by header block. This is one of the important header blocks used by intermediaries when the message gets routed through several nodes. Figure 3-7 illustrates a typical path a SOAP message may take on its way to its ultimate destination.

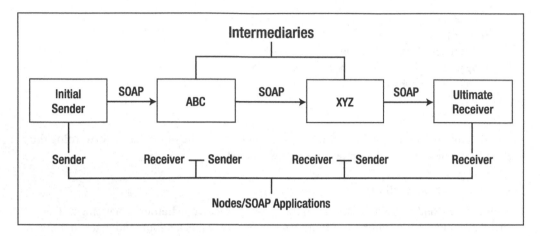

Figure 3-7. *A typical SOAP message path*

The initial sender sends a message to node ABC. After processing the message, node ABC forwards it to node XYZ. The XYZ node further processes the message and forwards it to the ultimate message recipient. The header blocks may contain the processing instructions for these intermediaries, ABC and XYZ.

Returning to our example of the stock brokerage from Chapter 2, suppose a customer places an online trade order with the broker. After processing the order, the broker forwards it to the main broker, that is, our stock brokerage. The stock brokerage further processes the order and forwards it to a stock exchange, which is the ultimate recipient of the trade order. The message path is illustrated in Figure 3-8.

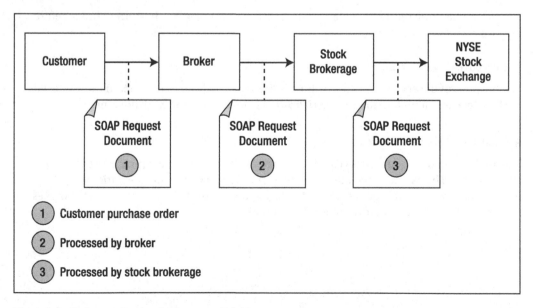

Figure 3-8. *Order processing by intermediaries*

As the order travels through different nodes, the stock exchange would like to track all the members who processed the order. Each member (node) can store the processed information in the header block of the message. This information can be captured in the processed-by header block, as shown in Listing 3-3.

Listing 3-3. *SOAP Header Blocks*

```
<?xml version="1.0" encoding="utf-8" ?>
<soap:Envelope
xmlns:soap="http://schemas.xmlsoap.org/soap/envelope/"
xmlns:NYSE="http://www.example.com/NYSE/Stocks/Tradeorder"
xmlns:processor="http://www.example.com/NYSE/trades/processed-by">
  <soap:Header>
    <NYSE:message-id>
    ...
    </NYSE:message-id>
    <processor:processed-by>
      <node>
        <name>
          broker
        </name>
        <time-in-millis>
          1015984780200
        </time-in-millis>
        <identity>
          http://www.example.com/broker
        </identity>
      </node>
      <node>
        <name>
          Brokerage
        </name>
        <time-in-millis>
          1015984780210
        </time-in-millis>
        <identity>
          http://www.example.com/brokerage/trades
        </identity>
      </node>
    </processor:processed-by>
  </soap:Header>
  <soap:Body>
    <NYSE:scrip>
      MSFT
    </NYSE:scrip>
```

```
    <NYSE:quantity>
       1000
    </NYSE:quantity>
    <NYSE:price>
       25.25
    </NYSE:price>
  </soap:Body>
</soap:Envelope>
```

The processed-by header block contains a subelement called node. Each processing node will add this element to the processed-by header block. The node element contains subelements such as name, time-in-millis, and identity.

In Listing 3-3, the customer has placed a trade request for MSFT; the quantity equals 1,000 and the price equals $25.25. Before the order reaches the NYSE, it goes through the broker node and our stock brokerage node. The broker node has added its name, the processing time, and identity information to the processed-by header block by adding a node element to it.

Our brokerage has added similar information to this processed-by header block by adding another node element to it. Ultimately, when the order is received by the NYSE, the stock exchange will know who has processed the order on its way and also have the processing details at their disposal.

Note that this processing information is not relevant to the trade request and thus should not be placed in the document body, although nothing prevents you from doing so. It is a good practice to separate the application data from the other application-irrelevant data such as processing information by intermediaries.

The Body Element

All SOAP messages must contain exactly one Body element. The Body element contains the information that is exchanged with the message recipient. The information may be application-specific data, a method call on the remote application, or details on the application-generated exception.

A Body element can contain many child elements, known as *body entries*. Like the Body element, each body entry must be identified by its fully qualified element name consisting of the namespace URI and the local name.

Each body entry is encoded as an independent element. The encodingStyle attribute can be applied to each body entry to indicate the encoding style.

The Body element from Listing 3-3 is reproduced in Listing 3-4 for easy reference.

Listing 3-4. *Code Fragment Illustrating Use of the SOAP Body Element*

```
  <soap:Body>
    <NYSE:scrip>
      MSFT
    </NYSE:scrip>
    <NYSE:quantity>
       1000
    </NYSE:quantity>
```

```
<NYSE:price>
  100.25
</NYSE:price>
</soap:Body>
```

The Body element in this example contains scrip, quantity, and price body entries.

A Body element may contain a Fault entry to describe the exception, as shown in Listing 3-5.

Listing 3-5. *Code Fragment Illustrating* Fault

```
<?xml version="1.0" encoding="UTF-8"?>
<soap:Envelope
xmlns:soap="http://schemas.xmlsoap.org/soap/envelope/">
  <soap:Body>
    <soap:Fault>
       ...
    </soap:Fault>
  </soap:Body>
</soap:Envelope>
```

The Fault element, in turn, contains subelements that describe the generated exception. Use of this element is discussed next.

The Fault Element

A SOAP Body element can contain a Fault element to indicate that a fault was generated during message processing. Such messages containing a Fault element are called *fault messages*. They provide a mechanism by which an application reports an error to upstream nodes in the message path.

A fault message might be generated by the ultimate receiver or any intermediary. In the request/response model, the receiver must send a SOAP fault back to its sender. In one-way messaging, the receiver might store the fault somewhere for postoperation auditing.

If a Fault element is present, it must appear as a body entry and it must not appear more than once within a Body element. The Fault element contains the following subelements:

- faultcode
- faultstring
- faultactor
- detail

The faultcode element

This element identifies the type of fault and is a mandatory subelement of a Fault element. The SOAP specifications define the following standard codes:

- Client
- Server
- VersionMismatch
- MustUnderstand

The Client faultcode The Client faultcode indicates that the sending node caused the current error. This might be because a message is not well formed or contains invalid data content. Sometimes the message is well formed but lacks the information the receiver is expecting. In this case too, the Client faultcode should be thrown to the sender. Listing 3-6 illustrates the use of Client faultcode.

Listing 3-6. *Example of* Client faultcode

```
<?xml version="1.0" encoding="UTF-8"?>
<soap:Envelope
xmlns:soap="http://schemas.xmlsoap.org/soap/envelope/">
  <soap:Body>
    <soap:Fault>
      <faultcode>
        soap:Client
      </faultcode>
      <faultstring>
        Too LARGE quantity
      </faultstring>
      <detail/>
    </soap:Fault>
  </soap:Body>
</soap:Envelope>
```

In this example, the client has placed a trade order for a quantity that exceeds his credit limit. The processing node, which may be the broker node, should send a fault message to the client, as given in Listing 3-6.

The Server faultcode The Server faultcode indicates that the receiving node has malfunctioned or it is unable to process the SOAP message. Listing 3-7 illustrates the use of Server faultcode.

Listing 3-7. *Example of* Server faultcode

```
<?xml version="1.0" encoding="UTF-8"?>
<soap:Envelope
xmlns:soap="http://schemas.xmlsoap.org/soap/envelope/">
<soap:Body>
  <soap:Fault>
    <faultcode>soap:Server</faultcode>
      <faultstring>
          The Order processing application is currently unavailable.➡
          Please try after some time.
      </faultstring>
      <detail/>
    </soap:Fault>
  </soap:Body>
</soap:Envelope>
```

In this example, the server could be too busy or the order processing application could be down. The server then generates a fault message as in Listing 3-7 and sends it to its sender.

The VersionMismatch faultcode The VersionMismatch faultcode indicates that the receiving node doesn't recognize the namespace of a SOAP message's Envelope element. Listing 3-8 illustrates the use of this faultcode.

Listing 3-8. *Example of* VersionMismatch faultcode

```
<?xml version="1.0" encoding="UTF-8"?>
<soap:Envelope
xmlns:soap="http://schemas.xmlsoap.org/soap/envelope/">
  <soap:Body>
    <soap:Fault>
      <faultcode>soap:VersionMismatch</faultcode>
        <faultstring>
          Order Request was not SOAP 1.1-conformant
        </faultstring>
        <detail/>
      </soap:Fault>
  </soap:Body>
</soap:Envelope>
```

The MustUnderstand faultcode If the SOAP request sets the mustUnderstand attribute to 1, the receiving node must process the message. However, if it does not recognize the header block, it will generate and send a fault message to the sender, as illustrated in Listing 3-9.

Listing 3-9. *Example of* MustUnderstand faultcode

```
<?xml version="1.0" encoding="UTF-8"?>
<soap:Envelope
xmlns:soap="http://schemas.xmlsoap.org/soap/envelope/">
  <soap:Body>
    <soap:fault><soap:Fault>
      <faultcode>
        soap:MustUnderstand
      </faultcode>
      <faultstring>
        Mandatory header block not understood.
      </faultstring>
      <detail/>
    </soap:Fault>
  </soap:Body>
</soap:Envelope>
```

Nonstandard SOAP faultcodes In addition to the standard faultcodes, you may be required to report other fault conditions to the sender. For example, a sender may send a previously obtained security token to the server while making a fresh request. If this token has become invalid by this time, the server will send an invalid security token fault message to the sender. The message is illustrated in Listing 3-10.

Listing 3-10. *Example of a Nonstandard* faultcode

```
<?xml version="1.0" encoding="UTF-8"?>
<soap:Envelope
xmlns:soap="http://schemas.xmlsoap.org/soap/envelope/"
xmlns:wsse="http://schemas.xmlsoap.org/ws/2002/06/secext">
  <soap:Body>
    <soap:Fault>
      <faultcode>
        wsse:InvalidSecurityToken
      </faultcode>
      <faultstring>
        Session timed out. Please logon again!
      </faultstring>
      <detail/>
    </soap:Fault>
  </soap:Body>
</soap:Envelope>
```

The faultstring Element

This is a mandatory element that provides a human-readable description of the fault. Different people may write different descriptions for the same fault. So far, there is no standardization on the text contents of this element. The text message can be written in any language. The special attribute xml:lang indicates the language used. Listing 3-11 illustrates use of the faultstring element.

Listing 3-11. *Example of a* faultstring *Element*

```
<?xml version="1.0" encoding="UTF-8"?>
<soap:Envelope
xmlns:soap="http://schemas.xmlsoap.org/soap/envelope/">
  <soap:Body>
    <soap:Fault>
      <faultcode>
        soap:Client
      </faultcode>
      <faultstring xml:lang="en">
        Order contains Invalid Stock Code
      </faultstring>
      <detail/>
    </soap:Fault>
  </soap:Body>
</soap:Envelope>
```

The `faultactor` element

The `faultactor` element indicates which node encountered the error and generated the fault. This is a required element if the faulting node is an intermediary. If the faulting node is an ultimate receiver, this element is optional. Listing 3-12 illustrates the use of the `faultactor` element.

Listing 3-12. *Example of a* `faultactor` *Element*

```
<?xml version="1.0" encoding="UTF-8"?>
<soap:Envelope
xmlns:soap="http://schemas.xmlsoap.org/soap/envelope/">
  <soap:Body>
    <soap:Fault>
      <faultcode>
        soap:MustUnderstand
      </faultcode>
      <faultstring>
        Mandatory header block not understood.
      </faultstring>
      <faultactor>
        http://www.example.com/brokerage/trades
      </faultactor>
      <detail/>
    </soap:Fault>
  </soap:Body>
</soap:Envelope>
```

In this example, the faulting node is `www.example.com/brokerage/trades` as indicated by the contents of the `faultactor` element.

The `detail` Element

This element is included if the fault was caused by the contents of the `Body` element. This must not be included if the error occurred while processing a header block. This may contain other application-specific elements. The use of the `detail` element is illustrated in Listing 3-13.

Listing 3-13. *Example of a* `detail` *Element*

```
<?xml version="1.0" encoding="UTF-8"?>
<soap:Envelope
xmlns:soap="http://schemas.xmlsoap.org/soap/envelope/"
xmlns:NYSE="http://www.example.com/NYSE/Stocks/Tradeorder">
  <soap:Body>
    <soap:Fault>
      <faultcode>
        soap:Client
      </faultcode>
      <faultstring>
        Invalid Purchase Order
      </faultstring>
```

```
    <detail>
      <NYSE:invalidOrderDetail>
        <NYSE:offending-scrip>
          MSFT
        </NYSE:offending-scrip>
        <NYSE:reason>
            The requested stock price for the buy order is too large as ➡
            compared to the current market price.
        </NYSE:reason>
      </NYSE:invalidOrderDetail>
    </detail>
  </soap:Fault>
 </soap:Body>
</soap:Envelope>
```

In this example, the client has placed a buy order with an astronomically high purchase price on the NYSE for MSFT. The server sends a fault message by giving out the offending details in the detail element. The detail element contains application-specific tags, offending-scrip and reason.

You have so far studied the structure of a SOAP document. After a document is constructed, it is dispatched by using a messaging server. SOAP defines two messaging modes that dictate how the message is dispatched. This topic is discussed next.

SOAP Messaging Modes

A SOAP message can be transported in one of two modes: Document-style or RPC-style. In Document-style mode, the entire document is sent within the body of the message or as an attachment to the message. In RPC-style mode, a particular method call is embedded in the document. After processing the message, the server may return a response to the client.

Either of these modes can use literal or SOAP encoding. In literal encoding, the document fragment can be validated against its XML schema. SOAP encoding is described in section 5 of the SOAP 1.1 specification.[8] SOAP encoding causes interoperability problems. The XML schema makes the use of SOAP encoding obsolete.

Based on the type of messaging and the encoding style, there are four distinct messaging modes:

- Document/Literal

- RPC/Literal

- RPC/Encoded

- Document/Encoded

The last two modes are not currently supported by the WS-I and thus are not covered in this book.

---

8. http://www.w3.org/TR/2000/NOTE-SOAP-20000508/#_Toc478383512

Document/Literal

In this mode, a SOAP Body element contains an XML document fragment. The XML document fragment is a well-formed XML element that contains arbitrary application data conforming to an XML schema. The document fragment uses a namespace separate from the SOAP message's namespace. Listing 3-14 shows a code fragment that illustrates how a document fragment is embedded in the SOAP Body element.

Listing 3-14. *Document/Literal Message*

```
<?xml version="1.0" encoding="UTF-8"?>
<soap:Envelope
xmlns:soap="http://schemas.xmlsoap.org/soap/envelope/"
xmlns:NYSE="http://www.example.com/NYSE/Stocks/Tradeorder">
  <soap:Body>
    <po:purchaseOrder orderDate="2005-08-25"
        xmlns:po="http://www.example.com/brokerage/orders/PO">
      <po:accountName>
        Poornachandra Sarang
      </po:accountName>
      <po:accountNumber>
        7219
      </po:accountNumber>
      ...
      <NYSE:scrip>
      MSFT
      </NYSE:scrip>
      <NYSE:quantity>
        1000
      </NYSE:quantity>
      <NYSE:price>
        100.25
      </NYSE:price>
      ...
    </po:purchaseOrder>
  </soap:Body>
</soap:Envelope>
```

The SOAP Body element contains a purchaseOrder element. This element belongs to the www.example.com/brokerage/orders/PO namespace prefixed po. This namespace is distinct from the global namespace NYSE. The po namespace is application specific. The receiver after parsing the document acts on the Body contents.

RPC/Literal

This mode enables SOAP messages to model calls to procedures with parameters and return values. An RPC request message contains the following items:

- Method name

- Input parameters (optional)

An RPC response message contains these items:

- Return value

- Any output parameters (optional)

- Fault (optional)

RPC/Literal messaging is used to expose traditional components as web services. A traditional component might be a servlet, stateless session bean, Java Remote Method Invocation (RMI) object, Common Object Request Broker Architecture (CORBA) object, or Distributed Component Object Model (DCOM) object. You will learn how to create web services by using some of these components in the next chapter.

RPC/Literal Request Message

In RPC-style messaging, the operation to be invoked on the web service is listed in the SOAP Body element. Listing 3-15 shows a typical RPC/Literal request SOAP message.

Listing 3-15. *RPC-Style Request Message*

```
<?xml version="1.0" encoding="UTF-8"?>
<soap:Envelope
xmlns:soap="http://schemas.xmlsoap.org/soap/envelope/"
xmlns:NYSE="http://www.example.com/NYSE/Stocks/Tradeorder">
  <soap:Body>
    <NYSE:getStockQuote>
      <NYSE:StockSymbol>
        MSFT
      </NYSE:StockSymbol>
    </NYSE:getStockQuote>
  </soap:Body>
</soap:Envelope>
```

In this case, the client sends a quote request to www.example.com/NYSE for the current price of MSFT stock. The method to be invoked on the remote server is getStockQuote, and the requested symbol is listed in the StockSymbol element.

RPC/Literal Response Message

After the message request in Listing 3-15 is executed, the server may send a response message. This response is shown in Listing 3-16.

Listing 3-16. *RPC-Style SOAP Response Message*

```
<?xml version="1.0" encoding="UTF-8"?>
<soap:Envelope
xmlns:soap="http://schemas.xmlsoap.org/soap/envelope/"
xmlns:NYSE="http://www.example.com/NYSE/Stocks/Tradeorder">
  <soap:Body>
    <NYSE:getStockQuoteResponse>
     <NYSE:StockSymbol>
       MSFT
     </NYSE:StockSymbol>
     <NYSE:price>
       26.81
     </NYSE:price>
    </NYSE:getStockQuoteResponse>
  </soap:Body>
</soap:Envelope>
```

The server returns the stock price for the requested symbol specified by the StockSymbol element in the contents of the price element.

SOAP over HTTP

So far you have learned how to create a SOAP request message and how to interpret a SOAP response document. Once constructed, a SOAP message needs an underlying transport—HTTP for instance. When you use HTTP as transport, SOAP messages are placed in its payload. In this section, I will illustrate both SOAP request and response messages riding on top of HTTP.

SOAP Request over HTTP

Consider our RPC-style request message in Listing 3-15. When this message is sent over HTTP, the data shown in Listing 3-17 would be sent to the server.

Listing 3-17. *SOAP Request over HTTP*

```
POST /IndigoService4/Service.svc HTTP/1.1
Host: localhost:8079
Content-Type: text/xml; charset="utf-8"
Content-Length: 282
SOAPAction: ""
Accept: text/html, image/gif, image/jpeg, *; q=.2, */*; q=.2
Connection: close
<?xml version="1.0" encoding="UTF-8" ?>
<soap:Envelope
  xmlns:soap="http://schemas.xmlsoap.org/soap/envelope/"
  xmlns:NYSE="http://www.example.com/NYSE/Stocks/Tradeorder">
```

```
  <soap:Body>
    <NYSE:getStockQuote>
      <NYSE:StockSymbol>
        MSFT
      </NYSE:StockSymbol>
    </NYSE:getStockQuote>
  </soap:Body>
</soap:Envelope>
```

Note the addition of the HTTP header information on top of the SOAP message. The client stub in your application adds this header information to your SOAP request. If you open the socket connection directly on the server, you will be responsible for generating this header information and adding it to the SOAP document.

■**Note** As you go along, you will understand the meaning of each and every statement in the SOAP request. Keep reading.

SOAP Reply over HTTP

After processing the request, the server sends a response to the client as a SOAP document. Such a response may consist of the result value of the method call or exception information. The server adds the header information to the SOAP response document as shown in Listing 3-18.

Listing 3-18. *SOAP Response over HTTP*

```
HTTP/1.1 200  OK
Content-Type:text/xml; charset='utf-8'
Content-Length: 311
<?xml version="1.0" encoding="UTF-8"?>
<soap:Envelope
xmlns:soap="http://schemas.xmlsoap.org/soap/envelope/"
xmlns:NYSE="http://www.example.com/NYSE/Stocks/Tradeorder">
  <soap:Body>
    <NYSE:getStockQuoteResponse>
      <NYSE:StockSymbol>
        MSFT
      </NYSE:StockSymbol>
      <NYSE:price>
        26.81
      </NYSE:price>
    </NYSE:getStockQuoteResponse>
  </soap:Body>
</soap:Envelope>
```

You will now study the next important component of web services architecture, that is, WSDL.

WSDL

As noted earlier in this chapter, WSDL is an acronym for *Web Services Description Language*. A WSDL document is an XML document used for describing the interface of a web service. It specifies the service's location, and describes both how to bind to it and which operations may be invoked on it. In other words, WSDL tells us where the service is located and how to use it. Like SOAP, WSDL has become another industry standard, with endorsements by major standards organizations such as the W3C, WS-I, and OASIS.

Why WSDL?

When you create a web service, you need to tell others how to use it. WSDL provides a standard means for doing so. For instance, to use the service, you need to know the kind of message you need to send to the service provider. Also, when the service sends you a reply, the client application should be able to interpret it. WSDL describes the structure for both these request and response messages.

A service may be connected to the client by using a particular Internet protocol, such as HTTP or FTP. WSDL describes the Internet protocol required by the service. Finally, the service is deployed at a specific URI. WSDL describes this URI.

Using the preceding information, the client connects to the specified URI by using the specified transport. After the connection is obtained, the client sends a request message conforming to the structure defined in the WSDL document and waits for the server response. The server response message conforms to the structure defined in the WSDL document. The client interprets the message by using the message structure information read from the WSDL.

How to Use WSDL

WSDL is ideally suited for code generators that generate the client stub code by using the information available in a WSDL document. The client application then uses this stub to consume the service.

However, in some situations you may want to construct the SOAP request message yourself. This is the case with APIs such as SAAJ, Apache SOAP,[9] and others. In such cases, the human readability of a WSDL document becomes useful. By examining the WSDL document, you can understand the operations on the remote service along with the parameters it requires.

You can hand-code a SOAP request to invoke the desired operation. The response can be interpreted by parsing the SOAP response document and using the message structure information available in the WSDL document.

WSDL Document Structure

A WSDL document is an XML-based document that conforms to the WSDL schema definition. Listing 3-19 illustrates the document structure.

---

9. Apache SOAP is discussed in depth in Chapter 4.

Listing 3-19. *Structure of a WSDL Document*

```
<definitions>
  <types>
    type definitions
  </types>
  <message>
    definitions of request/response messages
  </message>
  <portType>
    abstract interface
  </portType>
  <binding>
    protocol assignment and encoding style
  </binding>
  <service>
    Internet address of a web service
  </service>
    ...
</definitions>
```

The definitions element is the root element of the WSDL document. It contains several nested elements:

- types

- import

- message

- portType

- operations

- binding

- service

- documentation

The purpose of each of these elements is described in the following subsections.

The definitions Element

This is the root element of the WSDL document. This declares the namespace for the WSDL 1.1 XML schema and other namespaces required by the current document. The following code fragment illustrates the use of the definitions element:

```
<definitions
  name="MyHelloService"
  xmlns="http://schemas.xmlsoap.org/wsdl/"
  xmlns:tns="urn:Foo"
  xmlns:xsd="http://www.w3.org/2001/XMLSchema"
  xmlns:soap="http://schemas.xmlsoap.org/wsdl/soap/"
  targetNamespace="urn:Foo">

  ...
</definitions>
```

The name attribute defines the name of this document. The name of the current document is MyHelloService. Note the declarations of multiple namespaces in the definitions element.

The types Element

The types element contains the data type definitions used by the current document. The data types are defined by using XML schema language. Chapter 1 discussed how to define data types in XML. Remember those SimpleType and ComplexType declarations in Chapter 1? The following code fragment illustrates the use of the types element:

```
<types>
  <schema
    targetNamespace="http://example.com/stockquote.xsd"
    xmlns="http://www.w3.org/2000/10/XMLSchema">
    <element name="TradePriceRequest">
      <complexType>
        <all>
          <element name="ticker" type = "string"/>
        </all>
      </complexType>
    </element>
  </schema>
</types>
```

In this example, we declare a new element type called TradePriceRequest. Note the use of the schema element to encapsulate the types declarations. As mentioned, we use XML schema language to declare new types. The types element can contain any number of such declarations. These declarations are visible within the scope of the current document.

The import Element

The import element specifies references to other WSDL documents from which you want to import the definitions in your current document. The following code fragment imports the definitions from stockquote.wsdl from the URI specified by the location attribute:

```
<import
  namespace="http://example.com/stockquote/definitions"
      location=http://example.com/stockquote/stockquote.wsdl
/>
```

The message Element

The message element describes a message's payload. It describes both outgoing and incoming messages. The message element contains a nested element called part that describes the method parameter and its data type. The following code fragment declares a message called getStockQuote that requires one parameter called symbol of type XML string:

```
<message name="getStockQuote">
  <part name="symbol" type="xs:string"/>
</message>
```

The message element describes payloads for both RPC-style and Document-style web services, discussed next.

The RPC-Style Message

The following code fragment declares two RPC-style messages. The getStockQuote is a request message that takes a parameter called symbol of type string. The getStockQuoteResponse is a response message that returns a value called price of type string:

```
<message name="getStockQuote">
  <part name="symbol" type="xs:string"/>
</message>
<message name="getStockQuoteResponse">
  <part name="price" type="xs:string"/>
</message>
```

The Document-Style Message

The following code fragment defines a Document-style message called SubmitPurchaseOrderMessage. This element uses a parameter called order. The order element is of type purchaseOrder. Note that the part element uses the element attribute. In RPC-style messaging, it uses the type attribute.

In Document-style messaging, the part name specifies the name of the document, and the type attribute specifies the element that defines the structure of this document. In RPC-style messaging, the part name specifies the parameter to a method of a type specified by the type attribute:

```
<definitions name="PurchaseOrderDefinitions"
  xmlns:PO="http://www.example.com/brokerage/orders/PO">
  <types>
    <xsd:schema
      targetNamespace="http://www.example.com/brokerage/subbrokers">
      <xsd:import namespace="http:// www.example.com/brokerage/orders/PO"
      schemalocation="http:// www.example.com/brokerage/orders/po.xsd" />
    </xsd:schema>
  </types>
  <message name="SubmitPurchaseOrderMessage">
    <part name="order" element="PO:purchaseOrder" />
  </message>
</definitions>
```

The portType and operation Elements

The portType element defines a web service's abstract interface. This can be compared to a Java interface. The portType element has a name attribute. The name attribute defines a unique name for this abstract interface in the scope of the enclosing WSDL document.

Just as a Java interface contains method declarations, the portType element contains one or more operation elements. The operation specifies the method that may be invoked on a web service. The operation has input and output subelements. The input and output elements can occur at most one time within a given operation element.

The operation may generate SOAP faults. Thus, the operation element may have any number of Fault elements.

The following code fragment illustrates the use of the portType and operation elements:

```
<portType name="StockQuote">
  <operation name="getStockQuote">
    <input name="symbol" message="getStockQuoteRequest"/>
    <output name="price" message="getStockQuoteResponse"/>
  </operation>
</portType>
```

In this example, the abstract interface name of the portType is StockQuote. It defines one operation called getStockQuote, which requires a single parameter called symbol. The request message structure is given by getStockQuoteRequest. The operation returns a response message defined by the getStockQuoteResponse element. The name of the output parameter is price.

From this definition, you can conclude that you can invoke a getStockQuote operation on the StockQuote service. To invoke the operation, you need to send a message of type getStockQuoteRequest. On the operation's return, the server sends you a message of type getStockQuoteResponse.

You can include multiple operation elements within a single service interface to define several operations defined in the interface.

The binding Element

The binding element provides the mapping between an abstract portType and concrete protocols. It also defines the messaging styles (RPC or Document) and the encoding styles (Literal or Encoded). Listing 3-20 illustrates the use of the binding element.

Listing 3-20. *Code Fragment Illustrating Use of* binding *Element*

```
<binding type="stockorders" name="StockQuoteBinding">
  <soap:binding style="document"
                transport="http://schemas.xmlsoap.org/soap/http"/>
  <operation>
    <soap:operation soapAction="http://www.example.com/broker/placeOrder"/>
    <input>
      <soap:body use="literal"/>
    </input>
```

```
    <output>
      <soap:body use="literal"/>
    </output>
  </operation>
</binding>
```

This example uses SOAP protocol-specific binding as specified by the use of the soap:binding element. The style attribute specifies the document type of binding. The other option is rpc style. The binding specifies one operation called placeOrder. The operation input is a Document Literal, and its output also is Document Literal as specified by the contents of the input and output elements, respectively.

The service Element

The service element lists one or more ports defined earlier and associates a URL with each port. The following code fragment declares a service called StockQuoteService:

```
<service name="StockQuoteService">
  <documentation>
    Provides latest stock quotes for stocks traded on NYSE
  </documentation>
  <port name="StockQuote" binding="broker:StockQuoteBinding">
    <soap:address location="http://www.example.com/broker/stockquote"/>
  </port>
</service>
```

The documentation element provides the human-friendly description of the service. This example declares one port called StockQuote. To bind to this port, you use binding specified by the StockQuoteBinding element. It associates the specified www.example.com/broker/stockquote URI with the StockQuote port.

You can associate more than one URL to the same binding. This is illustrated in the following code fragment:

```
<port name="StockQuote" binding="broker:StockQuoteBinding">
  <soap:address location="http://www.example.com/broker/stockquote"/>
</port>
<port name="StockQuote_alternate" binding="broker:StockQuoteBinding">
  <soap:address location="http://www.example.com/brokerage/stockquote"/>
</port>
```

The purpose behind providing two URLs to the same binding is that if one URL is not available because of network or server failure, the service can be obtained from the alternate URL.

So far, you have studied how to define messages in a WSDL document. Now, you will study the different modes for exchanging messages.

Messaging Exchange Pattern

There are four distinct ways of exchanging messages between the two applications:

- *One-way*: The client sends a message to the server endpoint.

- *Request/response*: The endpoint first receives a message and then sends a correlated message.

- *Solicit/response*: The endpoint first sends a message and then receives a correlated message.

- *Notification*: The endpoint sends a message to the client.

One-Way Messaging

In one-way messaging, the client sends a message to the server endpoint and does not expect a response from the server. The message flow is thus one-way, from client to server. The following code snippet illustrates one-way messaging:

```
<message name="lastTradePrice">
  <part name="symbol" type="xs:string"/>
  <part name="price" type="xs:string"/>
</message>
<portType name="TradePrices">
  <operation name="setLastTradePrice">
    <input name="newPrice" message="lastTradePrice"/>
  </operation>
 </portType >
```

In this example, first we create a message type called lastTradePrice. The message takes two parameters, symbol and price, both of type string. The abstract interface is TradePrices that defines one operation called setLastTradePrice. The operation uses only the input element, thus making it a one-way operation. The input message for this operation is lastTradePrice. You use this operation to set the last trade price for a desired stock.

Request/Response Messaging

In request/response messaging, the sender sends a message to some endpoint and expects a response message from it. The following code snippet illustrates this:

```
<message name="getStockQuoteRequest">
  <part name="symbol" type="xs:string"/>
</message>
<message name="getStockQuoteResponse">
  <part name="price" type="xs:string"/>
</message>
```

```
<portType name="StockQuotes">
  <operation name="getStockQuote">
    <input message="getStockQuoteRequest"/>
    <output message="getStockQuoteResponse"/>
  </operation>
</portType>
```

First, we define two message types required by our getStockQuote operation. The getStockQuoteRequest message defines the input message and uses one parameter called symbol of type string. The getStockQuoteResponse defines the response message type that returns a parameter called price of type string.

The abstract service interface is called StockQuotes that defines one operation called getStockQuote. The operation uses the two messages as input and output messages. The use of both input and output elements indicates that this operation is of request/response type.

Solicit/Response Messaging

In solicit/response messaging, the client subscribes to the service and waits for a message from the server. On receipt of the server message, the client sends a request message to the endpoint. The following code snippet illustrates the solicit/response type of messaging:

```
<message name="getStockQuoteRequest">
  <part name="symbol" type="xs:string"/>
</message>
<message name="ReadyForQuote"/>
<portType name="StockQuotes">
  <operation name="getStockQuote">
    <output message="ReadyForQuote"/>
    <input message="getStockQuoteRequest"/>
  </operation>
</portType>
```

In this example, the getStockQuote message waits for the server to get ready. The server sends a message called ReadyForQuote whenever it gets ready for serving the stock quotes. On receipt of this message from the server, the client sends a getStockQuoteRequest message to the server. Note that the ReadyForQuote message does not have any input parameters.

Notification Messaging

This is similar to the solicit/response type of messaging, except that the client does not send any message back to the server after it receives a message from the server. Thus, as the name suggests, the notification is one-way from server to client. The following code snippet illustrates notification of messaging:

```
<message name="ShutDownMessage">
  <part name="reason" type="xs:string"/>
</message>
```

```
<portType name="StockServer">
<operation name="ShutDown">
  <output message="ShutDownMessage"/>
</operation>
</portType>
```

In this example, the client registers with the server for some notification such as server shutdown. Whenever the server shuts down, it sends a ShutDownMessage to the client. The message contains a parameter called reason of type string that describes the reason for shutting down.

So far, we have dissected different parts of a WSDL document. Now you will study the WSDL document in its totality.

The Complete WSDL Example

Listing 3-21 presents a complete WSDL listing.

Listing 3-21. *Sample Complete WSDL Document*

```
1. <?xml version="1.0" encoding="UTF-8"?>
2. <definitions xmlns="http://schemas.xmlsoap.org/wsdl/"
                 xmlns:tns="urn:Foo"
                 xmlns:xsd="http://www.w3.org/2001/XMLSchema"
                 xmlns:soap="http://schemas.xmlsoap.org/wsdl/soap/"
                 name="MyHelloService" targetNamespace="urn:Foo">
3. <types/>
4.    <message name="HelloIF_sayHello">
5.      <part name="String_1" type="xsd:string"/>
6.    </message>
7.    <message name="HelloIF_sayHelloResponse">
8.      <part name="result" type="xsd:string"/>
9.    </message>
10.    <portType name="HelloIF">
11.      <operation name="sayHello" parameterOrder="String_1">
12.        <input message="tns:HelloIF_sayHello"/>
13.        <output message="tns:HelloIF_sayHelloResponse"/>
14.      </operation>
15.    </portType>
16.    <binding name="HelloIFBinding" type="tns:HelloIF">
17.      <soap:binding transport=
                  "http://schemas.xmlsoap.org/soap/http" style="rpc"/>
18.      <operation name="sayHello">
19.        <soap:operation soapAction=""/>
20.        <input>
21.          <soap:body
                  encodingStyle=http://schemas.xmlsoap.org/soap/encoding/
                  use="encoded" namespace="urn:Foo"/>
22.        </input>
```

```
23.              <output>
24.                <soap:body
                      encodingStyle=http://schemas.xmlsoap.org/soap/encoding/
                      use="encoded" namespace="urn:Foo"/>
25.              </output>
26.          </operation>
27.      </binding>
28.  <service name="MyHelloService">
29.          <port name="HelloIFPort" binding="tns:HelloIFBinding">
30.              <soap:address location=http://PGS:8080/hello-jaxrpc/hello
                                xmlns:wsdl="http://schemas.xmlsoap.org/wsdl/"/>
31.          </port>
32.      </service>
33.  </definitions>
```

Line 1 indicates that this is an XML document.

Line 2 declares the top-level element called definitions, making the current document a WSDL document. The name of the document is specified by the name attribute that is set to MyHelloService. Line 2 also declares the use of required namespaces.

Line 3 begins and ends with the types element. Thus, the current document does not declare any custom types.

Lines 4–6 declare a message called HelloIF_sayHello that takes one parameter called String_1 of type string.

Lines 7–9 declare another message type called HelloIF_sayHelloResponse that returns a result called result of type string.

Lines 10–15 define an abstract interface called HelloIF with the help of the portType element.

Lines 11–14 define an operation within this interface. The operation uses the request/response type of messaging as indicated by the use of both input and output subelements.

Line 11 names this operation sayHello and specifies that it takes one parameter called String_1. If the operation requires more than one parameter, the parameterOrder defines the sequence for these parameters by listing these parameter names in the desired order.

Line 12 specifies that the input to the sayHello operation is provided by the message called HelloIF_sayHello. Note that this message was defined earlier in the document.

Line 13 declares that sayHello sends a response message to the caller of type HelloIF_sayHelloResponse.

Lines 16–27 define binding for the HelloIF interface.

Line 16 assigns the name to this binding. The name is HelloIFBinding. The binding type is HelloIF as defined earlier.

Line 17 declares a protocol-specific binding with the use of the soap:binding element. The transport for this binding is http, and the messaging style is rpc.

Lines 18–26 define operations in this binding by using the operation element. The name of the operation is sayHello.

Line 19 declares this as a SOAP operation with no action required.

Lines 20–22 declare the input message bindings.

Line 21 declares the encoding style for the input message.

Lines 23–25 declare the output message bindings.

Line 24 declares the encoding style for the output message.

Lines 28–33 use the `service` element to bind the `HelloIF` service to a specific service URL.
Line 28 names this service `MyHelloService`.

Lines 29–31 declare a `port` within this service. Remember, we could declare more than one port within a service.

Line 29 names the current port as `HelloIFPort` and sets its binding to `HelloIFBinding` declared previously.

Line 30 specifies the address for this port. The address is specified by the `location` attribute.

Line 33 closes our WSDL document definition.

UDDI

UDDI is an acronym for *Universal Description, Discovery, and Integration.* UDDI is one of the standards for creating an XML-based registry. The other standard is Electronic Business Using XML (ebXML).[10]

The UDDI standard defines a way to centrally store information about businesses that is accessible on the World Wide Web. The standard also defines a mechanism for accessing this information in an efficient manner.

As seen earlier, businesses develop web services and publish their service interfaces in WSDL documents. The location of these WSDL documents is published in the UDDI registry. Additionally, the registries may be used to store general information about the businesses. A client can search the registry for the desired service as well as this general information on businesses. Access to the UDDI registry is SOAP based. A client can access, update, and search a UDDI registry by using a SOAP request/response mechanism.

Public and Private Registries

Registries can be public or private. A *public registry* is accessible to all users, and a *private registry* restricts its access to only authorized members. Two popular public registries are hosted by Microsoft and SAP, and are accessible through the following URLs:

- Microsoft: `http://test.uddi.microsoft.com/`

- SAP: `http://udditest.sap.com/`

■**Note** IBM used to offer a public registry. As of Jan 12, 2006, IBM decided to shut down its registry and it is thus no longer available. Refer to `http://uddi.ibm.com/testregistry/registry.html`.

The use of a public registry requires you to create a user account. Currently, such user accounts are free for test purposes. Private registries are generally used for intranet applications and are not accessible outside the organization's network.

---

10. ebXML was designed to meet the needs of business-to-business applications and is not covered in this book.

Having seen the purpose of the UDDI registry, you will now learn the internal data structures of the registry. Knowledge of these structures is required to understand the format in which the data is stored in the registry.

UDDI Data Structures

The UDDI specification defines five core data structures to express information in the UDDI registry (see Figure 3-9).

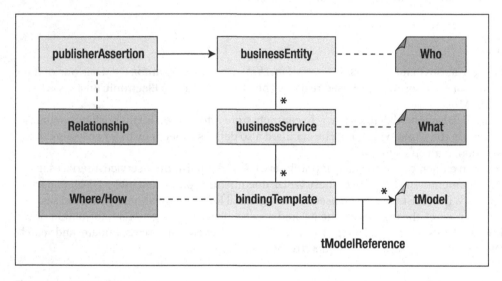

Figure 3-9. *UDDI data structures*

These data structures are defined in the UDDI version 2.0 API schema. Additionally, this schema defines approximately 40 SOAP messages that are used as requests and responses while communicating with the registry. The client uses these messages for accessing, updating, and searching the registry.

The businessEntity structure holds the information about a business. The businessEntity answers the question *who* in the registry. A businessService holds the information about the services offered by a business and answers *what* in the registry. The businessEntity has a one-to-many relationship to the businessService. This indicates that a business might offer more than one service.

Each businessService structure contains a specific instance of a bindingTemplate structure. The bindingTemplate instance provides information on where the service is running and how to bind to the service. The bindingTemplate answers the question *where/how* in the registry. A bindingTemplate is modeled based on the tModel instance.

A business may call another business as its associate. When such information is published by the first business in the registry, the second business must assert it. The publisherAssertion structure describes the "relationship" between two parties asserted by one or both.

Figure 3-9 also gives the containment hierarchy for the various structures. It is important that this hierarchy is strictly followed. For example, a businessEntity contains a businessService. A businessService cannot contain a businessEntity. Thus, a single instance of businessService cannot be associated with more than one instance of a businessEntity.

Whenever you store the information in the registry by using any of these data structures, the registry generates a Universally Unique Identifier (UUID) that identifies this information.

You will now study each of these data structures and learn how to use them.

The businessEntity Structure

The businessEntity structure is a top-level data structure that contains information about a business or entity. It contains the descriptions of the various services offered by the business. Listing 3-22 gives an XML schema definition for the businessEntity.

Listing 3-22. *Schema Defintion for* businessEntity *Structure*

```
<element name = "businessEntity">
  <complexType>
    <sequence>
      <element ref = "discoveryURLs" minOccurs = "0"/>
      <element ref = "name" maxOccurs = "unbounded"/>
      <element ref = "description" minOccurs = "0" maxOccurs = unbounded"/>
      <element ref = "contacts" minOccurs = "0"/>
      <element ref = "businessServices" minOccurs = "0"/>
      <element ref = "identifierBag" minOccurs = "0"/>
      <element ref = "categoryBag" minOccurs = "0"/>
    </sequence>
    <attribute ref = "businessKey" use = "required"/>
    <attribute ref = "operator"/>
    <attribute ref = "authorizedName"/>
  </complexType>
</element>
```

As seen in Listing 3-22, the businessEntity structure stores business information such as its name, description, contacts, and other items. The businessServices element holds a list of one or more logical business service descriptions. The categoryBag holds taxonomy information under which the entity is classified. The taxonomies define different classification schemes for businesses. It is the job of the publisher to list the business in one of the appropriate classifications. The find_business method provides a search on categoryBag elements.

The businessKey element contains the UUID for the current instance.

Also, note the authorizedName and operator elements. The authorizedName element specifies the publisher's name. The operator element specifies the name of the certified authority controlling the registry. The controlling operator generates both the authorizedName and operator elements while saving the businessEntity instance. The registry client should not supply these fields.

The businessService Structure

The businessService structure describes the service offered by a business. Listing 3-23 gives the schema definition for this structure.

Listing 3-23. *Schema Definition for* businessService *Structure*

```
<element name = "businessService">
  <complexType>
    <sequence>
      <element ref = "name" maxOccurs = "unbounded"/>
      <element ref = "description" minOccurs = "0"
        maxOccurs = "unbounded"/>
      <element ref = "bindingTemplates"/>
      <element ref = "categoryBag" minOccurs = "0"/>
    </sequence>
      <attribute ref = "serviceKey" use = "required"/>
      <attribute ref = "businessKey"/>
  </complexType>
</element>
```

Each service is described by its name, description, bindingTemplate, and categoryBag. The bindingTemplate describes the binding information to the service. As before, the categoryBag element holds the taxonomy classification for the service. The serviceKey element holds the UUID for the current instance. The businessKey element holds a reference to the parent businessEntity object. This is how we connect the service to a business instance. Note that we can connect each service to only a single business instance.

The bindingTemplate Structure

The bindingTemplate structure contains the technical descriptions of a web service. Each instance of the bindingTemplate structure has a single logical businessService parent. Listing 3-24 gives the schema definition for the bindingTemplate structure.

Listing 3-24. *Schema Definition for* bindingTemplate *Structure*

```
<element name = "bindingTemplate">
  <complexType>
    <sequence>
      <element ref = "description" minOccurs = "0" maxOccurs = "unbounded"/>
        <choice>
          <element ref = "accessPoint" minOccurs = "0"/>
          <element ref = "hostingRedirector" minOccurs = "0"/>
        </choice>
      <element ref = "tModelInstanceDetails"/>
    </sequence>
      <attribute ref = "bindingKey" use = "required"/>
      <attribute ref = "serviceKey"/>
  </complexType>
</element>
```

Each bindingTemplate instance contains its description in the description element. The accessPoint element is the required attribute and specifies the entry point address for the web service. The entry point address may be supplied as a URL, an e-mail, or even a telephone number. The hostingRedirector element is required if the value for the accessPoint is not specified. When specified, this refers to an alternate bindingTemplate that should be used for obtaining technical information about the service.

The bindingKey holds the UUID for the current instance. The serviceKey element corresponds to the serviceKey of the parent businessService object.

The tModel Structure

The tModel structure provides a URL that, in turn, provides information about the specifications and the standards that a web service complies with. The tModel structure also provides further information on how the web service behaves and what conventions it follows. It is metadata that describes the service. It describes the service's compliance with a specification or a concept. This is described with the help of description and overviewDoc elements. The identifierBag element contains name-value pairs that record identification numbers for the tModel. These IDs are used during a search operation on tModel. The categoryBag element specifies the taxonomy under which the service is listed. Listing 3-25 gives the schema definition of the tModel structure.

Listing 3-25. *Schema Definition of* tModel *Structure*

```
<element name = "tModel">
  <complexType>
    <sequence>
      <element ref = "name"/>
      <element ref = "description" minOccurs = "0"maxOccurs = "unbounded"/>
      <element ref = "overviewDoc" minOccurs = "0"/>
      <element ref = "identifierBag" minOccurs = "0"/>
      <element ref = "categoryBag" minOccurs = "0"/>
    </sequence>
    <attribute ref = "tModelKey" use = "required"/>
    <attribute ref = "operator"/>
    <attribute ref = "authorizedName"/>
  </complexType>
</element>
```

The tModelKey element contains the current instance's UUID. The values for operator and authorizedName elements are generated by the controlling operator during save. The overviewDoc holds references to remote descriptive information or instructions related to the tModel.

The publisherAssertion Structure

The publisherAssertion structure enables two cooperating businesses to make their relationship visible in the registry. Both businesses in the relationship must publish their own publisherAssertion with exactly the same information to make the relationship visible in the registry. If a single publisher is responsible for both businesses, only one of the assertions is sufficient to make the relationship visible in the registry. Listing 3-26 presents the schema definition for the `publisherAssertion` structure.

Listing 3-26. *Schema Definition for* `publisherAssertion` *Structure*

```
<element name = "publisherAssertion">
  <complexType>
    <sequence>
      <element ref = "fromKey"/>
      <element ref = "toKey"/>
      <element ref = "keyedReference"/>
    </sequence>
  </complexType>
</element>
```

The `fromKey` element is a required element and represents the first `businessEntity` in the relationship. The `toKey` element is also required and represents the second `businessEntity` in the relationship. The `keyedReference` is required and represents the relation type. The relation type is specified in terms of the key name–key value pair within a `tModel`.

Having seen all the data structures in a UDDI registry, you will now study UDDI APIs that allow you to publish your data in the registry and also search the registry for the desired information.

UDDI APIs

The UDDI specification defines a contract for publishing, locating, and inspecting business services in the registry. This contract lists the message structures that you need to use while requesting a service from the UDDI registry. The UDDI specification categorizes the APIs as follows:

- Publishing API

- Inquiry API

The publishing API allows a service provider to publish its services in the UDDI registry. The inquiry API allows you to search a desired service in the registry and retrieve information about a located service.

Publishing API

The publishing API provides several message structures for saving and deleting information in the registry. There is no message structure for modifying the information; in fact, the save operation itself can be used for modifying the data in the registry. As you have seen in the data structures description, each entry in the registry is identified by a key (UUID) that is generated by the registry during the first save operation. The subsequent save with the same key value modifies the record in the registry.

Authorization is required to publish anything in the registry. You acquire authorization by obtaining an authentication token from the registry. The publishing API provides a method for obtaining an authentication token. This must be supplied in all publishing requests made to the registry.

Inquiry API

You use the inquiry API to locate a desired service in the registry and retrieve information about the located service. You search the registry by using the inquiry API. After a search returns a list of matching services, you can retrieve their details by using other methods in the inquiry API. The inquiry API defines several find and get methods for searching the registry and obtaining object details.

Because the registry is XML-based, you invoke the methods listed in the publishing and inquiry APIs by sending SOAP requests to the registry. You will now study these publishing and inquiry messages.

Publishing API Save Messages

The UDDI publishing API defines four messages for saving information to the UDDI registry:

- save_business
- save_service
- save_binding
- save_tModel

As the name suggests, each message saves the corresponding registry object. For example, the save_business message is used for saving a businessEntity instance, and the save_service message saves a businessService instance. Each of these messages can also be used for modifying the data in the registry. To modify an existing instance, supply the same key value as in the original record while saving the modified field values.

If the save operation succeeds, the registry will send you a message containing the newly registered information. The save_business message returns a businessDetail message that contains the information on the newly registered business.

In case of error, a SOAP fault is generated and a dispositionReport structure is returned to the client. The dispositionResult element details the error.

Publishing API Delete Messages

Similar to save messages, the publishing API defines four corresponding delete messages:

- delete_business
- delete_service
- delete_binding
- delete_tModel

Once again, as the name suggests, each message deletes the corresponding object type from the registry. While deleting an object from the registry, you must supply the existing key value in the registry. If the key does not exist or if any other error occurs during processing, the registry generates a SOAP fault and returns a dispositionReport structure in the response message.

The delete_tModel message requires more explanation. Remember, the tModel instance may be referred by multiple entities in the registry. The delete_tModel message removes or retires the specified tModel instance. If other entities refer the specified tModel instance, the instance is not removed, but is marked as hidden. Such hidden instances are still accessible to their owner, but are not visible in the result set of the find_tModel method call. To make a hidden model visible again, you need to send the save_tModel message with the key for the hidden model instance. To permanently remove all the details of the tModel instance, you need to send the save_tModel message with empty values in the data field. Follow this save_tModel message with the delete_tModel message to permanently remove the instance.

Publishing API Security Messages

The security messages consist of the following two messages:

- get_authToken: The get_authToken message accepts a user ID and credentials as parameters and returns an authentication token to the caller. The token is an opaque value that is used in all other publisher API calls.

- discard_authToken: The discard_authToken message informs the operator site to discard a specified authentication token. The operator site generally retains the security token for managing the client session state.

Inquiry API Find Messages

The UDDI inquiry API defines four messages for searching information based on a certain search criterion:

- find_business

- find_service

- find_binding

- find_tModel

Each of these messages accepts a partial search string and returns a collection of the appropriate object types. For example, the find_business message returns a businessList message to the caller. The businessList message contains a list of businessInfo objects. Likewise, the find_service message returns a serviceList message to the client containing businessServices objects. If there are no records found, the list contains zero objects. The default behavior of the search functionality can be modified by specifying the desired search qualifiers in the findQualifier element in the message.

You can specify the number of rows you want to retrieve during the search operation. For a large number of results, the registry may truncate the list before sending it to the client. In such a case, it also sets the truncated attribute in the message to indicate this to the client.

Inquiry API Get Messages

As with find messages, the publishing API defines four get messages:

- `get_businessDetail`

- `get_serviceDetail`

- `get_bindingDetail`

- `get_tModelDetail`

Each of these messages require you to provide the key (UUID) as a parameter in the request message. On return, each message returns an appropriate object type. For example, the `get_businessDetail` message returns the `businessEntity` instance; the `get_serviceDetail` message returns the `serviceDetail` instance, and so on.

Summary

In this chapter, you studied one of the important architectures in today's IT industry: the web services architecture. A web service is essentially an application component that exposes its functionality by using standard web protocols. These web protocols are SOAP and WSDL.

Web services architecture consists of three major parts: the service provider, service requestor, and UDDI registry. The third component, the registry, is optional. A service provider creates a service and publishes the location of its service description in the UDDI registry. The service provider may supply the description directly to the service requestor. In such a case, the use of the registry becomes redundant.

A web service has three major components: SOAP, WSDL, and UDDI. All three components, which were discussed in depth, are XML based.

SOAP allows you to call operations on the remote service and also exchange data between two applications. WSDL describes the interface for the service, and the UDDI stores the business and its services information in the registry. The UDDI defines APIs for publishing and accessing information in the registry.

Web services heavily rely on the use of XML. This chapter described several XML-based message structures for web services operations. In the next chapter, you will study the implementations with several code examples that illustrate how to use these XML-based messages.

CHAPTER 4

■ ■ ■

Apache SOAP

Chapter 3 covered the SOAP standard theoretically, without discussing the practical implementations. This chapter introduces Apache's SOAP implementation.

Several major organizations have implemented SOAP. The Apache Software Foundation is one of them. Although nothing prevents you from hand-coding SOAP requests and manually interpreting SOAP responses, it's much easier to use the standard libraries provided by these SOAP implementers to construct the SOAP requests and electronically interpret SOAP responses.

In this chapter, you will learn how to install the Apache SOAP toolkit on Tomcat. You will then see an overview of the SOAP implementation architecture. You will create both RPC- and Document-style web services and will develop the client applications that access these services. You will examine the SOAP requests and responses created by the SOAP toolkit. You will learn how to handle exceptions in web services and how to use user-defined data types in your web services implementations. Finally, you will learn about the deployment issues with web services.

The chapter covers several programming examples. If you want to try experimenting with the code, you will need to download and install the SOAP implementation. Because you need to deploy your web service on a server, you will also have to install an HTTP server with servlet support. The Apache SOAP implementation supports several popular HTTP servers, such as Apache Tomcat, BEA WebLogic, IBM's WebSphere, Sun Microsystems' Sun ONE (previously known as iPlanet), the open source Jetty, Macromedia JRun, and Caucho Technology's Resin. Because this book is mainly about Apache implementations of XML APIs, I have used Apache Tomcat for the examples in this chapter.

Installing Apache SOAP and Related Software

Installing Apache SOAP is fairly easy. However, before installing these SOAP libraries on your machine, you need to install several other software packages. Specifically, you need three packages in order to use Apache SOAP:

- *The Java Runtime Environment (JRE) 1.5*: This is required for running any Java application on your machine.

- *Apache Tomcat*: This is the web server on which you will deploy the web services.

- *Apache SOAP*: This is the Apache implementation of the SOAP specifications.

Installing JRE 1.5

Tomcat version 5.5.9[1] was used for running the web services throughout this chapter. This version of Tomcat requires JRE 1.5. Therefore, if you do not have JRE 1.5 installed on your machine, download it from the following URL:

```
http://java.sun.com/j2se
```

The installation procedure is usually very simple. For example, for the Windows platform, an installer is provided. When you download the software, you get a Windows installer named `jdk-1_5_0-windows-i586.exe`. Double-clicking on this installer guides you through the various steps of installation. These steps are not exhaustive; they simply ask you to accept the license agreement and specify the folder where you would like to install the software.

Note For those of you installing on Linux, Appendix A provides detailed installation instructions for all the chapters in this book.

Installing Apache Tomcat

The latest version of Tomcat can be downloaded from the following URL:

```
http://jakarta.apache.org/
```

The download is available in various formats supporting different platforms. The entire source is also available for download. You can download the source and build it for your desired platform.

For Windows, you can download the zip archive. If you download the `.zip` version, simply unzip the software to your desired folder. The `.zip` version (`apache-tomcat-5.5.9.zip`[2]) does not come with administrator software for the server. This has to be downloaded (`apache-tomcat-5.5.9-admin.zip`) separately and unzipped to the same folder as Tomcat. The administrator software can be downloaded from the archives listed on the Apache site.[3]

For the Windows platform, the software is also supplied as an executable that you can download (`apache-tomcat-5.5.9.exe`). Running this executable results in it asking you to select the components you want to install, the installation folder, the port number, and the user name and password for the server. After you enter this information, the installer installs Tomcat on your machine, ready for testing. If you install by using this installer, you will still need to install the administrator service separately as explained in the previous paragraph. This is required only if you need to administer the server.

---

1. This is the latest stable build available at the time of this writing.
2. The filename will vary depending on the version you are downloading.
3. http://jakarta.apache.org/

Note For those of you installing on Linux, Appendix A provides detailed installation instructions for all the chapters in this book.

Testing the Installation

To start Tomcat, run the `startup.bat` batch file (if you are running Windows) or the `startup.sh` script (if you are running Linux).

Note If you have installed Tomcat as a Windows service, you need not run the `startup.bat` file because Windows automatically starts Tomcat at boot.

Open your browser and type in the following URL:

`http://localhost:8080`

This should open the Apache Tomcat/5.5.9 opening screen in your browser, as shown in Figure 4-1.

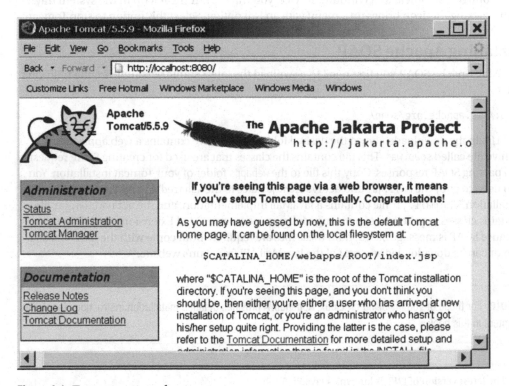

Figure 4-1. *Tomcat server welcome screen*

To run the administrator utilities, use the links listed under the Administration panel on the left side of the opening screen. When invoked, these links will ask you to enter credentials before they grant access to web server administration. For this, you will need to create an `admin` account for your server, if you have not done so during installation. You create the administrator account by modifying the `tomcat-users.xml` file under the `config` folder in your Tomcat installation. The modified configuration file is shown in Listing 4-1. You will need to add the lines shown in bold to the existing file.

Listing 4-1. *The* `tomcat-users.xml` *Configuration File*

```
<?xml version="1.0" encoding="utf-8" ?>
  <tomcat-users>
    <role rolename="tomcat" />
    <role rolename="role1" />
    <role rolename="manager" />
    <role rolename="admin" />
    <user username="tomcat" password="tomcat" roles="tomcat" />
    <user username="both" password="tomcat" roles="tomcat,role1" />
    <user username="role1" password="tomcat" roles="role1" />
    <user username="admin" password="admin" roles="admin,manager" />
  </tomcat-users>
```

To shut down the server, run `shutdown.bat` (on Windows) or `shutdown.sh` (on Unix). If you have configured Tomcat as a Windows service, you will see a Tomcat icon in the system tray. Right-clicking this icon brings up a menu with an Exit option. Select this option to stop Tomcat.

Installing Apache SOAP

To install Apache SOAP, you first need to download the latest stable version from the following URL:

`http://ws.apache.org/soap/`

Unzip the downloaded file to the desired folder. The archive contains a web application archive file called `soap.war`. This file contains the classes that are used for creating SOAP requests and parsing SOAP responses. Copy this file to the `webapps` folder of your Tomcat installation. You also need to copy the `mail.jar` and `activation.jar` files to the `\shared\lib` folder of your Tomcat installation. The `mail.jar` file contains a JavaMail implementation, and the `activation.jar` file contains classes required for supporting Mulipurpose Internet Mail Extensions (MIME) types. Because SOAP is message based, both these files are required. Both come with the J2EE[4] installation or can be downloaded as a part of the JavaMail API from Sun's website.[5]

■**Note** For those of you installing on Linux, Appendix A provides detailed installation instructions for all the chapters in this book.

---

4. The latest version of J2EE is known as Java EE 5.

5. http://java.sun.com/products/javamail/downloads/index.html

Testing the Installation

Test your installation by typing the following URL in your browser:

`http://localhost:8080/soap`

You should see a welcome screen, as shown in Figure 4-2.

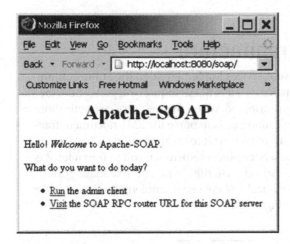

Figure 4-2. *Apache SOAP welcome screen*

The welcome screen contains two hyperlinks:

- Run the Admin Client: This hyperlink takes you to a screen that allows you to deploy and undeploy web services. The admin client screen also allows you to retrieve the list of deployed services.

- Visit the SOAP RPC router URL: This hyperlink takes you to the URL `http://localhost: 8080/soap/servlet/rpcrouter`. It prints a SOAP RPC router message on your browser. This is an important URL for us. All our clients will be sending the web service requests to this URL.

You can try clicking both the links to ensure that the correct pages open in your browser. Additionally, test the message-routing servlet by typing the following URL in your browser:

`http://localhost:8080/soap/servlet/messagerouter`

This prints a message similar to the RPC router on your browser. You will be using this router for calling Document-style web services.

This completes our server-side installation of Apache SOAP. If you are using a different machine for client development, you will need to follow the instructions in the Apache SOAP documentation to set up your client machine. If you use the same machine for both client and server deployment (which would be the case for most of us), you are ready for some real coding of web services.

You can test your client installation by using the following command at the command prompt:

```
C:\>java org.apache.soap.server.ServiceManagerClient ➥
http://localhost:8080/soap/servlet/rpcrouter list
```

This should print the list of all deployed services (which at this stage could be none at all) on your console.

SOAP Implementation Architecture

As you learned in the previous chapter, in a web services implementation the entire communication between a client and a server takes place by using SOAP request/response documents. A SOAP call can be RPC-oriented or document-oriented. When the web service application receives one of these SOAP requests, the application needs to parse the XML document fragment to understand the request and then needs to convert it to an appropriate binary request to the implementing service object. When the service object returns a result to the caller, it is mapped into a SOAP response first and then dispatched to the client. This marshalling and unmarshalling of messages is exactly what the Apache SOAP server implementation provides. The implementation architecture is shown in Figure 4-3.

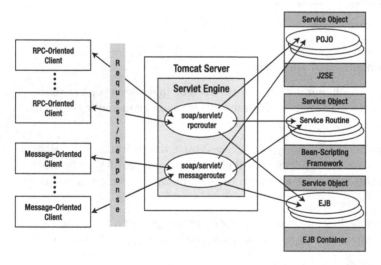

Figure 4-3. *Apache SOAP server implementation*

Apache's SOAP implementation provides two servlets called rpcrouter and messsagerouter, which together provide the desired functionality of transforming the messages from XML to binary and vice versa. The rpcrouter servlet services all the RPC-based requests, and the messagerouter servlet services all document-oriented requests. When the client makes a SOAP request to the SOAP server, it specifies the Uniform Resource Name (URN) for the service.

Note The URN is a unique identifier consisting of any text string for each defined service. At the time of deployment, this URN is mapped to the server implementation class. The deployment process is explained in depth later in this chapter.

Each deployed service has an associated unique identifier specified by this URN. The SOAP server uses this URN to invoke the call on the appropriate service object. How does the SOAP server know the appropriate service object? This is resolved with the help of a deployment descriptor (deployment descriptors are described in depth later in this chapter). The deployment descriptor associates a URN with the service object and its methods. Thus, looking at the deployment descriptor, the SOAP server knows which method on which Java class is to be invoked.

The service object itself can be implemented by using different technologies. You can implement the service object as a Plain Old Java Object (POJO), an Enterprise JavaBean (EJB), or a method written in a scripting language. As Figure 4-3 illustrates, both rpcrouter and messagerouter servlets can redirect the requests to any of these service objects. When the service object returns a response to the caller, the underlying runtime maps this into a SOAP response document and dispatches the response to the caller via the same servlets.

As you can see, the use of a Tomcat server is not unique. You can use any web server that provides the servlet support. Ensure that your web server supports the minimum servlet API version that is required by the Apache SOAP implementation.

Developing Web Services

As you learned in Chapter 3, a web service can be RPC-style or Document-style. In this section, we will develop both RPC- and Document-style web services and write clients for both.

Remember that a web service is essentially a component that exposes its interface by using standard web protocols. This component can be written as a simple Java class, a JavaBean, an EJB, a servlet, or even a .NET component or a Common Object Request Broker Architecture (CORBA) server object. To keep the component development simple so as to concentrate more on the SOAP implementation, we will be using only POJOs to develop the example web services.

Creating an RPC-Style Web Service

We will develop an RPC-style web service for our stock brokerage as discussed in Chapter 3. The web service will provide the requesting client with the latest trade price for a particular stock symbol.

The web service development consists of the following steps:

1. Developing the service that is deployed on the server

2. Developing a client that consumes this service

3. Running the client

Each of these tasks is described in detail here.

Developing the Service

Developing and deploying our web service comes as a result of completing two tasks. First we'll write the server code, and then we'll need to deploy it.

Writing the Server Code

The server code can consist of a POJO or an EJB or scripting language code. We will develop the server using POJO. The server code for our stock brokerage web service is shown in Listing 4-2.

Listing 4-2. *The Stock Quote Service Server Class* (`<working folder>\Ch04\RPC\ StockQuoteService.java`)

```
package StockBroker;
public class StockQuoteService
  {
    // A web service method
    public float getStockQuote(String symbol)
      {
        // We return the hard-coded value for simplicity
        return ((float)25.35);
      }
  }
```

This is a simple Java class with one public method called getStockQuote. The method receives a parameter of String type that represents the stock symbol for which the trade price is sought. The method returns a float value to the requesting client that contains the last traded price. The method implementation simply returns a fixed value to the client. In real life, the method would read the live database of the stock exchange to retrieve the last traded price.

Compile the code in Listing 4-2 by using the following command line:

```
C:\<working folder>\Ch04\RPC>javac -d . StockQuoteService.java
```

Copy the generated .class file (`<working folder>\Ch04\RPC\StockBroker\ StockQuoteService.class`) to the following folder:

```
<Tomcat Installation Folder>\webapps\soap\WEB-INF\classes\StockBroker
```

Deploying the Service

After you develop the service, you can choose from two techniques to deploy it on the server:

- Using a GUI-based admin tool

- Using a command-line interface

I will describe both methods of deployment.

Deploying by Using a GUI tool

To deploy the service, you use the Admin tool. Type the following URL in your browser to invoke the Admin tool:

```
http://localhost:8080/soap/admin/
```

Click the Deploy button on the Admin screen. This opens a screen as shown in Figure 4-4. All the fields on this screen are initially blank. The screen output shows the values that you will be filling in.

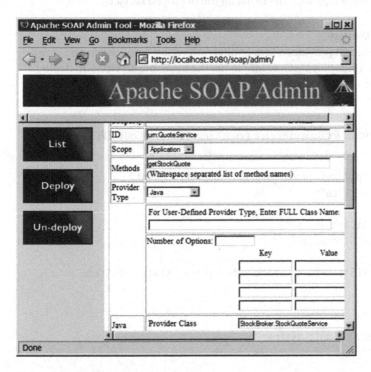

Figure 4-4. *Deployment wizard*

Complete the following steps to fill in the displayed form and deploy the web service:

1. In the ID field, type **urn:QuoteService**. The client supplies this URN in the request. The rpcrouter servlet redirects the client request to this URN on the server side.

2. Set the Scope combo box to Application. This option decides the lifetime of the server object. The lifetime may be Request, Session, or Application.

3. In the Methods text box, type **getStockQuote**. Remember, this is the method that our web service wants to expose as a web method that can be invoked by using SOAP.

4. As the Provider Type, select Java. This is the default selection. You can select the Script provider type if your server implementation uses a script code.

5. In the Java Provider group, set the Provider Class as StockBroker.StockQuoteService. Note that this is the fully qualified name of our web service class.

6. Use defaults for the rest of the selections.

7. Click the Deploy button on the left side of the screen to deploy the service.

8. If the deployment is successful, you will see a "Service urn:QuoteService deployed" message on your browser.

9. You can click the List button at any time to list all the deployed services.

Deploying by Using a Command Interface

The Apache SOAP implementation provides a Java application called ServiceManagerClient that allows you to deploy and undeploy services and to list the available services. To deploy the service by using this command-line utility, you first need to write a deployment descriptor. The deployment descriptor for QuoteService is given in Listing 4-3.

Listing 4-3. *Deployment Descriptor for* QuoteService (<working folder>\Ch04\RPC\ DeploymentDescriptor.xml)

```
<isd:service xmlns:isd="http://xml.apache.org/xml-soap/deployment"
             id="urn:QuoteService">
  <isd:provider type="java"
                scope="Application"
                methods="getStockQuote">
    <isd:java
      class="Apress.XMLBook.StockBroker.StockQuoteService" static="false"
    />
  </isd:provider>
  <isd:faultListener>
     org.apache.soap.server.DOMFaultListener
  </isd:faultListener>
</isd:service>
```

The service element defines an id attribute and sets its value to a namespace that is unique within the current deployment environment. In our case, this is set to urn:QuoteService. The provider element defines type, scope, and the web methods to be called. If the service exposes more than one method as a web method, all such methods are listed in the methods attribute, each separated by a space from the other. The class attribute in the isd:java element defines the name of the POJO class that implements the service. The deployment descriptors are discussed in depth later in the chapter.

After you write the deployment descriptor for your service, you can deploy the service by using the following command line:

```
C:\<working folder>\Ch04\RPC>java org.apache.soap.server.ServiceManagerClient➥
 http://localhost:8080/soap/servlet/rpcrouter deploy DeploymentDescriptor.xml
```

You can verify that the service has been deployed successfully by listing all the deployed services via the following command line:

```
C:\<working folder>\Ch04\RPC>java org.apache.soap.server.ServiceManagerClient ➥
http://localhost:8080/soap/servlet/rpcrouter list
```

The program will list all the deployed services, as shown here:

```
Deployed Services:

       urn:QuoteService
       urn:AddressFetcher
       urn:Hello
```

To undeploy a deployed service, use the following command line:

```
C:\<working folder>\Ch04\RPC>java org.apache.soap.server.ServiceManagerClient ➥
 http://localhost:8080/soap/servlet/rpcrouter undeploy urn:QuoteService
```

The URN (such as urn:QuoteService shown in the preceding statement) uniquely identifies the service to be undeployed.

Developing the Client

Developing a client is a simple process that requires you to write an application that constructs a call to the web service and invokes it. Such a client application can be written in any programming language of your choice. For this example, we will use Java.

To construct a call, you do not need to construct a SOAP request. You simply use provided Java classes to input the desired information for the web service. The underlying SOAP implementation converts the call to an XML SOAP request. Similarly, when the web service returns a response to the client, it does so as a SOAP response. The SOAP response document is interpreted by the SOAP runtime, and the result is returned to the client as a Java object.

Writing the Client Code

We will write a console-based Java application for the purpose of developing a client for our web service. Listing 4-4 provides the complete listing for the console application.

Listing 4-4. *Client Program for Stock Quote Service* (<working folder>\Ch04\RPC\ StockQuoteRequest.java)

```
package StockClient;
import java.net.*;
import java.util.*;
import org.apache.soap.*;
import org.apache.soap.rpc.*;
```

```java
public class StockQuoteRequest {
  public static void main (String[] args) throws Exception {
    if (args.length != 1)
      {
        System.err.println ("Usage: java StockQuoteRequest symbol");
        System.exit (1);
      }

    String ServiceURL = "http://localhost:8080/soap/servlet/rpcrouter";
    URL url = new URL (ServiceURL);
    String symbol = args[0];

    // Build the call.
    Call call = new Call ();
    call.setTargetObjectURI ("urn:QuoteService");
    call.setMethodName ("getStockQuote");
    call.setEncodingStyleURI(Constants.NS_URI_SOAP_ENC);
    Vector params = new Vector ();
    params.addElement (new Parameter("symbol", String.class, symbol, null));
    call.setParams (params);

    Response resp = call.invoke (/* router URL */ url, /* actionURI */ "" );

    // Check the response.
    if (resp.generatedFault ())
      {
        Fault fault = resp.getFault ();

        System.err.println("Generated fault: " + fault);
      }
    else
      {
        Parameter result = resp.getReturnValue ();
        System.out.println (symbol + " last trade: $" + result.getValue ());
      }
  }
}
```

The program sets the service URL in the following statement:

```java
String ServiceURL = "http://localhost:8080/soap/servlet/rpcrouter";
```

This is the URL of our rpcrouter servlet. The client sends a request to this URL, and the router servlet redirects the request to our POJO providing the service. The underlying implementation converts the request to a binary request required by our POJO service object. Next, the program constructs a URL object that points to this service URL, which will be used while invoking this service:

```java
URL url = new URL (ServiceURL);
```

Next, the program constructs a Call object for invoking the service:

```
Call call = new Call ();
```

We call the setTargetObjectURI method on the call object to set the target URI:

```
call.setTargetObjectURI ("urn:QuoteService");
```

Note that this is the ID used while deploying the service. Using this information, the rpcrouter servlet routes the requests to the appropriate service.

We call the setMethodName method on the call object to set the desired method call on the web service:

```
call.setMethodName ("getStockQuote");
```

The getStockQuote is the web method exposed by our stock quote web service.

We set the encoding style URI for the request by using the predefined constant:

```
call.setEncodingStyleURI(Constants.NS_URI_SOAP_ENC);
```

The value of this predefined constant is http://schemas.xmlsoap.org/soap/encoding/.

Next, we construct the parameter to our web method by using following code snippet:

```
Vector params = new Vector ();
params.addElement (new Parameter("symbol", String.class, symbol, null));
call.setParams (params);
```

The code constructs the parameters for the method by creating a Vector and adding Parameter objects to it. Thus, for multiple parameters, you construct the appropriate desired number of Parameter objects and add them to the Vector object.

Now, you are ready to invoke the call on the web service. You invoke the web service by calling the invoke method on the call object:

```
Response resp = call.invoke (/* router URL */ url, /* actionURI */ "" );
```

The invoke method takes two parameters. The first parameter is the router URL, which is the URL of our rpcrouter servlet. The second parameter is the action URI, which is set to a null string. This parameter is currently not used and will be implemented in future versions. The invoke method returns a Response object to the caller. The Response object may contain valid data returned by the service or a SOAP fault.

The program checks for the exception by using the following code snippet:

```
if (resp.generatedFault ())
  {
    Fault fault = resp.getFault ();
    System.err.println("Generated fault: " + fault);
  }
```

If the generatedFault method of the Response class returns true, the server has reported a fault condition. We retrieve the fault information by calling the getFault method on the response object. The program simply prints the fault information on the user console.

On success from the server, the program retrieves the returned value and prints it on the console by using the following code snippet:

```
Parameter result = resp.getReturnValue ();
System.out.println (symbol + " last trade: $" + result.getValue ());
```

Running the Client

Compile the client code by using the following command line:

```
C:\<working folder>Ch04\RPC>javac -d . StockQuoteRequest.java
```

To run the client, you use a `java` command in your command line with the appropriate parameter that represents a stock symbol. The client invocation and its output are shown here:

```
C:\<working folder>Ch04\RPC>java StockClient.StockQuoteRequest MSFT
MSFT last trade: $25.35
```

Investigating the RPC Implementation

As seen in both the client and server code examples, the developer does not have to deal with any SOAP code. The underlying implementation on both sides takes care of marshalling and unmarshalling the SOAP request and response. If you want to look up the SOAP request and response generated by the underlying implementation, you need to snoop around the network traffic. Fortunately, Apache's SOAP implementation provides a tool for this very purpose.

Running the Network Traffic Interceptor

You invoke the network snooping tool by running the provided Java console application via the following command line:

```
C:\ >java org.apache.soap.util.net.TcpTunnelGui 8079 localhost 8080
```

When you run this program, the screen will appear as shown in Figure 4-5.

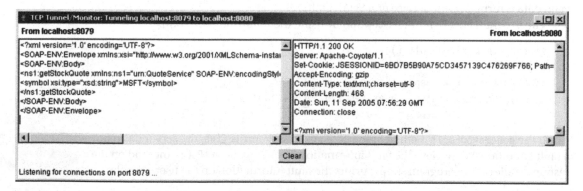

Figure 4-5. *Network traffic sniffer*

Note When you run the TcpTunnelGui tool, both the panes initially will be blank. Only when you modify and rerun your client application (as described later in this section) will you see the SOAP request and response displayed in the two panes, as seen in Figure 4-5.

This TCP Tunnel/Monitor program sets up a server socket to listen to incoming requests. In our case, we specify 8079 as the port on which this server socket should be listening. When a request is received, the program dumps the request contents in the edit field on the left side of the screen. Then it forwards the request to the URL and the port specified by the second (localhost) and the third (8080) parameters on the program invocation command line. When the service returns a response, the program dumps the response contents in the second edit field on the right side of the screen.

Intercepting network traffic by using this tool gives us an opportunity to examine the generated SOAP request and response. For this, you will need to modify the client application and set the ServiceURL port to 8079 from the earlier value of 8080. You do this by modifying the source to the following:

```
String ServiceURL = "http://localhost:8079/soap/servlet/rpcrouter";
```

Now, when you run the program (you will need to open another command prompt), the request will be sent to port 8079 on which the Tunnel/Monitor program is listening. The Tunnel/Monitor tool then redirects the request to port 8080.

This modified program is provided with the source download at the path <working folder>\Ch04\RPC\StockQuoteRequestNTS.java. You can compile this program and run it on a separate command window to see the SOAP request and response displayed in the TCP Tunnel/Monitor.

Examining SOAP Requests

When you capture the SOAP request by using the monitor tool, you will see the request in the left panel of the network traffic sniffer window. Listing 4-5 shows this request.

Listing 4-5. *SOAP Request with HTTP Header*

```
POST /soap/servlet/rpcrouter HTTP/1.0
Host: localhost:8079
Content-Type: text/xml;charset=utf-8
Content-Length: 452
SOAPAction: ""
Accept-Encoding: gzip

<?xml version="1.0" encoding="UTF-8" ?>
```

```
<SOAP-ENV:Envelope
  xmlns:xsi="http://www.w3.org/2001/XMLSchema-instance"
  xmlns:xsd="http://www.w3.org/2001/XMLSchema"
  xmlns:SOAP-ENV="http://schemas.xmlsoap.org/soap/envelope/"
>
  <SOAP-ENV:Body>
    <ns1:getStockQuote
      xmlns:ns1="urn:QuoteService"
      SOAP-ENV:encodingStyle="http://schemas.xmlsoap.org/soap/encoding/">
      <symbol xsi:type="xsd:string">
        MSFT
      </symbol>
    </ns1:getStockQuote>
  </SOAP-ENV:Body>
</SOAP-ENV:Envelope>
```

You may want to refer to Chapter 3 to understand the various parts of the SOAP request shown in Listing 4-5. The SOAP request starts with an xml declaration that is followed by an Envelope element. The Envelope element encapsulates the Body element and does not contain an optional header. The SOAP body contains a getStockQuote element; this is our web method. Note the declaration of urn:QuoteService as an XML namespace. The parameter to the method is specified by the symbol element of type xsd:string. The element text contents are set to MSFT.

At the top of the XML declaration, note the use of an HTTP header (refer to the "SOAP over HTTP" section in Chapter 3). The HTTP header contains the required information for transporting the XML document payload to the destination. We use HTTP *post* to invoke the web service. You cannot use HTTP *get* for this purpose. The request is posted to the rpcrouter at localhost:8079. From this port, it is redirected to port 8080 by the TCP Tunnel/Monitor tool.

Examining the SOAP Response

After executing the request, the server returns a SOAP response to the client. This response indicates either success of the request's execution or failure (in which case a SOAP fault is generated due to an application exception or network error). Listing 4-6 shows a SOAP response document that results from successful execution of the SOAP request in Listing 4-5. The response appears in the right-hand panel of the network traffic sniffer window.

Listing 4-6. *SOAP Response with HTTP Header*

```
HTTP/1.1 200 OK
Server: Apache-Coyote/1.1
Set-Cookie: JSESSIONID=8BA93045F0253C0A654A1458D15A3A29; Path=/soap
Accept-Encoding: gzip
Content-Type: text/xml;charset=utf-8
Content-Length: 468
Date: Sun, 11 Sep 2005 07:47:04 GMT
Connection: close
```

```
<?xml version="1.0" encoding="UTF-8" ?>

<SOAP-ENV:Envelope
  xmlns:xsi="http://www.w3.org/2001/XMLSchema-instance"
  xmlns:xsd="http://www.w3.org/2001/XMLSchema"
  xmlns:SOAP-ENV="http://schemas.xmlsoap.org/soap/envelope/"
>
  <SOAP-ENV:Body>
    <ns1:getStockQuoteResponse
      xmlns:ns1="urn:QuoteService"
      SOAP-ENV:encodingStyle="http://schemas.xmlsoap.org/soap/encoding/"
    >
      <return
        xsi:type="xsd:float"
      >25.35</return>
    </ns1:getStockQuoteResponse>
  </SOAP-ENV:Body>
</SOAP-ENV:Envelope>
```

The XML document is identified by the xml declaration as in the previous example. The Envelope element is the root element and encapsulates the mandatory Body element. The optional Header element is not used. The Body element contains the return value of float type. The return value is identified by the return element, whose value is set to 25.35 in the current example.

As in the SOAP request (Listing 4-5), an HTTP header is on top of the XML payload in the SOAP response (Listing 4-6). The header contains an HTTP 200 response code, which indicates an OK response. It also contains information on the server that returned the response. The server has also sent a cookie to the client as indicated by the Set-Cookie element. The server indicates the date and time of response.

Creating a Document-Style Web Service

Continuing with our stock brokerage example, we will now create a Document-style web service. This service will process a purchase order sent by a client as an XML document fragment. Our web service will receive the purchase order as part of a SOAP request. The web service will parse the request to extract the XML document fragment containing the purchase order. We will parse the XML fragment by using the DOM API (discussed in Chapter 2) to extract the order details. The web service will then generate a confirmation response to the client. The response will be another XML document fragment.

We will write a client that dispatches the purchase order to our web service. We will use a messaging API to send the XML document. Listing 4-7 shows the XML code that we will use as the input document containing the purchase order to be placed on our server.

Listing 4-7. *The* po.xml *Document (*<working folder>\Ch04\Messaging\BrokerApp\po.xml*)*

```
<s:Envelope xmlns:s="http://schemas.xmlsoap.org/soap/envelope/">
<s:Body >
<purchaseOrder xmlns="urn:po-processor"
               xmlns:NYSE="http://www.example.com/NYSE/Stocks/Tradeorder">
    <NYSE:scrip>
      MSFT
    </NYSE:scrip>
    <NYSE:quantity>
      1000
    </NYSE:quantity>
    <NYSE:price>
      25.25
    </NYSE:price>
</purchaseOrder>
</s:Body>
</s:Envelope>
```

Developing the Service

Like the RPC-style web service, the development of a document-style web service consists of
two parts: writing the server code and deploying the service. Both tasks are described in this
section.

Writing the Server Code

We will implement the server in a POJO, as we did for the RPC-style web service. In the RPC-style
web service, the Java class was registered with the rpcrouter servlet. In this case we will register
the class with the messagerouter servlet. After receiving the message, the messagerouter servlet
passes it to the registered Java class. Listing 4-8 shows the complete program for the server code.

Listing 4-8. *Document-Style Web Service (*<working folder>\Ch04\Messaging\BrokerApp\
StockOrderProcessor.java*)*

```java
package StockBroker;

import java.util.Vector;
import org.w3c.dom.Attr;
import org.w3c.dom.Element;
import org.w3c.dom.Node;
import org.w3c.dom.NodeList;
import org.apache.soap.*;
import org.apache.soap.rpc.SOAPContext;

/* The StockOrderProcessor defines a method called purchaseOrder that
 * is SOAP-aware
 */
```

```
public class StockOrderProcessor {
    // purchaseOrder method is a SOAP-method
    public void purchaseOrder(Envelope env, SOAPContext reqCtx,
            SOAPContext resCtx)
            throws Exception {

        // Create variable for storing node values
        String scripName = null;
        String quantity = null;
        String price = null;

        // Extract SOAP body
        Body b = env.getBody();
        // Get all the entries in the body and iterate through the list
        Vector entries = b.getBodyEntries();
        for (int i = 0; i < entries.size(); i++) {
            // get the element
            Element e = (Element) entries.elementAt(i);
            // Read the node name
            String nodeName = e.getNodeName();
            // Check if it is purchaseOrder
            if (nodeName.equals("purchaseOrder")) {
                // Iterate through the list of child nodes
                NodeList children = e.getChildNodes();
                for (int j = 0; j < children.getLength(); j++) {
                    Node n = children.item(j);
                    switch (n.getNodeType()) {
                        // for each type of element node, extract the
                        // text contents into appropriate variable
                        case Node.ELEMENT_NODE:
                            if (n.getNodeName().equals("NYSE:scrip"))
                                scripName = n.getTextContent();
                            else if (n.getNodeName().equals("NYSE:quantity"))
                                quantity = n.getTextContent();
                            else if (n.getNodeName().equals("NYSE:price"))
                                price = n.getTextContent();
                            else
                                throw new Exception("Unknown element: " + n.getNodeName());
                            break;
                        case Node.ATTRIBUTE_NODE:
                            break;
                    }
                }
            }
        }
    }
```

```
        // Create a buffer for user response
        StringBuffer response = new StringBuffer(1024);
        // Create SOAP response for the client
        response.append(Constants.XML_DECL)
        .append("<SOAP-ENV:Envelope ➡
                xmlns:SOAP-ENV=\"http://schemas.xmlsoap.org/soap/envelope/\">")
        .append("<SOAP-ENV:Body>")
        .append("<purchaseOrderResponse xmlns=\"urn:po-processor\">")
        .append("<return>")
        .append("Thanks, Received Order for ")
        .append(scripName)
        .append(" quantity= ")
        .append(quantity)
        .append(" price= " + price)
        .append("</return>")
        .append("</purchaseOrderResponse>")
        .append("</SOAP-ENV:Body>")
        .append("</SOAP-ENV:Envelope>");
        resCtx.setRootPart(response.toString(), "text/xml");
    }
}
```

We call our class StockOrderProcessor and define a method called purchaseOrder in it:

```
public class StockOrderProcessor {
    // purchaseOrder method is a SOAP-method
    public void purchaseOrder(Envelope env, SOAPContext reqCtx,
            SOAPContext resCtx)
            throws Exception {
```

The method is SOAP aware, that is, it is invoked with a SOAP request and returns a SOAP response to the client. The request/response process is achieved through the method parameters.

We expect that the SOAP request will contain the stock name, desired trade quantity, and price elements. The purchaseOrder method retrieves the values of these elements from the request document and stores them into the class variables declared as follows:

```
        // Create variable for storing node values
        String scripName = null;
        String quantity = null;
        String price = null;
```

The method then extracts the SOAP body by calling the getBody method of the Envelope class:

```
        // Extract SOAP body
        Body b = env.getBody();
```

The program retrieves all the entries in the body by calling its getBodyEntries method:

```
// Get all the entries in the body and iterate through the list
Vector entries = b.getBodyEntries();
for (int i = 0; i < entries.size(); i++) {
```

The getBodyEntries method retrieves a Vector object containing all the entries in the body. These entries consist of elements and their attributes. The program reads the element at each node in the vector and retrieves its name:

```
// get the element
 Element e = (Element) entries.elementAt(i);
 // Read the node name
 String nodeName = e.getNodeName();
```

If the node name equals purchaseOrder, we obtain its children by calling the getChildNodes method of the Element class:

```
if (nodeName.equals("purchaseOrder")) {
    // Iterate through the list of child nodes
    NodeList children = e.getChildNodes();
```

The getChildNodes method returns a NodeList object. The NodeList object contains a list of child nodes. We iterate through this list to retrieve each child node:

```
for (int j = 0; j < children.getLength(); j++) {
    Node n = children.item(j);
```

A switch statement is used to distinguish between the different node types. The node may be an element node or an attribute node:

```
switch (n.getNodeType()) {
        case Node.ELEMENT_NODE:
```

Our request document elements do not contain any attributes. Thus, we process only element nodes. We check the name of each node and copy the contents into an appropriate string variable depending on its name:

```
if (n.getNodeName().equals("NYSE:scrip"))
    scripName = n.getTextContent();
else if (n.getNodeName().equals("NYSE:quantity"))
    quantity = n.getTextContent();
else if (n.getNodeName().equals("NYSE:price"))
    price = n.getTextContent();
else
    throw new Exception("Unknown element: " + n.getNodeName());
```

After the SOAP body is processed, we will generate a SOAP response to the client. For this, first we declare a buffer for storing the response:

```
// Create a buffer for user response
StringBuffer response = new StringBuffer(1024);
```

Then we build the response by adding appropriate XML statements into the buffer. First, we add the XML declaration (available in the `Constants` class) to indicate that the current document is an XML document:

```
// Create SOAP response for the client
response.append(Constants.XML_DECL)
```

Next, we add the `Envelope` element indicating that this is going to be a SOAP document:

```
.append("<SOAP-ENV:Envelope xmlns:SOAP- ➥
                ENV=\"http://schemas.xmlsoap.org/soap/envelope/\">")
```

Next, we add the `Body` element:

```
.append("<SOAP-ENV:Body>")
```

Inside the `Body` element, we create a `purchaseOrderResponse` element and another subelement, `return`, within it:

```
.append("<purchaseOrderResponse xmlns=\"urn:po-processor\">")
.append("<return>")
```

Within the `return` element, we add the `scripName`, `quantity`, and `price` details obtained earlier:

```
.append("Thanks, Received Order for ")
.append(scripName)
.append(" quantity= ")
.append(quantity)
.append(" price= " + price)
```

Finally, all the tags are closed in the appropriate order, and the created buffer is copied to the response context:

```
.append("</return>")
.append("</purchaseOrderResponse>")
.append("</SOAP-ENV:Body>")
.append("</SOAP-ENV:Envelope>");
resCtx.setRootPart(response.toString(), "text/xml");
```

This completes our server code. Next, we will compile and deploy this server code on the Tomcat server.

Deploying the Service

Compile the server code by using a `javac` compiler and the following command line:

```
C:\<working folder>\Ch04\Messaging\BrokerApp>javac -d . StockOrderProcessor.java
```

Copy the generated `.class` file (`<working folder>\Ch04\Messaging\BrokerApp\ StockBroker\StockOrderProcess.class`) to the folder `<Tomcat Installation Folder>\webapps\ soap\WEB-INF\classes\StockBroker`.

You can deploy the server by using the GUI tool discussed earlier or you can deploy it from the command line. To deploy the server from the command line, use the following command:

```
C:\<working folder>\Ch04\Messaging\BrokerApp>java org.apache.soap.server.➥
ServiceManagerClient http://localhost:8080/soap/servlet/rpcrouter deploy ➥
DeploymentDescriptor.xml
```

You will need to set the appropriate Internet Protocol (IP) address and the port number for your server. You will also need the deployment descriptor shown in Listing 4-9.

Listing 4-9. *Deployment Descriptor for Deploying* StockOrderProcessor *Application (*<working folder>\Ch04\Messaging\BrokerApp\DeploymentDescriptor.xml*)*

```
<isd:service xmlns:isd="http://xml.apache.org/xml-soap/deployment"
             id="urn:po-processor" type="message">
  <isd:provider type="java"
                scope="Application"
                methods="purchaseOrder">
    <isd:java class="StockBroker.StockOrderProcessor"
              static="false"/>
  </isd:provider>

  <isd:faultListener>org.apache.soap.server.DOMFaultListener</isd:faultListener>
</isd:service>
```

Note that the service type is declared as message by specifying the value of the type attribute in the service element. The service provider is declared by the provider element. The attributes for this element declare the provider type as java. The methods attribute lists all the service methods separated by a space. In our service class, we provide only one method called purchaseOrder that we want to expose as a SOAP-aware method.

The name of the Java class is defined in the isd:java element by setting its class attribute. This is set to our Java class called StockOrderProcessor with its fully qualified name.

The faultListener element declares DOMFaultListener as the Java class that listens to generated faults.

Our next task is to write a client application that transmits the purchase order XML document to the server.

Developing the Client

Developing the client consists of two parts: writing the client code and running it. Both tasks are described in this section.

Writing the Client Code

Our client is a console-based Java application called SendMessage and is shown in Listing 4-10.

Listing 4-10. *Java Client Application That Consumes Document-Style Web Service* (<working folder>\Ch04\Messaging\BrokerApp\SendMessage.java)

```java
package StockClient;

import java.io.*;
import java.net.*;
import javax.xml.parsers.*;
import org.w3c.dom.*;
import org.xml.sax.*;
import org.apache.soap.*;
import org.apache.soap.messaging.*;
import org.apache.soap.transport.*;
import org.apache.soap.util.xml.*;

public class SendMessage {
  public static void main(String[] args) throws Exception {
    if (args.length != 2) {
      System.err.println
              ("Usage: java SendMessage SOAP-router-URL envelope-file");
      System.exit(1);
    }

    // Read input XML document file
    FileReader reader = new FileReader(args[1]);
    // Build document tree
    DocumentBuilder builder = XMLParserUtils.getXMLDocBuilder();
    Document doc = builder.parse(new InputSource(reader));
    if (doc == null) {
      throw new SOAPException(Constants.FAULT_CODE_CLIENT, "parsing error");
    }
    // get SOAP Envelope
    Envelope msgEnv = Envelope.unmarshall(doc.getDocumentElement());

    // send the message
    Message msg = new Message();
    msg.send(new URL(args[0]), "urn:action-uri", msgEnv);

    // receive response
    SOAPTransport st = msg.getSOAPTransport();
    BufferedReader br = st.receive();
    // Dump the response to user screen
    String line;
    while ((line = br.readLine()) != null) {
      System.out.println(line);
    }
  }
}
```

The client application is a command-line Java application called SendMessage:

```
public class SendMessage {
  public static void main (String[] args) throws Exception {
```

The main method receives two command-line parameters:

```
if (args.length != 2) {
  System.err.println
          ("Usage: java SendMessage SOAP-router-URL envelope-file");
  System.exit (1);
}
```

The first command-line argument specifies the URL for the messagerouter servlet, and the second parameter specifies the name of the XML document to be dispatched to the server. The method reads the input document file by creating a FileReader object on it:

```
// Read input XML document file
FileReader reader = new FileReader (args[1]);
```

We create the DocumentBuilder object by calling the getXMLDocBuilder static method of the XMLParserUtils class. We parse the input document by calling the parse method on the builder object:

```
// Build document tree
DocumentBuilder builder = XMLParserUtils.getXMLDocBuilder();
Document doc = builder.parse (new InputSource (reader));
```

The parse method on its successful completion returns the root node in the Document object. The program then extracts the envelope from the document by calling the unmarshall method of the Envelope class:

```
// get SOAP Envelope
Envelope msgEnv = Envelope.unmarshall (doc.getDocumentElement ());
```

To send the envelope in a message, we create a Message object:

```
// send the message
Message msg = new Message ();
```

The envelope is dispatched in a message by calling the send method on the Message object:

```
msg.send (new URL (args[0]), "urn:action-uri", msgEnv);
```

The client application now waits for the server response by obtaining the SOAPTransport object and calling the receive method on it:

```
// receive response
SOAPTransport st = msg.getSOAPTransport ();
BufferedReader br = st.receive ();
```

The receive method is a blocking call that waits until the server response is received. After receiving the response, the application dumps its contents on the user console:

```
    // Dump the response to user screen
    String line;
    while ((line = br.readLine ()) != null) {
      System.out.println (line);
    }
```

Running the Client

Compile the application by using the `javac` compiler. Copy the generated `.class` file to the Tomcat installation as described in the previous example.

Run the client application by using the following command line:

```
C:\<working folder>\Ch04\Messaging\BrokerApp>java StockClient.SendMessage ➡
http://localhost:8080/soap/servlet/messagerouter po.xml
```

When you run the application successfully, you should see the following output on your console:

```
<?xml version='1.0' encoding='UTF-8'?><SOAP-ENV:Envelope xmlns:SOAP-ENV="http://
schemas.xmlsoap.org/soap/envelope/"><SOAP-ENV:Body><purchaseOrderResponse xmlns=
"urn:po-processor"><return>Thanks, Received Order for
    MSFT
  quantity=
  1000
  price=
  25.25
  </return></purchaseOrderResponse></SOAP-ENV:Body></SOAP-ENV:Envelope>
```

Exception Handling

The Apache SOAP server provides an exception handler for processing any errors that may occur while invoking the web service. You have seen such exception handlers in our earlier example, where the exception handler class was listed in the deployment descriptor as the value of the `faultListener` element. The code fragment is reproduced here:

```
<isd:faultListener>org.apache.soap.server.DOMFaultListener</isd:faultListener>
```

The `DOMFaultListener` class augments the SOAP fault message with additional information about the fault. The Apache SOAP server also provides another class called `ExceptionFaultListener`. This class wraps the root exception in a parameter.

You can provide your own classes for exception handling to generate application-specific messages. To illustrate this, we will modify our `StockOrderProcessor` class from the previous example to use a custom exception handler. The order processor will check the order value, and will generate a custom exception message to the client if the value exceeds a preset credit limit.

To begin, we will write a custom exception handler.

Writing a Custom Exception Handler

A custom exception handler is a Java class that implements the SOAPFaultListener interface.
Listing 4-11 provides the code for the custom handler.

Listing 4-11. *Custom Exception Handler* (<working folder>\Ch04\Messaging\BrokerAppEx\
BrokerFaultHandler.java)

```
package StockBroker;

import org.apache.soap.*;
import org.apache.soap.rpc.SOAPContext;
import org.apache.soap.server.*;

/* The custom Fault Handler implements SOAPFaultListener interface
 */

public class BrokerFaultHandler implements SOAPFaultListener
  {

    /** Creates a new instance of BrokerFaultHandler */
    public BrokerFaultHandler() {
  }

    /* fault method receives SOAPFaultEvent object that may
     * be manipulated by the method
     */
  public void fault(SOAPFaultEvent evt) {
    Fault ft = evt.getFault();
    ft.setFaultString("Application Exception: Exceeded Credit Limit");
  }
}
```

As a part of the interface, the BrokerFaultHandler class needs to implement the sole
method fault. The fault method receives an argument type SOAPFaultEvent. After the
BrokerFaultHandler class is registered (this is shown later) with the SOAP server application,
the server instantiates this class at the time of deployment. If there is an error, the fault
method is called with the populated event object sent as a parameter to the fault method.
From this event object, we retrieve the Fault object by calling its getFault method. You may
now use the various methods of the Fault class to get and set its attributes. We use the
setFaultString method to set the value of the fault string to a desired message.

Modifying the StockOrderProcessor Class

You will need to modify the stock order processor class to compute the purchase order value.
If this value exceeds the predetermined limit, a custom exception is generated. Listing 4-12
shows the modification required in the StockOrderProcessor class.

Note The modified code is available under the name `StockOrderProcessorEx` class in the down-loaded files of this book's source code (`<working folder>\Ch04\Messaging\BrokerAppEx\ StockOrderProcessorEx.java>`).

Listing 4-12. *Throwing a Custom Exception*

```
case Node.ELEMENT_NODE:
  if (n.getNodeName().equals("NYSE:scrip"))
    scripName = n.getTextContent();
  else if (n.getNodeName().equals("NYSE:quantity"))
    quantity = n.getTextContent();
  else if (n.getNodeName().equals("NYSE:price"))
    {
       price = n.getTextContent();
       float Amount = Float.parseFloat(price)* Integer.parseInt(quantity);
     if (Amount > 1000)
       throw new Exception ();
    }
  else
    throw new Exception("Unknown element: " + n.getNodeName());
  break;
```

If the node element equals `NYSE:price`, we retrieve the price and multiply it by the previously obtained `quantity`. We compare the product with a predetermined value, and if it exceeds the limit, we throw an exception. Note that the exception will be handled by the exception handler defined in the deployment descriptor.

Our next task is to register the custom exception handler.

Registering a Custom Exception Handler

The exception handlers are registered in the deployment descriptor. Listing 4-13 provides the deployment descriptor for the application.

Note This deployment descriptor is available in the file `DeploymentDescriptorEx.xml` in the down-loaded files of this book's source code (`<working folder>\Ch04\Messaging\BrokerAppEx\ DeploymentDescriptor.xml>`).

Listing 4-13. *Deployment Descriptor (*`<working folder\Ch04\Messaging\BrokerAppEx\`
`DeploymentDescriptor.xml`*)*

```
<isd:service xmlns:isd="http://xml.apache.org/xml-soap/deployment"
             id="urn:po-processorEx" type="message">
  <isd:provider type="java"
                scope="Application"
                methods="purchaseOrder">
    <isd:java class="StockBroker.StockOrderProcessorEx"
              static="false"/>
  </isd:provider>
  <isd:faultListener>
    StockBroker.BrokerFaultHandler
  </isd:faultListener>
</isd:service>
```

The value for the faultListener element specifies the class to be used as a fault handler. Note that you can list multiple faultListeners in the deployment descriptor. These listeners will be called in the order they are listed.

Deploying the Application

Compile the source by using the following commands:

```
C:\<working folder>\Ch04\Messaging\BrokerAppEx>javac -d . BrokerFaultHandler.java
C:\<working folder>\Ch04\Messaging\BrokerAppEx>javac -d . StockOrderProcessorEx.java
```

Copy the generated .class files to the folder `<Tomcat Installation Folder>\webapps\`
`soap\WEB-INF\classes\StockBroker.`
To deploy the application on Tomcat, use the following command line:

```
C:\<working folder>\Ch04\Messaging\BrokerAppEx>java ➡
org.apache.soap.server.ServiceManagerClient ➡
http://localhost:8080/soap/servlet/rpcrouter deploy DeploymentDescriptorEx.xml
```

You can verify that the application is deployed by using the following command:

```
C:\<working folder>\Ch04\Messaging\BrokerAppEx>java ➡
org.apache.soap.server.ServiceManagerClient ➡
http://localhost:8080/soap/servlet/rpcrouter list
```

Be sure to use the appropriate port number for your installation.

Running the Application

You can run the application by using the following command line:

```
C:\<working folder>\Ch04\Messaging\BrokerAppEx>java StockClient.SendMessage ➡
http://localhost:8080/soap/servlet/messagerouter poEx.xml
```

The SendMessage client in the command line is the same as the one described in the earlier section. The poEx.xml (available in the downloaded source) that will cause an exception is given in Listing 4-14.

Listing 4-14. poEx.xml *That Causes an Exception During Processing (*<working folder>\Ch04\ Messaging\BrokerAppEx\poEx.xml*)*

```
<s:Envelope xmlns:s="http://schemas.xmlsoap.org/soap/envelope/">
<s:Body >
<purchaseOrder xmlns="urn:po-processorEx"
               xmlns:NYSE="http://www.example.com/NYSE/Stocks/Tradeorder">
    <NYSE:scrip>
      MSFT
    </NYSE:scrip>
    <NYSE:quantity>
      1000
    </NYSE:quantity>
    <NYSE:price>
      25.25
    </NYSE:price>
</purchaseOrder>
</s:Body>
</s:Envelope>
```

During processing of the poEx.xml document, the net order is computed as 1,000 multiplied by 25.25. This exceeds the predefined value of 1,000 and thus causes an exception generation. The output produced by running the client application is given here:

```
<?xml version='1.0' encoding='UTF-8'?>
<SOAP-ENV:Envelope xmlns:xsi="http://www.w3.org/2001/XMLSchema-instance" xmlns:x
sd="http://www.w3.org/2001/XMLSchema" xmlns:SOAP-ENV="http://schemas.xmlsoap.org
/soap/envelope/">
<SOAP-ENV:Body>
<SOAP-ENV:Fault>
<faultcode>SOAP-ENV:Server</faultcode>
<faultstring>Application Exception: Exceeded Credit Limit</faultstring>
<faultactor>/soap/servlet/messagerouter</faultactor>
</SOAP-ENV:Fault>

</SOAP-ENV:Body>
</SOAP-ENV:Envelope>
```

Note that the fault string element contains the application-specific message. To appreciate the importance of custom exception handling, replace the fault handler class in the deployment descriptor with the org.apache.soap.server.DOMFaultListener class and run the application one more time. This time you will see a message on the screen with a long stack trace describing the error.

Such types of error screens do the end user little good. Using the custom exception handlers, you will be able to generate messages that are application-domain specific and more meaningful to the end user.

Data Type Mappings

When you invoke a web service, you may occasionally want to send or receive user-defined data types in addition to the predefined data types. Note that any data type must be marshalled/unmarshalled to an XML data type. Apache SOAP defines mappings for several data types. In addition to primitive data types such as int and float, the list also contains data types such as GregorianCalendar, Date, Vector, Hashtable, TreeMap, and List. The list is quite exhaustive, and you can refer to Apache SOAP documentation for the complete list.[6]

Creating mappings for user-defined data types is not a complex process. Continuing with our example of a stock brokerage, say we want to offer the client a web service that returns the latest stock information for a desired stock code. The stock information consists of today's high price, today's low price, and the current bid and offer prices. The user sends the stock code to the service as a parameter and expects the four details in the response. One way to implement this would be to send the four values individually in the response. However, if your brokerage application has a built-in-class, say StockInfo, that contains all the required information, it would be easy to serialize an instance of this class in the response to the client.

Creating a User-Defined Data Type

You can write your StockInfo class representing the user-defined data type as shown in Listing 4-15.

Listing 4-15. StockInfo *Class (*<working folder>\Ch04\StockInfoService\StockInfo.java*)*

```
package stockinfoservice;

public class StockInfo {
    private float TodayHigh;
    private float TodayLow;
    private float CurrBid;
    private float CurrOffer;

    public StockInfo() {
    }

    /** Creates a new instance of StockInfo */
    public StockInfo(String Symbol) {
        if (Symbol.equals("IBM")) {
            setTodayHigh(25);
            setTodayLow(20);
```

---

6. Refer to "Creating Type Mappings" in the Apache SOAP v2.3.1 documentation that is the part of the SOAP installation.

```
            setCurrBid(22);
            setCurrOffer(23);
        } else if (Symbol.equals("MSFT")) {
            setTodayHigh(55);
            setTodayLow(50);
            setCurrBid(52);
            setCurrOffer(53);
        } else {
            setTodayHigh(15);
            setTodayLow(10);
            setCurrBid(12);
            setCurrOffer(13);
        }
    }
    public float getTodayHigh() {
        return TodayHigh;
    }
    public void setTodayHigh(float TodayHigh) {
        this.TodayHigh = TodayHigh;
    }
    public float getTodayLow() {
        return TodayLow;
    }
    public void setTodayLow(float TodayLow) {
        this.TodayLow = TodayLow;
    }
    public float getCurrBid() {
        return CurrBid;
    }
    public void setCurrBid(float CurrBid) {
        this.CurrBid = CurrBid;
    }
    public float getCurrOffer() {
        return CurrOffer;
    }
    public void setCurrOffer(float CurrOffer) {
        this.CurrOffer = CurrOffer;
    }
}
```

The StockInfo class follows the JavaBeans convention and defines its members as private and provides public getter/setter (accessor/mutator) methods. We define two constructors. The constructor that takes a string argument initializes the object state depending on the value of its argument. We have used hard-coded values for the stock. In real-life situations, you would pick up the values from a real-time database. You need to define a no-argument constructor because it is required by the web service that instantiates this class.

Web Service Implementation

Your web service implementation provides a method that can be invoked by a client to obtain the stock information provided by the StockInfo class in Listing 4-15. Listing 4-16 provides the server code that instantiates the StockInfo class.

Listing 4-16. *The Stock Info Server That Uses the* StockInfo *Class (*<working folder>\Ch04\ StockInfoService\StockInfoServer.java*)*

```java
package stockinfoservice;

public class StockInfoServer {

    /** Creates a new instance of StockInfoServer */
    public StockInfoServer() {
    }

    public StockInfo getStockInfo (String Symbol)
    {
        StockInfo info = new StockInfo(Symbol);
        return info;
    }
}
```

The getStockInfo method simply constructs a StockInfo object and returns it to the caller. The underlying runtime marshals this data to the appropriate XML data types.

Modifying the Deployment Descriptor

You will need to make a few modifications to your deployment descriptor before deploying the web service. Listing 4-17 shows the modified deployment descriptor.

Listing 4-17. *Deployment Descriptor for Mapping Java Objects (*<working folder>\Ch04\ StockInfoService\DeploymentDescriptor.xml*)*

```xml
<isd:service xmlns:isd="http://xml.apache.org/xml-soap/deployment"
             id="urn:QuoteService">
  <isd:provider type="java"
                scope="Application"
                methods="getStockInfo">
    <isd:java class="stockinfoservice.StockInfoServer" static="false"/>
  </isd:provider>

  <isd:faultListener>org.apache.soap.server.DOMFaultListener</isd:faultListener>
```

```
<isd:mappings>
    <isd:map encodingStyle="http://schemas.xmlsoap.org/soap/encoding/"
        xmlns:x="urn:xml-stockinfoserver-demo" qname="x:info"
        javaType="stockinfoservice.StockInfo"
        java2XMLClassName="org.apache.soap.encoding.soapenc.BeanSerializer"
        xml2JavaClassName="org.apache.soap.encoding.soapenc.BeanSerializer"/>
</isd:mappings>

</isd:service>
```

You will need to add the mappings element as shown in Listing 4-17 to the deployment descriptor. The mappings element is a subelement of the service element. The mappings element may contain multiple mappings, each defined by using the map subelement.

The map element defines the encoding style by using its encodingStyle attribute. The qualified name for the XML data type is defined by using the qname attribute. The class to be marshalled/unmarshalled is defined by using the javaType attribute.

The map element defines how to serialize this class and uses two attributes that define the classes for serialization and deserialization. The java2XMLClassName attribute defines the class to be used for converting from Java to an XML data type. The BeanSerializer class provides this functionality. The xml2JavaClassName attribute provides the reverse mapping. Again, the Apache-provided BeanSerializer class provides this functionality. If you need custom functionality while serializing or deserializing, you can create your own classes and specify their names in these two attribute values.

Deploying the Service

Compile the two Java files in Listing 4-16 and Listing 4-17 by using the following commands:

```
C:\<working folder>\Ch04\StockInfoService\javac -d . StockInfo.java
C:\<working folder>\Ch04\StockInfoService\javac -d . StockInfoServer.java
```

Copy the generated .class files to the folder <Tomcat Installation Folder>\webapps\soap\WEB-INF\classes\stockinfoservice.

You are now ready to deploy the service. You can use the GUI tool or the following command line to deploy the service:

```
C:\<working folder>\Ch04\StockInfoService java ➡
org.apache.soap.server.ServiceManagerClient ➡
http://localhost:8080/soap/servlet/rpcrouter deploy DeploymentDescriptor.xml
```

This command is the same as the previous commands you have used while deploying web services.

After the service is deployed, our next task is to write the client that invokes this service.

Writing the Client

You will write a console-based Java application that invokes the web service. Listing 4-18 gives the source code for the client application.

Listing 4-18. *Client Application That Uses the* StockInfo *Service (*C:\<working folder>\Ch04\ StockInfoService\InvestorClient.java*)*

```java
package stockinfoservice;

// import required classes

public class InvestorClient {

  public static void main(String[] args) throws Exception {

    if (args.length != 2) {
      System.err.println("Usage:");
        System.err.println(
          " java stockinfoservice.InvestorClient SOAP-router-URL StockSymbol");
            System.exit(1);
    }

    String encodingStyleURI = Constants.NS_URI_SOAP_ENC;
    URL url = new URL(args[0]);
    String StockSymbol = args[1];
    SOAPMappingRegistry smr = new SOAPMappingRegistry();
    BeanSerializer beanSer = new BeanSerializer();

    // Map the types.
    smr.mapTypes(Constants.NS_URI_SOAP_ENC,
      new QName("urn:xml-stockinfoserver-demo", "info"),
      StockInfo.class, beanSer, beanSer);

    // Build the call.
    Call call = new Call();

    call.setSOAPMappingRegistry(smr);
    call.setTargetObjectURI("urn:QuoteService");
    call.setMethodName("getStockInfo");
    call.setEncodingStyleURI(encodingStyleURI);

    Vector params = new Vector();

    params.addElement(new Parameter("Symbol",
      String.class,
      StockSymbol, null));
    call.setParams(params);

    // Invoke the call.
    Response resp;
```

```
    try {
      resp = call.invoke(url, "");
    } catch (SOAPException e) {
      System.err.println("Caught SOAPException (" +
        e.getFaultCode() + "): " +
        e.getMessage());
      return;
    }

  // Check the response.
  if (!resp.generatedFault()) {
    Parameter ret = resp.getReturnValue();
    stockinfoservice.StockInfo info =
    (stockinfoservice.StockInfo) ret.getValue();
    System.out.println ("Stock Info for " + StockSymbol);
    System.out.println("Today High: " + info.getTodayHigh());
    System.out.println("Today Low: " + info.getTodayLow());
    System.out.println("Current Bid: " + info.getCurrBid());
    System.out.println("Current Offer: " + info.getCurrOffer());
  } else {
      Fault fault = resp.getFault();
    System.err.println("Generated fault: " + fault);
  }
 }
}
```

In the main method of the class, create instances of the SOAPMappingRegistry and BeanSerializer classes as shown here:

```
SOAPMappingRegistry smr = new SOAPMappingRegistry();
BeanSerializer beanSer = new BeanSerializer();
```

Next, you will need to map the data types. This is done by calling the mapTypes method of the SOAPMappingRegistry class:

```
// Map the types.
smr.mapTypes(Constants.NS_URI_SOAP_ENC,
        new QName("urn:xml-stockinfoserver-demo", "info"),
        StockInfo.class, beanSer, beanSer);
```

The mapTypes method accepts the encoding style as its first parameter. The second parameter specifies the XML data type that is to be marshalled and unmarshalled. The third parameter specifies the Java class name to which the XML data type is marshalled and unmarshalled. The fourth parameter specifies the serialization class that implements this marshalling, and the fifth parameter specifies the class to be used for reverse mapping.

After you register the mappings in the mapping registry, your next task is to construct a call to the server:

```
Call call = new Call();
```

You need to specify the mapping registry that will be used by the call:

```
call.setSOAPMappingRegistry(smr);
```

On the call object, you set the URN of the web service, the method to be called, and the encoding style URI:

```
call.setTargetObjectURI("urn:StockInfoServer");
call.setMethodName("getStockInfo");
call.setEncodingStyleURI(encodingStyleURI);
```

Next, you need to construct and set the method parameters:

```
Vector params = new Vector();
params.addElement(new Parameter("Symbol",
  String.class,
  StockSymbol, null));
call.setParams(params);
```

In our case, we set the stock code as the only parameter to the method. Note that our web service implementation uses the hard-coded values for two stock symbols, IBM and MSFT. For other stock symbols, it returns another set of hard-coded values. The service implementation can be modified to retrieve the real-time information for the requested stock code and return its value to the client. However, to keep things simple enough so that we keep our focus on mapping user-defined data types, I have avoided this additional coding.

After constructing the call object, we call its invoke method by passing the URL of the web service as a parameter:

```
Response resp;
String url = "http://localhost:8080/soap/servlet/rpcrouter";

try
{
  resp = call.invoke(url, "");
}
catch (SOAPException e)
{
    System.err.println("Caught SOAPException (" +
      e.getFaultCode() + "): " +
      e.getMessage());
    return;
}
```

The invoke method returns a response to the client. Any exceptions are caught in the SOAPException catch block.

The program then checks whether the response contains a fault by calling its generated-Fault method:

```
// Check the response.
if (!resp.generatedFault())
{
  Parameter ret = resp.getReturnValue();
  stockinfoservice.StockInfo info =
    (stockinfoservice.StockInfo)ret.getValue();
  System.out.println ("Stock Info for " + StockSymbol);
  System.out.println("Today High: " + info.getTodayHigh());
  System.out.println("Today Low: " + info.getTodayLow());
  System.out.println("Current Bid: " + info.getCurrBid());
  System.out.println("Current Offer: " + info.getCurrOffer());
}
else
{
  Fault fault = resp.getFault();
  System.err.println("Generated fault: " + fault);
}
```

If the program finds no fault, the program retrieves the response's returned value and prints it on the user console. Note how the return value is mapped to the StockInfo class. If the program finds a fault, the program prints the fault details on the console.

Examining the SOAP Request and Response

Use the SOAP message interceptor program described earlier to study the mappings between a Java class and XML in the SOAP request and response. You will need to change the service request port to 8079, where the interceptor is configured to listen to input requests.

The SOAP request is given in the following screen output:

```
POST /soap/servlet/rpcrouter HTTP/1.0
Host: localhost:8079
Content-Type: text/xml;charset=utf-8
Content-Length: 450
SOAPAction: ""
Accept-Encoding: gzip

<?xml version='1.0' encoding='UTF-8'?>
<SOAP-ENV:Envelope xmlns:xsi="http://www.w3.org/2001/XMLSchema-instance"
                   xmlns:xsd="http://www.w3.org/2001/XMLSchema"
                   xmlns:SOAP-ENV="http://schemas.xmlsoap.org/soap/envelope/">
<SOAP-ENV:Body>
<ns1:getStockInfo xmlns:ns1="urn:QuoteService"
          SOAP-ENV:encodingStyle="http://schemas.xmlsoap.org/soap/encoding/">
<Symbol xsi:type="xsd:string">MSFT</Symbol>
</ns1:getStockInfo>
</SOAP-ENV:Body>
</SOAP-ENV:Envelope>
```

Note how the getStockInfo method call is embedded in the SOAP body. Also, notice the presence of the xsd:string type parameter passed to the method.

When the server executes the request successfully, it returns a SOAP response to the client. The SOAP response is given here:

```
HTTP/1.1 200 OK
Server: Apache-Coyote/1.1
Set-Cookie: JSESSIONID=46E561B2B240F52681DDB0C90D4D8481; Path=/soap
Accept-Encoding: gzip
Content-Type: text/xml;charset=utf-8
Content-Length: 692
Date: Sun, 08 Jan 2006 16:13:19 GMT
Connection: close

<?xml version='1.0' encoding='UTF-8'?>
<SOAP-ENV:Envelope xmlns:xsi="http://www.w3.org/2001/XMLSchema-instance"
                   xmlns:xsd="http://www.w3.org/2001/XMLSchema"
                   xmlns:SOAP-ENV="http://schemas.xmlsoap.org/soap/envelope/">
<SOAP-ENV:Body>
<ns1:getStockInfoResponse xmlns:ns1="urn:QuoteService"
    SOAP-ENV:encodingStyle="http://schemas.xmlsoap.org/soap/encoding/">
<return xmlns:ns2="urn:xml-stockinfoserver-demo" xsi:type="ns2:info">
<currBid xsi:type="xsd:float">52.0</currBid>
<currOffer xsi:type="xsd:float">53.0</currOffer>
<todayHigh xsi:type="xsd:float">55.0</todayHigh>
<todayLow xsi:type="xsd:float">50.0</todayLow>
</return>
</ns1:getStockInfoResponse>
</SOAP-ENV:Body>
</SOAP-ENV:Envelope>
```

Note the presence of several xsd:float elements that map to the individual data members of our StockInfo class.

The mappings for both the SOAP request and response are performed by the Apache-provided BeanSerializer class.

Deployment Descriptors

You have seen the use of deployment descriptors in the previous examples. You will now learn about their structure and purpose.

Purpose of the Deployment Descriptor

A *deployment descriptor* provides information on the runtime services required by the running application with the help of the service element. The service element describes the URN for the service, the method and the class name of the POJO class, and more. Note that the service can be provided not only by a POJO, but also by EJBs or by a service routine written in a scripting language. The scripting languages supported by the Bean Scripting Framework (BSF) are described later in this chapter. The contents of the deployment descriptor vary depending on the artifact that is exposed via SOAP.

Deployment Descriptor Structure

The deployment descriptor is basically an XML document. This XML document has a root element called service, which is defined in the http://xml.apache.org/xml-soap/deployment namespace:

```
<isd:service xmlns:isd="http://xml.apache.org/xml-soap/deployment"
             id="urn:QuoteService">

    ...
</isd:service>
```

The service element also contains an id attribute that defines the URN for the service. When the client invokes the service by using the specified URN, the SOAP server will redirect the call to the provider defined in the service element. How to define this provider is discussed next.

Depending on the artifact that is exposed via SOAP, we get three versions of the deployment descriptor:

- Standard Java class deployment descriptor

- EJB deployment descriptor

- BSF script deployment descriptor

Standard Java Class Deployment Descriptor

You have used the standard Java class deployment descriptors in the previous examples. To describe the structure, I have reproduced in Listing 4-19 a descriptor from Listing 4-3.

Listing 4-19. *Structure of a Deployment Descriptor for a POJO*

```
<isd:service xmlns:isd="http://xml.apache.org/xml-soap/deployment"
             id="urn:QuoteService">
  <isd:provider type="java"
                scope="Application"
                methods="getStockQuote">
    <isd:java
        class="StockBroker.StockQuoteService"
        static="false"/>
  </isd:provider>
  <isd:faultListener>
    org.apache.soap.server.DOMFaultListener
  </isd:faultListener>
</isd:service>
```

The provider subelement provides provider details such as its type, scope, and methods. The code in bold shows the provider used by the service. The type attribute specifies that the provider is a Java class. The `scope` attribute specifies the lifetime of the Java object. This can be `Request`, `Session`, or `Application`. The `scope` of the object (lifespan) will be the scope as indicated by one of these values. The `methods` attribute defines the methods of the class that are exposed as SOAP-aware methods. If more than one method needs to be exposed, these will be separated by a space.

The `java` element defines the fully qualified path of the Java class that provides the service. The fully qualified name is specified as the value for the `class` attribute. The `static` attribute specifies whether the class methods are static.

The `faultListener` element specifies the class to be used for processing faults.

EJB Deployment Descriptor

Listing 4-20 provides an example of an EJB deployment descriptor.

Listing 4-20. *Deployment Descriptor for EJB Provider*

```xml
<?xml version="1.0"?>
<isd:service xmlns:isd="http://xml.apache.org/xml-soap/deployment"
             id="urn:testprovider">
  <isd:provider type="org.apache.soap.providers.StatelessEJBProvider"
                scope="Application"
                methods="create">
  <isd:java class="samples/MyHelloService"/>
  <isd:option key="FullHomeInterfaceName" value="samples.MyHelloServiceHome" />
  <isd:option key="ContextProviderURL" value="iiop://localhost:9000" />
  <isd:option key="FullContextFactoryName"
              value="com.ibm.ejs.ns.jndi.CNInitialContextFactory" />
  </isd:provider>
  <isd:faultListener>org.apache.soap.server.DOMFaultListener
  </isd:faultListener>
</isd:service>
```

The `id` attribute of the `service` element defines a unique identifier that is used by the SOAP server to redirect the call to the appropriate service provider. The type of provider in Listing 4-20 is `StatelessEJBProvider`. This indicates that the service is provided by a stateless EJB. Note that an EJB can be a stateless bean, a stateful bean, or an entity bean. If the service is provided by a stateful EJB, you specify the type as `StatefulEJBProvider`. If the service is provided by an entity bean (both bean-managed and container-managed persistence beans), you specify the type as `EntityEJBProvider`.

Because the life cycle of an EJB is controlled by the EJB container, the only allowed value for the `scope` attribute is `Application`. The value for the `methods` attribute lists all the SOAP-aware bean methods.

The `java` element defines the name of the bean class as a value of its `class` attribute. This specifies the local or the remote interface of your EJB.

The `option` element is specified more than once. The `key` attribute differentiates between multiple occurrences of the `option` element. The key value of `FullHomeInterfaceName` specifies the fully qualified name of your EJB home class. The `ContextProviderURL` key specifies the

Internet InterOperable Protocol (IIOP) listener on your EJB server. Note that the communication between the EJB client and the server is done using IIOP. You will specify the URL of your EJB's IIOP listener as the value of the value attribute. You will need to specify both the IP and the port number while specifying the IIOP listener. The key value of FullContextFactoryName specifies the name of the initial context factory class. This class is specific to the application server provider and thus varies depending on the application server you are using.

BSF Script Deployment Descriptor

Listing 4-21 shows the deployment descriptor for a web service provided by a method written in a scripting language.

Listing 4-21. *Deployment Descriptor for BSF Script Language Service*

```xml
<?xml version="1.0"?>

  <isd:service xmlns:isd="http://xml.apache.org/xml-soap/deployment"
              id="urn:soap-calculator">
  <isd:provider type="script"
                scope="Application"
                methods="ADD SUBTRACT MULTIPLY DIVIDE">
    <isd:script language="javascript">
      function ADD (x, y) {
        return x + y;
      }

      function SUBTRACT (x, y) {
        return x - y;
      }

      function MULTIPY (x, y) {
        return x * y;
      }

      function DIVIDE (x, y) {
        return x / y;
      }
    </isd:script>
  </isd:provider>
  <isd:faultListener>org.apache.soap.server.DOMFaultListener
  </isd:faultListener>
</isd:service>
```

In Listing 4-21, the service provider type is defined as script. The scope can be Request, Session, or Application as in the case of the POJO class. The methods attribute lists all the exposed methods separated by a space character. The script element defines these various methods. The language attribute specifies the script language. Listing 4-21 defines four JavaScript methods.

Specifying Fault Listeners

You have learned how to create your own fault listeners for providing custom exception handling. Such fault listeners are registered in the deployment descriptor by using the faultListener element. In the faultListener element, you simply specify the fully qualified Java class name that receives fault events. You can list multiple fault listeners by using the faultListener element. Such fault listeners will be invoked in the order they are specified.

Specifying Type Mappings

If you want to map Java class types to XML types, you specify the type mappings in the deployment descriptor. The deployment descriptor provides an element called mappings for this purpose. Inside the mappings, you can include multiple occurrences of the map element. Each map element maps a Java class type to an XML data type. The map element defines attributes for specifying a Java class type, an XML data type, and classes used for serializing and deserializing data. You have studied how to specify such type mappings in the earlier section.

Summary

SOAP has been widely accepted as a standard of communication in distributed computing. Apache SOAP provides an important implementation of this SOAP standard. Web services use SOAP for communication between client and server. SOAP is XML based. Thus, a client requesting a service needs to create an XML-based SOAP request and receives an XML-based SOAP response from the server. On the server side, the server must be capable of interpreting a SOAP request and generating a SOAP response.

The Apache SOAP implementation provides the entire framework for generating SOAP requests and responses and parsing SOAP messages. This chapter discussed the architecture of the SOAP engine. The SOAP engine uses two servlets, one for RPC-type calls and another one for Document-type calls. Both servlets use configuration files by way of a deployment descriptor to redirect the calls to the appropriate server objects.

This chapter covered the development and deployment of both RPC-style and Document-style web services based on the Apache SOAP implementation. Both server and client applications were developed. The application may generate runtime errors. The chapter discussed how to handle the exceptions by using provided exception handlers or creating custom exception handlers.

When you invoke a web service, you may need to send a few parameters to the service. The mapping between the standard Java types and XML data types is desired. The Apache SOAP implementation provides such mappings for many standard data types and allows the developer to extend these mappings to other user-defined Java data types. The chapter covered how to map a user-created Java data type to an XML data type.

In a web service implementation, the service object can be a POJO, EJB, or a script code. You specify the type of service object in a deployment descriptor. The deployment descriptor defines the mapping between the service URN and the service object. The deployment descriptor also allows you to declare the custom exception handlers and type mappings. This chapter covered the structure and use of deployment descriptors.

CHAPTER 5

■ ■ ■

XSLT and Apache Xalan

In the preceding two chapters, you studied web services architecture and the Apache SOAP implementation that helps in developing applications based on that architecture. Because web services make your application globally available, you will need to internationalize your applications so that people in different parts of the world can use them.

Your application delivers information to users through documents. So far you have written such documents in English. However, these documents must be translated into a language of the user's choice before that user can understand them. You need a translator to do this. Similarly, an XML document that is read by different devices must be translated to the device-specific language before that device can understand its contents.

XML provides an excellent means of data transport and can be easily interpreted by humans. However, interpretation may not always be easy for applications, machines, and devices that must work with XML documents. In other words, XML is not easily discernible by other software applications and electronic devices.

In this chapter, you will learn how to transform an XML document from one form to another. Specifically, you will learn the following:

- Transformation changes a given XML document from one format to another. You will learn about these transformations and why they are needed.

- XSL is the language used for transformation. You will learn how to perform transformations using the Apache implementation of XSL.

- The transformation of a document requires searching the nodes in that document and converting them into another node. The nodes in a given XML document are located by using XPath specifications. This chapter provides a quick introduction to XPath.

- You will learn how XML documents are processed using instructions specified in an XSLT document and you will learn the structure of XSLT documents.

- Apache provides a full implementation of XSL and XPath specifications. This Apache project is called *Xalan*. You will use Xalan in this chapter to learn transformations.

- XSL transformations can be performed in either the client or the server applications. We will develop both client-side and server-side applications for transformations.

- A given XML document need not be fully transformed using XSL. You may transform only part of the document. You will learn how to perform such partial transformations.

- A series of transformations can be cascaded. Such transformations are based on the push model or pull model. You will create applications based on both models.

- Translets provide a sort of precompilation on transformations. In this chapter, you will learn how to create and use translets.

What Is Transformation?

The process of converting an XML document from one form into another is called *transformation*. Transformation can also result in an XML document itself conforming to a different schema than the original document's schema. The transformed document can then be further translated into device-specific commands so its contents can be rendered on the desired device. Thus, you can visualize transformation as a two-step process:

1. Transforming a given document into another XML document that can be interpreted by a particular device

2. Formatting the contents of the transformed document to render it on the device

Accordingly, there are two specifications: The first is called Extensible Stylesheet Language (XSL), and the second is called XSL-Formatting Objects (XSL-FO). You will study XSL in this chapter and XSL-FO in the next chapter.

Need for Transformation

Consider a web browser that can render an HTML document. If you input an XML document, what is displayed? The browser renders the unformatted document as is, because the browser is not capable of making any sense of the XML tags as it would with HTML tags.

We would prefer that the browser could render the document contents in a format that is more appealing to a human reader. For example, an XML document may contain a list of items. Presenting a human reader with a tabular format of this data makes more sense to the reader than presenting the original XML document in its core format containing several tags.

Consider another example in which XML is used to transport data from a front-end application to a back-end storage device such as Oracle Database, MySQL, or Microsoft SQL Server. Because the database engine requires input data in SQL format, you'll need to generate appropriate SQL statements. Thus, the XML document that contains the data must be converted into the corresponding SQL dialect before it can be used meaningfully by the database engine.

Consider yet another example of a business-to-business (B2B) scenario. Imagine that one partner company places a purchase order with another partner company. The purchase order is an XML document that adheres to the schema specifications of the first partner. However, the other partner does not follow the same schema definition. Thus, the purchase order document must undergo a transformation to another form that conforms to the schema definition of the receiving partner.

From these discussions, you can easily understand the need to devise a methodology for transforming an XML document to another XML format. The language used for defining transformations is called XSL.

The Apache Xalan project provides implementation for XML transformations based on XSL.

Apache Xalan Project

The Apache Xalan project provides a robust Java processor for transforming XML documents using XSL. This open source project is a result of contributions from IBM, Lotus, Oracle, Sun Microsystems, and others. Apache Xalan was initially a subproject of the Apache XML project but in October 2004 became an independent project in its own right. This was done to facilitate collaborative development for providing commercial-quality, full-featured support for XSLT on a wide variety of platforms. There are currently two subprojects under the Xalan project: Xalan-C++ and Xalan-Java. Both are compliant to XSLT (1.0) and XPath (1.0) specifications controlled by the W3C. You will be using Xalan-Java in this book.

The Xalan-Java project provides an XSLT processor, a command-line utility that transforms a specified XML document by using a stylesheet document specified on the command line. The processor libraries can also be invoked through your Java application code.

To use Xalan, you first need to download it from the Apache site and install it on your machine. This process is described next.

Downloading Xalan

You can download the Xalan distributions from the following URL:

http://xalan.apache.org/

The site contains the following binary distributions:

- xalan-j_2_7_0-bin.zip (for Windows) or xalan-j_2_7_0-bin.tar.gz (for Linux)

- xalan-j_2_7_0-bin-2jars.zip (for Windows) or xalan-j_2_7_0-bin-2jars.tar.gz (for Linux)

Both contain the same distribution but are packaged differently. The first one contains a Xalan interpretive processor, a compiled processor, and the runtime support packages in a single JAR file called xalan.jar. The second one contains the Xalan interpretive processor in xalan.jar, and the compiled processor and the runtime support packages in xsltc.jar. There is no advantage of one over the other. Both are identical, and you can download either one. You will need to add the corresponding JAR files (based on which version you download) in your classpath.

If you are interested in the implementation details, you can download the complete source code from the Apache download site.

Installing Xalan

Installing Xalan is as simple as most of the other Apache software installations. Just unzip the previously downloaded file to a desired folder. That folder will then contain many JAR files that you need to add to your classpath environment variable. Minimally, you need to add the following files to your classpath:

- xalan.jar or (xalan.jar and xsltc.jar): Processor and runtime libraries.

- serializer.jar: Contains serialization classes that are used by the Xalan processor.

- `xml-apis.jar`: Implementation of Java API for XML Parsing (JAXP) APIs.

- `xercesImpl.jar`: Implementation of XML parsers. You used this file in Chapter 2 for parsing XML documents.

After this is done, you are ready to test the Xalan installation.

Testing the Installation

The Xalan installation package contains Java source files for several sample programs located in the `samples` folder under your installation directory. The `samples` folder also contains a `xalansamples.jar` file that contains some of the compiled sources. Include this file in your classpath or copy it into the `webapps` folder of your Tomcat installation. If you are using some other application server or a servlet engine, follow the appropriate instructions to install the application JAR.

To test your installation, you can try compiling the SimpleTransform program. This is located in the `<xalan installation folder>\samples\SimpleTransform` folder. Compile the `SimpleTransform.java` file by using the following command line:

`C:\<xalan installation folder>\samples\SimpleTransform>javac SimpleTransform.java`

Run the program by using the following `java` command line. On success, you will see the following output:

```
C:\xalan-j_2_7_0\samples\SimpleTransform>java SimpleTransform
************* The result is in birds.out *************
```

The SimpleTransform application takes `birds.xml` as the input document and applies the transformation commands stored in the `birds.xsl` file to create as output the `birds.out` file. Both the `birds.xml` and `birds.xsl` files are in the same folder.

Alternatively, you can test the installation by running the command-line transformation processor as shown here:

```
C:\<xalan installation folder>\samples\SimpleTransform>java ➥
org.apache.xalan.xslt.Process -IN birds.xml -XSL birds.xsl -OUT birds.out
```

This creates the `birds.out` file in your working folder. If you are curious to see the transformation results, open the `birds.out` and `birds.xml` files in your favorite text editor. You can even examine `birds.xsl` to look at XSL commands used for performing transformations.

The Extensible Stylesheet Language (XSL)

Now that you understand the need for transformation and have successfully installed the required software, you are ready to try some real-life transformations and develop programs to do these transformations.

You are probably familiar with Cascading Style Sheets (CSS), which grant the user considerable control over how HTML elements are rendered. CSS helps in rendering HTML contents in a nicely formatted document. CSS is not XML based. XSL is another standard similar to CSS, but it is XML based.

As mentioned earlier, XSL is a language used for transformation. Such transformations usually consist of two parts: converting a given document from one XML form to another and formatting the resultant output so it is suitable for rendering on a desired device. Though XSL was created with the intention of transforming and formatting the output, its purpose soon evolved into two distinct specifications in order to better separate its transformation and formatting functionalities. These two specifications are as follows:

- XSLT[1] (XSL Transformations): a specification for transforming XML documents

- XSL-FO (XSL Formatting Objects): a specification for formatting documents

As stated earlier, this chapter introduces XSLT, while the next introduces XSL-FO. More specifically, the purpose of this chapter is to introduce XSLT in conjunction with the Apache implementation of XSLT (Xalan project) that defines several classes and utilities for transforming XML documents. We will focus on various programming techniques used in XML transformations.

While performing transformations, our program should be able to locate and extract any desired portion of a given XML document. This is where the XPath specifications come into the picture. XPath defines the syntax for locating any part of a given XML document. Therefore, before delving into the details of XSLT, let's have a quick tour of XPath specifications.

Quick Tour of XPath

XPath is a language for finding information in an XML document. A W3C standard since November 1999, it can be used for navigating through elements and attributes of an XML document. Specifically, XPath is capable of the following tasks:

- Locating parts of an XML document by using a specially defined syntax

- Navigating in an XML document by using path expressions, which allow the selection of nodes or node-sets in the document

- Performing complex node manipulation through its 100 functions, which are available for node comparisons, node manipulations, sequence manipulations, and more

A well-formed XML document can be represented as a tree containing nodes. Every node has a unique path in the tree with respect to the root node. This is similar to your hard drive's folder hierarchy, which consists of a root folder containing several subfolders. You can uniquely identify any folder or file on your disk by specifying the path starting from the root folder. Similarly, XPath defines the syntax for locating any element or attribute in an XML document with respect to the document's root node.

Also, in your hard drive's folder hierarchy, given any folder name, you can locate other folders or files on the hard drive starting from this given name. That is to say, you can specify the path for any folder or file relative to a known location. Similarly, XPath defines syntax for relative paths. The relative paths can be used for locating any node relative to a given node or for navigating to other nodes.

---

1. XSLT is now simply called XSL.

The operating system provides utilities (for example, search on Windows and find on Unix and Linux) for locating any file or folder on your hard drive. You create search expressions to narrow your search. Similarly, XSL defines several functions that can be used for comparisons during search operations to restrict your searches, with other functions available for performing node and sequence manipulations. Interested readers are referred to the XPath specifications for further details.[2]

XSLT depends heavily on XPath. Without XPath, you will not be able to use XSLT. So you will look at XPath syntax next.

XPath Syntax

To understand the XPath syntax, consider an example. Listing 5-1 displays a sample XML document first presented in Chapter 2.

Listing 5-1. *Sample XML Document for Illustrating XPath Syntax* (Ch05\src\po.xml)

```
<?xml version="1.0" encoding="utf-8" ?>
<PurchaseOrder>
  <PersonalComputer Type="Desktop">
    <Price>
      $995
    </Price>
    <Quantity>
      10
    </Quantity>
  </PersonalComputer>
  <PersonalComputer Type="Portable">
    <Price>
      $1295
    </Price>
    <Quantity>
      5
    </Quantity>
  </PersonalComputer>
  <Scanner Type="Desktop">
    <Price>
      $165
    </Price>
    <Quantity>
      2
    </Quantity>
  </Scanner>
  <Printer Type="Inkjet">
```

---

2. XPath specifications: http://www.w3.org/TR/xpath

```
    <Price>
      $85
    </Price>
    <Quantity>
      4
    </Quantity>
  </Printer>
  <Printer Type="LaserPrinter">
    <Price>
      $485
    </Price>
    <Quantity>
      1
    </Quantity>
  </Printer>
</PurchaseOrder>
```

We will now create various XPath expressions to locate the various nodes in this document. First, you will look at the XPath syntax for locating nodes.

Locating Nodes

To locate and select the nodes found in an XML document, we use the expression syntax shown in Table 5-1.

Table 5-1. *XPath Syntax for Locating Nodes in an XML Document*

Expression	Description
nodename	Selects all child nodes of the node
/	Selects from the root node
//	Starting at the current node, selects nodes in the document that match the selection
.	Selects the current node
..	Selects the parent of the current node
@	Selects an attribute

For example, the XPath expression (/) selects all the nodes in the preceding XML tree starting with the root element. In Listing 5-1, the root element is PurchaseOrder. Thus, the / expression selects all the nodes under the PurchaseOrder node. You use such selections to extract and operate on a part of the tree. Refer to the following tip for help in displaying the selection output for a given XPath expression.

Tip Later in the chapter, you will be developing a Java console application that takes an XML document as a first command-line parameter and the XPath expression as the second command-line parameter. The application displays the selected nodes by way of the user console. The application is called `PathSelector`, which is available from the Source Code area of the Apress website (`http://www.apress.com`). Compile the program by using following command line:

`C:\<working folder>\Ch05\src>javac -d . PathSelector.java`

You can use the following command to run the application:

`C:\<working folder>\Ch05\src>java xslt.PathSelector po.xml /PurchaseOrder/Printer`

This command uses a sample XML document called `po.xml` from Listing 5-1 as an input source (`po.xml` is available from the Source Code area of the Apress website, at the path `<working folder>/Ch05/src/po.xml`). Note that you will need to specify the appropriate path depending on where `po.xml` is located on your system. The application searches the document by using the XPath expression `/PurchaseOrder/Printer`. The output in this case will be as follows:

```
Querying DOM using /PurchaseOrder/Printer
<output>
<Printer Type="Inkjet">
    <Price>
      $85
    </Price>
    <Quantity>
      4
    </Quantity>
  </Printer><Printer Type="LaserPrinter">
    <Price>
      $485
    </Price>
    <Quantity>
      1
    </Quantity>
  </Printer></output>
```

Use this utility for testing the various XPath expressions that you create in this section. You can try other XPath expressions yourself to understand its syntax fully.

Building on this, the expression `/PurchaseOrder/PersonalComputer` selects all elements that are children of `PersonalComputer`, which itself is a child of the `PurchaseOrder` element. Thus, it will select `Price` and `Quantity` elements of each `PersonalComputer` node along with the text nodes that denote the text values for these nodes. Further, the expression `//PersonalComputer` selects all `PersonalComputer` elements in the document.

Locating Specific Nodes

To locate a specific node in the document, you use predicates. For example, the expression
/PurchaseOrder/PersonalComputer[1] selects the first PersonalComputer element that is the
child of the PurchaseOrder element. If you use the PathSelector utility (mentioned in the tip)
to try this XPath expression, you will see the following output:

```
Querying DOM using /PurchaseOrder/PersonalComputer[1]
<output>
<PersonalComputer Type="Desktop">
   <Price>
     $995
   </Price>
   <Quantity>
     10
   </Quantity>
 </PersonalComputer></output>
```

The expression /PurchaseOrder/PersonalComputer[last()] selects the last
PersonalComputer element that is the last child of the PurchaseOrder element. The program
output for this XPath query is as follows:

```
Querying DOM using /PurchaseOrder/PersonalComputer[last()]
<output>
<PersonalComputer Type="Portable">
   <Price>
     $1295
   </Price>
   <Quantity>
     5
   </Quantity>
 </PersonalComputer></output>
```

The expression /PurchaseOrder/PersonalComputer["Quantity>5"] selects all the
PersonalComputer elements of PurchaseOrder that have a Quantity element having a value
greater than 5. The program output is shown here:

```
Querying DOM using /PurchaseOrder/PersonalComputer[Quantity>5]
<output>
<PersonalComputer Type="Desktop">
   <Price>
     $995
   </Price>
   <Quantity>
     10
   </Quantity>
 </PersonalComputer></output>
```

Using Wildcards

You can use wildcards as shown in Table 5-2 to select one or more nodes matching the given criterion.

Table 5-2. *Wildcards for Matching Nodes in an XPath Query*

Wildcard	Description
*	Matches any element node
@*	Matches any attribute node
node()	Matches any node of any kind

Let's consider a few examples. To begin, the expression //PersonalComputer/* selects all child nodes of the PersonalComputer element. The program output is shown here:

```
Querying DOM using //PersonalComputer/*
<output>
<Price>
    $995
    </Price><Quantity>
    10
    </Quantity><Price>
    $1295
    </Price><Quantity>
    5
    </Quantity></output>
```

Note Compare this output with the output produced by the query //PersonalComputer from the previous example. In the current query, only the child elements of PersonalComputer are displayed, whereas in the earlier case the element PersonalComputer is also displayed in the output.

The expression //Printer[@*] selects all Printer elements irrespective of their attributes. The program output is shown here:

```
Querying DOM using //Printer[@*]
<output>
<Printer Type="Inkjet">
    <Price>
    $85
    </Price>
```

```
  <Quantity>
    4
  </Quantity>
</Printer><Printer Type="LaserPrinter">
  <Price>
    $485
  </Price>
  <Quantity>
    1
  </Quantity>
</Printer></output>
```

Finally, the expression //* selects all elements in the document. The program output is not shown for brevity.

Combining Paths

You can combine several paths by using the pipe character (|) to select multiple nodes. For example, the expression "//Scanner | //Printer" selects all Scanner and Printer elements in the document.

■**Note** If you try this expression by using the PathSelector utility, enclose the expression in double quotes as illustrated.

The expression //Printer/Price | //Printer/Quantity selects the Price and Quantity elements of all the Printer elements in the document. You can try this query to see the output for yourself.

XPath Axes

XPath defines what is known as an *axis* that locates a node-set relative to the current node. With respect to a given node, you can specify both its ancestors and descendants. As the name suggests, ancestors point to the parent of the current node, and descendants point to its children. You can also specify the siblings as following and preceding axes. All the nodes that are at the same level in the tree as the current node and also follow the current node will be addressed by using the following axis. Similarly, all nodes that precede the current node at the same level will be addressed by using the preceding axis. The relative positioning of the ancestor, descendant, following, and preceding axes are illustrated in Figure 5-1.

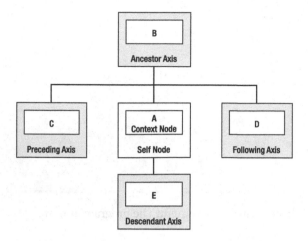

Figure 5-1. *XPath axes*

XPath specifications define several constant strings for navigating the tree by using the axes described in Figure 5-1. These names and their meanings are shown in Table 5-3. The meaning assigned to each axis is always with respect to the current node unless otherwise stated.

Table 5-3. *XPath Axes*

Axis Name	Meaning
ancestor	Selects all ancestors
ancestor-or-self	Selects all ancestors and the current node
attribute	Selects all attributes
child	Selects all children
descendant	Selects all descendants
descendant-or-self	Selects all descendants and the current node
following	Selects all nodes after the closing tag of the current node
following-sibling	Selects all following siblings
namespace	Selects all namespace nodes
parent	Selects the parent
preceding	Selects all nodes before the start tag of the current node
preceding-sibling	Selects all preceding siblings
self	Selects the current node

For example, the expression child::Printer selects all Printer nodes that are children to the current node. The expression child::text() selects all text nodes of the current node. The expression ancestor::Printer selects all Printer ancestors of the current node.

Finally, you will look at the various operators defined in the XPath specifications.

XPath Operators

XPath defines several operators that can be used in XPath expressions. These operators are provided in Table 5-4.

Table 5-4. *XPath Operators*

Operator	Description
|	Computes two node-sets
+	Addition
-	Subtraction
*	Multiplication
div	Division
=	Equals
!=	Not equal to
<	Less than
<=	Less than or equal to
>	Greater than
>=	Greater than or equal to
or	Or
and	And
mod	Modulus (division remainder)

Most of the operators have conventional meanings and thus do not require additional explanation. Multiple operators can be combined in an expression, and they then follow conventional precedence rules.

A Quick Tour of XSLT

XSL transforms an XML document into another document format, or perhaps more precisely, it transforms a source tree into a result tree. Note that every well-formed XML document can be represented as a tree. The output produced by XSLT can also be represented as a well-formed tree.

XSLT is not restricted to just transforming one document type to another. It can also be used to add elements and attributes to an output file, or to remove elements and attributes from the source file while creating an output file. You can also rearrange the source document, sort it on certain elements, and hide and display elements based on user-defined criteria, and more.

To perform these operations, XSLT must navigate the source tree. It uses XPath expressions discussed in the previous sections to navigate and select the desired part of the tree and then transforms the selected portion of the source tree into a result tree.

XSLT Processing Model

The XSLT processing model is illustrated in Figure 5-2.

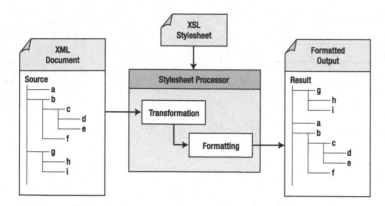

Figure 5-2. *XSLT processing model*

A stylesheet processor accepts two inputs:

- The XML document that is to be transformed

- The XSL stylesheet that contains the transformation instructions

The stylesheet processor uses XPath to locate the various parts of the input document. When a part is located, it is transformed by using a template defined in the stylesheet. The stylesheet contains several templates. The processor applies the template to a part of the input document that is selected using the XPath expression. The output of the processor is a tree that may represent another XML document, or even some other type of document such as HTML.

XSLT Example

Before getting into the XSL syntax, let's consider an example of how XSLT works. Listing 5-2 shows a sample XML document that we will transform into HTML by using XSL.

Note Only part of the XML document is shown here. The full listing for `CustomerOrders.xml` is available from the Source Code area of the Apress website (`http://www.apress.com`).

Listing 5-2. *Sample XML Document for XSL Transformation* (Ch05\src\CustomerOrders.xml)

```xml
<?xml version="1.0" encoding="utf-8" ?>
<?xml-stylesheet type="text/xsl" href="OrderProcessing.xslt"?>

<customers>

  <customer>
    <name>Hillary A. Johnston</name>
    <order>GFW</order>
    <quantity>50</quantity>
    <price>$25.35</price>
  </customer>

  <customer>
    <name>Leslie Doherty</name>
    <order>GFZ</order>
    <quantity>75</quantity>
    <price>$25.30</price>
  </customer>

  <customer>
    <name>Don Mrskos</name>
    <order>SXA</order>
    <quantity>29</quantity>
    <price>$25.23</price>
  </customer>
    ...
  <customer>
    <name>C. W. Southport</name>
    <order>ECT</order>
    <quantity>125</quantity>
    <price>$25.41</price>
  </customer>

</customers>
```

The XSLT file that we will use for transformation is shown in Listing 5-3.

Listing 5-3. *XSLT Document Used for Transformation* (Ch05\src\OrderProcessing.xslt)

```xml
<?xml version="1.0" encoding="UTF-8" ?>
<xsl:stylesheet version="1.0"
  xmlns:xsl="http://www.w3.org/1999/XSL/Transform"
  >
```

```
<xsl:template match="/">
  <TABLE BORDER="1">
    <TR bgcolor="0x0000ff">
      <TD>
        <font color="#FFFFFF">
          Customer Name
        </font>
      </TD>
      <TD>
        <font color="#FFFFFF">
          Order Scrip
        </font>
      </TD>
      <TD>
        <font color="#FFFFFF">
          Order Quantity
        </font>
      </TD>
      <TD>
        <font color="#FFFFFF">
          Order Price
        </font>
      </TD>
    </TR>
    <xsl:apply-templates select ="customers"/>
  </TABLE>
</xsl:template>

<xsl:template match="customers">
  <xsl:apply-templates select ="customer">
    <xsl:sort select="price" order="ascending"/>
  </xsl:apply-templates>
</xsl:template>
<xsl:template match="customer">
  <TR>
    <TD>
      <font color="#0000ff" size="+1">
        <xsl:value-of select ="name"/>
      </font>
    </TD>
    <TD bgcolor="#00FFFF">
      <xsl:value-of select="order"/>
    </TD>
    <TD>
      <p align="right">
        <xsl:value-of select="quantity"/>
      </p>
    </TD>
```

```
    <TD bgcolor="#00FFFF">
      <p align="right">
        <xsl:value-of select="price"/>
      </p>
    </TD>
  </TR>
</xsl:template>
</xsl:stylesheet>
```

We tell the browser to apply the template by including the following line in the XML document after the XML declaration:

```
<?xml-stylesheet type="text/xsl" href="OrderProcessing.xslt"?>
```

Make sure that the OrderProcessing.xslt file shown in Listing 5-3 resides in the same folder as the CustomerOrders.xml file also shown in that listing. If you now open the CustomerOrders.xml file in a browser that supports XSLT, you will see a nicely formatted output in your browser window. The output as seen in Microsoft Internet Explorer 6 is shown in Figure 5-3.[3]

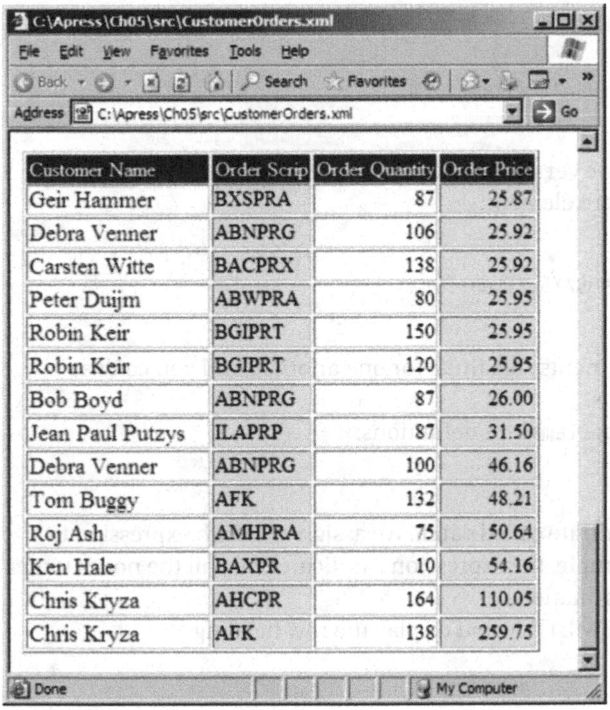

Figure 5-3. *Screen output of* CustomerOrders.xml *(Ch05\src\CustomerOrders.xml)*

---

3. Some of the other browsers that support XSLT are Firefox 1.0.2, Mozilla 1.7.8, Netscape 8, and Opera 8.

Tip You can try the output in the browser after removing the preceding XSLT processing line to understand the significance of transformation.

Note that using the built-in transformer in your browser is not an ideal way of transforming your XML documents. To perform the transformations, you can use the programming API (discussed later) or the command-line processor provided by Xalan as shown here:

```
C:\<working folder>\Ch05\src>java org.apache.xalan.xslt.Process -in ➥
 CustomerOrders.xml –xsl OrderProcessing.xslt -out test.html
```

XSLT Document Structure

Having seen how an XSLT sample document transforms the given XML document into another format, you will now study the structure of an XSLT document to learn XSL syntax.

The XSLT document begins with an XML declaration followed by the stylesheet element, which is the root element:

```
<?xml version="1.0" encoding="UTF-8" ?>
<xsl:stylesheet version="1.0"
  xmlns:xsl="http://www.w3.org/1999/XSL/Transform"
  >
```

The stylesheet element defines the version attribute and the xsl namespace. Instead of stylesheet, you can use the transform element:

```
<xsl:transform version="1.0"
  xmlns:xsl="http://www.w3.org/1999/XSL/Transform"
  >
```

The stylesheet and transform elements substitute for one another, and you can use either one in your stylesheet definitions.

This is now followed by one or more template definitions:

```
<xsl:template match="/">
```

The template element uses an attribute called match. We assign an XPath expression to this match attribute. In the current example, the expression / indicates that all the nodes under the root will be selected during transformation.

The subsequent lines create an HTML table and display the row heading:

```
<TABLE BORDER="1">
  <TR bgcolor="0x0000ff">
    <TD>
      <font color="#FFFFFF">
        Customer Name
      </font>
    </TD>
```

```
    <TD>
      <font color="#FFFFFF">
        Order Scrip
      </font>
    </TD>
    <TD>
      <font color="#FFFFFF">
        Order Quantity
      </font>
    </TD>
    <TD>
      <font color="#FFFFFF">
        Order Price
      </font>
    </TD>
  </TR>
```

Following this, we have this statement:

```
<xsl:apply-templates select ="customers"/>
```

This statement indicates that we will apply the customers template to all the selected nodes. The customers template is defined next:

```
<xsl:template match="customers">
  <xsl:apply-templates select ="customer">
    <xsl:sort select="price" order="ascending" data-type="number"/>
  </xsl:apply-templates>
</xsl:template>
```

For elements located under customers, we further apply the customer template. We arrange all the located customer elements by sorting them on the price subelement. The sorting order is ascending.

Next, we define the customer template itself:

```
<xsl:template match="customer">
```

Here, we create a row for our HTML table and display the contents of the name subelement in the first column:

```
<TR>
  <TD>
    <font color="#0000ff" size="+1">
      <xsl:value-of select ="name"/>
    </font>
  </TD>
  ...
</TR>
```

We use the value-of element with the select attribute set to the desired subelement. Likewise, we display order, quantity, and price subelements in the subsequent HTML table columns. Note that the value of the select attribute is an XPath expression that is used for navigating the XML document.

When you apply this template to CustomerOrders.xml shown in Listing 5-2, the various templates will be applied during transformation and you will see the output as illustrated in Figure 5-3.

With this brief introduction to XSLT completed, we will now proceed to the Apache Xalan implementation so you can learn how transformations are achieved through the provided tools and user-written Java code. While discussing the various programming techniques, you will also learn more about XSL.

Xalan's Transformation Capabilities

Apache Xalan provides a set of classes for performing XSL transformations through Java program code. It also provides a command-line utility to perform transformation. In this section, you will study several programming examples to learn how to do the following:

- Perform transformations through a stand-alone program

- Perform transformations on a server

- Cascade multiple transformations

You will begin by learning the command-line tool to perform transformations.

Using the Command-Line Transformation Tool

The Xalan implementation provides a command-line utility for performing transformations. For example, to perform the transformation on our CustomerOrders.xml file from Listing 5-2, you will run the following command at the command prompt:

```
C:\<working folder>\Ch05\src>java org.apache.xalan.xslt.Process -in ➥
 CustomerOrders.xml -xsl OrderProcessing.xslt -out test.html
```

The org.apache.xalan.xslt.Process utility defines several command-line switches. The -in switch specifies the name of the XML file to be processed. The -xsl switch specifies the name of the XSLT file used for transformation, and the -out switch specifies the name of the output file to be generated as a result of transformation.

After running the preceding command-line utility, you will find a test.html file created in your current folder. You can now open this file in your browser to view the output. This will be the same as the one displayed in Figure 5-3.

Additionally, this command-line tool provides several other switches. For example, the -XML switch uses an XML formatter to format the output and also adds an XML header to the output. The -TEXT switch uses a simple Text formatter, and the -HTML switch uses an HTML formatter. For further details, refer to Xalan documentation.

Writing Your First Transformation Program

Performing transformations through a Java application is easy. Listing 5-4 gives the complete listing of a Java console application that performs such XSL transformations.

Listing 5-4. *A Console-Based Java Application for XSL Transformations* (Ch05\src\ TransformTest.java)

```java
package xslt;

public class TransformTest {

  public static void main(String[] args) {
    if (args.length != 2)
    {
      System.out.println ("Usage: java TransformTest xsltFile xmlFile");
      System.exit(1);
    }
    String xsltFile = args[0];
    String xmlFile = args[1];

    // Create a TransformerFactory instance
    javax.xml.transform.TransformerFactory tFactory =
                      javax.xml.transform.TransformerFactory.newInstance();

      try {
          // Create a Transformer for the specified stylesheet
          javax.xml.transform.Transformer transformer = tFactory.newTransformer
            (new javax.xml.transform.stream.StreamSource(xsltFile));

          //Transform an XML Source and send the
          // output to a Result object
          transformer.transform (
              new javax.xml.transform.stream.StreamSource(xmlFile),
              new javax.xml.transform.stream.StreamResult (
                  new java.io.FileOutputStream("SortedOrders.html")
              )
          );
      } catch (Exception e){}
  }
}
```

The application first creates a factory instance by calling the newInstance static method of the TransformerFactory class. We create transformers from this factory object. A Transformer object is created by calling the newTransformer method of the factory. The newTransfomer method takes one argument of XSLT document type. The XSLT document source can be input as a DOMSource, SAXSource, or StreamSource. In the current example, we use a StreamSource object.

After a Transformer object is created, you can use it to transform any XML document with the transformation instructions (templates) embedded in the Transformer object. We call the transform method of the Transformer object to perform the transformations. The transform method takes two arguments. The first argument is an XML file source to be processed, and the second argument is the target output to which the result is serialized.

The XML source can be specified as any of the three sources specified earlier: `DOMSource`, `SAXSource`, or `StreamSource`. Additionally, it can be specified as an `XSLTCSource` object. The `XSLTCSource` object is created from a JAXP[4] source. In the current example, we use a file stream as a source.

The target object can be specified by using one of the three source types: `DOMSource`, `SAXSource`, or `StreamSource`. In the current situation, we use a `StreamSource` object to specify a physical file source called `SortedOrders.html`. Thus, the program output will create a file with this name and output the target object to this file.

Compiling and Running the Application

Compile the preceding code by using a `javac` compiler:

```
C:\<working folder>\Ch05\src>javac -d . TransformTest.java
```

Run the application by using the following command:

```
C:\<working folder>\Ch05\src>java xslt.TransformTest OrderProcessing.xslt ➥
 CustomerOrders.xml
```

The arguments specify the XSLT file to be used for transformation and the XML source document that is to be transformed. The download site contains the two files ready for your use. The `OrderProcessing.xslt` file is the transformation file, and `CustomerOrders.xml` is the source document to be transformed into an HTML file.

When you run the application, you will find the `SortedOrders.html` file created in your working folder. You can open this file in your browser to examine the processing result. The output is shown in Figure 5-4.

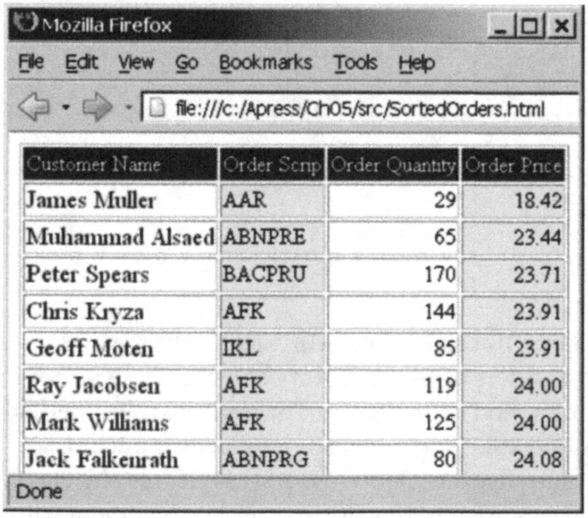
Mozilla Firefox
File Edit View Go Bookmarks Tools Help
file:///c:/Apress/Ch05/src/SortedOrders.html
Customer Name | Order Scrip | Order Quantity | Order Price
James Muller | AAR | 29 | 18.42
Muhammad Alsaed | ABNPRE | 65 | 23.44
Peter Spears | BACPRU | 170 | 23.71
Chris Kryza | AFK | 144 | 23.91
Geoff Moten | IKL | 85 | 23.91
Ray Jacobsen | AFK | 119 | 24.00
Mark Williams | AFK | 125 | 24.00
Jack Falkenrath | ABNPRG | 80 | 24.08
Done

Figure 5-4. *The result of transformation* (`Ch05\src\SortedOrders.html`)

4. Java API for XML Processing—refer to Chapter 2 for details.

Many times, you may want to perform XSL transformation at the server end and present the output as HTML in the user's browser. You will learn how to perform transformations at the server end in the following section.

Server-Side Transformations

To perform transformations on the server, you will need to write server-side code in a language such as Java, which might be embedded in a servlet or a JSP page. For demonstrational purposes, we will create a JSP page for our Sorted Orders example from the previous section.

Performing Transformation in JSP

The program listing for a JSP page that performs XSL transformations is given in Listing 5-5.

Listing 5-5. *Performing XSL Transformations* (Ch05\src\SortedOrders.jsp)

```jsp
<%@ page language="java" contentType="text/html" %>
<%@ page pageEncoding="UTF-8"%>
<%@ page import="javax.xml.transform.*"%>
<%@ page import="javax.xml.transform.stream.*"%>

<html>
  <head>
    <meta http-equiv="Content-Type" content="text/html; charset=UTF-8">
    <title>Customer Orders</title>
  </head>
  <body>

    <h1>Customer Orders</h1>

      <%! String FS = System.getProperty("file.separator"); %>
      <%
      String xmlFile = request.getParameter("XML");
      String xslFile = request.getParameter("XSL");

      // get the real path for xml and xsl files;
      String ctx = getServletContext().getRealPath("") + FS;
      xslFile = ctx + xslFile;
      xmlFile = ctx + xmlFile;

      TransformerFactory tFactory =
        TransformerFactory.newInstance();
      Transformer transformer =
        tFactory.newTransformer(new StreamSource(xslFile));
      transformer.transform(
        new StreamSource(xmlFile), new StreamResult(out));
      %>
  </body>
</html>
```

To begin, you need to import the required class libraries by using the following statements:

```
<%@ page import="javax.xml.transform.*"%>
<%@ page import="javax.xml.transform.stream.*"%>
```

In the HTML body tag, we first obtain the file-separator character:

```
<%! String FS = System.getProperty("file.separator"); %>
```

We use this file separator while constructing the input and XSLT filename path. We read the two input parameters:

```
String xmlFile = request.getParameter("XML");
String xslFile = request.getParameter("XSL");
```

We now obtain the context path and create the paths for the two input files:

```
String ctx = getServletContext().getRealPath("") + FS;
xslFile = ctx + xslFile;
xmlFile = ctx + xmlFile;
```

The rest of the code is the same as the code used in a stand-alone Java application discussed in the earlier section. We first create the TransformerFactory instance, followed by a Transformer instance based on the XSLT file input:

```
TransformerFactory tFactory =
  TransformerFactory.newInstance();
Transformer transformer =
  tFactory.newTransformer(new StreamSource(xslFile));
```

Finally, we perform the transformation by calling the transform method of the Transformer class:

```
transformer.transform(
  new StreamSource(xmlFile), new StreamResult(out));
```

The two parameters to this method specify the input and output source. The output source in our example is the JSP out object. Thus, the output of the transformation is displayed in the browser.

Invoking JSP

To run the preceding JSP, first copy it to the appropriate folder under the webapps\jsp-examples folder of your Tomcat installation. Run JSP by passing the appropriate parameters as shown here:

```
http://localhost:8080/jsp-examples/SortedOrders.jsp?XML=CustomerOrders.xml&➡
XSL=OrderProcessing.xslt
```

Make sure that you replace the context root jsp-examples with the appropriate context root of your installation, if you copy the files into another folder. Also ensure that the CustomerOrders.xml and OrderProcessing.xslt files are copied to the appropriate folder under the webapps\jsp-examples folder of your Tomcat installation.

Program Output

When you open the JSP page in your browser, you will see the output shown in Figure 5-5.

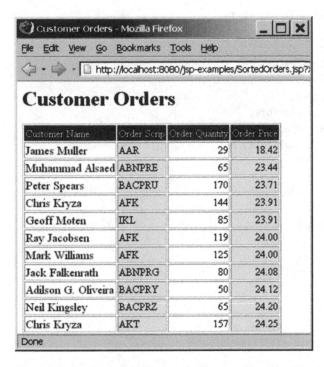

Figure 5-5. *Performing XSL transformation* (Ch05\src\SortedOrders.jsp)

Transforming Selected Contents

So far you have seen the processing and transforming of an entire XML document. Yet sometimes you might want to process only part of the document and transform it to another format. We will use XPath expressions for selecting parts of the input XML document.

Xalan provides the XPathAPI class for this purpose. This class's selectNodeIterator method allows you to specify an XPath expression as input and return a NodeList matching the requested path. Yet all the methods of this class are static and slow. To remedy this inefficiency, the CachedXPathAPI class provides a cached version of this class and is faster than using the static methods of the XPath class.

We will write a console-based Java application to illustrate how to use XPath expressions for processing only parts of an XML input file.

Partially Processing Documents

The source listing for a Java console application that processes and transforms part of a given input XML document is shown in Listing 5-6.

Listing 5-6. *Processing XML Documents Partially* (Ch05\src\PathSelector.java)

```java
package xslt;

import com.sun.org.apache.xpath.internal.XPathAPI;
import java.io.FileInputStream;
import java.io.OutputStreamWriter;
import javax.xml.parsers.DocumentBuilderFactory;
import javax.xml.transform.OutputKeys;
import javax.xml.transform.Transformer;
import javax.xml.transform.TransformerFactory;
import javax.xml.transform.dom.DOMSource;
import javax.xml.transform.stream.StreamResult;
import org.w3c.dom.Document;
import org.w3c.dom.Node;
import org.w3c.dom.traversal.NodeIterator;
import org.xml.sax.InputSource;
import org.apache.xpath.CachedXPathAPI;

public class PathSelector{
  public static void main(String[] args)
  throws Exception {
    String filename = null;
    String xpath = null;
    filename = args[0];
    xpath = args[1];

    // Set up a DOM tree to query.
    InputSource in = new InputSource(new FileInputStream(filename));
    DocumentBuilderFactory dfactory = DocumentBuilderFactory.newInstance();
    dfactory.setNamespaceAware(true);
    Document doc = dfactory.newDocumentBuilder().parse(in);

    // Set up transformer.
    Transformer transformer = TransformerFactory.newInstance().newTransformer();
    transformer.setOutputProperty(OutputKeys.OMIT_XML_DECLARATION, "yes");

    // Use the simple XPath API to select a nodeIterator.
    System.out.println("Querying DOM using "+ xpath);
    CachedXPathAPI path = new CachedXPathAPI();
    NodeIterator nl = path.selectNodeIterator(doc, xpath);

    // Serialize the found nodes to System.out
    System.out.println("<output>");
```

```
Node n;
while ((n = nl.nextNode())!= null)
  transformer.transform(new DOMSource(n),
      new StreamResult (new OutputStreamWriter(System.out)));

System.out.println("</output>");
  }
}
```

The application receives two command-line arguments. The first argument specifies the name of the input file to be processed, and the second argument specifies the XPath expression that is used for selecting a node list in the input document.

We first build a DOM[5] tree from the input file. We create an instance of DocumentBuilderFactory and create a DocumentBuilder by using the factory object. We then call the parse method of DocumentBuilder to parse the input document and build a Document object that gives the DOM representation of the input document.

As in the earlier examples, we create a Transformer object by first creating a TransformerFactory and then calling its newTransformer method. We set a property on the transformer object as follows:

```
transformer.setOutputProperty(OutputKeys.OMIT_XML_DECLARATION, "yes");
```

This instructs the transformer object to omit the XML declaration statement in the output.

Note The Transformer class has several predefined properties that can be set by the user programmatically.

To select the desired nodes based on the input XPath expression, CachedXPathAPI is instantiated:

```
CachedXPathAPI path = new CachedXPathAPI();
```

We now call the selectNodeIterator method on the CachedXPathAPI instance:

```
NodeIterator nl = path.selectNodeIterator(doc, xpath);
```

The selectNodeIterator method takes two arguments. The first argument is of Document type. We input the Document object obtained earlier in this argument. The second argument is the XPath expression that was obtained from the command line. The method creates a node list satisfying the XPath expression and returns an iterator to iterate through the list.

---

5. DOM and its API are covered in Chapter 2.

The program now iterates through the returned list of nodes until a leaf node (null) is reached:

```
Node n;
while ((n = nl.nextNode())!= null)
  transformer.transform(new DOMSource(n), new StreamResult ➡
                        (new OutputStreamWriter(System.out)));
```

In each iteration, a transformation is performed by passing the node object as the first argument to the transform object.

Note The node object is passed by constructing a DOMSource instance representing the node. In earlier examples, we used a stream source as input to the transform method. The other input sources could be any of the following: DOMSource, SAXSource, StreamSource, or XSLTCSource.

The second argument to the transform method specifies the output tree. In this example, we set this to the console output. Thus, as each node is processed, the transformation output is printed on the user console.

The program emits the opening output tag before the transformation begins and emits the closing output tag at the end of transformation.

Compiling and Running the Application

You compile the application by using a javac compiler and run the application by using the following command line:

```
C:\<working folder>\Ch05\src>java xslt.PathSelector CustomerOrders.xml ➡
 /customers/customer[order='AFK']
```

The input document is CustomerOrders.xml, and the XPath expression is /customers/customer[order='AFK']. The XPath expression selects all the customers who have placed an order on AFK stock. When you run the application, the following output will be generated:

```
Querying DOM using /customers/customer[order='AFK']
<output>
<customer>
  <name>Ray Jacobsen</name>
  <order>AFK</order>
  <quantity>119</quantity>
  <price>$24.00</price>
</customer><customer>
  <name>Mark Williams</name>
  <order>AFK</order>
  <quantity>125</quantity>
  <price>$24.00</price>
```

```
</customer><customer>
  <name>Tom Buggy</name>
  <order>AFK</order>
  <quantity>132</quantity>
  <price>$48.21</price>
</customer><customer>
  <name>Chris Kryza</name>
  <order>AFK</order>
  <quantity>138</quantity>
  <price>$259.75</price>
</customer><customer>
  <name>Chris Kryza</name>
  <order>AFK</order>
  <quantity>144</quantity>
  <price>$23.91</price>
</customer><customer>
  <name>Chris Kryza</name>
  <order>AFK</order>
  <quantity>151</quantity>
  <price>$25.51</price>
</customer></output>
```

You can change the XPath expression to select a different set of nodes. For example, you may want to list all the orders for which the quantity is greater than or equal to 170. Use the following command line to list all such orders:

```
C:\<working folder>\Ch05\src>java xslt.PathSelector CustomerOrders.xml ➥
  /customers/customer["quantity>=170"]
```

When you run the application, you will see the following output:

```
Querying DOM using /customers/customer[quantity>=170]
<output>
<customer>
  <name>Martin Dean</name>
  <order>AFE</order>
  <quantity>170</quantity>
  <price>$25.29</price>
</customer><customer>
  <name>Peter Spears</name>
  <order>BACPRU</order>
  <quantity>170</quantity>
  <price>$23.71</price>
</customer></output>
```

To list all the orders placed by the customer called Martin Dean, you use the following command line:

```
C:\<working folder>\Ch05\src>java xslt.PathSelector customer.xml ➥
 /customers/customer["name='Martin Dean'"]
```

To list the fifth order in the orders document, you use the following command line:

```
C:\<working folder>\Ch05\src>java xslt.PathSelector customer.xml ➥
 /customers/customer[5]
```

Likewise, you can input the appropriate XPath expression to select and process the desired portion of the input XML document.

Filters

Just as in Chapter 2's brokerage example, you will encounter situations when a purchase order placed by a customer passes through several approval stages. Each order initially needs an immediate manager's approval, followed by a broker's approval, and finally by the brokerage house's approval before it is placed on the stock exchange. We can run the XML-based orders document through a series of filters, where at each stage the document is examined, modified, and forwarded to the next stage. Xalan provides such filtering capabilities.

Java XSLT-Filtering Application

We will develop a Java application that applies a series of transformations to the orders document as illustrated in Figure 5-6.

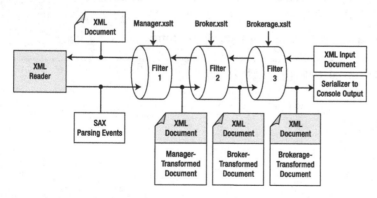

Figure 5-6. *XSLT filtering*

The orders document is our CustomerOrders.xml file that contains the consolidated orders from all the customers. The first transformation that we apply to this document is to provide the manager approval on a selected customer's order. We will add a tag and text to the orders document indicating the manager's approval. The next transformation that we apply will be the broker transformation. The broker receives the transformed document from the manager and appends approval to the document. Finally, the resultant document goes through another transformation at the stock brokerage, which also adds its approval to the document. We will now look at the various transformation files.

Manager XSLT Document

The XSLT document used by the manager is shown in Listing 5-7.

Listing 5-7. Manager.xslt *Document* (Ch05\src\Manager.xslt)

```
<?xml version="1.0"?>
<xsl:stylesheet xmlns:xsl="http://www.w3.org/1999/XSL/Transform" version="1.0">
  <xsl:template match="customers">
    <xsl:apply-templates select ="customer">
      <xsl:sort select="name" order="ascending"/>
    </xsl:apply-templates>
  </xsl:template>
  <xsl:template match="/customers/customer[name='Jim Morey']">
    <Manager>
      <xsl:value-of select="." />
      Manager Approved</Manager>
  </xsl:template>
</xsl:stylesheet>
```

The transformation first creates a template for arranging all the orders in the ascending order of customer names. Then it applies another template for selecting all the orders from the customer called Jim Morey. The template adds the Manager tag and the message Manager Approved to all the orders placed by Jim. The transformed document along with this additional text will now be processed by the broker transformation document.

Broker XSLT Document

The transformation document used at the broker end is shown in Listing 5-8.

Listing 5-8. Broker.xslt *Document* (Ch05\src\Broker.xslt)

```
<?xml version="1.0"?>
<xsl:stylesheet xmlns:xsl="http://www.w3.org/1999/XSL/Transform" version="1.0">
  <xsl:template match="Manager">
    <Broker>
    <xsl:value-of select="."/>
      Broker Approved</Broker>
  </xsl:template>
</xsl:stylesheet>
```

In this transformation, we search for the Manager tag. If one is found, we add the Broker tag to the located nodes and add the message Broker Approved to it. The document will now be further processed by the brokerage.

Brokerage House XSLT Document

The transformation document used by the brokerage is shown in Listing 5-9.

Listing 5-9. Brokerage.xslt *Document* (Ch05\src\Brokerage.xslt)

```
<?xml version="1.0"?>
<xsl:stylesheet xmlns:xsl="http://www.w3.org/1999/XSL/Transform" version="1.0">
  <xsl:template match="Broker">
    <xsl:value-of select="."/>
      Brokerage House Approved
  </xsl:template>
</xsl:stylesheet>
```

The transformation looks for the Broker tag. Remember, this was added to the input document by the broker transformation for all manager-approved orders. The transformation simply appends the text Brokerage House Approved to the selected node.

Let's now look at the application code that implements this filtering.

Filtering Application

The complete source of the filtering application is shown in Listing 5-10.

Listing 5-10. *Chaining Filters—Pull Model* (Ch05\src\PullFilter.java)

```
package xslt;

import org.apache.xml.serializer.Serializer;
import org.apache.xml.serializer.SerializerFactory;
import org.apache.xml.serializer.OutputPropertiesFactory;
import java.io.IOException;
import javax.xml.transform.TransformerConfigurationException;
import javax.xml.transform.TransformerException;
import javax.xml.transform.TransformerFactory;
import javax.xml.transform.sax.SAXResult;
import javax.xml.transform.sax.SAXSource;
import javax.xml.transform.sax.SAXTransformerFactory;
import javax.xml.transform.stream.StreamSource;
import org.xml.sax.InputSource;
import org.xml.sax.SAXException;
import org.xml.sax.XMLFilter;
import org.xml.sax.XMLReader;
import org.xml.sax.helpers.XMLReaderFactory;

public class PullFilter{
  public static void main(String[] args)
  throws TransformerException, TransformerConfigurationException,
         SAXException, IOException {
```

```
    // Instantiate a TransformerFactory.
    SAXTransformerFactory saxTFactory =
            ((SAXTransformerFactory) TransformerFactory.newInstance());

    // Create an XMLFilter for each stylesheet.
    XMLFilter ManagerFilter = saxTFactory.newXMLFilter
            (new StreamSource ("Manager.xslt"));
    XMLFilter BrokerFilter = saxTFactory.newXMLFilter
            (new StreamSource ("Broker.xslt"));
    XMLFilter HouseFilter = saxTFactory.newXMLFilter
            (new StreamSource ("Brokerage.xslt"));

    // Create an XMLReader.
    XMLReader reader = XMLReaderFactory.createXMLReader();

    // ManagerFilter uses the XMLReader as its reader.
    ManagerFilter.setParent(reader);

    // BrokerFilter uses ManagerFilter as its reader.
    BrokerFilter.setParent(ManagerFilter);

    // HouseFilter uses BrokerFilter as its reader.
    HouseFilter.setParent(BrokerFilter);

    // HouseFilter outputs SAX events to the serializer.
    java.util.Properties xmlProps = OutputPropertiesFactory.➡
                                    getDefaultMethodProperties("xml");
    Serializer serializer = SerializerFactory.getSerializer(xmlProps);
    serializer.setOutputStream(System.out);
    HouseFilter.setContentHandler(serializer.asContentHandler());

    HouseFilter.parse(new InputSource("CustomerOrders.xml"));
  }
}
```

As in the earlier cases, the application first creates a factory instance for performing transformations:

```
    SAXTransformerFactory saxTFactory =
            ((SAXTransformerFactory) TransformerFactory.newInstance());
```

We will use the SAX[6] model for parsing during transformations. Thus, we typecast the factory object to the SAXTransformerFactory class.

---

6. SAX is covered in Chapter 2.

Note The `SAXTransformerFactory` class extends the `TransfomerFactory` class to support the SAX model. It provides two types of `ContentHandlers`. One is used for creating `Transformer` objects, and the other is used for creating `Template` objects.

Next, we create filters by calling the `newXMLFilter` method on the factory object:

```
XMLFilter ManagerFilter = saxTFactory.newXMLFilter
        (new StreamSource ("Manager.xslt"));
XMLFilter BrokerFilter = saxTFactory.newXMLFilter
        (new StreamSource ("Broker.xslt"));
XMLFilter HouseFilter = saxTFactory.newXMLFilter
        (new StreamSource ("Brokerage.xslt"));
```

The `newXMLFilter` method receives the appropriate XSLT file input as a stream source. We will pass the input document to the `parse` method of the `HouseFilter`:

```
HouseFilter.parse(new InputSource("CustomerOrders.xml"));
```

We set the parent for the `HouseFilter` to `BrokerFilter` and its parent in turn to `ManagerFilter`:

```
HouseFilter.setParent(BrokerFilter);
BrokerFilter.setParent(ManagerFilter);
```

The parent of `ManagerFilter` is set to an instance of `XMLReader`:

```
XMLReader reader = XMLReaderFactory.createXMLReader();
ManagerFilter.setParent(reader);
```

Thus, the document that is input into the `HouseFilter` will be read by this reader and passed to the `ManagerFilter` first. The `ManagerFilter` applies its transformations and serializes the output to `BrokerFilter`. The `BrokerFilter` applies further transformations as discussed earlier and sends its output to `HouseFilter`. The `HouseFilter`, after performing its own transformations, serializes the output to the system console:

```
Serializer serializer = SerializerFactory.getSerializer(xmlProps);
serializer.setOutputStream(System.out);
```

Thus, after the input document undergoes transformations defined by three filters, the result is printed on the user console.

Running the Application

If you run the preceding application, you will see a sorted list of orders on your system console. If you scroll through the list and locate the orders placed by the customer Jim Morey, you will see the following output:

```
...
Jean Paul Putzys
  ILAPRP
  87
  $31.50

  Jim Morey
  BAXPR
  75
  $25.26

        Manager Approved
        Broker Approved
        Brokerage House Approved

  Jim Morey
  BSCPRX
  75
  $24.26

        Manager Approved
        Broker Approved
        Brokerage House Approved

  Jody Hornor
  ABNPRF
  87
  $24.83
...
```

Note that only the orders placed by Jim have been marked as approved, while on other orders no such annotation is added.

The filtering technique discussed here is based on the *pull model*. Using this model, each filter pulls the contents from the previous filter. However, there is another filtering technique based on what is termed the *push model*. This model is discussed next.

The Push Filtering Model

In the *push model*, every filter pushes its output to the next filter. The first filter reads the contents from an input source document and therefore becomes the content handler for that document. The second filter becomes the content handler for the output of the first filter. The third filter becomes the content handler for the output of the second filter, and so on. We will illustrate this technique by writing a Java console application that processes our CustomerOrders.xml file by using the three filters discussed in the previous section.

Filtering Application

The complete listing of a Java application (PushFilter.java) for filtering that is based on the push model is shown in Listing 5-11.

Listing 5-11. *Chaining Filters—Push Model* (Ch05\src\PushFilter.java)

```java
package xslt;

import java.io.IOException;

import javax.xml.transform.TransformerConfigurationException;
import javax.xml.transform.TransformerException;
import javax.xml.transform.TransformerFactory;
import javax.xml.transform.sax.SAXResult;
import javax.xml.transform.sax.SAXSource;
import javax.xml.transform.sax.SAXTransformerFactory;
import javax.xml.transform.sax.TransformerHandler;
import javax.xml.transform.stream.StreamSource;

import org.apache.xml.serializer.Serializer;
import org.apache.xml.serializer.SerializerFactory;
import org.apache.xml.serializer.OutputPropertiesFactory;
import org.xml.sax.SAXException;
import org.xml.sax.XMLReader;
import org.xml.sax.helpers.XMLReaderFactory;

public class PushFilter{
  public static void main(String[] args)
  throws TransformerException, TransformerConfigurationException,
           SAXException, IOException {
    // Instantiate a TransformerFactory.
    SAXTransformerFactory saxTFactory = ((SAXTransformerFactory)
           TransformerFactory.newInstance());

    // Create a TransformerHandler for each stylesheet.
    TransformerHandler tHandler1 = saxTFactory.newTransformerHandler
           (new StreamSource("Manager.xslt"));
    TransformerHandler tHandler2 = saxTFactory.newTransformerHandler
           (new StreamSource("Broker.xslt"));
    TransformerHandler tHandler3 = saxTFactory.newTransformerHandler
           (new StreamSource("Brokerage.xslt"));

    // Create an XMLReader.
    XMLReader reader = XMLReaderFactory.createXMLReader();
    reader.setContentHandler(tHandler1);
    reader.setProperty
            ("http://xml.org/sax/properties/lexical-handler", tHandler1);
```

```
tHandler1.setResult(new SAXResult(tHandler2));
tHandler2.setResult(new SAXResult(tHandler3));

// transformer3 outputs SAX events to the serializer.
java.util.Properties xmlProps = OutputPropertiesFactory.
        getDefaultMethodProperties("xml");
Serializer serializer = SerializerFactory.getSerializer(xmlProps);
serializer.setOutputStream(System.out);
tHandler3.setResult(new SAXResult(serializer.asContentHandler()));

// Parse the XML input document.
reader.parse("CustomerOrders.xml");
    }
}
```

As in the earlier example, we first create a SAXTransformerFactory instance. We then create a TransformerHandler for each stylesheet:

```
TransformerHandler tHandler1 = saxTFactory.newTransformerHandler
        (new StreamSource("Manager.xslt"));
TransformerHandler tHandler2 = saxTFactory.newTransformerHandler
        (new StreamSource("Broker.xslt"));
TransformerHandler tHandler3 = saxTFactory.newTransformerHandler
        (new StreamSource("Brokerage.xslt"));
```

Next, we create an XMLReader for reading our input document and set its content handler to the first handler we created:

```
XMLReader reader = XMLReaderFactory.createXMLReader();
reader.setContentHandler(tHandler1);
```

Thus, the input document that is read by XMLReader will be handled by a content handler based on the Manager.xslt transformation file.

We now set the content handler for the output of the first content handler:

```
tHandler1.setResult(new SAXResult(tHandler2));
```

The output of the first content handler is handled by tHandler2, which is based on the Broker.xslt transformation file.

The output of the second content handler is handled by tHandler3, which is based on the Brokerage.xslt transformation file.

```
tHandler2.setResult(new SAXResult(tHandler3));
```

The output of the third content handler will be dumped to the user console. This is done by creating a Serializer for the console output and setting it as the content handler for tHandler3:

```
Serializer serializer = SerializerFactory.getSerializer(xmlProps);
serializer.setOutputStream(System.out);
tHandler3.setResult(new SAXResult(serializer.asContentHandler()));
```

After the filter chain is created, you need to simply read the input file by using the first `XMLReader`:

```
reader.parse("CustomerOrders.xml");
```

The file is now transformed by using transformation filters defined in the chain, and the output tree is produced.

Running the Application

When you run this application, you will get an output exactly identical to the program output of the previous section.

The only difference between the two applications is the processing model that is employed for filtering.

Translets

Xalan-Java provides an XSLT compiler and a runtime processor collectively called *XSLTC*. This can be used for compiling a stylesheet into a set of classes, known as the *translet*. This translet can later be applied to an XML document to perform transformations. In this section, you will learn how to create translets and use them to transform XML documents. A command-line tool is provided for creating translets and using them to transform documents. You can also do the same through a programmatic interface. You will learn both techniques here.

Command-Line Tool

To create a translet at the command prompt, the Xalan implementation provides a Java application called `org.apache.xalan.xsltc.cmdline.Compile`. To perform the transformation, it provides another application called `org.apache.xalan.xsltc.cmdline.Transform`. We will use these applications to compile our `OrderProcessing.xslt` file that we have used in our earlier examples. We will then apply the created translet to the `CustomerOrders.xml` file.

Creating a Translet

To create a translet, use the following command line:

```
C:\<working folder>\Ch05\src>java org.apache.xalan.xsltc.cmdline.Compile ➥
OrderProcessing.xslt
```

This compiles the specified XSLT file and creates a set of Java classes, namely `OrderProcessing.class` and `OrderProcessing$0.class` in your working folder. Alternatively, you can request that the tool emit a JAR file containing all these created classes by using the `-j` switch on the command line as follows:

```
C:\<working folder>\Ch05\src>java org.apache.xalan.xsltc.cmdline.Compile ➥
-j Orders.jar OrderProcessing.xslt
```

This creates an `Orders.jar` file in your working folder containing all the created classes.

Performing Transformation by Using a Translet

You can use the translet created in the previous step to perform transformations on any number of XML documents. To transform the CustomerOrders.xml file from our earlier examples, use the following command line:

```
C:\<working folder>\Ch05\src>java org.apache.xalan.xsltc.cmdline.Transform ➡
CustomerOrders.xml OrderProcessing
```

This outputs the transformed document to the console.

If you have archived the classes into a JAR file called Orders.jar, use the following command line to perform the transformation:

```
C:\<working folder>\Ch05\src>java org.apache.xalan.xsltc.cmdline.Transform ➡
 -j Orders.jar CustomerOrders.xml OrderProcessing
```

Before running this command, make sure that the Orders.jar file is placed in your system classpath.

Programming Interface for Translets

Translets can be created through your program code at runtime. You can use such translets to transform your documents through your application program. A console-based Java application that creates and uses translets to transform documents is shown in Listing 5-12.

Listing 5-12. *Console Application Illustrating Use of Translets* (Ch05\src\Translets.java)

```java
package xslt;

import java.io.FileNotFoundException;
import java.io.FileOutputStream;
import java.util.Properties;
import javax.xml.transform.Transformer;
import javax.xml.transform.TransformerException;
import javax.xml.transform.TransformerFactory;
import javax.xml.transform.stream.StreamResult;
import javax.xml.transform.stream.StreamSource;
import javax.xml.transform.Templates;

public class Translets{
  public static void main(String argv[]) {
    // Set the TransformerFactory system property to generate and use translets.
    Properties props = System.getProperties();
    props.put("javax.xml.transform.TransformerFactory",
            "org.apache.xalan.xsltc.trax.TransformerFactoryImpl");
    System.setProperties(props);
```

```
        try {
          // Instantiate the TransformerFactory
          TransformerFactory tFactory = TransformerFactory.newInstance();
          // Create a translet based on the specified XSLT file
          Templates translet = tFactory.newTemplates(new StreamSource
                    ("OrderProcessing.xslt"));

          // Perform transformations
          Transformer transformer = translet.newTransformer();
          transformer.transform( new StreamSource("CustomerOrders.xml"),
            new StreamResult(new FileOutputStream("SortedOrders.html")));
          System.out.println("Produced SortedOrders.html");

          transformer.transform( new StreamSource("CustomerOrders1.xml"),
            new StreamResult(new FileOutputStream("SortedOrders1.html")));
          System.out.println("Produced SortedOrders1.html");
        } catch (Exception e) {
          e.printStackTrace();
        }
    }
}
```

As in the earlier cases, we will instantiate a transformer factory and a transformer.
For a transformer factory, Xalan provides an implementation in the class called
TransformerFactoryImpl. To instantiate this class, we set a system property called
TransformerFactory. The newInstance method of the TransformerFactory class uses this
property to instantiate the factory class.

We set the required system property by using the following code snippet:

```
Properties props = System.getProperties();
props.put("javax.xml.transform.TransformerFactory",
          "org.apache.xalan.xsltc.trax.TransformerFactoryImpl");
System.setProperties(props);
```

Next, we instantiate the transformer factory:

```
TransformerFactory tFactory = TransformerFactory.newInstance();
```

To create a translet based on a certain XSLT file, we call the newTemplates factory method:

```
Templates translet = tFactory.newTemplates(new StreamSource
            ("OrderProcessing.xslt"));
```

The method receives the XSLT file as a stream source and returns an object of type
Templates.

We create a transformer based on this Templates object by calling its newTransformer
method:

```
Transformer transformer = translet.newTransformer();
```

After a transformer is created, it can be applied to an XML document to transform it to another form by using the templates defined in the `Templates` object:

```
transformer.transform(new StreamSource("CustomerOrders.xml"),
    new StreamResult(new FileOutputStream("SortedOrders.html")));
```

The `transform` method, as seen in the earlier examples, receives the source tree as the first argument and a reference to the output tree as the second argument. When the method completes, it will create an output tree. In our example, a file called `SortedOrders.html` would be created in the working folder.

The created translet can now be applied to another XML document:

```
transformer.transform( new StreamSource("CustomerOrders1.xml"),
    new StreamResult(new FileOutputStream("SortedOrders1.html")));
```

The output will be a `SortedOrders1.html` file, the same as the one shown earlier.

Summary

In this chapter, you studied one of the important features in XML processing: transforming XML documents. XML documents are ideally suited for data transport. Though they are easily read by humans, they cannot be easily interpreted by other software applications. Thus, the XML documents need to be converted into a format that is understandable to other applications. The Extensible Stylesheet Language (XSL) is used for defining such transformations.

When a document is transformed, it can be transformed fully or partially. To transform a document partially, you need a way to identify and locate the parts of the document. The XPath specification allows you to locate a desired part of the document and returns you a node list containing the located part. The desired part itself is specified as an XPath expression. In this chapter, you studied XPath syntax and its application in locating the parts of the XML document.

The original XSL specifications have been split into two parts: XSLT and XSL-FO. The XSLT specification (now simply known as XSL) defines how transformations are performed on a given XML document, and XSL-FO defines how a transformed document is formatted. In this chapter, you studied XSLT. The transformation commands are written in an XSLT file. The XML document can specify the desired transformation file in its definition immediately following the XML declaration. The browsers enabled for XSLT interpret the commands in the specified transformation file and transform the document contents before presenting those in the output window.

The transformations can also be performed by using the API provided in the Xalan implementation. In this chapter, you learned how to use this API to perform your transformations through application code. First, we wrote a stand-alone console application to perform transformations. Next, we wrote transformation code in a JSP so as to perform the transformations on the server side.

You also learned the techniques of chaining multiple transformations. Both push and pull models for chaining and filtering were discussed.

Finally, we covered the concept of translets, through which any desired XSLT file is converted into a set of Java classes. The created translet can then be applied to multiple XML documents for transformations. Both command-line interfaces and programmatic interfaces of translets were covered.

In the next chapter, you will learn how to format the transformed document by using XSL-FO specifications.

CHAPTER 6

■ ■ ■

XSL-FO

In the preceding chapter, you learned how to transform XML by using XSLT. Often these transformations convert an XML document into another XML variant; however, it's also possible to convert these documents into other formats such as HTML and plain text. If you want to render a document for use within a format-specific device, you need to transform it into the format required by that device. If the desired output device is a printer, the difficulties can quickly compound because hundreds of printer models are available. Thus, to print the document to any user-specific printer, you would have to provide transformation instructions for each of these printer-specific document formats. Obviously, this task would be not only impractical, but likely impossible. An ideal alternative solution is available.

XSL-Formatting Objects (XSL-FO) provides for the formatting of objects intended for display on multiple media outlets. Thus, it promotes a "write once, display anywhere" philosophy. Fortunately, the Portable Document Format (PDF) supports several output devices. If you transform your document into PDF, it can be printed on any printer in the world for which you have a printer driver available.

The Apache *Formatting Objects Processor (FOP)* project offers a Java implementation for print formatting based on XSL-FO specifications.[1] The implementation provides both a command-line tool and the program libraries for use in your applications. It reads a formatting object (FO) tree and renders the result to various output formats. The default output target is PDF. However, the FOP also supports a variety of other output formats, including AWT, MIF, PCL, Print, PS, SVG, TXT, and XML.

In this chapter, you will learn to use both the FOP's command-line utility and a programmatic interface for creating PDF files from an XML document. To convert a given input XML document, you will need to create an XSL-FO document that contains the formatting commands written in XSL-FO. You will learn XSL-FO syntax and its use for creating PDF documents that can contain not only plain text, but also graphics, tables, multicolumnar reports, and more.

Installing FOP

Before we proceed with XSL-FO specifications, you need to download and install the software on your machine so that you can try out the various examples illustrated in this chapter.

---

1. http://www.w3.org/TR/xsl/slice6.html#fo-section

Downloading and Installing FOP

You need to download FOP from the Apache website. You can download the binaries from the following URL:

```
http://xmlgraphics.apache.org/fop/download.html
```

You may download the source if you wish to build the binaries locally or to study its implementation.

Like all other earlier Apache software that you have seen in this book, the installation of FOP is easy. You need to unzip the downloaded archive to a desired folder. After installing the software, make sure that you add the installation folder to your environment PATH and the several library JAR files to your classpath environment variable.

Note In addition to the JAR files in the `<installation folder>\lib` folder, you also need to add the `fop.jar` file from `<installation folder>\build` folder to your classpath.

Note For those of you installing on Linux, Appendix A gives detailed installation instructions for all the chapters in this book.

Testing the Installation

You can test the installation by running the FOP command-line utility. The installation provides several examples. Open a command prompt and change the directory to `<installation folder>\ examples\fo\basic`. Here you will find several FO files (which have the `.fo` extension). Run the `fop` command on any of the FO files. The sample command line is as follows:

```
C:\fop-0.20.5\examples\fo\basic>fop simple.fo simple.pdf
```

The formatting processor takes the input from the specified FO file and creates a PDF file with the specified name. You will see the following output on the screen:

```
C:\fop-0.20.5\examples\fo\basic>fop simple.fo simple.pdf
 [INFO] Using org.apache.xerces.parsers.SAXParser as SAX2 Parser
[INFO] FOP 0.20.5
[INFO] Using org.apache.xerces.parsers.SAXParser as SAX2 Parser
[INFO] building formatting object tree
[INFO] setting up fonts
[INFO] [1]
[INFO] Parsing of document complete, stopping renderer
```

Check for the presence of the `simple.pdf` file in your working directory. You can open this in Adobe Reader to see its contents.

First FO Example

Now that you have installed the software, you are ready to learn the XSL-FO syntax. We will continue our case study from Chapter 2 and design a few PDF reports required by our stock brokerage. Imagine that the stock brokerage needs to send some confidential reports to its customers periodically. Every report begins with a cover page. We will write an FO document to create this cover page, which we will call Cover.fo. The complete listing of Cover.fo is shown in Listing 6-1.

Listing 6-1. *Formatting Document for Cover Page* (Ch06\src\Cover.fo)

```xml
<?xml version="1.0" encoding="utf-8" ?>

<fo:root xmlns:fo="http://www.w3.org/1999/XSL/Format">

  <fo:layout-master-set>
    <fo:simple-page-master master-name="Cover Page">
      <fo:region-body/>
    </fo:simple-page-master>
  </fo:layout-master-set>

  <fo:page-sequence master-reference="Cover Page">
    <fo:flow flow-name="xsl-region-body">
      <fo:block
        font-family="Helvetica"
        font-size="36pt"
        font-weight="bold"
        space-before ="360pt"
        text-align="center"
        >
        Stock Brokerage
      </fo:block>
      <fo:block
        font-family="Times Roman"
        font-size="24pt"
        font-style="italic"
        space-before ="12pt"
        text-align="center"
        >
        Confidential Report
      </fo:block>
    </fo:flow>
  </fo:page-sequence>
</fo:root>
```

We will now analyze the Cover.fo document so you will understand how the document formatting is achieved.

Note If you are curious to see the output produced after processing the Cover.fo document in Listing 6-1, refer to Figure 6-1.

The first line is an XML declaration indicating that this is an XML document. The second line declares the required namespaces:

```
<fo:root xmlns:fo="http://www.w3.org/1999/XSL/Format">
```

The fo:root element forms the root of the XSL-FO document. The various FO elements are defined in the fo namespace specified by the URI http://www.w3.org/1999/XSL/Format.

Within the root element we define the page layout templates:

```
<fo:layout-master-set>
  <fo:simple-page-master master-name="Cover Page">
    <fo:region-body/>
  </fo:simple-page-master>
</fo:layout-master-set>
```

The layout-master-set element defines the layouts for the various pages in the document. We are creating only one layout that is used by our cover page. Later, we will create more layouts for documents requiring multiple output templates.

Page masters are created by adding subelements to the layout-master-set element. As its name suggests, the simple-page-master element is used for creating simple page layouts. The master-name attribute of this element specifies the name of our template. We name this master Cover Page. We will refer to this master name later while defining pages in the document.

Each master defines the geometry of a page. A page is divided into several areas, or regions. The region-body subelement defines the body of the output page. This body is similar to an HTML body element in which you write your content. In addition to the body region, the master defines regions such as those before and after the body. We will look at these areas and other areas on a page later in this chapter.

After defining the master page layouts, we start creating pages. This is done with the help of a page-sequence element:

```
<fo:page-sequence master-reference="Cover Page">
```

The page-sequence element specifies how to create a sequence of pages within a document. We specify the master page layout to be used while creating pages by specifying the value for the master-reference attribute. Note that the value for this attribute is defined in the layout master set created earlier.

Within a page we define the content flow by using the flow element:

```
<fo:flow flow-name="xsl-region-body">
```

The flow element is a container for the flow objects. A flow object may be text or an image. The flow-name attribute defines the region for the flow. This should map to the predefined names. In this case, we will flow our content in the body area of the document. Other areas, as said before, could be regions before and after.

Within the flow, we now define one or more `flow` objects. A `flow` object is defined by using a `block` subelement:

```
<fo:block
   font-family="Helvetica"
   font-size="36pt"
   font-weight="bold"
   space-before ="360pt"
   text-align="center"
   >
   Stock Brokerage
</fo:block>
```

We write the desired content within the opening and closing `block` tag. In the preceding example, we use the text `Stock Brokerage` as our content. This text will be rendered on the output page.

We define the text formatting with the help of various attributes of the `block` element. For example, the `font-family` attribute defines the font to be used. The `font-size` and `font-weight` define the font size and weight, respectively. The `space-before` attribute defines the leading space before the content. In the current example, this is set to `360pt`. Thus, the space before the text content with respect to the previous block will be 360 points. Note that publishers use points as units for page measurement; however, these dimensions can also be specified in inches and centimeters.

The `text-align` attribute defines the alignment for the block content. The alignment can be left, center, right, or other predefined values in the schema.

After the heading block, another block is defined as follows:

```
<fo:block
   font-family="Times Roman"
   font-size="24pt"
   font-style="italic"
   space-before ="12pt"
   text-align="center"
   >
   Confidential Report
</fo:block>
```

Here, we use the text `Confidential Report` as the block content. We use a different font, font size, and style than the previous block. The space before the content now equals 12 points.

Performing Transformation

Your next task is to use the FOP engine to create a PDF document based on the layout specified in Listing 6-1. The screen output when you run `fop` is shown here:

```
Ch06\src>fop Cover.fo Cover.pdf
[INFO] Using org.apache.xerces.parsers.SAXParser as SAX2 Parser
[INFO] FOP 0.20.5
[INFO] Using org.apache.xerces.parsers.SAXParser as SAX2 Parser
[INFO] building formatting object tree
[INFO] setting up fonts
[INFO] [1]
[INFO] Parsing of document complete, stopping renderer
```

Viewing Output

After a successful run, the FOP utility creates a Cover.pdf file in the working folder. You can use Adobe Reader to open this file. The screen output is shown in Figure 6-1.

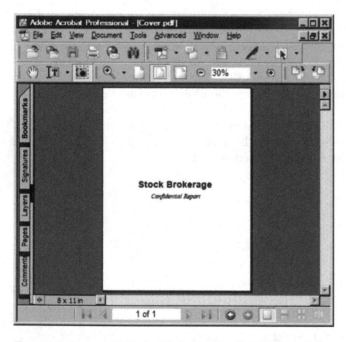

Figure 6-1. Cover.pdf *file in Adobe Reader* (Ch06\PDFDocs\Cover.pdf)

From this you can gauge how easy it is to create a nicely formatted document by using XSL-FO and the provided print formatter.

The XSL-FO Document Structure

The XSL-FO document is a well-formed XML document that should conform to the schema definition provided by the W3C. In this section, you will look at the various elements of this schema and how the entire document is structured.

The Top-Level Document Structure

An XSL-FO document is ultimately an XML document and thus always begins with an XML declaration. Listing 6-2 shows the top-level structure of an XSL-FO document.

Listing 6-2. *Top-Level Structure of XSL-FO Document*

```
<?xml version="1.0" encoding="ISO-8859-1"?>
<fo:root xmlns:fo="http://www.w3.org/1999/XSL/Format">

<fo:layout-master-set>
  <fo:simple-page-master master-name="A4">
    <!-- Page template goes here -->
  </fo:simple-page-master>
</fo:layout-master-set>

<fo:page-sequence master-reference="A4">
  <!-- Page content goes here -->
</fo:page-sequence>
</fo:root>
```

The root element of the document is called root. This is declared in the namespace http://www.w3.org/1999/XSL/Format. After the root element, we declare the set of layout master pages with the help of the layout-master-set element. Each master page is given a unique name in the current context. As seen earlier, while ordering the content, we use this page name. You can define multiple master templates here. You will look at how to define the template shortly.

After the page master templates are declared, we declare a sequence of pages for defining our page content. Before we discuss how to add the page content, let's examine the various regions of the page where such page content can be placed.

XSL-FO Areas

To organize the content on a page, the entire page is divided into several rectangular areas. XSL-FO defines several such rectangular areas, or boxes:

- *Page*: Each page consists of several regions.

- *Region*: Each region contains several blocks.

- *Block*: Each block contains several lines.

- *Line*: A line contains the matter to be rendered.

- *Inline*: Certain characters in a line, such as bullets or the first character of a paragraph, may be formatted differently by using the inline subelement within a line element.

The output of XSL-FO goes into pages. The output may go into a single page or multiple pages depending on the amount of content and the type of output device. If you are outputting to a printer, multiple pages may be output, whereas if you are outputting to a browser, you may get a single long page.

I will now describe each of these areas in additional detail.

Pages

The output of an XSL-FO document runs into one or more pages. Each page can contain static information such as a header or footer. A page can display a page number. The formatting engine tracks the page numbers as the contents are laid out in multiple pages. A page can be odd- or even-numbered. An odd-numbered page may use a different formatting style than an even-numbered page.

Each page is divided into regions as shown in Figure 6-2.

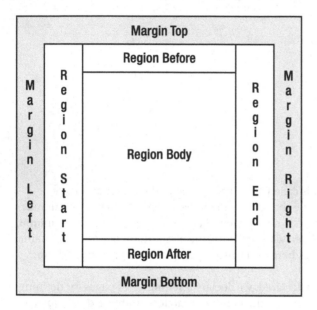

Figure 6-2. *Page structure*

Regions

A page consists of five distinct regions:

- region-body: This refers to the body of the page. This is where your document content will flow across multiple pages.

- region-before: This refers to the page header. This generally contains the static content that will be displayed on every page.

- region-after: This refers to the page footer. This again contains static content (such as page numbers) that will be displayed on every page.

- region-start: This refers to the left sidebar of the page. Typically, this may not be very useful. If you place any content in this region, it will appear on all subsequent pages, just like the header and the footer.

- region-end: This refers to the right sidebar of the page. This has a similar purpose to region-start, except that the static content will be placed on the right side of the region body and will be repeated on each page.

Blocks

Each region on a page consists of blocks. A block generally consists of paragraphs, tables, lists, images, and so on. Remember, in Listing 6-1 we used blocks to define the text on our cover page document. Several attributes of the block element allow you to define the formatting for its content. For example, you can specify the font to be used, its size, style, and more. You can also specify the content alignment such as left, center, right, and other items. For each block, you can also specify the white space around the content by using margins and various space attributes.

A block can contain line areas.

Lines

The line area defines the formatting for its line content. As with a block, for each line you can specify a different formatting style. You can put inline areas inside the line.

Inlines

The inline areas define the formatting of the text inside lines. Typically, this is used for defining line bullets, graphics, and other items. For example, you might want to place a graphic in front of the current line or you might simply decide to make the first character of the line bigger than the rest of the text. In such cases, you would use the inline tag to specify formatting different from the formatting used by the rest of the content.

XSL-FO Page Templates

Now that you have seen the various areas in which the page content will flow, you are ready to look at how to define a page template that uses these various areas. A *page template* defines the layout of a page. As seen earlier, you can define multiple templates, each with a unique name within the layout master set. For example, you can define a template for the cover page, left page, right page, index page, and so on. Additionally, we use the simple-page-master element to define the template page. This element has attributes that define the page height, width, orientation, and other items. The following example illustrates how to format a page with a specified height, width, and margins:

```
<fo:simple-page-master master-name="left"
   page-height="297mm"
   page-width="210mm"
   margin-top="1cm"
   margin-bottom="2cm"
   margin-left="2.5cm"
   margin-right="2.5cm"
>
<!-- The various regions are defined here -->
</fo:simple-page-master>
```

Here we have defined a page master called left with a height equal to 297 millimeters (mm) and a width equal to 210 mm. We have also defined the various sizes for the page margins.

Within this page, we will now define regions as follows:

```
<fo:region-body   margin="3cm"/>
<fo:region-before extent="2cm"/>
<fo:region-after  extent="2cm"/>
<fo:region-start  extent="2cm"/>
<fo:region-end    extent="2cm"/>
```

As mentioned earlier (and shown in Figure 6-2), the page has five regions. The purpose of each region was specified earlier.

For each region, several attributes are defined that determine the content alignment, orientation, background, padding, and more. Additionally, the region-body element has a column-count attribute that determines the number of columns in the document. Thus, you can flow the content in multiple columns easily by setting the attribute value for this element.

After you define the various page masters, you are ready to set the content on the page.

Organizing Content

You start laying out the page and putting content on it by using the page-sequence element. You declare the page-sequence element as follows:

```
<fo:page-sequence master-reference="first">
```

The master-reference attribute specifies the master page to be used. The master pages were defined earlier in the page templates.

Within the page-sequence element, you use the flow element that defines the various blocks:

```
<fo:flow flow-name="xsl-region-body">
```

The flow element has only one attribute, called flow-name. We set this to xsl-region-body, indicating that we want to flow the content in the region body. You can specify other regions if you want to organize the contents into those regions. The various regions were discussed earlier, and the allowed values for flow-name are as follows:

- xsl-region-body: Content is placed in the page body.

- xsl-region-before: Content is placed in the region-before area depicted in Figure 6-2. This is the header area of the page.

- xsl-region-after: Content is placed in the region-after area depicted in Figure 6-2. This is the footer area of the page.

- xsl-region-start: Content is placed in the region-start area depicted in Figure 6-2.

- xsl-region-end: Content is placed in the region-end area depicted in Figure 6-2.

A flow consists of block elements.

Blocks

A typical block element is shown here:

```
<fo:block font-family="Helvetica" font-size="14pt">
  This text is displayed in Helvetica font.
</fo:block>
```

A block contains the text or image to be rendered in the output. In the current example, the following text will be rendered in the output: "This text is displayed in Helvetica font." This will be displayed by using 14-point Helvetica font. The block has various attributes that define the fonts, margins, alignment, borders, background, and other items.

The block contains various areas as shown in Figure 6-3.

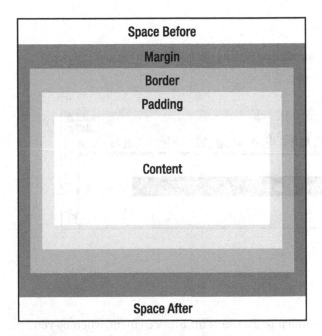

Figure 6-3. *Various areas in a block*

The content area contains the actual content, such as the text, image, and so on. On four sides of the content, we define the padding. Outside the padding, the border is defined. Surrounding the border, we have margins. Outside the margins, we define the space-before and space-after areas. Values for each of these areas can be specified with their respective attributes.

The various attributes together define the block decoration and the format of its content. The FOP schema defines several common properties that are then applied to various elements. The margin properties, for example, are applied to a block to define the top, bottom, left, and right margins. The border properties are used for defining the border styles. The border style can be independently set for top, bottom, left, and right borders. Similarly, the border color can be independently set for the four areas. Likewise, you can set the individual width and the padding for each border area. The background-color attribute sets the background color, and the background-image attribute sets the background image for the block.

For the content within the block, the various attributes are provided to define the font style, size, text alignment, and so on.

A typical block with the various properties set is shown here:

```
<fo:block font-size="18pt"
  font-family="sans-serif"
  line-height="24pt"
  background-color="rgb(0,0,255)"
  color="rgb(255,255,255)"
  text-align="center"
  padding-top="3pt">
  Cover Page
</fo:block>
```

When you render this block to an output device, you will see the output as shown in Figure 6-4.

Figure 6-4. *A typical formatted output*

Lines and Inlines

The use of line and inline elements is similar to the use of the block element, whereby you can set the formatting style of the line contents. The inline element, as stated earlier, allows you to control the appearance of part of the line contents. The use of these elements will be discussed through the code examples later in the chapter.

Incorporating Graphics

Now that you've learned the page template structure and how to write an XSL-FO document for creating a simple page, you're ready to look at how to enhance the formatted document. In this section, you'll learn how to incorporate graphics images. First you'll learn how to add any type of image, such as a GIF or JPG image. Then you'll focus on two techniques for including SVG images.

Adding Images

Adding an image to a page is a simple matter. You need to add a block that specifies the image file as its contents. We will add an image of the company logo for our stock brokerage cover page. We add the image by including the following block in the content flow:

```
<fo:block text-align="center">
  <fo:external-graphic src="url(../Ch06/src/ais.JPG)"/>
</fo:block>
```

The image file is specified by using the external-graphic element. The src attribute specifies the path where this file is located. In our example, the path is specified as a relative URL with respect to the current folder. The image file is a JPG file. When you render this block along with the other two text blocks containing the text, the output looks like Figure 6-5.

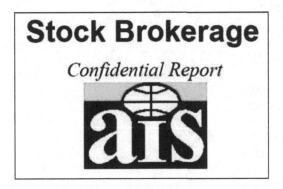

Figure 6-5. *Incorporating an image* (Ch06\PDFDocs\CoverImage.pdf)

The images that can be rendered like this can be any of the several formats, with extensions such as .gif, .jpg, .bmp, or .tif.

Including SVG Images

Scalable Vector Graphics (SVG)[2] is an XML-based language for describing two-dimensional graphics. Just as we have incorporated a graphics image in other formats in an XSL-FO document, we can also incorporate an SVG image that is stored in an external file. Because SVG is written in XML, we can embed the graphics definition directly in an XSL-FO document. You will learn both techniques of incorporating SVG images next.

Using an External Definition

An SVG image can be defined in an external file and included as a reference URL by using the external-graphic element as in the earlier examples. Listing 6-3 provides the definition of an

---

2. The SVG specifications can be downloaded from http://xml.apache.org/batik or http://www.w3.org/TR/SVG11/

SVG image that consists of a series of embedded rectangles, where the color values increment from red to black as you move to the inner rectangle.

Listing 6-3. *SVG Definition* (Ch06\src\boxes.svg)

```
<?xml version="1.0" standalone="no"?>
<!DOCTYPE svg PUBLIC "-//W3C//DTD SVG 20000802//EN"
          "http://www.w3.org/TR/2000/CR-SVG-20000802/DTD/svg-20000802.dtd">

<svg width="100" height="100" xml:space="preserve">
  <g style="fill:red; stroke:#000000">
    <rect x="0" y="0" width="100" height="100"/>
  </g>
  <g style="fill:rgb(200,0,0); stroke:#000000">
    <rect x="5" y="5" width="90" height="90"/>
  </g>
  <g style="fill:rgb(150,0,0); stroke:#000000">
    <rect x="10" y="10" width="80" height="80"/>
  </g>
  <g style="fill:rgb(100,0,0); stroke:#000000">
    <rect x="15" y="15" width="70" height="70"/>
  </g>
  <g style="fill:rgb(50,0,0); stroke:#000000">
    <rect x="20" y="20" width="60" height="60"/>
  </g>
  <g style="fill:rgb(0,0,0); stroke:#000000">
    <rect x="25" y="25" width="50" height="50"/>
  </g>
</svg>
```

To render this image to your output document, you would need to include following blocks in your document flow:

```
<fo:block
  space-before ="12pt"
  text-align="center">
    Including SVG image
</fo:block>
<fo:block
  space-before ="12pt"
  text-align="center">
    <fo:external-graphic src="url(../Ch06/src/boxes.svg)"/>
</fo:block>
```

The first block displays a text message, while the second block includes the SVG image from the external file boxes.svg. When you render this to the output device, you will see output similar to Figure 6-6.

Including SVG image

Figure 6-6. *Output from incorporating SVG image from an external source file*
(Ch06\PDFDocs\FileSVG.fo)

Embedding SVG

In the previous example, we used the SVG definition stored in an external file. Because SVG is
an XML document, we can embed the SVG code directly into the XSL-FO document. The block
shown in Listing 6-4 does this.

Listing 6-4. *Embedding SVG in a Block*

```
<fo:block xmlns:svg="http://www.w3.org/2000/svg"
  text-align="center"
  space-before="15pt">

    <fo:instream-foreign-object
      content-width="6cm"
      content-height="6cm">

        <svg:svg width="6cm" height="6cm" xml:space="preserve">
          <svg:g style="fill:rgb(211,211,211);">
            <svg:circle cx="100" cy="100" r="50"/>
          </svg:g>
          <svg:g style="fill:rgb(175,175,175);">
            <svg:circle cx="100" cy="100" r="40"/>
          </svg:g>
          <svg:g style="fill:rgb(150,150,150);">
            <svg:circle cx="100" cy="100" r="30"/>
          </svg:g>
          <svg:g style="fill:rgb(100,100,100);">
            <svg:circle cx="100" cy="100" r="20"/>
          </svg:g>
          <svg:g style="fill:rgb(75,75,75);">
            <svg:circle cx="100" cy="100" r="10"/>
          </svg:g>

        </svg:svg>
      </fo:instream-foreign-object>

  </fo:block>
```

The program first declares the SVG namespace in the `block` element. The use of the `instream-foreign-object` element allows you to enter the SVG definition in the block. The `instream-foreign-object` element takes `content-width` and `content-height` as attributes that determine the overall size of the image. This is followed by the SVG code that draws concentric circles of different shades of grey. The program output is shown in Figure 6-7.

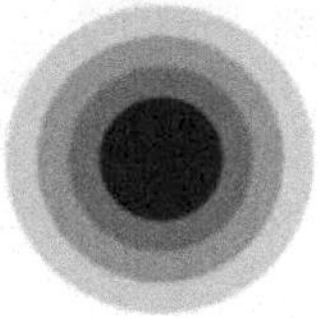

Figure 6-7. *Image produced by embedded SVG (*`Ch06\src\EmbeddingSVG.fo`*)*

Note Use the embedding technique of incorporating SVG files in your document only if such image definitions are small and do not change periodically. If the definition changes too often or if it is too large, it will raise document maintenance issues.

Having studied how to incorporate graphics in your document, you will now learn to create tabular reports.

Creating Tables

Continuing with the stock brokerage theme, suppose the firm would like to send the confirmation report for the orders received from the customer. We would like to print this report in a nice tabular form. XSL-FO allows you to create tabular reports easily. We will create a tabular order report that will list out all the trade orders requested by the customer. The table will list the stock name, code, quantity ordered, desired price, and the type of order (buy or sell). In earlier chapters, this kind of data was generated as HTML. Now, we will create a nice-looking PDF document for this data. Listing 6-5 provides the complete code of an XSL-FO document that creates such a tabular report.

Listing 6-5. *XSL-FO Document That Generates Tabular Report (*`Ch06\src\OrderReport.fo`*)*

```
<?xml version="1.0" encoding="utf-8"?>

<fo:root xmlns:fo="http://www.w3.org/1999/XSL/Format">

  <!-- defines the layout master -->
  <fo:layout-master-set>
    <fo:simple-page-master
      master-name="first"
      page-height="29.7cm"
```

```
      page-width="21cm"
      margin-top="1cm"
      margin-bottom="2cm"
      margin-left="1.5cm"
      margin-right="1.5cm">
    <fo:region-body margin-top="3cm" margin-bottom="1.5cm"/>
    <fo:region-before extent="3cm"/>
    <fo:region-after extent="1.5cm"/>
  </fo:simple-page-master>
</fo:layout-master-set>

<!-- starts actual layout -->
<fo:page-sequence master-reference="first">

<fo:flow flow-name="xsl-region-body">
  fo:block font-size="18pt"
    font-family="sans-serif"
    font-weight="bold"
    line-height="24pt"
    space-after="15pt"
    background-color="Blue"
    color="white"
    text-align="center"
    padding-top="3pt">
      Stock Brokerage
  </fo:block>

  <!-- normal text -->
  <fo:block text-align="start" line-height="24pt">
    We have received the following trade orders from you.
  </fo:block>

  <!-- table start -->
  <fo:table table-layout="fixed"
    font-size="10pt"
    line-height="24pt"
    border-color="black"
    border-style="solid"
    border-width=".5mm" >
      <fo:table-column column-width="70mm" />
      <fo:table-column column-width="30mm" />
      <fo:table-column column-width="25mm" />
      <fo:table-column column-width="25mm" />
      <fo:table-column column-width="30mm" />
      <fo:table-body>
```

```
<fo:table-row background-color="Cyan" font-weight="bold" >
  <fo:table-cell >
    <fo:block>Scrip Name</fo:block>
  </fo:table-cell>
  <fo:table-cell >
    <fo:block>Scrip Code</fo:block>
  </fo:table-cell>
  <fo:table-cell >
    <fo:block>Quantity</fo:block>
  </fo:table-cell>
  <fo:table-cell >
    <fo:block>Price</fo:block>
  </fo:table-cell>
  <fo:table-cell >
    <fo:block>Order Type</fo:block>
  </fo:table-cell>
</fo:table-row>
<fo:table-row background-color="White">
  <fo:table-cell >
    <fo:block>American Financial Group Inc.</fo:block>
  </fo:table-cell>
  <fo:table-cell >
    <fo:block>AFE</fo:block>
  </fo:table-cell>
  <fo:table-cell >
    <fo:block>170</fo:block>
  </fo:table-cell>
  <fo:table-cell >
    <fo:block>$25.29</fo:block>
  </fo:table-cell>
  <fo:table-cell >
    <fo:block>Buy</fo:block>
  </fo:table-cell>
</fo:table-row>
<fo:table-row background-color="rgb (200,200,200)">
  <fo:table-cell >
    <fo:block>BAC Capital Trust IV</fo:block>
  </fo:table-cell>
  <fo:table-cell >
    <fo:block>BACPRU</fo:block>
  </fo:table-cell>
  <fo:table-cell >
    <fo:block>170</fo:block>
  </fo:table-cell>
  <fo:table-cell >
    <fo:block>$23.71</fo:block>
  </fo:table-cell>
```

```
        <fo:table-cell >
          <fo:block>Sell</fo:block>
        </fo:table-cell>
      </fo:table-row>
      <fo:table-row background-color="White">
        <fo:table-cell >
          <fo:block>Dominion Resources, Inc.</fo:block>
        </fo:table-cell>
        <fo:table-cell >
          <fo:block>DPRU</fo:block>
        </fo:table-cell>
        <fo:table-cell >
          <fo:block>87</fo:block>
        </fo:table-cell>
        <fo:table-cell >
          <fo:block>$53.53</fo:block>
        </fo:table-cell>
        <fo:table-cell >
          <fo:block>Sell</fo:block>
        </fo:table-cell>
      </fo:table-row>
      <fo:table-row background-color="rgb (200,200,200)">
        <fo:table-cell >
          <fo:block>Delphi Financial Group Inc.</fo:block>
        </fo:table-cell>
        <fo:table-cell >
          <fo:block>DPRU</fo:block>
        </fo:table-cell>
        <fo:table-cell >
          <fo:block>29</fo:block>
        </fo:table-cell>
        <fo:table-cell >
          <fo:block>$26.04</fo:block>
        </fo:table-cell>
        <fo:table-cell >
          <fo:block>Sell</fo:block>
        </fo:table-cell>
      </fo:table-row>

    </fo:table-body>
  </fo:table>
  <!-- table end -->

  <!-- normal text -->
  <fo:block text-align="center" space-before="12pt" font-size="6pt" >
    This is just for your notification.
    You need not respond to this mail.
```

```
    </fo:block>

    </fo:flow>
  </fo:page-sequence>
</fo:root>
```

As in the earlier examples, the document starts with an XML declaration followed by the root element called root. This is followed by the declaration of page masters. We create only one master page layout called first:

```
<fo:layout-master-set>
  <fo:simple-page-master
    master-name="first"
      ...
  >
  ...
  </fo:simple-page-master>
</fo:layout-master-set>
```

The various attributes of the simple-page-master define the page size, margins for the region-body, and so on. After defining the set of master pages, we start the actual page sequence where we would organize the contents. The contents are displayed in the region body:

```
<!-- starts actual layout -->
<fo:page-sequence master-reference="first">
<fo:flow flow-name="xsl-region-body">
```

In the region body, we declare a block that prints the name of our stock brokerage in a reverse background. The various attributes define the font, size, background color, and so on:

```
<fo:block font-size="18pt"
    ...>
    Stock Brokerage
</fo:block>
```

After this, we print another block displaying a text message. At this point, we start the definition of the table structure. The table definition starts with an fo:table element. We set the table layout to fixed dimensions by setting its table-layout attribute:

```
<fo:table table-layout="fixed"
    ...
  border-color="black"
  border-style="solid"
  border-width=".5mm" >
```

We define the border for the table by setting the border color, style, and width attributes. Within the table, we will now create the desired number of columns. This is done by using the fo:table-column element. We create five columns as follows:

```
<fo:table-column column-width="70mm" />
<fo:table-column column-width="30mm" />
<fo:table-column column-width="25mm" />
<fo:table-column column-width="25mm" />
<fo:table-column column-width="30mm" />
```

For each column, we set the width by using the column-width attribute. After the table structure is defined, we flow the content in the table by opening a table-body element:

```
<fo:table-body>
  ...
</fo:table-body>
```

Within the body of the table, we define various rows by using the table-row element. For the first row, we set the background color to cyan and the font weight to bold. Thus, the text in this row will be shown in bold font:

```
<fo:table-row background-color="Cyan" font-weight="bold" >
```

Within each row, we define various table cells by using the fo:table-cell element. Within a table cell we create a block element to flow the text content:

```
<fo:table-cell>
  <fo:block>Stock Name</fo:block>
</fo:table-cell>
```

In the first cell, we display Stock Name as our text. Likewise, in subsequent table columns, we will display headings such as Stock Code, Quantity, Price, and Order Type. After this, we close the row by using the closing table-row element:

```
</fo:table-row>
```

We now begin another row by using the table-row element again. This time, we set the background color to white:

```
<fo:table-row background-color="White">
```

As with the previous row, we will declare various table cells for this row and display the desired data in them.

Likewise, you can create as many rows as you wish in a table. After you are finished inputting all the desired rows, you close the table by using the appropriate closing tags for the table body and table itself:

```
  </fo:table-body>
</fo:table>
<!-- table end -->
```

After the table is closed, we create one more block to display a notification message to the user. Finally, we close the flow and the page-sequence by using the appropriate closing tags before the closing tag of our document:

```
    </fo:flow>
  </fo:page-sequence>
</fo:root>
```

You may now run the FOP utility on this FO document to generate the PDF. If you view the generated PDF in a PDF reader, you will see the output shown in Figure 6-8.

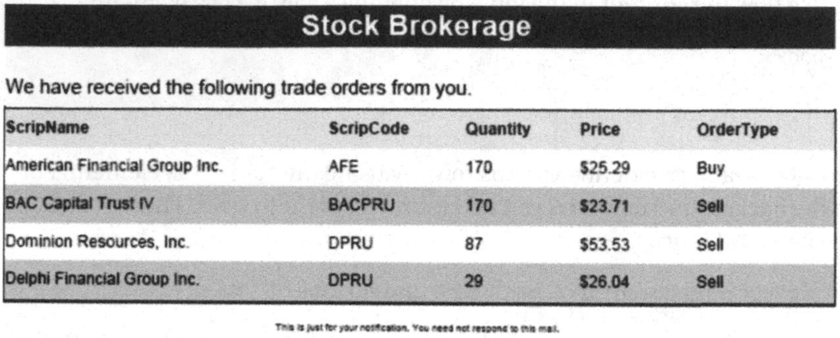

Stock Brokerage				

We have received the following trade orders from you.

ScripName	ScripCode	Quantity	Price	OrderType
American Financial Group Inc.	AFE	170	$25.29	Buy
BAC Capital Trust IV	BACPRU	170	$23.71	Sell
Dominion Resources, Inc.	DPRU	87	$53.53	Sell
Delphi Financial Group Inc.	DPRU	29	$26.04	Sell

This is just for your notification. You need not respond to this mail.

Figure 6-8. *Generated tabular report of Listing 6-5* (Ch06\PDFDocs\OrderReport.pdf)

Columnar Text

You may occasionally want to present text by using a multicolumn format. XSL-FO allows you to easily accomplish this task. In fact, after a page is defined, you can change the number of columns and the content will automatically flow into the newly defined layout. In this section, you will learn how to create a multicolumn report. First you will create the XSL-FO document and then you will render it as a PDF file.

Creating the XSL-FO Document

We will develop an XSL-FO document that creates a multicolumn output. To demonstrate, a short paragraph from Chapter 3 will be used as the text content. We will repeat this paragraph multiple times, each time applying a different style. The entire matter will flow over four pages. The page height has been reduced so that you can see the effect of flowing text over multiple pages.

We will also use the inline element to format the first character and the first two words of the first two paragraphs. The XSL-FO document that produces a columnar report page is shown in Listing 6-6.

Listing 6-6. *XSL-FO for Generating Columnar Report* (Ch06\src\MultiColumn.fo)

```
<?xml version="1.0" encoding="utf-8"?>

<fo:root xmlns:fo="http://www.w3.org/1999/XSL/Format">
```

```
<!-- defines page layout -->
<fo:layout-master-set>

  <fo:simple-page-master master-name="columnarPage"
              page-height="6in"
              page-width="8.5in"
              margin-top="1in"
              margin-bottom="1in"
              margin-left="0.75in"
              margin-right="0.75in">
    <fo:region-body
            margin-top="1in" margin-bottom="1in"
            column-count="3" column-gap="0.25in"/>
    <fo:region-before extent="1in"/>
    <fo:region-after extent="1in"/>
  </fo:simple-page-master>

</fo:layout-master-set>

<!-- actual layout -->
<fo:page-sequence master-reference="columnarPage">

  <fo:static-content flow-name="xsl-region-before">
    <fo:block font-size="16pt"
            font-family="sans-serif"
            line-height="normal"
            text-align="start"
                        color="blue">Multi-Columnar Report</fo:block>
    </fo:static-content>

  <fo:static-content flow-name="xsl-region-after">
    <fo:block font-size="10pt"
            font-family="sans-serif"
            line-height="12pt"
                        space-before.optimum="6pt"
            text-align="end"
                        color="blue">Page # <fo:page-number/></fo:block>
    </fo:static-content>

  <fo:flow flow-name="xsl-region-body">
    <fo:block font-size="12pt"
            font-family="sans-serif"
            line-height="15pt"
            space-after.optimum="3pt"
            text-align="start"
                        span="none">
```

```
                    <fo:inline color="blue"
                      font-weight="bold"
                      font-size="24pt">
                      W<fo:inline
                      font-size="12pt">
                          eb services
                    </fo:inline>
                </fo:inline>
```

technology connects two applications by using XML-based protocols. An application requests a service from another cooperating application by sending an XML-based message to it. This message is called a SOAP request. The requestor embeds a method call for the remote application within the message. In addition, this message contains the parameters required by the remote method. The remote application executes the requested method and may send another XML-based message in response to the requestor. Like the requesting message, the response is also in SOAP format and contains the return value of the remote procedure call.

```
        </fo:block>
        <fo:block font-size="12pt"
                  font-family="sans-serif"
                  color="green"
                  line-height="15pt"
                  space-after.optimum="3pt"
                  space-before="5pt"
                  text-align="start"
                span="none">
                <fo:inline color="blue"
                  font-weight="bold"
                  font-size="24pt">
                  W<fo:inline
                      font-size="12pt">
                      eb services
                </fo:inline>
            </fo:inline>
```

technology connects two applications by using XML-based protocols. An application
...

```
        </fo:block>
        <fo:block font-size="12pt"
                  font-family="Times Roman"
                  font-style="italic"
                  line-height="15pt"
                  space-after.optimum="3pt"
                  text-align="start"
                    background-color="yellow"
                    span="none">
```

Web services technology connects two applications by using XML-based protocols. An
...

```
      </fo:block>
      <fo:block font-size="14pt"
                font-family="Helvetica"
                line-height="15pt"
                space-after.optimum="3pt"
                text-align="start"
               span="none">
```
Web services technology connects two applications by using XML-based protocols. An
...

```
      </fo:block>

          </fo:flow>
    </fo:page-sequence>
</fo:root>
```

We start by defining master page layouts. We create a master page called `columnarPage`:

```
<fo:simple-page-master master-name="columnarPage"
```

We set the page height, width, and various margins to the desired values. We then create the regions within the page: `region-body`, `region-before`, and `region-after`. The `region-body` element is important to us because this is where we will be flowing page content:

```
<fo:region-body
   margin-top="1in" margin-bottom="1in"
   column-count="2" column-gap="0.25in"/>
```

In the `region-body` element, we define the `column-count` as 2. This attribute determines the number of columns for the text. Later, you will try changing the value of this attribute to flow the text in more than two columns.

After defining the page layout masters, we will start placing the content. First, we place content in the region-before area:

```
<fo:static-content flow-name="xsl-region-before">
   <fo:block font-size="16pt"
             font-family="sans-serif"
             line-height="normal"
             text-align="start"
             color="blue">Multi-Columnar Report</fo:block>
   </fo:static-content>
```

After this, we define content for the region-after area:

```
<fo:static-content flow-name="xsl-region-after">
   <fo:block font-size="10pt"
             font-family="sans-serif"
             line-height="12pt"
```

```
                    space-before.optimum="6pt"
                    text-align="end"
                    color="blue">Page # <fo:page-number/></fo:block>
        </fo:static-content>
```

In the region-after area that appears at the bottom of each page, we place the page number. Note how the page numbers are automatically generated with the help of the fo:page-number element. The space-before.optimum attribute for this block element sets the optimum spacing to 6 points. Thus, the space before this block may not always equal 6 points, but could be more depending on how the rest of the page content is placed.

Now, we define the flow for the region-body area:

```
<fo:flow flow-name="xsl-region-body">
```

For each paragraph in this area, we create a block element. Each block will use a different formatting style. We declare the first block as follows:

```
<fo:block font-size="12pt"
          font-family="sans-serif"
          line-height="15pt"
          space-after.optimum="3pt"
          text-align="start"
          span="none">
```

The block defines the formatting for its content by using its various attributes. Within this block, we use the inline element to set different formatting for the first character and the first two words of the paragraph:

```
        <fo:inline color="blue"
          font-weight="bold"
          font-size="24pt">
          W<fo:inline
            font-size="12pt">
            eb services
        </fo:inline>
```

Note the use of nested inline elements to set the formatting of the first character different from the other characters in the first two words. The first character is displayed in blue color in bold 24-point size. The first character, which is W, is placed as the content of the inline element. The rest of the characters (that is, eb services) are displayed in 12 points and the same blue color.

After the first two words are placed, we place the rest of the matter for the paragraph as the content of the outer block element. This text will be displayed using the font style defined for this block element.

We repeat this block along with its content three more times, changing the block style each time.

Rendering Columnar Output

You can now run the FOP utility on this FO document to generate the PDF. If you view the generated PDF in a PDF reader, you will see a four-page document. The first page of the output is shown in Figure 6-9.

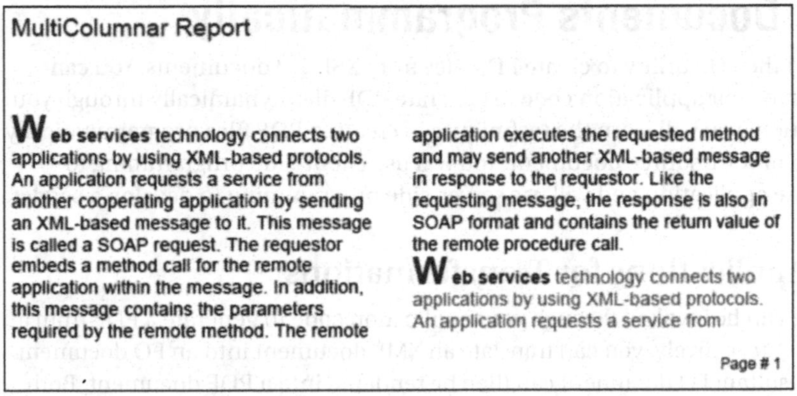

MultiColumnar Report

Web services technology connects two applications by using XML-based protocols. An application requests a service from another cooperating application by sending an XML-based message to it. This message is called a SOAP request. The requestor embeds a method call for the remote application within the message. In addition, this message contains the parameters required by the remote method. The remote application executes the requested method and may send another XML-based message in response to the requestor. Like the requesting message, the response is also in SOAP format and contains the return value of the remote procedure call.

Web services technology connects two applications by using XML-based protocols. An application requests a service from

Page # 1

Figure 6-9. *Two-column output*

You can generate the document yourself to see how the text flows nicely across multiple pages in two columns. Also, note the page number as it autoincrements on each page count.

Note Because this book is printed in black-and-white, some of the formatting effects, such as font color and highlights, will not be visible here. You will need to observe these effects on your color monitor.

Now you can try changing the column count to 3. Figure 6-10 shows the generated output for page 2.

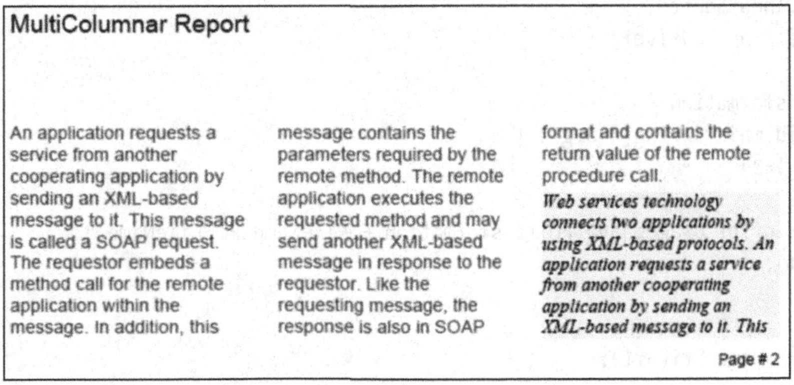

MultiColumnar Report

An application requests a service from another cooperating application by sending an XML-based message to it. This message is called a SOAP request. The requestor embeds a method call for the remote application within the message. In addition, this message contains the parameters required by the remote method. The remote application executes the requested method and may send another XML-based message in response to the requestor. Like the requesting message, the response is also in SOAP format and contains the return value of the remote procedure call.

Web services technology connects two applications by using XML-based protocols. An application requests a service from another cooperating application by sending an XML-based message to it. This

Page # 2

Figure 6-10. *Three-column report* (Ch06/PDFDocs/MultiColumn.pdf)

The XSL-FO specification provides several such elements for producing nicely formatted documents. You can refer to this specification to understand the use of other elements. The use of such elements is not complicated, and whatever knowledge you have gained in this chapter so far should be enough to help you learn the rest of the elements on your own.

Processing Documents Programmatically

So far, you have used the FOP utility to create PDF files from XSL-FO documents. You can also use the FOP API in your application code to generate PDF files dynamically through your program. In this section, you will learn the techniques of creating PDF files programmatically from a given XSL-FO or XML source document. You will use client-side programming to develop a stand-alone application and will use server-side programming to develop a servlet.

Stand-Alone Applications for Transformations

Apache's FOP engine can be invoked through your application code to generate a PDF from a given FO document. Alternatively, you can translate an XML document into an FO document by using XSLT. The resultant FO document can then be rendered into a PDF document. Both of these techniques are described next.

The FO to PDF Transformation

The programmatic creation of a PDF file from an XSL-FO document is an easy process. The complete code for a console-based Java application is given in Listing 6-7.

Listing 6-7. *Console Application for PDF Creations* (Ch06\src\FOTransformation.java)

```java
package xmlfo;

import java.io.File;
import java.io.IOException;
import java.io.InputStream;
import java.io.OutputStream;
import org.xml.sax.InputSource;
import org.xml.sax.InputSource;
import org.apache.fop.apps.Driver;

public class FOTransformation {
  public static void main(String[] args) {
    if(args.length !=2)
    {
      System.out.println("Usage:java FOTransformation FOFileName PDFFileName");
      System.exit(1);
    }
    try {
      Driver driver = new Driver();
```

```
        // set the logger

    //Setup Renderer (output format)
        driver.setRenderer(Driver.RENDER_PDF);

        //Setup output
        OutputStream out = new java.io.FileOutputStream(args[1]);
        try {
            driver.setOutputStream(out);
            //Setup input
            InputStream in = new java.io.FileInputStream(args[0]);
            try {
                driver.setInputSource(new InputSource(in));
                //Process FO
                driver.run();
            } finally {
                in.close();
                }
            } finally {
                out.close();
        }
        System.out.println("Output file created successfully!");
    } catch (Exception e) {
        e.printStackTrace();
        System.exit(-1);
    }
  }
}
```

The FOP implementation provides the Driver class for performing the transformation. You simply need to instantiate this class, set its input and output streams, and call the run method to produce the output. The class is instantiated as follows:

```
Driver driver = new Driver();
```

After you have instantiated it, you will need to set up the renderer by calling the setRenderer method on the Driver class:

```
//Setup Renderer (output format)
driver.setRenderer(Driver.RENDER_PDF);
```

In the current example, we set the renderer to PDF by using the Driver.RENDER_PDF predefined constant as an argument to the setRenderer method.

You set the output for the renderer by constructing a file output stream and assigning it to the driver by calling its setOutputStream method as follows:

```
//Setup output
OutputStream out = new java.io.FileOutputStream(args[1]);
try {
    driver.setOutputStream(out);
```

Likewise, you set the input stream for the driver by first constructing an input stream object and then assigning it to the driver by calling its setInputSource method:

```
//Setup input
InputStream in = new java.io.FileInputStream(args[0]);
try {
    driver.setInputSource(new InputSource(in));
```

At this stage, your driver is set up and you are ready to perform the transformations, which you do by simply calling the run method on the driver object:

```
driver.run();
```

If the run method runs to its success, the specified PDF file will be created in the current folder. In case of errors while processing, the program captures the exceptions and prints them on the user console.

Compiling and Running the Application

You can compile the code by using the javac compiler on the command line as follows:

```
C:\<installation folder>\Ch06\src>javac -d . FOTransformation.java
```

After it is compiled, run the application from a command line by specifying the desired parameters:

```
C:\<installation folder>\Ch06\src>java xmlfo.FOTransformation Cover.fo Cover.pdf
```

Before compiling and running the application, ensure that you have all the required libraries in your environment's classpath. You will need to include the various JAR files from <your installation folder>\lib folder into your classpath.

■**Note** You will also need to include in your classpath the fop.jar file from <your installation folder>\build folder.

The XML to PDF Transformation

In the previous section, you learned how to convert an FO document into a PDF document through your application code. Now, you will learn how to convert a given XML document directly into a PDF document through application code. The application code that performs this transformation is given in Listing 6-8.

Listing 6-8. XML2PDF *Transformation—Stand-Alone Application* (Ch06\src\XMLTransformation.java)

```java
package xmlfo;
//Java
import java.io.File;
import java.io.IOException;
import java.io.OutputStream;

//JAXP
import javax.xml.transform.Transformer;
import javax.xml.transform.TransformerFactory;
import javax.xml.transform.TransformerException;
import javax.xml.transform.Source;
import javax.xml.transform.Result;
import javax.xml.transform.stream.StreamSource;
import javax.xml.transform.sax.SAXResult;

//FOP
import org.apache.fop.apps.Driver;

public class XMLTransformation {

    public static void main(String[] args) {
        if(args.length !=2)
        {
            System.out.println
                ("Usage:java XMLTransformation XMLFileName PDFFileName");
            System.exit(1);
        }
try {
            //Setup input and output files
            File xmlfile = new File("args[0]");
            File xsltfile = new File("args[1]");

            //Construct driver
            Driver driver = new Driver();

            // set the logger

            //Setup Renderer (output format)
            driver.setRenderer(Driver.RENDER_PDF);

            //Setup output
            OutputStream out = new java.io.FileOutputStream("Result.pdf");
            try {
                driver.setOutputStream(out);
```

```
                   //Setup XSLT
                   TransformerFactory factory = TransformerFactory.newInstance();
                   Transformer transformer = factory.newTransformer
                                                (new StreamSource(xsltfile));

                   //Setup input for XSLT transformation
                   Source src = new StreamSource(xmlfile);

                   //Resulting SAX events (the generated FO) must be
                   //piped through to FOP
                   Result res = new SAXResult(driver.getContentHandler());

                   //Start XSLT transformation and FOP processing
                   transformer.transform(src, res);
               } finally {
                   out.close();
               }

           System.out.println("Success!");
       } catch (Exception e) {
           e.printStackTrace();
           System.exit(-1);
       }
   }
}
```

For transforming an XML document into a PDF file, you need to first transform the given XML document into an FO document. You do so by using transformations defined in another XSLT document. The application accepts two command-line parameters that specify the name of the input XML file as the first parameter and the name of the XSLT file as the second parameter. The application first constructs the File objects on these two input files:

```
           //Setup input and output files
           File xmlfile = new File("args[0]");
           File xsltfile = new File("args[1]");
```

The application then creates a Driver instance and sets its renderer type to a predefined value of Driver.RENDER_PDF:

```
           //Construct driver
           Driver driver = new Driver();

           //Setup Renderer (output format)
           driver.setRenderer(Driver.RENDER_PDF);
```

We set the output for the transformation result by creating a stream object for the Result.pdf file and assigning it to the driver instance:

```
//Setup output
OutputStream out = new java.io.FileOutputStream("Result.pdf");
try {
    driver.setOutputStream(out);
```

Next, we create a transformer based on the specified XSLT file:

```
//Setup XSLT
TransformerFactory factory = TransformerFactory.newInstance();
Transformer transformer = factory.newTransformer
                                (new StreamSource(xsltfile));
```

■**Tip** XSLT transformations were discussed in Chapter 5.

Next, we create a StreamSource object for input to XSLT transformations:

```
//Setup input for XSLT transformation
Source src = new StreamSource(xmlfile);
```

The output of the XSLT transformation must be piped through to FOP, where another transformation will convert FO to PDF:

```
//Resulting SAX events (the generated FO) must be piped through to FOP
Result res = new SAXResult(driver.getContentHandler());

//Start XSLT transformation and FOP processing
transformer.transform(src, res);
```

The transformer finally transforms the XML source document to a resultant output stream by using its transform method. Note that it does first perform transformation of XML to intermediate FO by using the specified XSLT document.

Compiling and Running the Application

You can use the javac compiler to compile the preceding application code by using the following command line:

```
C:\<installation folder>\Ch06\src>javac -d . FOTransformation.java
```

To run the application, use the command as follows:

```
C:\<installation folder>\Ch06/src>java xmlfo.XMLTransformation ➡
CustomerOrders.xml Process.xsl
```

When the application runs successfully, you will find the Result.pdf file created in the working folder.

Creating a Server-Side Transformation Application

Now we will look at the development of the server-side code, which will enable us to create a PDF file on the server and render its output in the client browser. To perform transformations on the server side, we will create a servlet and deploy it on a Tomcat server. We will consider both techniques of converting FO to PDF and converting XML to PDF.

The FO to PDF Transformation

The process for server-side transformation is identical to the one described in the console application in the previous section. Again, we will use the provided `Driver` class to perform the transformation. The complete code for the servlet that performs this transformation is given in Listing 6-9.

Listing 6-9. `Fop2PDFServlet` *Performs FO to PDF Transformation on Server* (Ch06\src\ Fop2PDFServlet.java)

```java
import java.io.*;

import javax.servlet.*;
import javax.servlet.http.*;

import org.xml.sax.InputSource;

import org.apache.fop.apps.Driver;

public class Fop2PDFServlet extends HttpServlet {
  public void doGet(HttpServletRequest request,
      HttpServletResponse response) throws ServletException {
  try {
    String foParam = request.getParameter("fo");

    if (foParam != null) {
      FileInputStream file = new FileInputStream(foParam);

      try {
        ByteArrayOutputStream out = new ByteArrayOutputStream();
        response.setContentType("application/pdf");

        Driver driver = new Driver(new InputSource(file), out);
        driver.setRenderer(Driver.RENDER_PDF);
        driver.run();

        byte[] content = out.toByteArray();
        response.setContentLength(content.length);
        response.getOutputStream().write(content);
```

```
      response.getOutputStream().flush();
    } catch (Exception ex) {
    throw new ServletException(ex);
  }

  } else {
  PrintWriter out = response.getWriter();
  out.println("<html><head><title>Error</title></head>\n"+
        "<body><h1>Fop2PDFServlet Error</h1><h3>No 'fo' "+
        "request param given.</body></html>");
  }
} catch (ServletException ex) {
  throw ex;
}
catch (Exception ex) {
  throw new ServletException(ex);
}
}
}
```

The servlet takes one parameter that specifies the name of the XSL-FO file to be trans-formed and renders its output on the client browser:

```
String foParam = request.getParameter("fo");
if (foParam != null) {
  FileInputStream file = new FileInputStream(foParam);
```

As in the previous example, we first construct an input source object. The program reads the value of the fo parameter and constructs a FileInputStream object on it. The Driver object will use this as the input stream.

We construct the byte array output stream for the program output:

```
ByteArrayOutputStream out = new ByteArrayOutputStream();
```

The driver renders its output to the stream. As the driver renders the output of PDF type, we need to set the content type in the output stream. This is done by calling the setContentType method on the response object:

```
response.setContentType("application/pdf");
```

If you register the PDF reader application in your browser, the browser will display the content of the PDF file.

After setting the input and output streams and the content type for the output, we instantiate the Driver:

```
Driver driver = new Driver(new InputSource(file), out);
```

The driver is initialized with the desired input and output streams passed as parameters to its constructor.

As in the earlier example, we set the renderer to PDF type and call the run method on the driver object to perform the transformation:

```
driver.setRenderer(Driver.RENDER_PDF);
driver.run();
```

The output produced by the driver goes in the specified byte array stream. We need to copy this in the response object of the servlet. We read the contents of the byte array output stream into a byte array:

```
byte[] content = out.toByteArray();
```

We set the content length on the response object by calling its setContentLength method. The length equals the length of the byte array in which the response has been generated:

```
response.setContentLength(content.length);
```

We write the actual content to the response object by calling the write method on its output stream:

```
response.getOutputStream().write(content);
```

The output stream contents need to be flushed to the browser by calling its flush method:

```
response.getOutputStream().flush();
```

At this stage, the generated PDF output will be displayed on the user browser.

Compiling the Servlet

You can use the javac compiler from the command line to compile the servlet code given in Listing 6-5. In this case, you will need to ensure that all the required library files are available in your classpath. Also, you will need to create the WAR file for deployment on the web server.

The easier way to compile and deploy the servlet is to use the Apache-provided build file. The build.bat file is available in your <fop installation folder>\examples\servlet folder. Copy the servlet source file to your <fop installation folder>\examples\servlet\src folder. You will need to modify the build.xml file from the servlet folder. The only change you would need in the build.xml file is to change the value for the property name as follows:

```
<property name="name" value="Fop2PDFservlet"/>
```

Set the value attribute to the name of your servlet. When you build the project, the fop.war file will be created in your servlet\build folder. Drop this file in the webapps folder of your Tomcat installation and restart Tomcat. This will install the servlet and make it ready for invocation.

Note If you are using another web server, you will need to follow its instructions for installing the servlet.

Running the Servlet

You can run the servlet by typing the following URL in your browser:

```
http://localhost:8080/fop/Fop2PDFServlet?fo=c:\apress\ch06\src\Cover.fo
```

Note Before you run this URL, ensure that the Cover.fo file is available in the specified folder.

The Cover.fo file is shown in Listing 6-1 and is available from the Source Code area of the Apress website (http://www.apress.com). If you have registered Adobe Reader for reading PDF files in your browser, you will see the output as shown in Figure 6-11.

Figure 6-11. Fop2PDFServlet *Response Output* (Ch06\PDFDocs\Cover.pdf)

XML to PDF Transformation

The previous example showed the transformation of an FO file into PDF. Now we will write servlet code that takes XML and XSLT documents as input parameters. The content of the XML document will first be transformed into an intermediate FO document by using the transformation instructions given in the XSLT file. The content of the FO file will then be rendered on the output device as a PDF document.

The code for the XML2PDF servlet is given in Listing 6-10.

Listing 6-10. XML2PDF *Servlet* (Ch06\src\XML2PDFServlet.java)

```java
import java.io.*;
import javax.servlet.*;
import javax.servlet.http.*;
import org.xml.sax.InputSource;
import org.apache.fop.apps.Driver;
import org.apache.fop.apps.XSLTInputHandler;
```

```
public class XML2PDFServlet extends HttpServlet {
    public void doGet(HttpServletRequest request,
                      HttpServletResponse response) throws ServletException {
    String xmlParam = request.getParameter("xml");
    String xsltParam = request.getParameter("xslt");
      try {
        if ((xmlParam != null) && (xsltParam != null)) {
          XSLTInputHandler input =
            new XSLTInputHandler(new File(xmlParam),
              new File(xsltParam));
          try {
            ByteArrayOutputStream out = new ByteArrayOutputStream();

            response.setContentType("application/pdf");

            Driver driver = new Driver();
            driver.setRenderer(Driver.RENDER_PDF);
            driver.setOutputStream(out);
            driver.render(input.getParser(), input.getInputSource());

            byte[] content = out.toByteArray();
            response.setContentLength(content.length);
             response.getOutputStream().write(content);
            response.getOutputStream().flush();
            } catch (Exception ex) {
          throw new ServletException(ex);
        }

        } else {
          PrintWriter out = response.getWriter();
          out.println("<html><head><title>Error</title></head>\n"+
            "<body><h1>XML2PDFServlet Error</h1><h3>"+
            "request params not proper.</h3></body></html>");
        }
      }catch (ServletException ex) {
        throw ex;
      }
      catch (Exception ex) {
        throw new ServletException(ex);
      }
    }
  }
}
```

The servlet accepts two parameters, namely xml and xslt. The first parameter specifies the XML document whose contents are to be rendered to a PDF file. The second parameter specifies the XSLT file that transforms the input XML file to an intermediate FO document. The transformation output is directly rendered on the browser as in the previous example.

The servlet first reads the two input parameters into local variables:

```
String xmlParam = request.getParameter("xml");
String xsltParam = request.getParameter("xslt");
```

If the input parameters are not specified, the servlet displays a proper error message on the browser. If both parameters are specified, we construct an input handler that is later used by the driver object:

```
if ((xmlParam != null) && (xsltParam != null)) {
    XSLTInputHandler input =
        new XSLTInputHandler(new File(xmlParam),
            new File(xsltParam));
```

Apache provides a special class called XSLTInputHandler for creating an input to the Driver class that performs the rendering. The input handler class takes two parameters: The first parameter is the XML document, and the second parameter is the XSLT document that is used for transformation.

After constructing the input handler, we construct the output stream as in the previous example:

```
ByteArrayOutputStream out = new ByteArrayOutputStream();
```

We set the content type to PDF in the response object:

```
    response.setContentType("application/pdf");
```

We create the Driver instance, set its renderer type, and set the output stream:

```
        Driver driver = new Driver();
        driver.setRenderer(Driver.RENDER_PDF);
        driver.setOutputStream(out);
```

Next, we call the render method on the driver object to perform the transformation:

```
driver.render(input.getParser(), input.getInputSource());
```

The render method uses the parser passed in its first argument and uses the source document passed in the second argument. The driver will output its results to the byte stream as in the earlier example. We copy these contents into a byte buffer and output the buffer to the response object of the servlet:

```
        byte[] content = out.toByteArray();
        response.setContentLength(content.length);
        response.getOutputStream().write(content);
        response.getOutputStream().flush();
```

The output will now be displayed on the client browser.

Compiling and Running the XML2PDF Servlet

To compile the servlet, you can use the provided build.bat file as in the previous example.

■**Note** You will need to modify build.xml to specify the name of your servlet as XML2PDFServlet.

After a WAR file is created, deploy it on the web server. To test this servlet, you can use the provided XML (CustomerOrders.xml) and XSL (Process.xsl) files in the src folder of your code download. These are available in the <your installation folder>\Ch06\src folder. CustomerOrders.xml is the file you have used in the previous examples. The Process.xsl file defines the XSLT transformation to transform the CustomerOrders document into a tabular format as depicted in Figure 6-12.

Open the following URL in your browser:

```
http://localhost:8080/fop/XML2PDFServlet?xml=C:\Apress\Ch06\src\CustomerOrders.➡
xml&xsl= C:\Apress\Ch06\src\Process.xsl
```

You will see the output as shown in Figure 6-12.

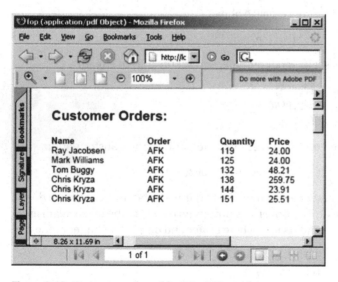

Figure 6-12. *Output produced by* XML2PDF *servlet*

Summary

XSL-FO is a powerful language for rendering the contents of an XML document to a format specific to an output device. In this chapter, you learned the transformation process by using the Apache-supplied FOP utility. This chapter covered the XSL-FO syntax so that you can create your own FO documents that can be easily transformed into PDF documents by using the FOP utility.

XSL-FO is XML based and allows you to create complicated page layouts easily. The specifications define several tags in an XML schema. You create an XML-FO document adhering to this schema. You use various elements from this schema in an FO document to specify the desired formatting for each paragraph in the document.

You learned how to create simple title pages in which you could control the font size, style, foreground color, and background color for your titles. You learned how to incorporate graphics in your output documents. XSL-FO specifications allow you to import graphics images from various popular formats including the latest SVG format.

XSL-FO specifications allow you to create tables in your output document. You learned the syntax for creating tabular outputs. In a continuation of our stock brokerage application from Chapter 2, you learned how the stock brokerage created a tabular report for its clients.

You also learned how to create a multicolumn page layout and flow the contents in multiple columns. The number of columns on a page can be easily changed by modifying a single attribute value. For a multipage document, the FOP engine keeps track of page numbering. You learned how to place an autocounting page number on your document.

Instead of using the command-line FOP utility, you can generate PDF documents through your application code. Such transformations can be done by writing a console application or can be performed on a server by using a servlet. You learned both techniques of client- and server-side processing.

The transformation through your application code can be done starting with an FO document or it can be performed directly on an XML source document. If you decide to use an XML document as the content input, it needs to be converted into an intermediate FO document before rendering its output to PDF. For this, we use XSLT. The XSLT document contains instructions for transforming an XML document into an FO document. You learned how to perform such transformations through your application code.

CHAPTER 7

∎∎∎

The Apache Cocoon Framework

In the first six chapters of this book, you have learned several XML technologies such as parsing, invoking web services, XSL transformations, and formatting objects. In this chapter, we will bring all of these technologies together to create a web application that people would like to use and application developers could manage with ease. This is exactly what the Apache Cocoon framework provides.

Apache Cocoon is an XML publishing framework that accepts XML data as the input source, transforms it by using the transformation rules defined by you, and eventually converts it to a presentation format of your choice. These three processes—document creation, transformation, and presentation—are loosely coupled, meaning that each can be respectively managed by an appropriate individual or group without interfering with efforts made by other individuals or groups working on the other components. For example, the person responsible for choosing the document content will not necessarily be tasked with how the content is transformed and rendered on the client's display. Apache Cocoon accounts for this separation, resulting in more efficient management of your web application.

In this chapter, you will learn web development techniques using Cocoon.

First, you will learn why this new publishing framework is needed, obtain some brief information about Cocoon's history, and download the software needed for this chapter. Then you will learn about Cocoon's pipeline architecture—how it isolates and defines the three aforementioned roles and manages the process flows. You will see an overview of the architecture's main components.

Next you will create a Cocoon application that builds on the stock brokerage case study from Chapter 2. You will then take a closer look at Cocoon's sitemap document and its various elements. You will learn to render the web page content into several formats by modifying the Cocoon pipeline. You will learn the purpose of various components such as transformers, generators, and serializers in the Cocoon pipeline and learn to create internationalized sites by modifying some of these components.

You will also learn about an important technology called XML server pages, which allows you to create dynamic websites and provides a better separation between content and presentation by using Logicsheets. Finally, you will learn to configure Cocoon for performance optimizations.

Why Another Web Framework?

In the Web's early days, content was served to the user in a static fashion. Although static HTML pages initially sufficed, developers soon realized that more power and flexibility could be had by generating content dynamically. This opened up the possibility of retrieving data from numerous sources (from a database, for instance) and then inserting that data into the page by using embedded logic. Thus came a barrage of languages such as JavaServer Pages (JSP), Active Server Pages (ASP), and PHP: Hypertext Processor (PHP). Although these technologies greatly enhanced the developer's capabilities in terms of creating dynamic content, they aren't without their problems.

Page designers who typically focus on HTML syntax generally are not so adept at the embedded application logic code written in a language such as Java or Perl. At the same time, application developers generally have little idea of how to present their content in a user-friendly manner. Therefore, to most effectively manage a website, ideally a method for separating the logic and presentation into components that can be managed irrespective of the maintainer would be available. While the *content provider* would choose the document structure and what is to be presented to the reader, the *logic provider* would develop application code to generate content. A *style provider* would be responsible for deciding how the content is formatted for rendering on the user device. Of course, a workflow would exist that coordinates the three entities; however, the requirements would stay independent of each other.

If the reader uses a different device for viewing a web page, the person who is responsible for rendering the output will be concerned with transforming the page content to a new format. Similarly, if the data source changes, only the logic programmer should be concerned with how to fetch the data from the new source. Finally, if the actual page content requires updating, only the content provider will decide what needs to be changed. Although the earlier technologies do not easily enable the separation of these three concerns, the Cocoon framework does so in a clear and structured way.

Formally defined, the three concerns are depicted in Figure 7-1.

Figure 7-1. *Three concerns of web page development and management*

Besides the three concerns, Figure 7-1 also depicts one additional role: the management role. This individual is responsible for site management and coordinates the three other roles.

To achieve a manageable separation between the three roles, we need to provide a loose coupling between the three so that each can be managed independently of the others and so changes in one would not necessitate changes in the others. This can be achieved by defining clear-cut contracts between the different concerns.

To begin, we will define a contract between the Logic and Content roles. The Logic role generates the data dynamically and passes it to the page structure by using a certain specified contract. The content provider defines the page structure. The style provider retrieves the page content and transforms it by using its own rules for rendering to the output device. The transformation rules are independent of what is being transformed. There is no need to have any contract between the Logic and the Style roles because they never talk to each other.

Apache Cocoon provides the separation of these concerns and their management by creating a framework for web development.

A Brief History of Cocoon

The Cocoon project was founded by Stefano Mazzocchi in 1998 as an open source project under the Apache Software Foundation. Mazzocchi realized that HTML allows people to render document content on an output device but fails to perform any semantic analysis on the document. XML solves this problem by allowing the creator to design her own meaningful tags. However, the semantic analysis of an XML document is again restricted to a human reader and does not extend to a machine. Consider the following XML document fragment:

```
<book>
  <title>
      Professional Apache XML
  </title>
  <author>
      Poornachandra Sarang
  </author>
</book>
```

Looking at this XML code, a human reader can easily see that the code describes a book having the title *Professional Apache XML* that is authored by Poornachandra Sarang. Thus, an author tag in an XML document makes sense to a human reader in understanding who has authored the document, but makes no sense to a machine reading this document. Even if some other document creator uses the tag writer instead of author, a human reader will understand that the book was written by Sarang. Human readers possess this capability of semantic analysis; machines do not.

By designing the Cocoon framework, Mazzocchi provided a model that is flexible enough to implement semantic analysis and provide functionality to meet the ever-changing needs of a typical web application. It provides the tools and mechanism to incorporate changes in the processing of a document.

The Cocoon project started as a simple servlet that would provide XSL transformation for styling XML content. It used the reactor design pattern for connecting components and was based on the DOM Level 1 API. As you saw in Chapter 2, DOM is expensive in terms of its memory and processing time requirements. This provided severe limitations in designing large, dynamic sites and thus failed quickly.

A new model was soon proposed that is currently known as Cocoon 2. This was designed to be scalable, fast, and memory efficient. It uses SAX instead of DOM for document processing. It provides separate management functionality for managing the components of a pipeline. It also supports precompilation, pregeneration, and caching for better performance. All this is explained in more detail later in this chapter.

Before you look into this framework and its architecture, you first need to install the software so that you can run the sample applications presented in the chapter while learning Cocoon.

Downloading the Software

The Cocoon source can be downloaded from the Apache site:

```
http://cocoon.apache.org
```

The latest version as of this writing and the one used in this chapter is 2.1.8. According to a policy instituted as of version 2.1, binaries are no longer provided. Therefore, you will need to download and build the source code regardless of platform. Note that this is a whopping 45+ MB download. You will also need to ensure that you have Java Development Kit (JDK) installed on your machine.

Building and Installing the Software

Unzip the downloaded source to a desired folder. Build the code by running the provided build script found in the extracted package. This will build the Cocoon source to generate all the required libraries. After the code is successfully built, run it by using the following command at the command prompt. For instance, on Microsoft Windows this process might look like this:

```
C:\{installation folder}>cocoon
```

This starts a light version of the Jetty server containing a servlet engine.

■**Note** A light version of the Jetty web server is provided as a part of Cocoon for quick deployment and testing of your Cocoon applications.

You will see a message similar to the following in the command window after the server starts successfully:

```
16:57:13.015 EVENT   Started SocketListener on 0.0.0.0:8888
16:57:13.031 EVENT   Started org.mortbay.jetty.Server@e94e92
```

The preceding build process generates a cocoon.jar file in the <installation folder>\ build folder. This file cannot be deployed on a Tomcat web server. To create an installation for Tomcat, use the following command line to build the source:

```
C:\{installation folder}>build war
```

This creates a cocoon.war file in the <installation folder>\build\cocoon folder. After it is successfully built, you will see screen output similar to the following:

```
...
war:
Trying to override old definition of task manifest
Writing: build/webapp/WEB-INF/Manifest.mf
Building jar: C:\cocoon-2.1.8\build\cocoon\cocoon.war

BUILD SUCCESSFUL
Total time: 3 minutes 15 seconds
```

Copy the cocoon.war file in the webapps folder of your Tomcat installation and restart Tomcat if it is already running.

Testing Your Installation

You can test the installation by opening the following URL in your browser (if you are using the provided Jetty web server):

http://localhost:8888

The Jetty server listens to the 8888 port by default. You will see the Cocoon welcome screen on your browser, as shown in Figure 7-2.

Figure 7-2. *Cocoon welcome screen*

If you have deployed the cocoon.war file on Tomcat, you will need to use the following URL:

```
http://localhost:8080/cocoon
```

■Note Use the appropriate port number for your Tomcat installation.

On success, you will see the welcome screen shown in Figure 7-2.

Now that you have successfully installed Cocoon, you are ready to study its architecture. Understanding the architecture is important in learning even how the conventional Hello World web page is developed and deployed in Cocoon.

Cocoon's Pipeline Architecture

The Web uses HTTP for communication, and its application model is based on a request/ response mechanism. A web client requests a web page from a site by making an HTTP request. The responding server parses the request and either reads a static page from local storage or generates a web page dynamically to fulfill the client request. The web page may then be transformed into HTML or any other desired format as an HTTP response to the client. The entire scenario can be visualized as a document flow that undergoes a series of transformations by various components. You can imagine that these components are placed in a pipeline, through which the document flows.

Cocoon follows a similar architecture, in which an XML document traverses through the various components placed in a pipeline. These components transform the XML document at each stage to produce the final desired output to the client. In this section, you'll see an overview of the Cocoon architecture and then take a closer look at its specific components. You'll also learn about the use of multiple pipelines.

Figure 7-3 shows the document flow through the various components in a pipeline.

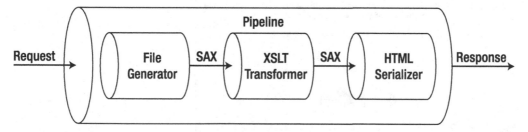

Figure 7-3. *Cocoon pipeline architecture*

The pipeline architecture results in breaking down processing of every web request into the following three stages:

- *File generator.* Responsible for parsing XML data to *generate* the desired content

- *XSLT transformer.* Responsible for *transforming* the content to a desired output format

- *HTML serializer.* Responsible for s*erializing* the transformed data, for rendering to the output device

Each component in the Cocoon pipeline is pluggable and can be individually replaced without affecting the functioning of other components in the pipeline. The communication between the components is event based and uses SAX for document processing. As you saw in Chapter 2, the SAX processing model generates events whenever it encounters an element in the input document.

The Cocoon pipeline can have three or more components. Figure 7-3 shows the three essential components. The pipeline begins with a generator component, which generates the document content. The output of a generator is fed into a transformer, where the document might undergo zero or more transformations. The transformed content can be aggregated by another aggregator component (not shown in the figure). Finally, the pipeline ends with a serializer.

If you are familiar with servlet chaining, you can compare the pipeline architecture to it. Just as servlets are chained to provide the desired processing of a client request and to generate a client response, the various components in a pipeline are chained to provide the desired processing on a client request and to produce the response to the client.

Generator

As I have said, the generator is the first component in Cocoon's pipeline. A typical (and the simplest) generator is FileGenerator. It picks up the document content from a local XML file, parses the document, and sends the SAX events on the occurrence of each element in the document down the pipeline. FileGenerator is just one of the generators provided by Cocoon. Cocoon provides implementations for several other generators that pick up the data from various input sources. For example, a request generator picks up the input from the client's HTTP request, whereas a JSP generator picks up its input from a JavaServer page. You will study these classes in later sections.

Transformer

A transformer takes its input from a generator and transforms the given input into another XML document. A typical transformer is an XSLT transformer that transforms an input source tree into an output tree based on the rules defined in an XSLT document. Other types of transformers are an SQL transformer, which queries the database and transforms the result into an XML document. The internationalization (i18n) transformer transforms the input document into various locale-specific code snippets. Again, Cocoon provides several such transformers that you will learn about later in this chapter.

Serializer

This component is the last in the Cocoon chain and is responsible for generating the final presentation to the client. A typical serializer is an HTML serializer that processes SAX events generated by the transformer and returns an HTML document to the user waiting on the other end of the pipeline. Cocoon defines several serializers. For example, in Chapter 6 you saw a serializer that serializes an XML document into a PDF document. Other useful serializers are XML, VRML, and WAP, which convert the input source into the corresponding output formats, as their names suggest. You will learn more about the different serializers later in this chapter.

Matchers

You have seen the important components of a pipeline. However, this process can quickly become a bit more involved, because a typical web application may require several pipelines. The need for more than one pipeline stems from the idea that client requests may use several URL patterns. Each URL pattern may require its own customized processing and thus a different pipeline. For example, all of the URLs requesting HTML documents (URLs ending with .html) would pass through a certain pipeline, while all the requests ending with .xml would pass through another pipeline.

The Cocoon processing model must parse the input request to determine which pipeline should be assigned for processing. This is done by creating a sitemap. A *sitemap* is an XML-based configuration document that allows the creator to define several pipelines, one for each distinct URL pattern. This is achieved by creating *matchers* in the sitemap. A matcher matches the input URL pattern with a predefined filter pattern in the sitemap. Figure 7-4 depicts this processing model.

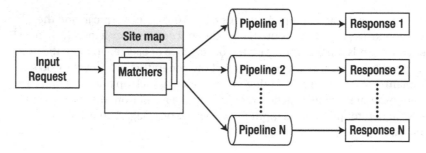

Figure 7-4. *Matching input requests for pipeline assignments*

The URL pattern in the input request is compared with each of the matchers in the sitemap until a match is found. Depending on the match result, the associated pipeline is assigned for processing the request. The response generated to the user depends on the processing pipeline used.

Thus far, we have covered the theory necessary to understand Cocoon's behavior. Before going further into implementation details, let's create our first Cocoon program.

Your First Cocoon Application

We will continue our case study of the stock brokerage from Chapter 2 and design a page for the brokerage. We will begin with the cover page for the confidential document generated by the brokerage. This page is same as the one first created in Chapter 6 (refer to Figure 6-5 for more information). We will use an XML input source that defines the structure for this page. We will then use an XSLT file to define the transformation of the input source into an HTML document. Finally, we will use the HTML serializer to serialize the generated HTML document to a browser, where the final output will be rendered. We will also need to create a sitemap that defines a pipeline consisting of these three components.

Creating the Input Source Document

The content provider decides on the page content. Suppose that the content provider decides that the cover page should contain the company name, the confidentiality statement, and the company logo. Thus, the content provider has to create a document structure that will provide the data for these three elements.

The structure of our cover page document that provides this data is given in Listing 7-1.

Listing 7-1. *Cover Page Document Structure* (Ch07\HTMLOutApp\coverpage.xml)

```xml
<?xml version="1.0"?>
<page>
  <CompanyName>
    Stock Brokerage
  </CompanyName>
  <Security>
    Confidential Report
  </Security>
  <Logo/>
</page>
```

The root element of this document is page. The page element has three subelements: CompanyName, Security, and Logo. The CompanyName element defines the company name, the Security element defines the confidentiality message, and the Logo element is a placeholder for the company logo. During the XSLT transformation, we will add to this placeholder the image tag that refers to the physical source of the image.

Note that nowhere does the content provider say what the output will look like, because this is of no concern to this team member. Rather, it is the page designer's job to decide how the output will look to the user.

Defining the Transformation

The next step is to define the transformation that converts the preceding XML document into an HTML document. Listing 7-2 shows how this transformation is performed.

Listing 7-2. *Transformation Document for Cover Page* (Ch07\HTMLOutApp\page2html.xsl)

```
<?xml version="1.0"?>

<xsl:stylesheet version="1.0" xmlns:xsl="http://www.w3.org/1999/XSL/Transform"
                              xmlns="http://www.w3.org/1999/xhtml">

  <xsl:template match="page">
    <html>
      <head>
        <title>
          <xsl:value-of select="CompanyName"/>
        </title>
      </head>
      <body>
        <xsl:apply-templates/>
      </body>
    </html>
  </xsl:template>

  <xsl:template match="CompanyName">
    <h1 align="center">
      <xsl:apply-templates/>
    </h1>
  </xsl:template>

  <xsl:template match="Security">
    <h2 align="center">
      <xsl:apply-templates/>
    </h2>
  </xsl:template>

  <xsl:template match="Logo">
    <p align="center">
      <img src="file:///ais.jpg" width="150" height="104"/>
    </p>
  </xsl:template>

</xsl:stylesheet>
```

You learned about XSL transformations in Chapter 5, so I will only briefly describe the XSL document in Listing 7-2. The transformation first looks for the root element of our cover page document and defines an HTML header and body structure. For the CompanyName and Security elements, we create the HTML headings with a center alignment. Last, for the Logo element, an img tag that specifies the JPG filename in its src attribute is created.

When the Cocoon engine applies this XSL transformation to the document source given in Listing 7-1, it will produce the desired HTML page.

Defining the Serializer

Though you can write your own serializer, Cocoon fortunately provides many classes that define serializers to standard output devices. Because we wish to render our cover page on a browser, we will use the provided HTML serializer. If you want to output the cover page as a PDF document, you use a different serializer. More on this later.

Creating a Sitemap

The last, but most important, part of our Cocoon application is to create a sitemap that defines the pipeline for processing the client requests. By default, the sitemap must be stored in a file named sitemap.xmap. However, you'll later learn how to change this default through the Cocoon configuration file. Listing 7-3 presents the sitemap definition.

Listing 7-3. *Sitemap for Cover Page Application* (Ch07\HTMLOutApp\sitemap.xmap)

```
<?xml version="1.0"?>

<map:sitemap xmlns:map="http://apache.org/cocoon/sitemap/1.0">

  <map:pipelines>
    <map:pipeline>

      <map:match pattern="coverpage.html">
        <map:generate src="coverpage.xml"/>
        <map:transform src="page2html.xsl"/>
        <map:serialize type="html"/>
      </map:match>

    </map:pipeline>
  </map:pipelines>
</map:sitemap>
```

The root element of the sitemap document is sitemap. We can define one or more pipelines within this sitemap element. In the current document, we create only one pipeline. The pipeline is defined by using the pipeline subelement within the pipelines element.

The input to the pipeline comes from a client request. We must match the client request to a particular pipeline. The pipeline element contains a subelement called match for this very purpose. The match subelement has an attribute called pattern that defines the URL pattern for matching with the input request. In our case, we define the pattern as coverpage.xml. Thus, if the client input request contains the URL pattern coverpage.xml, it is matched to the current pipeline and the request will be processed by the components defined in this pipeline.

The first component in the pipeline is a document generator. We use the src attribute to specify the source document to the generator. This is set to coverpage.xml. Thus, the generator reads the content of the coverpage.xml file and after parsing it, creates SAX events for the next component in the pipeline, that is, the transformer.

The transformer is defined by using the transform subelement. The source for the transformer is defined by using the src attribute. This is set to page2html.xsl. The input document will be transformed to HTML by using the transformation commands defined in this source file.

The last component in the pipeline is the serializer that is defined by using the serialize subelement. The type attribute defines the type of serializer. We use html as our type in the current example because the browser requires an HTML source.

The next task is to deploy this application and run it to examine the output.

Deploying and Running the Application

The deployment of our first Cocoon application is a simple XCOPY deployment process. If you are running Cocoon on Tomcat, create a folder structure called Ch07\HTMLOutApp in the webapps\cocoon\samples folder of your Tomcat installation. Copy the three files (Listings 7-1 through 7-3) created in the previous sections into the newly created HTMLOutApp folder.

Tip I recommend that you copy the entire Ch07 folder along with its subfolders into the webapps\cocoon\samples folder, following the same folder hierarchy as defined in the provided source. If you do not copy the entire source, you will need to copy at least the sitemap.xmap file from the Ch07 folder of the source download to the newly created Ch07 folder under the samples folder.

Now, run the application by typing the following URL in your browser:

http://localhost:8080/cocoon/samples/Ch07/HTMLOutApp/coverpage.html

When you open this URL in your browser, you will see the output as shown in Figure 7-5.

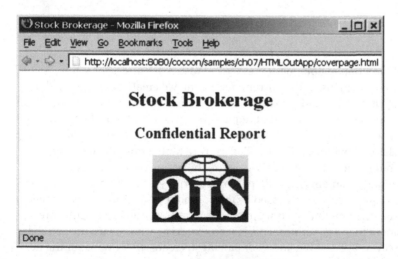

Figure 7-5. *Screen output of our first Cocoon application*

The Sitemap Document

Now that you have some hands-on experience creating a Cocoon application, you're ready to delve into the details of the sitemap that is the heart of the Cocoon framework.

The general structure of a sitemap is as follows:

```
<?xml version="1.0"?>
  <map:sitemap xmlns:map="http://apache.org/cocoon/sitemap/1.0">
    <map:components/>
    <map:views/>
    <map:resources/>
    <map:action-sets/>
    <map:pipelines/>
  </map:sitemap>
```

As seen in our first Cocoon application, a sitemap is an XML document that defines one or more pipelines for the web application. The root element of the sitemap document is sitemap. The various elements of the sitemap are defined in the namespace http://apache.org/cocoon/sitemap/1.0.

The sitemap contains various subelements, as shown in the preceding document structure. These subelements define the components, views, resources, actions, and pipelines. The purpose of each component is discussed throughout the rest of this section.

The components Element

The components element allows you to define components of different types that are then used in pipeline processing. You will generally create components if you want to reuse the same functionality in multiple pipelines. Under such situations, you create a component with a given name and reference it in a pipeline by using that assigned name.

All components have a few common attributes such as name and src. The name attribute specifies the component name that can be referenced later in the pipeline. The src attribute specifies the name of the .class file that implements this component. In our first application, we did not use the components element. You will use this element in later examples when you create components with given names and reuse them multiple times in your pipelines.

The views Element

The views element defines the exit point for the pipeline processing with the help of a view subelement. Every view is assigned a name. The user specifies the desired view by using this name on the command line while requesting a page. For example, the user may specify a view as shown here:

```
http://localhost:8080/cocoon/documents/broker.html?cocoon-view=fancyPage
```

In the preceding URL, the user is requesting the broker.html page from the specified path. The presentation made to the user is decided by the formatting defined in the fancyPage view. Each view in the sitemap defines the format in which a document is presented to the user; fancyPage is the name of the view that is defined in the views section of the sitemap.

The pipeline output undergoes the processing defined in the `fancyPage` view before the output is rendered on the device.

You can define one or more `view` elements within `views`, each defining a different output format to the user. Whatever is achieved with the view can also be achieved in the serializer component of the pipeline. However, defining views allows the user to select the format at runtime and does not require modifications to the sitemap. The user specifies the desired view on the command line at runtime to use it.

The resources Element

A sitemap can consist of many pipelines, and at the same time a given pipeline can be used multiple times in a document. The `resources` element allows you to create a name for a `pipeline` resource so that it can be used multiple times in a document without having to define it at every place where it is called. After you define a resource with a given name, you call the resource by using the `call` subelement within a pipeline. This is illustrated in Listing 7-4.

Listing 7-4. *Defining and Using Resources in a Sitemap*

```
<?xml version="1.0"?>
<map:sitemap xmlns:map="http://apache.org/cocoon/sitemap/1.0">
  <map:resources>

    <map:resource name="pipeline1" >
      <map:generate ... />
      <map:transform ... />
      <map:serialize ... />
    </map:resource>

    <map:resource name="pipeline2" >
      <map:generate ... />
      <map:transform ... />
      <map:serialize ... />
    </map:resource>

  </map:resources>

  <map:pipeline>

    <map:match pattern="default-processing/*/*">
      <map:call resource="pipeline1">
        ...
      </map:call>
    </map:match>
```

```
      <map:match pattern="custom-processing/*" >
        <map:call resource="pipeline2">
          ...
        </map:call>
      </map:match>
    </map:pipeline>
```

```
</map:sitemap>
```

In Listing 7-4, we create two pipelines, pipeline1 and pipeline2, by using the resource element. These resources are then called after the pattern matching is done in the match element. You can call the same pipeline for different patterns.

The first match in Listing 7-4 uses the pattern /*/*, indicating that any URL pattern such as /myfolder/mypage.html will be matched. The first * indicates a match between the two forward slashes, and the second * indicates a match after the last forward slash in the URL. The second match uses the pattern /*, indicating that anything after the last slash in the URL is selected. We use the default matching when no other match is found.

When a resource element is created, it need not contain all three components of a pipeline. For example, you can create a resource that contains only the generator component. When you define the pipeline, you can call this resource to incorporate the generator component and then use other transformer and serializer components of your own. This is illustrated in Listing 7-5.

Listing 7-5. *Creating and Using a Resource with the* generate *Component*

```
<?xml version="1.0"?>
  <map:sitemap xmlns:map="http://apache.org/cocoon/sitemap/1.0">
  <map:resources>

    <map:resource name="pipeline1" >
      <map:generate ...="" />
    </map:resource>

  </map:resources>

  <map:pipeline>

    <map:match pattern="default-processing/*/*">
      <map:call resource="pipeline1">
        ...
      </map:call>
      <map:serialize ...="" />
    </map:match>
```

```
    <map:match pattern="custom-processing/*" >
      <map:call resource="pipeline1">
        ...
      </map:call>
      <map:transform ...="" />
      <map:serialize ...="" />
    </map:match>
  </map:pipeline>

</map:sitemap>
```

Listing 7-5 defines a resource called pipeline1 that contains only one component of generator type:

```
<map:resource name="pipeline1" >
  <map:generate ...="" />
</map:resource>
```

The ellipsis (...) in the generate element will specify the name of the .class file used by the generator component. We use this resource whenever we want this generator for creating the content for our pipeline.

In Listing 7-5, we call this pipeline1 resource in two different pipelines. The first pipeline after calling this generator resource provides only the serialization, as shown here:

```
<map:call resource="pipeline1">
    ...
</map:call>
<map:serialize ...="" />
```

Note that we invoke this pipeline for default processing. For custom processing, we define another pipeline that calls the pipeline1 resource to generate the content and then performs a transformation before serializing the content to the output device, as shown here:

```
<map:call resource="pipeline1">
    ...
</map:call>
<map:transform ...="" />
<map:serialize ...="" />
```

The actions Element

So far, you have seen that a pipeline has an orderly set of components. These components are invoked in the order in which they are listed in the pipeline. What if you want to change the processing order depending on the output results of the intermediate processing? The actions element allows you to do this. Depending on the runtime results of a processed component, you can initiate a different action in the pipeline. Not only this, but actions can also be used to control the pipeline flow depending on the parameter values in the input request.

Defining actions in your sitemap is easy. The following code snippet shows how to define actions:

```
<map:actions>
  <map:action name="DoShopping" src="shopping.ShoppingAction"/>
  <map:action name="CommitCart" src="shopping.CommitAction"/>
  <map:action name="AbortCart" src="shopping.AbortAction"/>
  <map:action name="ValidateCart" src="shopping.ValidateAction"/>
</map:actions>
```

Here we have defined four actions for shopping, committing, aborting, and validating a shopping cart. Note that ShoppingAction, CommitAction, AbortAction, and ValidateAction actions are the Java classes that you must create, and you must make the corresponding .class files available to Cocoon at runtime. These action classes extend from the provided AbstractAction class. This class provides an abstract method called act that has access to the input request object. The class returns a Map object to the caller. It can also set parameters to be used as request parameters by the next action.

You call the action with the following code snippet:

```
<input type="submit" name="cocoon-action-ACTIONNAME" value="DoShopping">
```

This results in calling the implementation in the ShoppingAction class. This class may return a null or a valid Map object. If it returns a null, all other actions enclosed within the currently called action will be discarded. Depending on the result of the DoShopping action, you will call different components in your pipeline and invoke further actions such as CommitAction, AbortAction, and ValidateAction depending on your application logic.

It is also possible to define an action set in your sitemap with the help of the action-set element. The action set defines more than one action, which are called in the sequence they are defined.

Finally, we come to the most important element of the sitemap: the pipelines element.

The pipelines Element

A pipelines element can define one or more pipelines for processing. Each pipeline is defined by using a pipeline element. A pipeline element has several subelements. Out of these, the most frequently used element is match.

Within a pipeline, you can provide one or more match elements. Each match element specifies a URL pattern that is matched to the client request. Within a match, you define the pipeline with the help of generate, transform, and serialize elements in this order. The generate element specifies the source document. Note that this source need not have any resemblance to the URL pattern defined in the match, although it could be the same. For example, the URL pattern could be index.html, and the source document used by the generator could also be index.html. Alternatively, the URL pattern could be simply a wildcard such as *, and the input source could be welcome.html. In general, these two attribute values need not be the same as each other.

The generator output is fed to a transformer component as SAX events. The transformer is defined by using the transform element. The src attribute specifies the transformation document (XSLT) to be used for transformation.

Finally, the `serialize` element specifies the serializer component that transforms the SAX events into a stream of characters or binary digits for the final consumption of the output device.

Listing 7-6 shows a typical pipelines structure.

Listing 7-6. *The* `pipelines` *Element Structure (*Ch07\HTMLOutApp\sitemap.xmap*)*

```
<map:pipelines>
  <map:pipeline>
    <map:match pattern="coverpage.html">
      <map:generate src="coverpage.xml"/>
      <map:transform src="page2html.xsl"/>
      <map:serialize type="html"/>
    </map:match>
  </map:pipeline>
</map:pipelines>
```

As seen in Listing 7-6, whenever the URL request pattern contains `coverpage.html`, the pipeline defined here will be applied. The pipeline uses `coverpage.xml` as a source document that must exist on the server. This source is transformed into another format, in this case to HTML as the name suggests, by using the `page2html.xsl` transformation document. The output HTML document is then serialized into a character stream by the serializer component of type `html`. This component is implemented as a Java file that receives the SAX events from the previous component (that is, the transformer) and writes the document content into a character stream.

Besides these frequently used elements, the `pipeline` element contains many child elements such as `call` and `act`, which we have used earlier. The `pipeline` has other elements, including `select`, `when`, `redirect-to`, `aggregate`, and `handle-errors`. I will not cover the use of each of these elements in this text; refer to the Cocoon documentation for details.

Modifying Pipelines

In this section, you will study more programming examples to further understand pipeline processing and the creation of sitemaps. We will modify the sitemap used in our first Cocoon application so you can see how easy it is to alter pipeline processing to achieve different output. In our first application, we started out with an XML document created by the server and transformed it into an HTML document to be output on a browser. We will now render this document in different formats by modifying our pipeline.

Generating Text Output

The Cocoon library provides a special serializer to transform the document into text format. This serializer is called `text`.

Note Every serializer has an associated Java class.

To use this serializer in the serialize element of your pipeline, set the type attribute value to text. This is illustrated in the following code snippet:

```
<map:match pattern="coverpage.txt">
  <map:generate src="coverpage.xml"/>
  <map:serialize type="text"/>
</map:match>
```

Note that the matching pattern is set to coverpage.txt. If you examine the source code that is available in the downloaded file for this book, you will notice that there is no file called coverpage.txt provided. Similarly, you would not have found any file called coverpage.html used in our first application in the downloaded source. This is simply a URL context that is used for selecting the desired pipeline. This can be any text string, although we generally use explicit extensions such as .html or .txt so that the user knows what to expect in the output.

The generate element uses the same source document, coverpage.xml, as in the first application case. We do not provide any transformation in the current pipeline. Thus, the SAX events produced by the generator will be fed into the serializer, which is the next component in the pipeline. The serializer component is the text type. This component transforms the SAX input events into a stream of text.

To invoke this pipeline, you use the following URL:

```
http://localhost:8080/cocoon/samples/Ch07/TextOutApp/coverpage.txt
```

The output produced by this URL is shown in Figure 7-6. Note that the text output does not contain an image. Images are automatically removed if you render the output to text format.

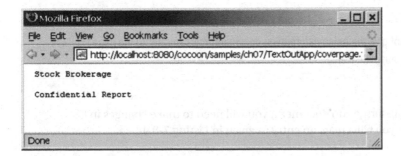

Figure 7-6. *Text output generated by the pipeline*

Generating PDF Output

To generate the PDF document from the XML source, you will need to create a transformation file that converts the XML document to an FO[1] tree. The FO tree will then be transformed into a PDF document by using the fo2pdf serializer. You learned how to convert an FO tree into a PDF document in Chapter 6. First, we will write a transformation that converts the source XML document into an FO document.

---

1. FOs (formatting objects) are covered in Chapter 6.

Transforming XML to FO

The code snippet in Listing 7-7 shows how the given XML document is transformed into FO commands.

Listing 7-7. *Code Snippet for XML-to-FO Transformation* (Ch07\PDFOutApp\page2fo.xsl)

```
<xsl:template match="CompanyName">
  <fo:block font-size="36pt" space-before.optimum="24pt" text-align="center">
    <xsl:apply-templates/>
  </fo:block>
</xsl:template>

<xsl:template match="Security">
  <fo:block font-size="12pt" space-before.optimum="12pt" text-align="center">
    <xsl:apply-templates/>
  </fo:block>
</xsl:template>

<xsl:template match="Logo">
  <fo:block space-before.optimum="12pt" text-align="center">
    <fo:external-graphic src="url(file:///ais.jpg"/>
    <xsl:apply-templates/>
  </fo:block>
</xsl:template>
```

■**Note** Listing 7-7 does not give the full transformation document. You can refer to the page2fo.xsl file in the download for the complete listing.

After writing the transformation document, you will need to make changes in the sitemap. In the sitemap, you will create an entry as given in Listing 7-8.)

Listing 7-8. *The Match Entry in the Sitemap for PDF Conversion* (Ch07\PDFOutApp\sitemap.xmap)

```
<map:match pattern="coverpage.pdf">
  <map:generate src="coverpage.xml"/>
  <map:transform src="page2fo.xsl"/>
  <map:serialize type="xml"/>
</map:match>
```

Here we define the match pattern as coverpage.pdf. Thus, when the user types this pattern as part of the request URL, he will see the input source document displayed in PDF format (initially we will output the intermediate XSL-FO document). The generator source is the same as in the earlier examples: coverpage.xml. The transformation is now performed by using the page2fo.xsl transformation file. The serializer is specified as xml. Thus, the output of this match operation would result in an XML document that is the FO document created from the input source coverpage.xml.

■Note You will first examine the generated FO document in your browser and later modify the serializer to output it as PDF.

After adding the preceding match entry in your sitemap, open the following URL in your browser:

```
http://localhost:8080/cocoon/samples/Ch07/PDFOutApp/coverpage.pdf
```

■Note Do not forget to make appropriate adjustments to the port number in the preceding URL for your installation.

When you open the preceding URL, you will see the document shown in Listing 7-9 in your browser.

Listing 7-9. *XSL-FO Document Created by Transformer (Ch07\PDFOutApp\page2fo.xsl)*

```
<?xml version="1.0" encoding="iso-8859-1" ?>
<fo:root xmlns:fo="http://www.w3.org/1999/XSL/Format">
  <fo:layout-master-set>
    <fo:simple-page-master margin-right="2.5cm" margin-left="2.5cm"
                           margin-bottom="2cm" margin-top="1cm"
                           page-width="21cm" page-height="29.7cm"
                           master-name="page">
      <fo:region-before extent="3cm" />
      <fo:region-body margin-top="3cm" />
      <fo:region-after extent="1.5cm" />
    </fo:simple-page-master>
    <fo:page-sequence-master master-name="all">
      <fo:repeatable-page-master-alternatives>
        <fo:conditional-page-master-reference page-position="first"
                                              master-reference="page" />
      </fo:repeatable-page-master-alternatives>
    </fo:page-sequence-master>
  </fo:layout-master-set>
  <fo:page-sequence master-reference="all">
    <fo:static-content flow-name="xsl-region-after">
      <fo:block line-height="14pt" font-family="serif"
                font-size="10pt" text-align="center">
```

```
        page
      <fo:page-number />
    </fo:block>
  </fo:static-content>
  <fo:flow flow-name="xsl-region-body">
    <fo:block text-align="center" space-before.optimum="24pt"
            font-size="36pt">Stock Brokerage</fo:block>
    <fo:block text-align="center" space-before.optimum="12pt"
            font-size="12pt">Confidential Report</fo:block>
    <fo:block text-align="center" space-before.optimum="12pt">
      <fo:external-graphic src="url(file:///C:/ais.jpg)" />
    </fo:block>
  </fo:flow>
</fo:page-sequence>
</fo:root>
```

This is the XSL-FO document created by the transformer component in our pipeline.

Transformations to PDF

We need to transform this further into a PDF. We do this by applying another transformation. Listing 7-10 shows these transformations.

Listing 7-10. *Pipelines for Converting FO Document to PDF* (Ch07\PDFOutApp\sitemap.xmap)

```
<map:match pattern="coverpage.pdf">
  <map:generate src="coverpage.xml"/>
  <map:transform src="page2fo.xsl"/>
  <map:serialize type="fo2pdf"/>
</map:match>
```

The serializer component is now fo2pdf, which is a Cocoon-supplied class that transforms FO document SAX events into a stream object used by a PDF reader. When you open the PDF URL (http://localhost:8080/cocoon/samples/Ch07/PDFOutApp/coverpage.pdf) listed earlier, you will see the PDF document as shown in Figure 7-7.

Figure 7-7. *PDF transformation output*

Generating Output in Other Formats

So far we have converted our input source document in HTML, text, PDF, and of course XML formats.

Note You can output in XML format by changing the `type` attribute of `serialize` to `xml`, just the way it was done for producing the XSL-FO document in the previous example.

To change the output format, you simply need to change the serializer in the pipeline. If the new serializer expects the input in a specific XML format, you need to provide an appropriate transformer in the pipeline. Changing the transformer requires writing an XSLT document to provide the desired transformation. The Cocoon samples provide examples of several such transformations.

Tip Refer to the `<Tomcat installation folder>\webapps\cocoon\samples\hello-world\style\xsl` folder for the list of transformation files.

The Cocoon Hello World example (`http://localhost:8080/cocoon/samples/hello-world/`) illustrates how to convert the input source document into XHTML, WML, CHTML, VoiceML, Zip Archive, RTF, XLS, and many other formats. Figure 7-8 shows the screen output of the Hello World application that is supplied as a part of Apache sample applications.

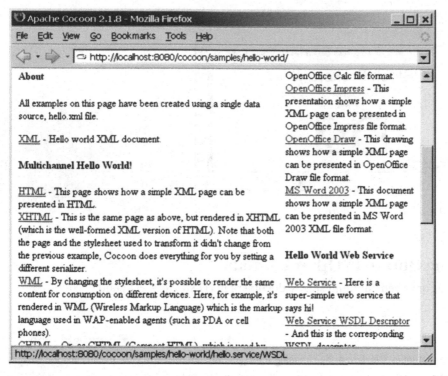

Figure 7-8. *Screen output of Apache Hello World sample application*

Clicking a link option shown on the screen (see Figure 7-8) renders the input document into that specified format.

The Transformers in Cocoon

You probably agree that the transformer is the most important component in the Cocoon pipeline. The transformers are placed between the generator and the serializer in the pipeline. You can place any number of transformers in a pipeline. The input message passes through each transformer in the order in which they are defined. Each transformer is associated with a Java class.

Cocoon provides several transformer classes ready for your use. A few are listed here:

- xslt: The default transformer

- i18n: Used for internationalization and localization

- log: Used for logging and debugging

- sql: Used for querying a database and translating the result to XML

- filter: Used for filtering the number of elements that can pass through a given block

There are many more transformers defined in the Cocoon framework. You can find further details in the Cocoon's user guide (`http://cocoon.apache.org/2.1/userdocs/transformers.html`).

I will now discuss one more application that uses one of these predefined transformers.

The i18n Transformer

The i18n transformer is useful for customizing your site for different countries and locales. In the example program, I will demonstrate how to format date, time, currency, and number in different locales. Our stock brokerage can use this feature while doing business with international clients.

First we will discuss the sitemap for this page.

The Sitemap for i18n

Listing 7-11 shows the sitemap used for our i18n page.

Listing 7-11. *The Sitemap for the i18n Application* (Ch07\i18n\sitemap.xmap)

```xml
<?xml version="1.0"?>

<map:sitemap xmlns:map="http://apache.org/cocoon/sitemap/1.0">

  <map:components>
    <map:generators default="file">
      <map:generator name="file"
        src="org.apache.cocoon.generation.FileGenerator"
        logger="sitemap.generator.file"/>
    </map:generators>
    <map:transformers default="xslt">
      <!-- Configure i18n transformer -->
      <map:transformer name="i18n"
        src="org.apache.cocoon.transformation.I18nTransformer">
        <catalogs default="messages">
          <catalog id="messages" name="messages" location="translations"/>
        </catalogs>
        <cache-at-startup>true</cache-at-startup>
      </map:transformer>
    </map:transformers>
  </map:components>

  <map:pipelines>
    <map:pipeline>
```

```
<map:match pattern="i18ntest.html">
  <map:generate src="i18ntest.xml"/>
  <map:transform type="i18n"/>
  <map:serialize type="html"/>
</map:match>
```

```
    </map:pipeline>
  </map:pipelines>
</map:sitemap>
```

The sitemap first defines the components for i18n transformation. The components are declared in the components element. We create two types of components here, a generator and a transformer. The generator is created by using the generator element:

```
<map:generators default="file">
  <map:generator name="file"
    src="org.apache.cocoon.generation.FileGenerator"
    logger="sitemap.generator.file"/>
</map:generators>
```

We create only one generator, which is named file. The src attribute defines the name of the .class file that is used by the generator. The logger attribute specifies the log file to be used for logging the errors and the output during the generation process. The default attribute for the generators element specifies the default generator to be used, if the pipeline does not specify any generator.

After defining generators, we define transformers. The transformers are specified in the transformers element. You can define one or more transformers under this element by using the transformer element for each. The default transformer is specified by using the default attribute of the transformers element:

```
<map:transformers default="xslt">
```

The transformer for i18n is declared by creating a transformer entry:

```
<!-- Configure i18n transformer -->
<map:transformer name="i18n"
  src="org.apache.cocoon.transformation.I18nTransformer">
```

The transformer is assigned the name i18n. We will use this name in our pipeline to call this transformer. The src attribute specifies the name of the .class file that is provided by Cocoon. A transformer requires one or more catalog elements specified by the catalogs tag.

```
<catalogs default="messages">
  <catalog id="messages" name="messages" location="translations"/>
</catalogs>
```

The default catalog is specified by using the default attribute of the catalogs element. The catalog itself has a unique id in the current context, a unique name, and the location of the catalog file that contains the language translations to be used for each defined key. You can cache all the catalogs at start-up by including the following line fragment:

```
<cache-at-startup>true</cache-at-startup>
```

The catalogs contain the equivalent text strings in different languages. Because we are not performing any text translations in our example, we will not use catalogs; however, the presence of the catalog element is mandatory. After the components are defined, we define the pipelines. We define only one pipeline in the current example that matches the pattern i18ntest.html in the request URL:

```
<map:pipeline>
  <map:match pattern="i18ntest.html">
    <map:generate src="i18ntest.xml"/>
    <map:transform type="i18n"/>
    <map:serialize type="html"/>
  </map:match>
</map:pipeline>
```

If a match is found, we use the source document specified as i18ntest.xml. The file is transformed by the i18n component defined in the components section. The pipeline serializes the output of transformation to HTML format.

We will now examine the i18ntest.xml test document.

The i18n Test Document

The XML input document that is used for testing internationalization features is given in Listing 7-12.

Listing 7-12. *The i18n Test Document (*Ch07\i18n\i18ntest.xml*)*

```
<?xml version="1.0" encoding="utf-8" ?>
<page xmlns:i18n="http://apache.org/cocoon/i18n/2.1">
  <para>
    <h3>Date in different formats</h3>
    <i18n:date-time pattern="short" locale="en_US"/>
    <br/>
    <i18n:date-time pattern="medium" locale="en_US"/>
    <br/>
    <i18n:date-time pattern="long" locale="en_US"/>
    <br/>
    <i18n:date-time pattern="FULL" locale="en_US"/>
    <br/>
    <h3>Different Locales</h3>
    US Full Date:
    <i18n:date-time pattern="FULL" locale="en_US"/><br/>
    German Full Date:
    <i18n:date-time pattern="FULL" locale="de_DE"/><br/>
    India Full Date:
    <i18n:date-time pattern="FULL" locale="hi_IN"/><br/>
    Japan Full Date:
    <i18n:date-time pattern="FULL" locale="ja_JP"/><br/>
    China Full Date:
    <i18n:date-time pattern="FULL" locale="zh_CN"/><br/><br/>
```

```
US Currency:
<i18n:number type="currency" value="2501.9845"/><br/>
German Currency:
<i18n:number type="currency" currency="de_DE" value="2501.9845"/><br/>
Indian Currency:
<i18n:number type="currency" currency="hi_IN" value="2501.9845"/><br/>
Japan Currency:
<i18n:number type="currency" currency="ja_JP" value="2501.9845"/><br/>
China Currency:
<i18n:number type="currency" currency="zh_CN" value="2501.9845"/><br/><br/>

US Number:
<i18n:number locale="en_US" value="10000000"/><br/>
German Number:
<i18n:number locale="de_DE" value="10000000"/><br/>
France Number:
<i18n:number locale="fr_FR" value="10000000"/><br/>
```

```
  </para>
</page>
```

The document first declares the namespace required for internationalization support:

```
<page xmlns:i18n="http://apache.org/cocoon/i18n/2.1">
```

We will print the current date and time in different formats by using the US English locale. The current date and time is printed by using the date-time element:

```
<i18n:date-time pattern="short" locale="en_US"/>
```

The locale attribute specifies the locale to be used while outputting the date. We will change this locale in the subsequent statements to see its effect. The pattern attribute defines several predefined values such as short, medium, long, and full. Additionally, you can also create your own patterns.

Next, we change the locale value as follows:

```
German Full Date:
<i18n:date-time pattern="FULL" locale="de_DE"/><br/>
India Full Date:
<i18n:date-time pattern="FULL" locale="hi_IN"/><br/>
```

This will print the current date and time in the full format, using German and Indian formats. The program similarly outputs the date and time in Japanese and Chinese formats.

Next, we print the currency in different formats specific to different locales:

```
US Currency:
<i18n:number type="currency" value="2501.9845"/><br/>
German Currency:
<i18n:number type="currency" currency="de_DE" value="2501.9845"/><br/>
```

This will print the number 2501.9845 in the currency format for the specified locale. Finally, we will print a large number in different locales by using the number element as follows:

```
US Number:
<i18n:number locale="en_US" value="10000000"/><br/>
German Number:
<i18n:number locale="de_DE" value="10000000"/><br/>
France Number:
<i18n:number locale="fr_FR" value="10000000"/><br/>
```

Page Output

If you open the i18n page given in Listing 7-12 with the URL http://localhost:8080/cocoon/ samples/Ch07/i18n/i18ntest.html, you will see the output as shown in Figure 7-9.

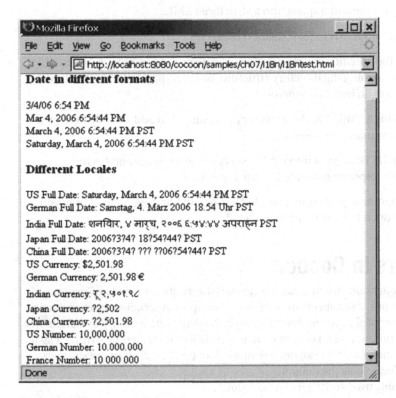

Figure 7-9. *The output of the i18n page*

From this example, you can understand how easy it is to extend the internationalization support to your website created by using Cocoon. Cocoon provides many useful transformers. It is beyond the scope of this book to cover all of the predefined transformers, but you can go through the online documentation for further details.

The Generators in Cocoon

As seen earlier, the generator is the starting component in a Cocoon pipeline. Every pipeline containing a generator must terminate with a serializer. A generator reads the input source document and generates the SAX events for the next component in the pipeline. You write a generator by creating a Java class that reads the input document, parses it, and generates the SAX events for consumption by the next component in the pipeline.

A generator is declared in the sitemap by using the generate element. A generator may take additional configuration information from the child elements of this generate tag. The generate element is a subelement of the generators element. You must declare one of the generators as the default in the generators element.

Cocoon provides several generators, including the following:

- file: Reads the input document from the local file system or any URL.

- request: Converts the current request into a structured XML.

- stream: Reads input from HTTPRequest InputStream.

- directory: Reads the specified source directory structure and generates a structured XML document containing the directory structure. You can specify the depth of the directory structure as an input parameter.

- xpathdirectory: This is similar to the directory generator, but additionally performs XPath queries on the input document.

- jsp: This feeds the HTTP request into the JSP servlet engine and generates the SAX events from the JSP response generated by the JSP engine.

There are several important generators provided in Cocoon libraries. Again, I urge you to go through the online documentation for more details.

The Serializers in Cocoon

Like transformers and generators, many ready-to-use serializers are provided in Cocoon. We have used different types of serializers in our earlier examples. A serializer is an end point of a Cocoon pipeline. A serializer transforms the input SAX events into a binary or a character stream for the final consumption of an output device. A serializer is created by writing a Java class to perform this serialization. You can declare more than one serializer in the sitemap. One serializer must be declared as the default.

Some of the commonly used serializers are as follows:

- *HTML*: This is the default serializer that serializes XML to HTML.

- *XML*: This is the simplest possible serializer because it simply serializes input SAX events generated from an XML source into another XML document format. This can be used for outputting to any of the XML formats such as SVG, VRML, and so on.

- *Text*: This serializes XML to plain text.

- *WML*: This serializes XML to WML (Wireless Markup Language).

- *PDF*: This takes SAX events generated from an XSL-FO document as input and generates a PDF output stream using FOP.[2]

- *SVG*: This is one of the advanced serializers that accepts input from an SVG document, encodes the SVG image as an image file using Batik's[3] transcoder, and renders the output like any other component in Cocoon. For example, the client may request a JPG image in its URL request. The source for this JPG may be an SVG image. The SVG image will then be transcoded into a JPG image and served to the client.

There are many useful serializers provided in Cocoon. Again, you can read the online documentation for further details.

Having seen the various transformers, generators, and serializers provided in Cocoon, we will now revisit the sitemap structure to discuss its components element in more detail.

The Sitemap Components

As you have already seen, a sitemap can contain one or more pipelines. A pipeline consists of components. Such components can be declared at the time of their use or prior to their use. Components are declared prior to their use by using the components element. A component, once created, can be used multiple times in the sitemap. In this section, you'll take a look at the sitemap's components element and then some of its subelements.

The components Element

The components element has following subelements:

```
<map:components>
   <map:generators/>
   <map:transformers/>
   <map:serializers/>
   <map:readers/>
   <map:selectors/>
   <map:matchers/>
   <map:actions/>
   <map:pipelines/>
</map:components>
```

As can be seen from the list, the components element allows you to define components of several types, which are then used in pipeline processing. All the components have a few common attributes such as name and src. The name attribute specifies the component's name, with which the component can be referenced later in the pipeline. The src attribute specifies the name of the .class file that implements this component.

---

2. FOP is covered in Chapter 6.

3. For details on the Batik project, refer to the Apache site: http://xml.apache.org/batik/.

The generators Element

As seen earlier, the generator is the first component in the Cocoon pipeline. The generator reads the input source document and generates the SAX events for the next component in the pipeline. A typical generators entry is shown in Listing 7-13.

Listing 7-13. *A Typical* generators *Entry*

```
<map:generators default="file">
  <map:generator name="file"
    src="org.apache.cocoon.generation.FileGenerator"/>
  <map:generator name="serverpages"
    src="org.apache.cocoon.generation.ServerPagesGenerator">
  <map:generator name="dir"
    src="DirectoryGenerator"/>

    ...

  </map:generator>
</map:generators>
```

A generators element defines one or more generator elements. Each generator specifies a different source of input. Listing 7-13 defines three such generators. The first generator is called file and uses the Cocoon-supplied FileGenerator as its input class. The second generator is called serverpages and uses the supplied ServerPagesGenerator class as its source. The third generator is called dir and uses a custom-defined class called DirectoryGenerator as its input source class. Note that it is your responsibility to provide the class definition and the fully qualified name for the .class file in the src attribute.

The generators element has a default attribute. The value of this attribute specifies the generator to use if none is specified in the pipeline definition.

The transformers Element

The next element in the components element is the transformers element. The transformers element defines a transformer component. The transformer component takes its input from the generator component as SAX events. After performing the transformations on the input source, the transformer then generates another set of SAX events for the next component in the pipeline. A typical transformers entry is shown in Listing 7-14.

Listing 7-14. *A Typical* transformers *Entry*

```
<map:transformers default="xslt">
  <map:transformer name="xslt"
    src="org.apache.cocoon.transformation.TraxTransformer">
  <map:transformer name="xinclude"
    src="org.apache.cocoon.transformation.XIncludeTransformer"/>
</map:transformers>
```

You can define one or more transformer components under the transformers element. In the example given in Listing 7-14, we create two transformer components. The first one is called xslt, and the second one is named xinclude. For each of these components, we define the src class. In both cases, the source class is provided by Cocoon. You can also create your own transformer classes.

The serializers Element

The serializers element defines the last component in the Cocoon pipeline. As seen earlier, the Cocoon libraries provide several predefined serializers for your ready use. The serializer component receives the SAX events from the previous component in the pipeline and transforms them into a stream for the final consumption of the output device. A typical serializers entry is shown in Listing 7-15.

Listing 7-15. *A Typical* serializers *Entry*

```
<map:serializers default="html">
  <map:serializer name="html" mime-type="text/html"
      src="org.apache.cocoon.serialization.HTMLSerializer"/>
  <map:serializer name="wap" mime-type="text/vnd.wap.wml"
      src="org.apache.cocoon.serialization.XMLSerializer"/>
  <map:serializer name="svg2jpeg" mime-type="image/jpeg"
      src="org.apache.cocoon.serialization.SVGSerializer"/>
  <map:serializer name="svg2png" mime-type="image/png"
      src="org.apache.cocoon.serialization.SVGSerializer"/>
</map:serializers>
```

The serializers element can contain definitions for one or more serializer components. Listing 7-15 defines four serializer elements. For each one, the mime-type is set to the appropriate value for the output device. The src attribute, as in earlier cases, defines the class to be used for converting the SAX events into a stream.

The selectors Element

The selectors element defines one or more selector components. A selector component allows you to implement conditional logic in your sitemap. It evaluates an expression and returns a boolean value. A typical selectors map entry is shown in Listing 7-16.

Listing 7-16. *A Typical* selectors *Entry*

```
<map:selectors default="browser">
  <map:selector name="media"
    src="org.apache.cocoon.selection.MediaSelector">
    ...
  </map:selector>
  <map:selector name="browser"
    src="org.apache.cocoon.selection.BrowserSelector">
    ...
  </map:selection>
  <map:selector name="mail"
    src="org.apache.cocoon.selection.MailCommandSelector">
```

```
    ...
  </map:selector>
</map:selectors>
```

In Listing 7-16, we have created three selectors. Each one uses the built-in classes for selection. For example, the `BrowserSelector` selects the browser, and the `MediaSelector` selects the media. All the selector classes internally implement the `Selector` interface. The `Selector` interface defines a `select` method that accepts `expression` as one of the parameters. The method signals a `boolean` depending on the result of expression evaluation.

The matchers Element

A `matchers` element defines a class that is used for matching the URL pattern against the client request. On a successful match, it returns a `Map` object; otherwise, it returns a `null`. The pattern itself can consist of wildcards or regular expressions. On success of the match operation, the wildcards or regular expressions in the pattern will be replaced with the values in the input request. The Cocoon libraries provide several predefined classes for pattern matching. Listing 7-17 shows a typical `matchers` entry in the sitemap.

Listing 7-17. *A Typical* matchers *Entry*

```
<map:matchers default="wildcard">
  <map:matcher name="wildcard"
    src="org.apache.cocoon.matching.WildcardURIMatcher">
      ...
  </map:matcher>
  <map:matcher name="regexp"
    src="org.apache.cocoon.matching.RegexpURIMatcher">
      ...
  </map:matcher>
  <map:matcher name="local"
    src="org.apache.cocoon.matching.LocaleMatcher">
      ...
  </map:matcher>
  <map:matcher name="requestParameter"
    src="org.apache.cocoon.matching.RequestParamMatcher">
      ...
  </map:matcher>
</map:matchers>
```

The `matchers` element in Listing 7-17 defines four matchers. The source class for each matcher is specified by its `src` attribute. Every matcher class implements the `Matcher` interface. The interface declares a method called `match` that takes a string pattern as one of the parameters.

Having discussed the architecture and the various components used in the pipeline, now we will turn our attention to another important aspect in the Cocoon framework. So far, all our Cocoon applications use static page content. You will now study how to generate dynamic XML content.

XML Server Pages

XML Server Pages, also known as XSP, is a Cocoon technology for generating dynamic XML content. The XML documents thus created are fed into the Cocoon pipeline for further transformation and presentation to the client. The data for these dynamic XML pages can come from various sources, such as databases, URLs, flat files, and more. XSP allows you to manipulate data before the output document is created. Thus, it contains programming logic that is written in Java for data retrieval and manipulations.

In this section, you will learn about the structure of an XSP document and how to process these documents. You will create a web page by using XSP for our brokerage site and will learn how XSP is internally processed. Finally, you will learn about Logicsheets.

Understanding the XSP Document Structure

The general structure of the XSP document is shown in Listing 7-18.

Listing 7-18. *General Structure of XSP Document*

```
<?xml version="1.0" encoding="utf-8" ?>
<xsp:page language="java" xmlns:xsp="http://apache.org/xsp">
  <xsp:structure>
    <xsp:include> ... </xsp:include>
    <xsp:include> ... </xsp:include>
    ...
  </xsp:structure>
  <document>
    <xsp:logic>
      ...
    </xsp:logic>
    <xsp:logic>
      ...
    </xsp:logic>
    ...
    <!-- other elements -->
  </document>
</xsp:page>
```

Being an XML document, the XSP starts with an XML declaration. The root element is called page. The language attribute sets the programming language. The current implementation that we are using in this chapter uses the Java language. Other implementations of XSP can use other programming languages. The page contains zero or more structure elements and any number of logic elements. Besides these, a page can contain a single user element that is not relevant to us in the current context.

An XSP page can contain Java logic code. This is put in one or more logic elements. Java code may require importing some Java packages. Such imports are put in structure/include elements.

Processing XSP Documents

For processing XSP documents, Cocoon provides a generator class called
ServerPagesGenerator. We will need to specify this class in our sitemap as a generator component in our pipeline. Our generators entry in the sitemap will look like the following:

```
<map:generators default="file">
  <map:generator name="xsp"
                 src="org.apache.cocoon.generation.ServerPagesGenerator"/>
</map:generators>
```

After the generator processes the input document, it will undergo further transformations
as defined by the rest of the components in the pipeline.

Creating a Web Page for Live Data Feed

We will now develop a simple web page for our stock brokerage that provides the live data
for the client-requested stock. We will create this web page based on XSP technology that
accepts the stock symbol on the command line as a parameter. The XSP will retrieve this
parameter, obtain the live data for the requested stock symbol, and generate an XML document for the next component in the pipeline. We will not be implementing the retrieval of
live data; instead, we will have a placeholder in our Java code where later on you can plug
in the Java code for retrieving live data from an external resource.

We will begin by writing the sitemap for our web page.

Writing the Sitemap for Processing XSP

Listing 7-19 shows the required sitemap content.

Listing 7-19. *The Sitemap for Processing XSP* (Ch07\XSP\sitemap.xmap)

```
<?xml version="1.0"?>

<map:sitemap xmlns:map="http://apache.org/cocoon/sitemap/1.0">
  <map:components>
    <map:generators default="file">
      <map:generator name="xsp"
                     src="org.apache.cocoon.generation.ServerPagesGenerator"/>
    </map:generators>
  </map:components>

  <map:pipelines>
    <map:pipeline>
      <map:match pattern="StockQuote.xsp">
        <map:generate type="xsp" src="StockQuote.xsp"/>
        <map:serialize type="xml"/>
      </map:match>
    </map:pipeline>
  </map:pipelines>
</map:sitemap>
```

We define a generator called xsp. The src attribute of this generator is set to the ServerPagesGenerator class. This generator will read the input document along with the parameter on the input request and process the document to produce a series of SAX events for the next component in the pipeline.

The sitemap defines only one pipeline that looks for the StockQuote.xsp URL pattern in the input request. It uses the xsp generator to process the specified XSP document. Without transforming the output further, it serializes the output by using the xml serializer. The output device will display the generated XML document.

In practice, this dynamically generated XML document will undergo a series of further transformations before it is output to a device.

Next, we will look at the XSP document.

Creating Live Data XSP

Listing 7-20 gives the complete listing of the XSP document that takes one input parameter specifying the stock code. The page obtains the live quote for the requested stock and generates an XML page for further processing by the Cocoon pipeline.

Listing 7-20. *XSP That Requests Live Quote* (Ch07\XSP\StockQuote.xsp)

```
<?xml version="1.0" encoding="utf-8" ?>
<xsp:page language="java"
xmlns:xsp="http://apache.org/xsp">
  <xsp:structure>
    <xsp:include>java.util.Calendar</xsp:include>
    <xsp:include>java.text.*</xsp:include>
  </xsp:structure>

  <document>
    <xsp:logic>
      String stockName = request.getParameter("stock").toString();
      String msg = "Last Trade";
      String price = "";
      if (stockName.equals("IBM")) {
        price = "$25.00";
      }
      else if (stockName.equals("MSFT")) {
        price = "$35.00";
      }
      else {
        price = "Unknown stock!";
      }
    SimpleDateFormat format = new SimpleDateFormat("EEE, MMM d, yyyy hh:mm:ss");
    String timestamp = format.format(java.util.Calendar.getInstance().getTime());
    </xsp:logic>
    <msg>
      <xsp:expr>msg</xsp:expr>
    </msg>
```

```
    <stock>
      <xsp:expr>stockName</xsp:expr>
    </stock>
    <price>
      <xsp:expr>price</xsp:expr>
    </price>
    <time>
      <xsp:expr>timestamp</xsp:expr>
    </time>
  </document>
</xsp:page>
```

The document starts with the root element xsp, in which we define the page language and the required namespace.

The Java code embedded in the page requires the two Java packages: java.util and java.text. We import these by using the <xsp:include> element. In the <xsp:logic> element, we write Java code for retrieving the stock prices. First, we read the value of the input parameter:

```
String stockName = request.getParameter("stock").toString();
```

The parameter name is stock. The request object is implicitly provided by Cocoon at runtime. We create two String variables:

```
String msg = "Last Trade";
String price = "";
```

The first variable is initialized to a constant string that is output in the resultant XML document as is. The second variable is assigned a null value and is later initialized in the Java code. The code now checks for the hard-coded string value of IBM:

```
if (stockName.equals("IBM")) {
  price = "$25.00";
}
```

If the input parameter value matches IBM, the program assigns a constant value to the price field. In reality, you will write code that sends the requested symbol as a parameter to the external service providing live quotes for traded stocks. Likewise, the program sets the price variable to a constant value for other stock inputs.

The following two lines retrieve the current system time and assign it to a timestamp variable:

```
SimpleDateFormat format = new SimpleDateFormat("EEE, MMM d, yyyy hh:mm:ss");
String timestamp = format.format(java.util.Calendar.getInstance().getTime());
```

Note that this timestamp may be different than the actual trade time. I have assigned the current time to the timestamp variable just to illustrate the use of some Java code here.

After the logic is defined, we start creating the XML document:

```
<msg>
  <xsp:expr>msg</xsp:expr>
</msg>
```

The `<xsp:expr>` element substitutes the value of the expression in the provided place-holder. When the preceding code is transformed into XML, you will get the following line:

```
<msg>Last Trade</msg>
```

Note that both the opening and closing `<msg>` tags will be added in the output as is. Likewise, we add other strings in the output along with the desired XML tags.

Finally, we close the `document` and `page` tags.

Opening the Live Data Page

To open the live data page, copy both the XSP (Listing 7-20) and sitemap (Listing 7-19) files into a desired folder of your Cocoon installation. You can now open the page by using a URL somewhat like this:

```
http://localhost:8080/cocoon/samples/Ch07/XSP/StockQuote.xsp?stock=IBM
```

This will process the XSP and produce the output as shown here:

```
<?xml version="1.0" encoding="ISO-8859-1" ?>
<document xmlns:xsp="http://apache.org/xsp">
  <msg>Last Trade</msg>
  <stock>IBM</stock>
  <price>$25.00</price>
  <time>Mon, Dec 19, 2005 02:01:40</time>
</document>
```

You can try different input parameter values and examine the output for its correctness.

Looking Under the Hood

Having seen how to create and open an XSP document, you will now look under the hood to understand Cocoon's implementation of XSP processing. Figure 7-10 shows the architectural model of XSP processing.

There is a lot of similarity between the JSP processing model and the Cocoon XSP processing model. In JSP, the JSP engine converts the JavaServer page into a servlet. In the XSP processing model, Cocoon converts the XSP into a generator class to be used in the pipeline. The XSL transformations create a Java source file from the XSP file. The engine adds _xsp to the filename while naming the created Java file. The Java compiler compiles this file into a .class file, which is finally used in the Cocoon pipeline. You can specify the compiler to use in the Cocoon configuration file. (Cocoon configuration is discussed later in this chapter.)

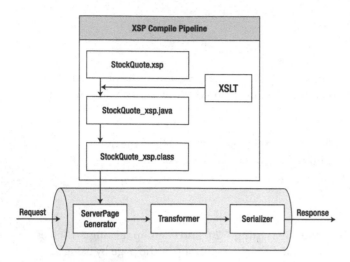

Figure 7-10. *XSP processing model*

■ **Tip** The Java source file for our example is created in the folder `<Tomcat Installation>\work\`
`Catalina\localhost\cocoon\cocoon-files\org\apache\cocoon\www\samples\Ch07\XSP\`
`StockQuote_xsp.java`.

Just as in the case of JSP, if the XSP changes, Cocoon will re-create the Java file and recompile it to produce a new generator. Once compiled, the same class definition will be used until XSP changes again.

The XSP compilation pipeline is independent of the processing pipeline that is used for client-request processing. Thus, the generated Java code does not have access to the input request parameters at compile time. However, the executing generator class has access to the request parameters.

Using Logicsheets in XSP

Now we will again compare XSP with JSP technology. JSPs were designed with the intention of separating the content from the logic; however, embedded Java code in JSP does not give a clear separation between the two. Thus came the taglibs, which provided a much better separation between the presentation and the logic. XSP faced the same problem, which is solved by using Logicsheets, a similar concept to taglibs.

A *Logicsheet* defines a markup to be used in your XSP files. This markup code is then converted into actual code enclosed in code-embedding directives for the XSP page. For example, there could be a markup such as `<sendmail:send-mail>`, where `sendmail` refers to the appropriate XML namespace. The `send-mail` will have several parameters specified by other markups. The entire code is translated into corresponding Java code.[4]

---

4. It may be some other language, depending on the XSP implementation.

I will illustrate the use of predefined Logicsheets with an example. Imagine that our stock brokerage wants to send an e-mail to its clients on every trade confirmation. The customer makes a trade request, and after the trade is confirmed, the stock brokerage sends an e-mail notification to the customer. I will discuss the fragment of the XSP page that generates and sends mail to the customer.

First, we will look up the sitemap definition.

Writing a Sitemap for XSP Processing

The sitemap that is used for processing the XSP that sends mail is shown in Listing 7-21.

Listing 7-21. *Sitemap for Processing XSP That Sends E-Mail Notifications*
(Ch07\LogicSheets\sitemap.xmap)

```
<?xml version="1.0"?>

<map:sitemap xmlns:map="http://apache.org/cocoon/sitemap/1.0">
  <map:components>
    <map:generators default="file">
      <map:generator name="xsp"
                     src="org.apache.cocoon.generation.ServerPagesGenerator"/>
    </map:generators>
  </map:components>

  <map:pipelines>
    <map:pipeline>
      <map:match pattern="mailtest.xsp">
        <map:generate type="xsp" src="mailtest.xsp"/>
        <map:serialize type="xml"/>
      </map:match>
    </map:pipeline>
  </map:pipelines>
</map:sitemap>
```

Here we define one generator called xsp. The source class for this generator is specified as ServerPagesGenerator, which you have used in earlier examples. We define one pipeline that recognizes the pattern mailtest.xsp and passes the input document through the xsp generator and xml serializer.

Creating an XSP Document for Sending Mail

We will now look up the XSP document that composes the mail dynamically by using predefined Logicsheets and sends them to the mail server. Listing 7-22 illustrates how to compose and send e-mail in an XSP document.

Listing 7-22. *XSP to Illustrate the Use of Predefined Logicsheets* (Ch07\LogicSheets\ `mailtest.xsp`)

```
<?xml version="1.0" encoding="ISO-8859-1"?>
<xsp:page language="java"
  xmlns:xsp="http://apache.org/xsp"
  xmlns:sendmail="http://apache.org/cocoon/sendmail/1.0">
  <email>
    <sendmail:send-mail>
      <sendmail:from>sarang@abcom.com</sendmail:from>
      <sendmail:to>sarang@abcom.com</sendmail:to>
      <sendmail:subject>Trade Confirmation</sendmail:subject>
      <sendmail:body>Your order has been successfully traded.</sendmail:body>

      <sendmail:smtphost>192.168.100.50</sendmail:smtphost>
      <sendmail:smtpuser>sarang</sendmail:smtpuser>
      <sendmail:smtppassword>ApacheXML</sendmail:smtppassword>

      <sendmail:on-success>
        <p>
          Email successfully sent.
        </p>
      </sendmail:on-success>
      <sendmail:on-error>
        <p style="color:red;">
          An error occurred: <sendmail:error-message/>
        </p>
      </sendmail:on-error>
    </sendmail:send-mail>
  </email>
</xsp:page>
```

In the root element, we create a namespace called `sendmail`:

```
xmlns:sendmail="http://apache.org/cocoon/sendmail/1.0">
```

The `send-mail` tag uses several parameters to specify the `from`, `to`, `subject`, and `body` for the e-mail message. As you can see in the code, you can easily compose an e-mail by using these tags. The `attachment` tag (not used in the current example) allows you to add attachments to the mail.

After the mail is composed, we set the SMTP authentication information by providing the content within `smtphost`, `smtpuser`, and `smtppassword` elements. Note that the SMTP server configuration is usually placed in the Cocoon configuration file discussed later in the chapter. By providing the content for the three mentioned `smtpXXX` elements, you will be overriding the settings in the Cocoon configuration.

The `on-success` element content will be executed if Cocoon sends the mail successfully. The `on-error` element is used for error notification.

Testing the Mail XSP Document

You may now open the XSP document given in Listing 7-22 by typing the following URL in your browser:

```
http://localhost:8080/cocoon/samples/Ch07/LogicSheets/mailtest.xsp
```

Do not forget to make adjustments for your installation in the preceding URL. If Cocoon successfully connects to your mail server and sends the mail, you will see the following screen output in your browser.

```
<?xml version="1.0" encoding="ISO-8859-1" ?>
<email xmlns:xsp="http://apache.org/xsp"
  xmlns:sendmail="http://apache.org/cocoon/sendmail/1.0">
  <p>Email successfully sent.</p>
  </email>
```

Using Other Predefined Logicsheets

Cocoon provides several Logicsheets ready for your use. These are categorized as follows:

- *Request*: Wraps XML tags around standard request operations

- *Session*: Wraps XML tags around standard session operations

- *ESQL*: Used for performing SQL queries and serializing the results as XML

- *Forms*: Provides input form functionality

- *Sendmail*: Provides notifications for composing and sending e-mail

It is beyond the scope of this book to cover all these predefined Logicsheets. For more information, you can refer to several other books, online documentation, and tutorials available on this topic.[5]

Cocoon Configurations

So far in this chapter, you have studied several Cocoon program examples. In this section, you will learn how to configure Cocoon. For this, you must have some knowledge of the internal workings of Cocoon.

Understanding Cocoon Internals

As you have seen as a part of the installation, Cocoon is deployed as a servlet on a servlet container. The servlet container, such as Tomcat, initializes the servlet at its start-up. The servlet

---

5. Online Cocoon user documentation can be found at http://cocoon.apache.org/2.1/userdocs.
   Tutorials are available at http://www.planetcocoon.com and at http://jsn-server5.com/cocoon/
   docs/userdocs/xsp/logicsheet.html.

initialization information is obtained from the `<cocoon installation>\WEB-INF\web.xml` file. The path to the configuration file (`cocoon.xconf`) is stored in this file. By default, this configuration file is stored in the same folder as the `web.xml` file.

Cocoon Servlet Initialization

During initialization of the servlet, the `cocoon.xconf` configuration file is loaded. The configuration contains the mappings of roles to classes. The role is a concept introduced by the Apache Avalon framework.[6] Each role is implemented by an executable class code defined in the configuration file.

The `cocoon.xconf` file is an XML file and thus an XML parser is required to parse this file. The parser is obtained from the environment variable `org.apache.cocoon.components.parser. Parser`. If this variable is not defined, a default parser called `org.apache.cocoon.components. parser.JaxpParser` is used. You can change this parser by modifying the `xml-parser`'s `class` attribute in the `cocoon.xconf` file. This is shown in the following code snippet:

```
<xml-parser class="org.apache.excalibur.xml.impl.JaxpParser"
  logger="core.xml-parser" pool-max="32">
   ...
</xml-parser>
```

During parsing and initializing, Cocoon loads the classes for each defined role. A role can be implemented by one or more classes. As a part of the initialization process, Cocoon also obtains the location of the sitemap. A default sitemap (`sitemap.xmap` file) is provided in the Cocoon installation folder. The sitemap is compiled during the `HttpRequest` handling.

Tip To understand the sequence of events that takes place during Cocoon start-up, you can refer to the Unified Modeling Language (UML) sequence diagram provided in the Cocoon documentation (`http://localhost:8080/cocoon/docs/developing/images/initialize_Cocoon.png`).

HttpRequest Handling

Once initialized, all the HTTP requests are passed to the Cocoon servlet. The servlet obtains the request, response, and servlet info objects as a part of the environment. The environment decides which sitemap to use. The path to the sitemap is passed to the `Manager` object. The `Manager` object determines whether the compiled version of the sitemap already exists. If not, it creates one. Finally, the handler forwards the request to the generated sitemap class. The sitemap class selects the pipeline based on the URL pattern matching and processes the request through the selected pipeline.

---

6. For more information, look up http://localhost:8080/cocoon/docs/developing/avalon.html in your Cocoon documentation.

Tip For more details, you can refer to the UML sequence diagram (`http://localhost:8080/cocoon/docs/developing/images/get_hello_html.png`) provided in the Cocoon documentation.

Setting Configuration Parameters

The cocoon.xconf file contains the configuration information that is later used by the Cocoon runtime during the execution of web requests. As a developer, you may be required to modify this configuration file in some situations. For example, to set up the data source, configure the mail server, or set up your own parser, you will need to modify this file. I will discuss a few such elements from the configuration file.

Configuring for Performance

During the development phase, you modify your sitemap several times. As mentioned earlier, the Manager object checks whether the compiled version of the sitemap is available for processing the request. If so, it does not generate the class for the sitemap. However, during the development, you will want this sitemap class to be generated on every change to the sitemap. The following entry in the configuration file (cocoon.xconf) allows you to do this:

```
<sitemap check-reload="yes" file="context://sitemap.xmap" logger="sitemap"/>
```

Set the check-reload flag to yes (which is the default) during the development. In a production environment, make sure that this flag is set to no; otherwise, it may seriously hamper the site's performance.

Configuring Your Own Parsers and Processors

As mentioned earlier, you can configure your own parser by modifying the entry for the xml-parser element:

```
<xml-parser class="org.apache.excalibur.xml.impl.JaxpParser"
            logger="core.xml-parser" pool-max="32">
```

You can set up your own XSLTC processor by modifying the entries in the following code:

```
<component class="org.apache.excalibur.xml.xslt.XSLTProcessorImpl"
           logger="core.xslt-processor"
           role="org.apache.excalibur.xml.xslt.XSLTProcessor/xsltc">
  <parameter name="use-store" value="true"/>
  <parameter name="transformer-factory"
             value="org.apache.xalan.xsltc.trax.TransformerFactoryImpl"/>
</component>
```

```
<component class="org.apache.excalibur.xml.xslt.XSLTProcessorImpl"
           logger="core.xslt-processor"
           role="org.apache.excalibur.xml.xslt.XSLTProcessor/xalan">
    <parameter name="use-store" value="true"/>
    <parameter name="incremental-processing" value="false"/>
    <parameter name="transformer-factory"
               value="org.apache.xalan.processor.TransformerFactoryImpl"/>
</component>
```

Note that the preceding entries refer to the Xalan XSLT processor. For the Saxon XSLT processor, refer to the corresponding entry in the configuration file.

To modify the XPath processor, you need to modify the following entry:

```
<xpath-processor class="org.apache.excalibur.xml.xpath.XPathProcessorImpl"
                 logger="core.xpath-processor"/>
```

Setting Up Data Sources

To set up a data source, you need to modify the entry for the datasources element:

```
<datasources>
    <jdbc logger="core.datasources.personnel" name="personnel">
        <pool-controller max="10" min="5"/>
        <auto-commit>false</auto-commit>
        <dburl>jdbc:hsqldb:hsql://localhost:9002</dburl>
        <user>sa</user>
        <password/>
    </jdbc>
</datasources>
```

In this entry, you need to set up the appropriate URL and the required user name/ password. Besides this, you will be able to set other features, including autocommit and the size of the connection pool.

Setting Up the Mail Server

To set the mail server configuration, you need to modify the following entry in the configuration file:

```
<component class="org.apache.cocoon.mail.MailMessageSender"
        logger="core.mail.MailSender" role="org.apache.cocoon.mail.MailSender">
    <!--+
        | SMTP host name, user name, and password.
        <smtp-host>127.0.0.1</smtp-host>
        <smtp-user>john</smtp-user>
        <smtp-password>john</smtp-password>
        +-->
</component>
```

After adding the host, user, and password information, do not forget to uncomment those entries. These are originally commented in the default sitemap.

Summary

The Cocoon framework provides an excellent framework for web development. Web developers were always concerned with separating program logic from the presentation while creating dynamic web pages. Cocoon solves this problem by providing a clear separation between the three concerns, namely logic, content, and style. It also addresses another important concern of web development: management of the web application.

The Cocoon framework is based on the pipeline processing model. In a Cocoon application, we create pipelines consisting of various components. An input request enters a selected pipeline and undergoes various transformations in several components defined in the pipeline until the response is generated at the other end. The components in a pipeline are categorized based on their functionality: generating content, transforming it, and serializing it to a device-specific format. Accordingly, the pipeline consists of three important components called generators, transformers, and serializers. You can include multiple transformers in a pipeline.

The management of the pipelines and the various components within it are achieved through the creation of a sitemap. Every Cocoon application creates an XML-based sitemap that defines the pipelines and the components in them. Being an XML document, the sitemap can be easily altered to modify the processing of the input request.

After introducing a basic application development in Cocoon, this chapter discussed several built-in components. The use of some of these components was discussed with the help of practical examples.

The chapter also introduced you to another important Cocoon technology: XSP. XSP allows you to create dynamic content that is processed by other components in the pipeline before a web page is rendered to the client. The XSP technology has lot of similarities to Java's JSP technology. Like JSP, the XSP technology contains embedded program code. The default programming language is Java; however, other implementations of XSP may use other languages. An XSP page is transformed by a built-in pipeline to another XML document that contains elements to embed Java code. The runtime generates a Java class that is compiled and used as a generator in the pipeline. The input request is piped through this generator to the next component, which is the transformer component.

The XSP technology that allows the generation of dynamic pages also suffers from a lack of clear-cut separation between the content generation and the presentation. Thus, XSP introduced what is known as Logicsheets, which are like JSP taglibs. A Logicsheet is transformed into a set of XML elements that embed Java code. Cocoon provides several ready-to-use Logicsheets. The chapter covered the use of one Logicsheet for composing and sending e-mail dynamically in an XSP document.

Finally, the chapter covered some internals of the Cocoon framework and its configuration. The Cocoon runtime is deployed as a servlet on a servlet container. Once deployed, all the web requests are first directed to this servlet. The servlet selects the appropriate sitemap for processing the request and passes control to the pipeline for processing the request.

The Cocoon configuration is defined in the `cocoon.xconf` file. We discussed a few entries in this configuration file to look up how to improve runtime performance, how to configure the parsers, how to configure data sources, how to configure mail servers, and more.

The Cocoon framework has a lot more to offer your web application development than what I could cover in the limited space provided by this chapter. I urge you to go through several other available sources such as books, websites, online tutorials, and user groups for further reading. Happy learning!

CHAPTER 8

■ ■ ■

XML-Security

In the last few chapters, you have seen the extensive use of XML for data transport. When such data is transported over public networks, is it secured? Could the data be read or even tampered with by a malicious third party? Further, will the receiver of the data be assured about the authenticity of the sender and integrity of the data? This chapter gives answers to all these questions.

I will discuss the need for security and cover important security concepts. Cryptography plays an important role in securing your applications and data, and in this chapter you will study both symmetric- and asymmetric-key cryptography. You will learn to create digital signatures and certificates and use them in your applications. XML signature specifications allow you to sign documents partially, and you will also learn about these specifications. Finally, you will learn the techniques of encrypting and decrypting data for protecting its contents from prying eyes.

Why Security?

Throughout this book, we have been working on a stock brokerage case study. Our stock brokerage accepts trade orders from its customers by using a web interface. As the orders pass through a public network, it is conceivable that somebody could monitor the network traffic, and read and modify the order, before sending the modified order to the brokerage. The stock brokerage, unaware of the modifications to the order, might execute it on the stock exchange and cause no end of grief for the customer.

When the brokerage receives the customer's order, how does it know that the order did indeed originate from the appropriate individual? In the case of trade losses, the customer might refuse to confirm the order. Similarly, whenever the customer places an order or makes an online payment to the broker, is the customer sure he's really talking to the broker and not some malicious third party masquerading as the organization?

The concepts of secure data transmission and the authentication of sender and receiver are not restricted to stock exchange operations. Data transmissions need to be secure in several other situations such as banking transactions, e-commerce shopping, and government operations. Further, should that data be intercepted, we need to ensure that it cannot be read by an intruder.

Before we look into the answers to the preceding questions and the implementations of security in this digital world, let's look at some of the important terms used in security.

Important Terms in Security

The answers to the questions presented in the previous section lie in the definitions of several important security terms: authentication, authorization, nonrepudiation, message integrity, and message confidentiality. Each of these terms is defined in this section.

Authentication

Authentication is a process of determining whether someone is in fact whosoever he or she claims to be.

When the customer places an order with the stock brokerage, the brokerage needs to authenticate itself to the customer. The customer can then be sure of sending the order to the appropriate destination. Similarly, the customer may have to authenticate himself to the broker. This is called *mutual authentication*, whereby both parties confirm the identity of the other party involved in the conversation.

Authorization

Authorization is a process of granting an authenticated user the authority to access certain resources, based on the access rights of that user.

After a user is authenticated by a web application, he will be allowed to perform various tasks. The scope of these tasks is decided by the user's privileges as defined by the system administrator. This process of allowing the user to perform certain operations is called *authorization*.

Nonrepudiation

Nonrepudiation is a process followed by two parties involved in a communication that will prevent either user from denying the conversation in the future.

As mentioned earlier, a customer might deny having placed an order that resulted in trade losses. In such cases, the stock brokerage should be able to prove to the customer that it has a valid order from the customer in question, that the order did indeed originate from that customer, and that the order was not tampered with on its way. This process is called *non-repudiation*, whereby the customer cannot deny having placed the order.

Message Integrity

Message integrity is a process by which the message receiver is guaranteed that the received message has not been tampered with on its way.

The stock brokerage needs to ensure that the various trade requests received from its customers have not been modified on their way. An intruder could intercept a message, modify its contents, and forward it to the ultimate receiver. The integrity of the message is guaranteed by generating message digests and creating digital signatures on digests. This is discussed in depth later in the chapter.

Message Confidentiality

Message confidentiality is a process that ensures both message sender and receiver that even if the message is intercepted by an intruder on its way, it would not make any tangible sense to the interceptor.

Whenever a customer sends a trade request to the stock brokerage, hiding the trade order details from an interceptor may not be required. However, when the customer sends credit card details to the brokerage, the content must be hidden from spying eyes. Message confidentiality is achieved by encrypting the message content.

Brief Introduction to Cryptography

Cryptography is the process of transforming data from one form to another in order to hide the message content from an interceptor and to prevent undetected modifications.

The original form of data is called *plaintext* in cryptography, and the transformed form is called *ciphertext*. The term *plaintext* refers to not only human-readable data, but also binary data such as images and database content. Ciphertext is the transformed human-unreadable data.

The cryptography process involves converting plaintext to ciphertext, and converting ciphertext back to its original form of plaintext. Transforming plaintext into ciphertext is known as *encryption*. This is illustrated in Figure 8-1.

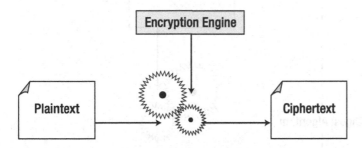

Figure 8-1. *Encryption transforms plaintext to ciphertext.*

Transforming ciphertext to plaintext is called *decryption*. This is illustrated in Figure 8-2.

Encryption ensures that the data is hidden from illegitimate users. But how does it prevent undetected modification of the data? In cryptography, we sign the data by creating a checksum on the data. This checksum may be generated by a simple algorithm, such as adding binary representations of each character in the message text. This checksum is called a *message digest*. At the receiver end, the receiver re-creates the checksum (message digest) by using the same algorithm as the sender. If the two digests match, the receiver can be sure that the data has not been tampered with on its way. It also ensures message authenticity—that the message did originate from the sender. This process is illustrated in Figure 8-3.

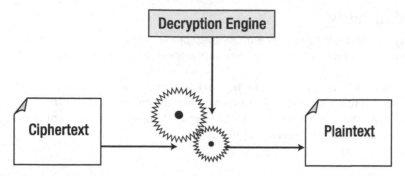

Figure 8-2. *Decryption transforms ciphertext to plaintext.*

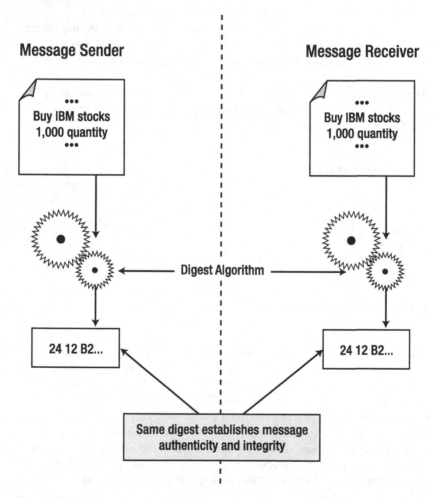

Figure 8-3. *Using a message digest for message authenticity and integrity checks*

In cryptography, we use a key for encryption and decryption. A *key* is a predefined character sequence. The encryption process that uses a key is shown in Figure 8-4.

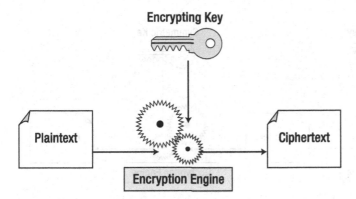

Figure 8-4. *Encryption algorithm that uses a key*

We can use one key or a matching pair of keys for encryption and decryption. We decrypt the encrypted data by using either the same key used for encryption or a matching key provided by the message sender. Because the one key or matching keys used for decryption are privately held by the two involved parties, the process ensures message confidentiality.

A key is also used for generating the message digest. The sender sends both the message and its generated digest to the intended receiver. The signing key or a matching key is shared with the receiver. The receiver uses the supplied key to generate a message digest on the received message. If the two message digests match, the message authenticity and integrity are established.

Thus, these cryptography techniques answer all the requirements of security:

- Hide information content

- Prevent undetected modification

- Prevent unauthorized use

Depending on whether a shared key or a matching pair of keys is used, two types of cryptography techniques are available: symmetric and asymmetric cryptography. You will learn about both in this section. You will also learn about the use of digital signatures and certificates.

Symmetric Cryptography

Symmetric cryptography uses the same key for both encryption and decryption, or for signing and verifying. (Its name reflects the symmetry of using the same key at both ends.) Figure 8-5 illustrates encryption and decryption using symmetric-key cryptography.

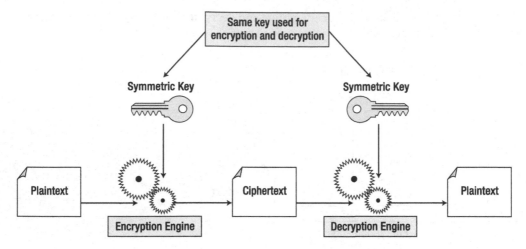

Figure 8-5. *Symmetric cryptography uses the same key for both encryption and decryption.*

Either party can generate the key for the conversation. This key should not be transmitted over unsecured channels such as the Internet and must be made available to the other party even before the conversation begins.

Symmetric cryptography has its roots deep into the early stages of computing. In World War II, symmetric cryptography was used extensively by many countries. The Germans confidently believed that messages sent via Enigma, an electromechanical rotor-based cipher system, could not be cracked. But the British cracked some of the Enigma codes early in the war and continued to decrypt important messages until the Allies' final victory.

Sharing the key with the legitimate user has posed the greatest challenge in symmetric-key cryptography and ultimately led to the invention of asymmetric cryptography. However, although asymmetric cryptography offers a solution to key sharing, it is slower than symmetric cryptography. Thus, in practice, and as you will see later in this chapter, we use a combination of the two techniques.

Asymmetric Cryptography

In *asymmetric cryptography*, the sender creates a pair of matching keys. It is assumed that the techniques used for creating the pair ensure that there is one and only one matching key. The two keys are called the *public key* and the *private key*. As its name indicates, the public key is truly public and is made available to everybody who asks for it. Likewise, the private key is totally private to the key generator and should never be lost or disclosed to anybody; doing so would compromise security.

It is also assumed in asymmetric cryptography that by knowing the public key, nobody can deduce its private key. This eliminates any risk that may be involved in making the key truly public.

The sender uses his private key to sign or encrypt the document. The receiver uses the matching public key obtained from the sender to verify the signature or to decrypt the *gibberish* (this is another term used in cryptography to refer to ciphertext) received from the sender. This process is illustrated in Figure 8-6.

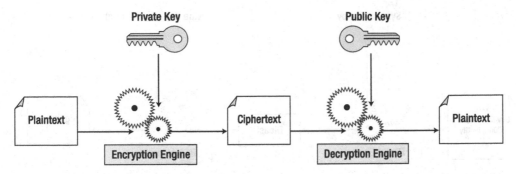

Figure 8-6. *Asymmetric cryptography uses different keys for encryption and decryption.*

■**Note** If encryption is carried out with one of the keys of the key pair, decryption is possible *only* with the matching key of the same key pair. The encrypted message cannot be decrypted with the same key.

Digital Signatures

A *digital signature* is the equivalent of a paper signature in the digital world. Just as you sign paper documents to establish their authenticity, you sign digital documents by creating and adding a digital signature. Signatures on paper cannot be forged easily; also, any changes made to the content of a document on physical paper can be detected easily.

In digital documents, we create a digital signature by creating a checksum based on the document contents. In bookkeeping, you typically take a total of all debit transactions and another total of all credit transactions. These are the two checksums. When they match, you know that your accounts tally. Similarly, in the digital world, a checksum can be generated with a simple algorithm such as adding binary representations of each character in the document.[1] This checksum is also known as a *message digest*. In fact, we create another checksum based on the message digest, which is then called the digital signature. Thus, a digital signature is a checksum of a checksum (message digest).

We use a mix of both symmetric and asymmetric cryptography while generating digital signatures. The process of signing and verifying the documents is as follows:

1. A sender creates a message digest on a document by using a message digest engine. A message digest algorithm might be seeded with a symmetric key if message authenticity is desired. The sender then uses asymmetric-key cryptography to encrypt the message digest along with the symmetric key (also called a secret) used for creating the digest. That means that two values, namely the message digest and the symmetric key, are encrypted by using the private key of the public/private key pair. This encrypted data (signature), along with the original document, is sent to the receiver. This process is illustrated in Figure 8-7.

---

1. The checksum algorithms used in practice are much more complicated and thereby more secure than the one suggested here.

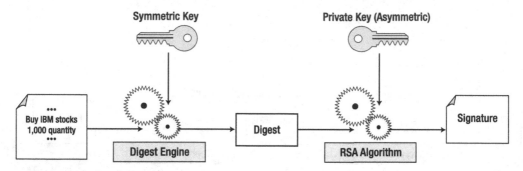

Figure 8-7. *Generating a digital signature*

2. After receiving the document along with its signature, the receiver uses the public key
   supplied by the sender to decrypt and thus obtain the message digest and the secret
   (the symmetric key used for encryption). The receiver re-creates the message digest by
   using the obtained secret. If the generated message digest matches the received message digest, the document origin is authenticated and the message integrity is assured.
   This process is illustrated in Figure 8-8.

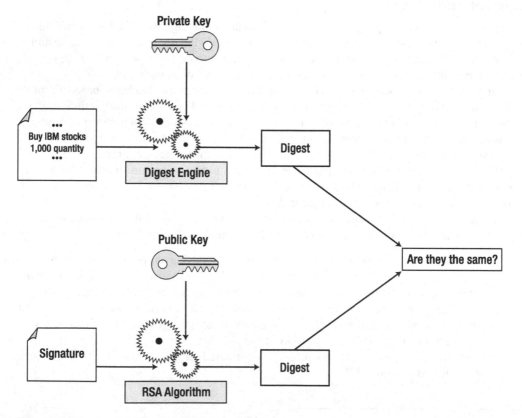

Figure 8-8. *Message verification using a public key*

This technique is ideally suited for large documents. For small documents, you can use asymmetric-key cryptography to sign the entire document.

Digital Certificates

There are many utilities available for generating a matching public/private key pair. Because public/private key pairs can be generated with ease, how can anyone be assured about the authenticity of the public key? It is possible for someone to create a public/private key pair and distribute the public key to everyone while claiming to be someone else. This is where digital certificates come into the picture.

After creating a public/private key pair, the creator should send the public key to a certification authority (CA) such as VeriSign.[2] After establishing the sender's identity, VeriSign creates a digital certificate for that sender. This certificate contains the sender's public key, name, and various other details. Itself a digital document, the certificate is signed by the CA by using its own private key. Figure 8-9 shows the structure of a digital certificate.

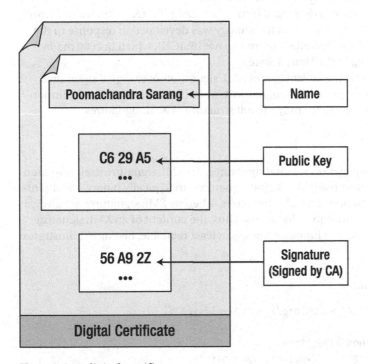

Figure 8-9. *A digital certificate*

The public key of the CA is available to the public, like any other public key. The document receiver now can verify the authenticity of the sender's public key by obtaining the certificate issued by the CA. In short, the CA vouches for the correctness of the sender's public key.

---

2. http://www.verisign.com

A widely used standard for defining digital certificates is X.509. This International Tele-communication Union (ITU) recommendation[3] is known as ITU-T X.509 (formerly CCITT[4] X.509) and as ISO/IEC/ITU 9594-8, which defines a standard certificate format for public-key certificates and certification validation.

Using XML Signatures

Digital signatures sign the entire document. XML signature is a specification that allows you to sign the document partially. It is similar to digital signatures.

XML signature technology embodies the concepts discussed in the previous sections. The only difference is that by using XML signatures, you can sign either the full document or only a specified portion of it. When using other digital signatures, you sign the entire document.

The XML signatures are not restricted to XML documents, but can be applied to any other type of digital data such as images or even HTML documents.

The XML signature technology was developed by the XML-DSig charter (http://www.w3.org/1999/05/XML-DSig-charter-990521.html). This technology was developed in response to the Electronic Signatures in Global and National Commerce Act (ESIGN), which in 2000 made digital signatures legally binding in the United States.

In this section, you will study the advantages of XML signatures over digital signatures. You will learn about the various types of XML signatures. You will also learn about the importance of canonical XML. Finally, you will study the full structure of XML signatures.

Advantages

XML signatures offer few advantages over digital signatures. An XML signature itself is written in XML and is thus somewhat user readable. Digital signatures are typically binary documents consisting of both printable and nonprintable characters, whereas XML signatures are always encoded so as to consist of only printable characters. Thus, the content of an XML signature, although it might not make sense to a human reader, is at least readable. Listing 8-1 illustrates a typical XML signature.

Listing 8-1. *A Typical XML Signature*

```
<ds:Signature xmlns:ds="http://www.w3.org/2000/09/xmldsig#">
  <ds:SignedInfo>
    <ds:CanonicalizationMethod Algorithm=
      "http://www.w3.org/TR/2001/REC-xml-c14n-20010315">
    </ds:CanonicalizationMethod>
    <ds:SignatureMethod Algorithm=
      "http://www.w3.org/2000/09/xmldsig#rsa-sha1">
    </ds:SignatureMethod>
```

---

3. http://www.itu.int/ITU-T/asn1/database/itu-t/x/x509/1997/

4. CCITT stands for Comite Consultatif Internationale de Telegraphie et Telephonie.

```
    <ds:Reference URI="">
      <ds:Transforms>
        <ds:Transform Algorithm=
          "http://www.w3.org/2000/09/xmldsig#enveloped-signature">
        </ds:Transform>
      </ds:Transforms>
      <ds:DigestMethod Algorithm=
        "http://www.w3.org/2000/09/xmldsig#sha1">
      </ds:DigestMethod>
      <ds:DigestValue>/EzketjAlFVxtuJG8Dg1bUYoKCE=</ds:DigestValue>
    </ds:Reference>
  </ds:SignedInfo>
  <ds:SignatureValue>
BHq3QeByVI7oAjLZOZsGDiCLjOLstBB2Z7O2jxPC88QGhQUKPxWhXOrGHDcNuS9mZYvbeO2HCnccTrC
Su1Uwys9v8GanL6akAMvdxO4tYTMwbNm+YXQgf3gBaWP/XXe6WibJzR2v2+aOIeWZnoR2gkHsIPnpL1
JeqiqYMxjMkR4=
  </ds:SignatureValue>
  <ds:KeyInfo>
    <ds:KeyValue>
      <ds:RSAKeyValue>
        <ds:Modulus>
ijqXBjmSWNbJmD7zZoauMRBYDh/1LeKhVljz/FCLhJofDQhXj+ZMY48/1J+KAGOtSa3U9UHOsAKeprX
24/tTkWiWTyIxQRHgCl/Z3B5fh/lylfvSN47WSPAgIZ6JpNfOxOa3XlVht/aCs+QbdKTk2qOs
        FlJjRu8N6Kw5pNa9slU=
        </ds:Modulus>
        <ds:Exponent>AQAB</ds:Exponent>
      </ds:RSAKeyValue>
    </ds:KeyValue>
  </ds:KeyInfo>
</ds:Signature>
```

As you can see in Listing 8-1, the signature consists entirely of only printable characters. A signature is an XML document. Because XML is text-based, so is the XML signature. The entire signature is enclosed in an opening and closing Signature tag. Unlike digital signatures, XML signatures include the name of the algorithm that was used to generate the signature. Look at the SignatureMethod and DigestMethod elements in Listing 8-1 for the algorithm they use. For digital signatures, there has to be a prior agreement between the sender and the receiver on the algorithms they are going to use for signing and creating message digests. Also, look at the DigestValue and SignatureValue element contents. They contain only printable characters.

Another major difference between digital signatures and XML signatures is that XML signatures can be used to selectively sign a part of the document. This offers an advantage of not breaking the original signature when the document is processed by multiple parties on its way to its final destination. The customer purchase order for our stock brokerage may pass through multiple stages of approval to its final destination. If the intermediaries modify the document, the original signature will break. However, with the XML signature's ability to sign only a partial document, the original signature and all the intermediary signatures can be retained to their final destination.

Signature Types

XML signatures are classified into three types, depending on their association with the document that is signed:

- *Enveloped*: The XML signature is embedded in the document that is being signed. That means that the Signature element will appear as one of the child elements in the original XML document.

- *Enveloping*: The entire document that is to be signed appears as one of the child elements of the Signature element.

- *Detached*: The XML signature appears in a document that is separate from the signed document. The Signature stores the reference to the signed document. This type of signature is useful for signing non-XML documents.

Canonical XML

You have seen in Listing 8-1 that the Signature contains a digest value specified by the DigestValue element. This digest is very sensitive to changes in the document. As a matter of fact, even the slightest change such as adding one white-space character to the document will change the digest drastically. As you might imagine, a digest algorithm should not generate a digest that is similar to the old one whenever the original document undergoes even a very minor change.

Unfortunately, different XML applications can generate XML documents that contain identical content but potentially have slight variations such as the amount of white space found within it. Also, there are no strict guidelines on how the entire document is structured as long as it is well formed. Thus, for each document, the generated digest will vary drastically and the signature verification on a signed document could fail due to minor differences in the two versions of the same logical document. To overcome this limitation, canonical XML was introduced.

Canonical XML is a normalized representation of any physical XML document. It is a standard for signature processing. Before a document is signed, it is transformed into a canonical XML document. Similarly, before the signature is verified, the received document is transformed again to canonical XML to regenerate the digest for verification.

XML Signature Structure

Listing 8-2 shows the general structure of an XML Signature element.

Listing 8-2. *XML Signature Structure*

```
<Signature ID="">
  <SignedInfo>
    <CanonicalizationMethod Algorithm=""/>
    <SignatureMethod Algorithm=""/>
    <Reference URI="">
      <DigestMethod Algorithm=""/>
      <DigestValue> ... </DigestValue>
```

```
    </Reference>
  </SignedInfo>
  <SignatureValue> ... </SignatureValue>
  <KeyInfo> ... </KeyInfo>
</Signature>
```

As seen in Listing 8-2, the Signature contains child elements called
CanonicalizationMethod and SignatureMethod. This is where you would specify the algorithms
used for creating canonical XML and for signing the document, respectively. Similarly, the
DigestMethod element allows you to specify the digest algorithm in its attribute value
(Algorithm). The Signature element also contains elements such as DigestValue,
SignatureValue, and KeyInfo, which contain the information that their names suggest.

Downloading and Installing Software

The Apache XML-Security project is available in source and binary distribution for both Java
and C++ libraries. If you use C++ for development, you will need to download C++ libraries. I
will use Java libraries in this book. You can download Java libraries from the following URL:

http://xml.apache.org/security/dist/java-library/

The download site contains both binary and source distributions:

- xml-security-bin-1_3_0.zip (binary distribution)

- xml-security-src-1_3_0.zip (source distribution)

You can download the source distribution and build it by using Apache Ant[5] to create
the libraries. Ant is a Java-based build tool that is similar to other build tools such as make,
gnumake, nmake, and others.

Alternatively, if you download the binary distribution, which is much larger than the
source distribution, simply unzip the file to a desired folder for installing the software. After
unzipping the binary, include the various JAR files from the libs folder of your installation
in your classpath and you are ready to go.

Signing XML Documents

In this section, we will start our programming exercises. Imagine that a customer wants to
place a trade order with our stock brokerage. Because the brokerage needs to authenticate the
customer, the customer must sign the purchase order (PO). The brokerage would verify the
purchase order before executing it.

To sign the PO, the customer generates a public and private key for his own use and then
signs the PO by using the generated private key. The customer sends the original document
along with the signature and the public key to the brokerage. The brokerage retrieves the public key from the received document and then verifies the authenticity and the integrity of the

---

5. http://ant.apache.org/

document. The brokerage performs this verification by using the algorithms specified in the Signature element of the received document to re-create and match the re-created message digest and the signature with those obtained as a part of the Signature element.

Note that this technique has one fallacy: the brokerage cannot be sure about the authenticity of the customer's public key itself. To authenticate the public key, the brokerage needs a digital certificate issued by a CA. We will use digital certificates in our future examples. To keep matters simple in this example, we will generate a public/private key pair dynamically and use it while signing and verifying the document.

Generating and Signing an XML Document

Listing 8-3 illustrates how to sign a dynamically created XML document.

Listing 8-3. *Signing Dynamically Generated XML Document* (Ch08\src\SignedPO.java)

```
/*
 * SignedPO.java
 */
package apress.ApacheXML.ch08;

// Import required classes
import java.io.File;
import java.io.FileOutputStream;
import java.security.KeyPair;
import java.security.KeyPairGenerator;
import java.security.PrivateKey;
import java.security.PublicKey;
import org.apache.xml.security.algorithms.MessageDigestAlgorithm;
import org.apache.xml.security.signature.XMLSignature;
import org.apache.xml.security.transforms.Transforms;
import org.apache.xml.security.utils.XMLUtils;
import org.w3c.dom.Document;
import org.w3c.dom.Element;
import javax.xml.parsers.DocumentBuilder;

public class SignedPO {

  static Document createDocument() throws Exception {
    // Obtain an instance of Docuement Builder Factory
    javax.xml.parsers.DocumentBuilderFactory dbf =
        javax.xml.parsers.DocumentBuilderFactory.newInstance();
    dbf.setNamespaceAware(true);
    javax.xml.parsers.DocumentBuilder db = dbf.newDocumentBuilder();

    // Create a new document
    Document doc = db.newDocument();
```

```java
// Create elements
Element root = doc.createElementNS(null, "PurchaseOrder");
Element contents = doc.createElementNS(null, "signedContents");

doc.appendChild(root);
root.appendChild(contents);
contents.appendChild(doc.createTextNode(
        "\nWe request that you EXECUTE the following trades\n"));

// Add Trade details
Element stock1 = doc.createElementNS(null, "stock");
contents.appendChild(stock1);
stock1.appendChild(doc.createTextNode("GFW"));
Element quantity1 = doc.createElementNS(null, "quantity");
contents.appendChild(quantity1);
quantity1.appendChild(doc.createTextNode("50"));
Element price1 = doc.createElementNS(null, "price");
contents.appendChild(price1);
price1.appendChild(doc.createTextNode("25.35"));
Element type1 = doc.createElementNS(null, "type");
contents.appendChild(type1);
type1.appendChild(doc.createTextNode("B"));

// Add one more Trade
// ...

return doc;
}

public static void main(String unused[]) throws Exception {

  org.apache.xml.security.Init.init();

  // Generate a public/private key pair for temporary use
  KeyPairGenerator kpg = KeyPairGenerator.getInstance("RSA");
  KeyPair keyPair = kpg.generateKeyPair();

  // Obtain reference to generated public/private keys
  PrivateKey privateKey = keyPair.getPrivate();
  PublicKey pubkey = keyPair.getPublic();

  // Create a po document
  Document doc = createDocument();

  // Obtain the root element
  Element root = doc.getDocumentElement();
```

```
    // Create file for writing output
    File f = new File("po.xml");
    // Create a XMLSignature instance that uses RSA_SHA1 algorithm
    XMLSignature signature = new XMLSignature(doc, f.toURL().toString(),
            XMLSignature.ALGO_ID_SIGNATURE_RSA_SHA1);

    // Create canonical XML
    Transforms transforms = new Transforms(doc);
    transforms.addTransform(Transforms.TRANSFORM_ENVELOPED_SIGNATURE);

    // Add canonicalized document to signature
    signature.addDocument("", transforms,
            MessageDigestAlgorithm.ALGO_ID_DIGEST_SHA1);

    // Add the public key information to signature
    signature.addKeyInfo(pubkey);

    // Add signature itself to the PO document
    root.appendChild(signature.getElement());

    // Sign the document
    signature.sign(privateKey);

    // Create an output stream
    FileOutputStream fos = new FileOutputStream(f);
    // Output the memory document using XMLUtils.
    XMLUtils.outputDOMc14nWithComments(doc, fos);
  }
}
```

We have to initialize the security libraries before invoking any of the Apache XML-Security library services. The main function first initializes the security libraries with the following code:

```
org.apache.xml.security.Init.init();
```

We then generate a public/private key pair for the current session:

```
// Generate a public/private key pair for temporary use
KeyPairGenerator kpg = KeyPairGenerator.getInstance("RSA");
KeyPair keyPair = kpg.generateKeyPair();
```

We are using RSA algorithms for key generation.[6] This is the most popular implementation of the Public Key Infrastructure (PKI). The other well-known implementations are Diffie-Hellman (DH)[7] and Elliptic Curve Diffie-Hellman (ECDH).[8]

---

6. The RSA algorithm was invented by Ron Rivest, Adi Shamir, and Len Adleman. The name RSA was coined after the initials of the inventors.

7. Refer to http://www.rsasecurity.com/rsalabs/node.asp?id=2126 for details.

8. Refer to http://www.rsasecurity.com/rsalabs/node.asp?id=2013 for details.

We retrieve the public and private keys from the generated key pair:

```
// Obtain reference to generated public/private keys
PrivateKey privateKey = keyPair.getPrivate();
PublicKey pubkey = keyPair.getPublic();
```

We then create a purchase order XML document by calling the createDocument method. The createDocument method uses the DOM API discussed in Chapter 2 to generate the PO document dynamically. It returns the reference to the Document object to the caller. We will add a Signature element to this document.

We construct the Signature element by using the following statement:

```
// Create a XMLSignature instance that uses RSA_SHA1 algorithm
XMLSignature signature = new XMLSignature(doc, f.toURL().toString(),
        XMLSignature.ALGO_ID_SIGNATURE_RSA_SHA1);
```

Note that we have specified the algorithm to be used for signature generation as one of the parameters. The XMLSignature class defines several IDs for the use of different algorithms. For example, you can use the ALGO_ID_SIGNATURE_RSA_SHA256 ID to create a 256-bit signature or you can use ALGO_ID_SIGNATURE_RSA_SHA512 to generate a 512-bit signature.

■**Note** The ALGO_ID_SIGNATURE_RSA_SHA1 generates a 172-bit signature and not a 1-bit signature as you might conclude from the previous statement.

■**Tip** Try these different algorithms to see their effect on the generated signature value in the signed document.

The first parameter to the XMLSignature constructor is the Document object that is to be signed, and the second argument is a reference to the output file where the signed document will later be serialized.

After constructing the Signature, the program transforms the input document to canonical XML:

```
// Create canonical XML
Transforms transforms = new Transforms(doc);
transforms.addTransform(Transforms.TRANSFORM_ENVELOPED_SIGNATURE);
```

We then add the document to the Signature element:

```
// Add canonicalized document to signature
signature.addDocument("", transforms,
        MessageDigestAlgorithm.ALGO_ID_DIGEST_SHA1);
```

We specify the digest algorithm to be used while adding the document.

Tip I again urge you to try the different digest algorithms to see their effect on the digest value.

We add the key info to the `signature` so that the receiver obtains the customer's public key as a part of the document:

```
// Add the key information to signature
signature.addKeyInfo(pubkey);
```

The `signature` node is then appended to the root of the document:

```
// Add signature itself to the PO document
root.appendChild(signature.getElement());
```

After this, the document itself is signed by calling the `sign` method of the `XMLSignature` class:

```
// Sign the document
signature.sign(privateKey);
```

During execution of this `sign` method, the signature is generated and inserted into the Signature element of the document. Our document is now signed. We need to serialize the document constructed in memory to a physical file. We do this by creating an output stream on the desired physical file and by calling the `outputDOMc14nWithComments` method of the `XMLUtils` class to perform the serialization:

```
// Create an output stream
FileOutputStream fos = new FileOutputStream(f);
// Output the memory document using XMLUtils.
XMLUtils.outputDOMc14nWithComments(doc, fos);
```

Running the Application

Compile the application by using the following command line:

```
C:\<working folder>\ch08\src>javac -d . SignedPO.java
```

Run the application by using the following command line:

```
C:\<working folder>\ch08\src>java apress.ApacheXML.ch08.SignedPO
```

On a successful run, you will find a `po.xml` file created in your working folder.

Examining the Signed Document

If you open the po.xml file in your browser or your console, you will see the following output:

```
<PurchaseOrder>
  <signedContents>
    We request that you EXECUTE the following trades
    <stock>GFW</stock>
    <quantity>50</quantity>
    <price>25.35</price>
    <type>B</type>
    <stock>ABNPRF</stock>
    <quantity>100</quantity>
    <price>24.83</price>
    <type>S</type>
  </signedContents>
  <ds:Signature xmlns:ds="http://www.w3.org/2000/09/xmldsig#">
    <ds:SignedInfo>
      <ds:CanonicalizationMethod Algorithm=
          "http://www.w3.org/TR/2001/REC-xml-c14n-20010315">
      </ds:CanonicalizationMethod>
      <ds:SignatureMethod Algorithm=
          "http://www.w3.org/2001/04/xmldsig-more#rsa-ha256">
      </ds:SignatureMethod>
      <ds:Reference URI="">
        <ds:Transforms>
          <ds:Transform Algorithm=
              "http://www.w3.org/2000/09/xmldsig#enveloped-signature">
          </ds:Transform>
        </ds:Transforms>
        <ds:DigestMethod Algorithm="http://www.w3.org/2001/04/xmlenc#sha256">
        </ds:DigestMethod>
        <ds:DigestValue>
          nkXWyyMrZ5WEfpXHUuWNqDUnF2xkmW5WkwoIkSn2nFk=
        </ds:DigestValue>
      </ds:Reference>
    </ds:SignedInfo>
    <ds:SignatureValue>
Fzi6hsoz3bkO2Bd2GfumTKzwqu5+i14Mfw1MW3Vd8u4bTyK3K5bJqmV7mz1DibcysdbSa3bxycVdCR9
XvuWC5XtRs9xABrU7+eNRK/IeRG1dsrQIIYgZ4XN97pLVU/iu5BJDERop/5CxqwnTjRWlvLselwdKnp
PqmGaFy6mrBks=
    </ds:SignatureValue>
    <ds:KeyInfo>
      <ds:KeyValue>
        <ds:RSAKeyValue>
          <ds:Modulus>
```

fL1AftPy9xQo6kEmE1Pw1Swe6HeCkNKWYdP7OfkFZu8PDJ43RzgflV5VYipD1u8J5YGqJg71XDIzMOQ
2IPcWU6NbCkcKrzeM4CMlw4d7Z8lQPPeIdQhVo/6+jCtqPemtwdpSZmiyfZhJyf/bXfezgBtPKM/5MP
KdepeUjOKVbhO=
```
            </ds:Modulus>
            <ds:Exponent>AQAB</ds:Exponent>
          </ds:RSAKeyValue>
        </ds:KeyValue>
      </ds:KeyInfo>
   </ds:Signature>
</PurchaseOrder>
```

The root element of the generated document is PurchaseOrder. The PurchaseOrder element contains a child element called signedContents, which in turn encapsulates the two trade orders. The element of interest to us is the ds:Signature element. This contains subelements that describe the algorithms used for canonicalization, signing, and creating the message digest. It also contains elements that describe the value for the message digest and the signature. The document also contains the key information specified by the KeyInfo element. This contains the public key of the signing customer. We will retrieve this key in our next application to verify the document.

Verifying the Purchase Order

In the previous section, you learned how the customer generates a purchase order dynamically, signs it by using its own private key, and sends the signed document to the stock brokerage. The brokerage now needs to verify the document and its integrity. In this section, we will develop an application that retrieves the public key of the customer from the received document and uses it to verify the document.

Developing an Application for Verifying the Document

Listing 8-4 illustrates how to verify a given signed document.

Listing 8-4. *Program to Verify a Signed Document (Ch08\src\VerifyPO.java)*

```
/*
 * VerifyPO.java
 */

package apress.ApacheXML.ch08;

// Import required classes
import java.io.File;
import java.io.FileInputStream;
import java.io.FileNotFoundException;
import java.security.PublicKey;
import org.apache.xml.security.keys.KeyInfo;
import org.apache.xml.security.samples.utils.resolver.OfflineResolver;
```

```java
import org.apache.xml.security.signature.XMLSignature;
import org.apache.xml.security.utils.Constants;
import org.apache.xml.security.utils.XMLUtils;
import org.apache.xpath.XPathAPI;
import org.w3c.dom.Element;

public class VerifyPO {

public static void main(String unused[]) {
  // Initialize security
  org.apache.xml.security.Init.init();

  // Obtain a builder factory instance
  javax.xml.parsers.DocumentBuilderFactory dbf =
          javax.xml.parsers.DocumentBuilderFactory.newInstance();
  dbf.setNamespaceAware(true);
  dbf.setAttribute("http://xml.org/sax/features/namespaces", Boolean.TRUE);

  try {
    // Open the file to be verified
    File f = new File("po.xml");
    System.out.println("Trying to verify " + f.toURL().toString());

    // Create a document builder
    javax.xml.parsers.DocumentBuilder db = dbf.newDocumentBuilder();
    db.setErrorHandler(
            new org.apache.xml.security.utils.IgnoreAllErrorHandler());

    // parse the input document
    org.w3c.dom.Document doc = db.parse(new java.io.FileInputStream(f));

    // Look for the Signature element in the required namespace
    Element nscontext = XMLUtils.createDSctx(doc, "ds",
        Constants.SignatureSpecNS);
    Element sigElement = (Element) XPathAPI.selectSingleNode(doc,
        "//ds:Signature[1]", nscontext);

    // Create signature element
    XMLSignature signature = new XMLSignature(sigElement,
        f.toURL().toString());

    // Add a resource resolver to enable the retrieval of resources
    signature.addResourceResolver(new OfflineResolver());

    // Retrieve the key information
    KeyInfo ki = signature.getKeyInfo();
```

```
        if (ki != null) {
          // Retrieve the public key from key information
          PublicKey pk = signature.getKeyInfo().getPublicKey();
          if (pk != null) {
            boolean result = signature.checkSignatureValue(pk);
            String str = null;
            if (result)
              str = "The document " + f.toURL().toString() + " is valid!";
            else
              str = "The document " + f.toURL().toString() + " is invalid!";
            System.out.println(str);
          } else {
            System.out.println("No public key found for document verification");
                }
        } else {
          System.out.println("Missing KeyInfo");
        }
      } catch (Exception ex) {
          ex.printStackTrace();
      }
    }
  }
}
```

The main function first initializes the security libraries and like the earlier program obtains the document builder factory instance, creates a document builder, and parses the specified XML document by using DOM APIs.

After the document is parsed, the Signature element is located by using the XPath APIs:

```
// Look for the Signature element in the required namespace
Element nscontext = XMLUtils.createDSctx(doc, "ds",
        Constants.SignatureSpecNS);
Element sigElement = (Element) XPathAPI.selectSingleNode(doc,
        "//ds:Signature[1]", nscontext);
```

We construct the Signature element by using the located instance of the Signature in the input document:

```
// Create signature element
XMLSignature signature = new XMLSignature(sigElement,
        f.toURL().toString());
```

We now add a resource resolver to the constructed signature to retrieve the resources:

```
// Add a resource resolver to enable the retrieval of resources
signature.addResourceResolver(new OfflineResolver());
```

The key information stored in the input document is retrieved by calling the getKeyInfo method of the XMLSignature class:

```
// Retrieve the key information
KeyInfo ki = signature.getKeyInfo();
```

After the key information is retrieved, we retrieve a public key from it. Note that in our case, the sender has sent his public key as part of the document:

```
// Retrieve the public key from key information
PublicKey pk = signature.getKeyInfo().getPublicKey();
```

Using the public key, the document is verified:

```
boolean result = signature.checkSignatureValue(pk);
```

The checkSignatureValue method returns a boolean value indicating the success or failure of the document verification. Note that the Signature element itself contains the digest value, signature value, the algorithms used, and so on. The checkSignatureValue method uses this information to validate the document.

If there are errors, the program prints the appropriate exception messages at the appropriate points in the program.

Running the Application

Compile the code by using the following command line:

```
C:\<working folder>\ch08\src>javac -d . VerifyPO.java
```

Run the application by using the following command line:

```
C:\<working folder>\ch08\src>java apress.ApacheXML.ch08.VerifyPO
```

When you run the program, you will see output similar to the following:

```
Trying to verify file:/C:/apress/ch08/src/po.xml
Feb 1, 2006 10:35:30 AM org.apache.xml.security.signature.Reference verify
INFO: Verification successful for URI ""
The document file:/C:/apress/ch08/src/po.xml is valid!
```

If the verification fails, you will get an appropriate failure message.

Tip Make a minor modification to po.xml (for example, adding a white-space character) and save it. Now rerun the application to verify that the document verification fails this time.

Using Digital Certificates

The example in the previous section used a dynamically generated key pair. This key pair is valid only during the current session, when the application is running. Thus, there is nobody to vouch for the public key of the sender. In fact, the sender himself will not remember this public key unless he stores it to secondary storage in the same session as when the key is created. In practice, each sender who wants to sign the documents must send the public key to a CA and obtain a digital certificate that authenticates the public key.

In this section, I will describe the entire procedure for using digital certificates in your application. The procedure consists of the following steps:

1. Creating a public/private key

2. Exporting the public key to a physical file

3. Requesting a certificate from a CA

4. Importing the CA's certificate into your database

To complete these steps, we will use the Keytool utility provided as a part of your JDK installation.

Creating a Key Pair

We will use the Keytool utility to create a key pair. The utility stores the generated keys in a local database. This is a flat file known as keystore. You can give any name and extension to this file. We will call our keystore file keystore.jks and create it in the root folder of your current drive.

To generate a key pair for yourself, go to the C:\ root folder (assuming you are running Windows) and run the Keytool utility at the command prompt with the -genkey option. You will also need to specify the alias name for your key and the path to the keystore file. When you run this utility, you will be asked a series of questions to gather information about the key signer, that is, you. Note that you will later send this information to a CA for ultimately including it in a digital certificate. The following transcript of the Keytool session was output when I ran it on my machine:

```
C:\>keytool -genkey -v -alias XMLBook -keystore c:\\keystore.jks
Enter keystore password:  sanjay
What is your first and last name?
  [Unknown]:  Poornachandra Sarang
What is the name of your organizational unit?
  [Unknown]:  Authoring
What is the name of your organization?
  [Unknown]:  ABCOM
What is the name of your City or Locality?
  [Unknown]:  Mumbai
What is the name of your State or Province?
  [Unknown]:  Maharashtra
What is the two-letter country code for this unit?
  [Unknown]:  IN
Is CN=Poornachandra Sarang, OU=Authoring, O=ABCOM, L=Mumbai, ST=Maharashtra,
C=I N correct?
  [no]:  y
```

```
Generating 1,024 bit DSA key pair and self-signed certificate (SHA1WithDSA)
        for: CN=Poornachandra Sarang, OU=Authoring, O=ABCOM, L=Mumbai,
            ST=Maharashtra, C=IN
Enter key password for <XMLBook>
        (RETURN if same as keystore password):  sanjay
[Storing c:\\keystore.jks]
```

You can input the information specific to you while generating the key. We will need the alias name to identify the key to be used while signing the document.

Listing Keys in Your Keystore

You can make a list of the keys in your keystore anytime by using the -list option on the Keytool utility. If you have created the keystore and added an XMLBook key entry to it as described in the previous section, you will get output similar to the following when you run Keytool with the -list option:

```
C:\>keytool -list -keystore c:\keystore.jks
Enter keystore password:  sanjay

Keystore type: jks
Keystore provider: SUN

Your keystore contains 1 entry

xmlbook, Dec 28, 2005, keyEntry,
Certificate fingerprint (MD5): 36:79:EB:27:66:17:17:8B:47:79:FC:AB:FF:E4:5D:08
```

Note that every time you open the keystore, you will be asked to enter the password.

Exporting the Certificate

After creating a public and private key pair for your use, you can send this pair to a CA for obtaining a CA's certificate that authenticates the validity of your public key. To do this, you export your public key to a physical file and send that to a CA. To export the public key, you use the -export option on the Keytool utility. The transcript of the session run on my machine is as follows:

```
C:\>keytool -export -alias XMLBook -file xmlbook.cer -keystore c:\keystore.jks
Enter keystore password:  sanjay
Certificate stored in file <xmlbook.cer>
```

Note that you need to specify the alias for which you want to extract and export the public key. The certificate containing your public key is stored in the file specified by the `-file` option, and the `-keystore` option specifies the path to your keystore.

Note You can create more than one keystore for use on the same machine.

Requesting a Certificate from a CA

After your public key is exported to a physical file, you send this to a CA for verification. In this step, you do not have to do anything except send your exported certificate to a CA and wait for its verification. After the CA is satisfied with your credentials, it will issue you another certificate (of course, they may charge some money for it). This certificate contains your public key and your company's information. It also contains information about the CA who issues the certificate. The certificate itself is signed using the private key of the CA.

We will now request a test certificate from a CA for the XMLBook alias that we created in the previous section. Export the XMLBook key to a text file and save that file as `xml.txt` by using the following command:

```
C:\>keytool -certreq -keystore c:\keystore.jks -file xml.txt -alias xmlcer
```

Thawte, a certification authority, provides free Secure Sockets Layer (SSL) digital certificates for testing purposes. You can get a test certificate from their website: `http://www.thawte.com/ssl-digital-certificates/ssl123/index.html`. Click on Free SSL Trial and follow the instructions. You have to paste the contents of the `xml.txt` file in the space provided for a certificate signing request. After submitting this request, your key will be processed and a certificate will be displayed on the next page. Copy this content and save it as `xml.cert`. In the next step, you will import this certificate in your keystore database.

Importing Certificates

After you receive a certificate from the CA, you can distribute it along with your signed documents to prove your identity. Just as you distribute your certificate, you can also receive certificates from other senders who want to prove their identities to you. You can import such certificates into your keystore database for your future use. To import a certificate, you use the `-import` option on the Keytool utility as shown in the following command:

```
C:\>keytool -import -file xml.cert -alias xmlcert -trustcacerts -keystore ➥
 c:\keystore.jks
```

The following is a transcript of importing a certificate into my database:

```
Enter keystore password:  sanjay
Owner: CN=Poornachandra Sarang, OU=Authoring, O=ABCOM, L=Mumbai,
       ST=Maharashtra, C=IN
Issuer: CN=Thawte Test CA Root, OU=TEST TEST TEST, O=Thawte Certification,
       ST=FOR TESTING PURPOSES ONLY, C=ZA
Serial number: d2d9c50eb3e45f46
Valid from: Thu Feb 02 18:32:17 GMT+05:30 2006 until: Thu Feb 23 18:32:17 GMT+0
       5:30 2006
Certificate fingerprints:
       MD5:  89:50:B8:1B:11:DF:B6:47:DA:97:06:72:DC:F2:0F:C5
       SHA1: C1:3F:8E:4F:E6:2C:5E:CE:62:34:25:5D:0D:8E:9F:DF:5F:0C:9F:45
Trust this certificate? [no]:  y
Certificate was added to keystore
```

If you list the certificates in your database, you will find two entries: one for XMLBook that you created earlier and one that you imported (alias xmlcert) in this step.

Now that we are ready with our certificates and keystore, let's look at how to use these certificates for signing and verifying our documents.

Using Digital Certificates for Document Signing

In this section, you will learn how to sign a document and attach a digital certificate to a signed document for establishing your identity to the client. We will use the same dynamically created PO document as in the earlier example in Listing 8-3. Listing 8-5 illustrates how to sign the document and attach a digital certificate to the signed document.

Listing 8-5. *Signing and Attaching a Digital Certificate* (Ch08\src\CertifiedPO.java)

```java
/*
 * CertifiedPO.java
 */
package apress.ApacheXML.ch08;

// Import Required Classes

public class CertifiedPO {

  static Document createDocument() throws Exception {
      // Same as in Listing 8-3 - SignedPO.java
    return doc;
  }

  public static void main(String unused[]) throws Exception {
```

```
org.apache.xml.security.Init.init();
Constants.setSignatureSpecNSprefix("");

String keystoreType = "JKS";
String keystoreFile = "c:\\keystore.jks";
String keystorePass = "sanjay";
String privateKeyAlias = "XMLBook";
String privateKeyPass = "sanjay";
String certificateAlias = "XMLBook";

KeyStore ks = KeyStore.getInstance(keystoreType);
FileInputStream fis = new FileInputStream(keystoreFile);

//load the keystore
ks.load(fis, keystorePass.toCharArray());

//get the private key for signing.
PrivateKey privateKey = (PrivateKey) ks.getKey(privateKeyAlias,
        privateKeyPass.toCharArray());

// Create a PO document
Document doc = createDocument();

// Obtain the root element
Element root = doc.getDocumentElement();

// Create file for writing output
File f = new File("PO-certified.xml");

// Create a XMLSignature instance that uses RSA_SHA1 algorithm
XMLSignature signature = new XMLSignature(doc, f.toURL().toString(),
        XMLSignature.ALGO_ID_SIGNATURE_DSA);

// Create canonical XML
Transforms transforms = new Transforms(doc);
transforms.addTransform(Transforms.TRANSFORM_ENVELOPED_SIGNATURE);

// Create canonicalized document to signature
 signature.addDocument("", transforms,
        MessageDigestAlgorithm.ALGO_ID_DIGEST_SHA1);

//Add in the KeyInfo for the certificate that we used the private key of
X509Certificate cert =
        (X509Certificate) ks.getCertificate(certificateAlias);
```

```
    // Add the information to signature
    signature.addKeyInfo(cert);
    signature.addKeyInfo(cert.getPublicKey());

    // Add signature itself to the PO document
    root.appendChild(signature.getElement());

    // Sign the document
    signature.sign(privateKey);

    // Create an output stream
    FileOutputStream fos = new FileOutputStream(f);

    // Output the memory document using XMLUtils.
    XMLUtils.outputDOMc14nWithComments(doc, fos);
  }
}
```

After initializing the security system, the main function creates a few variables that specify the details of our keystore and the key that we intend to use for signing the document:

```
String keystoreType = "JKS";
String keystoreFile = "c:\\keystore.jks";
String keystorePass = "sanjay";
String privateKeyAlias = "XMLBook";
String privateKeyPass = "sanjay";
String certificateAlias = "XMLBook";
```

The getInstance method of the KeyStore class obtains a reference to the KeyStore:

```
KeyStore ks = KeyStore.getInstance(keystoreType);
```

We open the keystore file by creating an input stream on it and then initialize the KeyStore instance with the data read from the file:

```
FileInputStream fis = new FileInputStream(keystoreFile);
//load the keystore
ks.load(fis, keystorePass.toCharArray());
```

For signing, we need the private key. We obtain this from the keystore by calling its getKey method. The getKey method requires the alias for the key and its password. The method returns an instance of PrivateKey to the caller:

```
//get the private key for signing.
PrivateKey privateKey = (PrivateKey) ks.getKey(privateKeyAlias,
        privateKeyPass.toCharArray());
```

The program then creates a document as in the earlier case (refer to Listing 8-3), obtains its root element for later adding the signature, and opens a file for writing the signed document. These steps are the same as the ones in Listing 8-3.

Next, we create an instance of XMLSignature by using the Digital Signature Algorithm (DSA):

```
// Create a XMLSignature instance that uses RSA_SHA1 algorithm
XMLSignature signature = new XMLSignature(doc, f.toURL().toString(),
        XMLSignature.ALGO_ID_SIGNATURE_DSA);
```

We perform canonicalization as in the earlier case and add the canonicalized document to the created signature:

```
// Create canonical XML
Transforms transforms = new Transforms(doc);
transforms.addTransform(Transforms.TRANSFORM_ENVELOPED_SIGNATURE);

// Create canonicalized document to signature
 signature.addDocument("", transforms,
        MessageDigestAlgorithm.ALGO_ID_DIGEST_SHA1);
```

We retrieve the certificate from the keystore by calling its getCertificate method. We will attach this certificate to the signed document:

```
//Add in the KeyInfo for the certificate that we used the private key of
X509Certificate cert =
        (X509Certificate) ks.getCertificate(certificateAlias);
```

The getCertificate method takes the certificate alias as its parameter and returns an instance of X509Certificate. We add this certificate and the public key associated with it to the signature object:

```
// Add the information to signature
signature.addKeyInfo(cert);
signature.addKeyInfo(cert.getPublicKey());
```

Finally, we add the signature object to the document root as in the earlier example:

```
// Add signature itself to the PO document
root.appendChild(signature.getElement());
```

The document is signed by using the sign method of the XMLSignature class:

```
// Sign the document
signature.sign(privateKey);
```

The signed document is serialized to an output file by using the XMLUtils class as in the earlier example:

```
// Create an output stream
FileOutputStream fos = new FileOutputStream(f);

// Output the memory document using XMLUtils.
XMLUtils.outputDOMc14nWithComments(doc, fos);
```

Running the `CertifiedPO` Application

Compile the source shown in Listing 8-5 by using the following command line:

```
C:\<working folder>\ch08\src>javac -d . CertifiedPO.java
```

Run the application by using the following command line:

```
C:\<working folder>\ch08\src>java apress.ApacheXML.ch08.CertifiedPO
```

On a successful run of the application, you will find the `PO-certified.xml` file created in your working folder. Outputting this file to your console or opening it in your browser would produce a screen output similar to the one shown here:

```
<PurchaseOrder>
  <signedContents>
    We request that you EXECUTE the following trades
    <stock>GFW</stock>
    <quantity>50</quantity>
    <price>25.35</price>
    <type>B</type>
    <stock>ABNPRF</stock>
    <quantity>100</quantity>
    <price>24.83</price>
    <type>S</type>
  </signedContents>
  <Signature xmlns="http://www.w3.org/2000/09/xmldsig#">
    <SignedInfo>
      <CanonicalizationMethod
        Algorithm="http://www.w3.org/TR/2001/REC-xml-c14n-20010315">
      </CanonicalizationMethod>
      <SignatureMethod
        Algorithm="http://www.w3.org/2000/09/xmldsig#dsa-sha1">
      </SignatureMethod>
      <Reference URI="">
        <Transforms>
          <Transform
            Algorithm="http://www.w3.org/2000/09/xmldsig#enveloped-signature">
          </Transform>
        </Transforms>
        <DigestMethod
          Algorithm="http://www.w3.org/2000/09/xmldsig#sha1">
        </DigestMethod>
        <DigestValue>KhvCkxATMSfEBakaOMscs1AaDmw=</DigestValue>
      </Reference>
    </SignedInfo>
    <SignatureValue>d9Z4Q3E7T+gJgQHBMCCtJm4hG6QzhU39B/bvbWZnizVFOMH3wc49vQ==
    </SignatureValue>
```

```
      <KeyInfo>
        <X509Data>
          <X509Certificate>
MIIDIzCCAuECBEPgThQwCwYHKoZIzjgEAwUAMHcxCzAJBgNVBAYTAklOMRQwEgYDVQQIEwtNYWhhcmF
zaHRyYTEPMAoGA1UEBxMGTXVtYmFpMQ4wDAYDVQQKEwVBQkNPTTESMBAGA1UECxMJQXV0aG9yaW5nMR
OwGwYDVQQDExRQb29ybmFjaGFuZHJhIFNhcmFuZzAeFwOwNjAyMDEwNTU4NDRaFwOwNjA1MDIwNTU4N
DRaMHcxCzAJBgNVBAYTAklOMRQwEgYDVQQIEwtNYWhhcmFzaHRyYTEPMAoGA1UEBxMGTXVtYmFpMQ4w
DAYDVQQKEwVBQkNPTTESMBAGA1UECxMJQXV0aG9yaW5nMRowGwYDVQQDExRQb29ybmFjaGFuZHJhIFN
hcmFuZzCCAbgwggEsBgcqhkjOOAQBMIIBHwKBgQD9f1OBHXUSKVLfSpwu7OTn9hG3UjzvRADDHj+Atl
EmaUVdQCJR+1k9jVj6v8X1ujD2y5tVbNeBO4AdNG/yZmC3a5lQpaSfn+gEexAiwk+7qdf+t8Yb+DtX5
8aophUPBPuD9tPFHsMCNVQTWhaRMvZ1864rYdcq7/IiAxmdOUgBxwIVAJdgUI8VIwvMspK5gqLrhAvw
WBz1AoGBAPfhoIXWmz3ey7yrXDa4V7l5lK+7+jrqgvlXTAs9B4JnUVlXjrrUWU/mcQcQgYCOSRZxI+h
MKBYTt88JMozIpuE8FnqLVHyNKOCjrh4rs6Z1kW6jfwv6ITVi8ftiegEkO8yk8b6oUZCJqIPf4Vrlnw
aSi2ZegHtVJWQBTDv+zOkqA4GFAAKBgQDfCQe9UlgB4/1k9gC9QqdwqTnJAzKQV+sCYkWWckmSL1LvT
jcX37pvOTO6azdSWDfdpWAH99TkrbTmX2wOopuKSTGCDNrf+bbmiWZeLg/36Vnm4F3lFLXzKk25sWx4
5DzkpW8cEu7T5G/3uwAgRVmkrHTqVOD7ezbwytDOEADOMDALBgcqhkjOOAQDBQADLwAwLAIUMKHnmQm
z4pJT1T37I7mUb7KjhfYCFCU+b7suEeRGHQ1k7ZNeSllb2xs7
          </X509Certificate>
        </X509Data>
        <KeyValue>
          <DSAKeyValue>
            <P>
/X9TgR11EilS30qcLuzk5/YRt1I87OQAwx4/gLZRJmlFXUAiUftZPY1Y+r/F9bow9subVWzXgTuAHTR
v8mZgt2uZUKWkn5/oBHsQIsJPu6nX/rfGG/g7V+fGqKYVDwT7g/bTxR7DAjVUE1oWkTL2dfOuK2HXKu
/yIgMZndFIAcc=
            </P>
            <Q>l2BQjxUjC8yykrmCouuEC/BYHPU=</Q>
            <G>
9+GghdabPd7LvKtcNrhXuXmUr7v6OuqC+VdMCzOHgmdRWVeOutRZT+ZxBxCBgLRJFnEj6EwoFhO3zwk
yjMim4TwWeotUfIOo4KOuHiuzpnWRbqN/C/ohNWLx+2J6ASQ7zKTxvqhRkImog9/hWuWfBpKLZl6Ae1
UlZAFMO/7PSSo=
            </G>
            <Y>
3wkHvVJYAeP9ZPYAvUKncKk5yQMykFfrAmJFlnJJki9S7043F9+6b9Ezums3Ulg33aVgB/fU5K20519
sNKKbikkxggza3/m25olmXi4P9+lZ5uBd5RS18ypNubFseOQ85KVvHBLuO+Rv97sAIEVZpKxO6lTg+3
s28MrQ9BAA9DA=
            </Y>
          </DSAKeyValue>
        </KeyValue>
      </KeyInfo>
    </Signature>
</PurchaseOrder>
```

Note that the output document now contains an X509Certificate element that contains the encoded data for the certificate. The receiver will use this certificate to establish trust in the sender-provided public key.

We will now develop an application for verifying this document.

Verifying Documents Containing Digital Certificates

Like the earlier example of Listing 8-3, the document verification process using a digital certificate is easy. The entire application for document verification is available in the VerifyCertifiedPO.java file in your downloaded code. I will discuss only the relevant code, shown here:

```java
// Retrieve the key information
KeyInfo ki = signature.getKeyInfo();

if (ki != null) {
    X509Certificate cert = signature.getKeyInfo().getX509Certificate();

    if (cert != null) {
      boolean result = signature.checkSignatureValue(cert);
      String str = null;
      if (result)
        str = "The document " + f.toURL().toString() + " is valid!";
      else
        str = "The document " + f.toURL().toString() + " is invalid!";
          System.out.println(str);
    } else {
      System.out.println("Did not find a Certificate");
    }

} else {
  System.out.println("Missing KeyInfo");
}
```

As in the earlier case, we retrieve the Signature element from the received document and obtain the key information from it. From the key information, we retrieve the embedded certificate by calling its getX509Certificate method:

```java
X509Certificate cert = signature.getKeyInfo().getX509Certificate();
```

We verify the document by calling the checkSignatureValue method on the signature. The method takes the preceding cert as its parameter. The method returns a boolean value that indicates the success or failure of the verification:

```java
boolean result = signature.checkSignatureValue(cert);
```

■**Note** The sender need not attach a certificate to every signed document, if such a certificate is made available to the intended receiver in advance. The receiver can store the certificate in his own keystore and refer to it whenever the authenticity of the sender's public key is to be established.

Running the VerifyCertifiedPO Application

Compile the provided `VerifyCertifiedPO.java` file by using the following command line:

```
C:\<working folder>\ch08\src>javac -d . VerifyCertifiedPO.java
```

Run the application by using the following command line:

```
C:\<working folder>\ch08\src>java apress.ApacheXML.ch08.VerifyCertifiedPO
```

You will see output similar to the following:

```
Trying to verify file:/C:/apress/ch08/src/PO-certified.xml
Feb 4, 2006 4:07:43 PM org.apache.xml.security.signature.Reference verify
INFO: Verification successful for URI ""
The document file:/C:/apress/ch08/src/PO-certified.xml is valid!
```

So far you have seen how to sign a document and how a receiver of the document establishes the document's authenticity and integrity. However, in all of these cases, the document content always remains readable to an interceptor. You will now study the techniques of encryption and decryption so that the document content would make sense only to a legitimate intended receiver and not to an interceptor.

Using XML Encryption/Decryption

As stated earlier in this chapter, encryption transforms the document content known as plaintext to gibberish, or ciphertext. The encrypted document makes little or no sense to anybody receiving it. A legitimate receiver has to decrypt the document by using a shared secret key to retrieve the document in its original format.

In this section, I will illustrate encryption and decryption techniques by using an example. We will use the dynamic PO document from Listing 8-3 as a sample document for encryption. We will encrypt the content of this document and output it to a file. Later, the receiver will decrypt this document to read the original content.

Developing an Application for Encrypting the PO

As mentioned earlier, we will use a symmetric key for encryption because of its quicker processing time as compared to asymmetric-key cryptography. We will create a symmetric key during the application session. This symmetric key, which is valid only during the application session, must be given to the receiver. Thus, we will serialize the key to a file and distribute it along with the encrypted file. We will encrypt the symmetric key by using another key called the key encryption key (KEK) so that even if an interceptor gets his hands on the symmetric key, it would not be useful to him unless he decrypts the received key. The entire process is illustrated in Figure 8-10.

The key generator uses salt[9] to randomize the password.

---

9. Refer to *RSA Security's Official Guide to Cryptography* by Steve Burnett and Stephen Paine (McGraw-Hill, 2001).

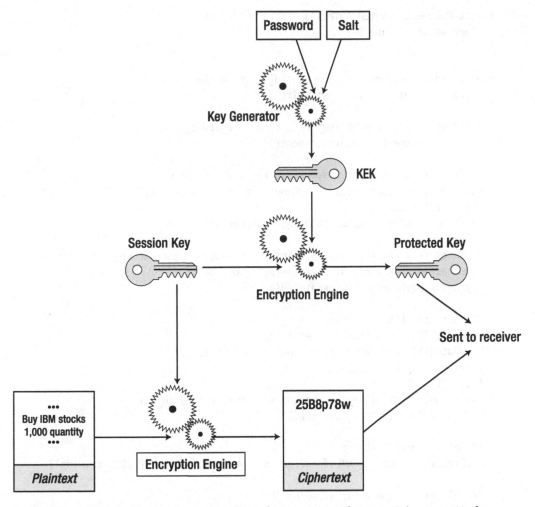

Figure 8-10. *Encryption based on combination of symmetric and asymmetric cryptography*

So let's now look at the application that encrypts our PO. Listing 8-6 illustrates how to encrypt a source XML document.

Listing 8-6. *Application for Encrypting the PO* (Ch08\src\EncryptPO.java)

```
/*
 * EncryptPO.java
 */
package apress.ApacheXML.ch08;

// import required classes

public class EncryptPO{
```

```java
static Document createDocument() throws Exception {
// Same as in Listing 8-3
}

public static void main(String unused[]) throws Exception {
  org.apache.xml.security.Init.init();

  // Create a PO document that we intend to encrypt
  Document document = createDocument();

  // Generate a 128 bit AES symmetric key for encryption
  KeyGenerator keyGenerator = KeyGenerator.getInstance("AES");
  keyGenerator.init(128);
  Key symmetricKey = keyGenerator.generateKey();

  // Generate a key (KEK) for encrypting the above symmetric key
  keyGenerator = KeyGenerator.getInstance("DESede");
  Key kek = keyGenerator.generateKey();

  // Store the KEK to a file
  File kekFile = new File("SecretKEK");
  FileOutputStream f = new FileOutputStream(kekFile);
  f.write(kek.getEncoded());
  f.close();
  System.out.println("Key encryption key (KEK) stored in " +
          kekFile.toURL().toString());

  // Get a Cipher instance
  XMLCipher keyCipher = XMLCipher.getInstance(XMLCipher.TRIPLEDES_KeyWrap);

  // Initialize Cipher for wrapping KEK
  keyCipher.init(XMLCipher.WRAP_MODE, kek);

  // Encrypt symmetric key with KEK
  EncryptedKey encryptedKey = keyCipher.encryptKey(document, symmetricKey);

  // Obtain document root element reference for encypting the document
  Element rootElement = document.getDocumentElement();

  // Create and initalize cipher for encyption using our symmetric key
  XMLCipher xmlCipher = XMLCipher.getInstance(XMLCipher.AES_128);
  xmlCipher.init(XMLCipher.ENCRYPT_MODE, symmetricKey);

  // Add the document to be signed and the encryption key into
  // a KeyInfo instance
  KeyInfo keyInfo = new KeyInfo(document);
  keyInfo.add(encryptedKey);
```

```
// Add the key information to cipher
EncryptedData encryptedData = xmlCipher.getEncryptedData();
encryptedData.setKeyInfo(keyInfo);

// This is where actual encryption takes place
xmlCipher.doFinal(document, rootElement, true);

// Open file for storing encrypted document
File encryptionFile = new File("encryptedPO.xml");
f = new FileOutputStream(encryptionFile);

// Create transformer for outputting encrypted document to a stream
Transformer transformer =
        TransformerFactory.newInstance().newTransformer();
transformer.setOutputProperty(OutputKeys.OMIT_XML_DECLARATION, "yes");

// Perform the transformation
DOMSource source = new DOMSource(document);
StreamResult result = new StreamResult(f);
transformer.transform(source, result);

f.close();
System.out.println("Wrote encrypted document to " +
        encryptionFile.toURL().toString());
    }
}
```

After initializing the security system, the main function creates the PO document as in our earlier examples.

Next, we generate a 128-bit symmetric key by using the Advanced Encryption Standard (AES) algorithm:

```
// Generate a 128 bit AES symmetric key for encryption
KeyGenerator keyGenerator = KeyGenerator.getInstance("AES");
keyGenerator.init(128);
Key symmetricKey = keyGenerator.generateKey();
```

■**Note** The discussion of AES or any other algorithm for key generation is beyond the scope of this book. You can refer to a local copy of the Java Cryptography Extension (JCE) reference guide (`<JDK installation folder>\docs\guide\security\JCERefGuide.html`) or its online version (at http://java.sun.com/products/jce/reference/docs/index.html) for more general information on cryptography.

Next, we will generate a key for encrypting this symmetric key so that if it landed in the wrong hands en route to the intended receiver, the interceptor would not be able to use it to decrypt the original document (unless the interceptor figured out how to decrypt the received key to retrieve the original symmetric key). As noted earlier in this chapter, a key that is used for encrypting another key (symmetric key) is generally called a KEK—a key that encrypts another key.

We generate the KEK like the earlier key generation, by using the generateKey method of the KeyGenerator class, except that we use a different algorithm for key generation. This is an additional safety provided for securing the document contents. The point is that even if somebody breaks the algorithm used for encryption, he will have to now break two such algorithms:

```
// Generate a key (KEK) for encrypting the above symmetric key
keyGenerator = KeyGenerator.getInstance("DESede");
Key kek = keyGenerator.generateKey();
```

After the KEK is generated, we store it to a file for transporting it to the intended receiver:

```
// Store the KEK to a file
File kekFile = new File("SecretKEK");
FileOutputStream f = new FileOutputStream(kekFile);
f.write(kek.getEncoded());
f.close();
System.out.println("Key encryption key (KEK) stored in " +
        kekFile.toURL().toString());
```

We will now look into how to encrypt our document by using these keys. As mentioned earlier, the encrypted data is called ciphertext. Apache defines a class called XMLCipher for representing this ciphertext. We create an instance of this class by calling its getInstance method. The getInstance method receives the algorithm that we intend to use for encryption as a parameter:

```
// Get a Cipher instance
XMLCipher keyCipher = XMLCipher.getInstance(XMLCipher.TRIPLEDES_KeyWrap);
```

We use a Triple DES (Digital Encryption Standard) algorithm in the current case.

Note Many more algorithms are available in the Apache implementation of XML signatures. Refer to the documentation of the XMLCipher class for a list of implemented algorithms.

Next, we initialize the cipher for wrapping the KEK:

```
// Initialize Cipher for wrapping KEK
keyCipher.init(XMLCipher.WRAP_MODE, kek);
```

The first parameter to the init method specifies whether the cipher is used for encryption and decryption, or for key wrapping and unwrapping. We will use the encryption mode later in our code when we create a cipher for encrypting our document.

We now encrypt the symmetric key using our KEK by calling the encryptKey method on the cipher:

```
// Encrypt symmetric key using KEK
EncryptedKey encryptedKey = keyCipher.encryptKey(document, symmetricKey);
```

After encrypting the key, we encrypt the document. We first obtain the reference to the root node:

```
// Obtain document root element reference for encypting the document
Element rootElement = document.getDocumentElement();
```

We create another cipher for encrypting our document, initialize it for the appropriate mode, and specify the use of the previously generated symmetric key:

```
// Create and initalize cipher for encption using our symmetric key
XMLCipher xmlCipher = XMLCipher.getInstance(XMLCipher.AES_128);
xmlCipher.init(XMLCipher.ENCRYPT_MODE, symmetricKey);
```

Before we perform the actual encryption, we need to inform the cipher about the whereabouts of our document to be encrypted and the encryption key. For this, we construct a KeyInfo object that refers to the document to be signed. We use its add method to add the encryption key to it:

```
// Add the document to be signed and the encryption key into
// a KeyInfo instance
KeyInfo keyInfo = new KeyInfo(document);
keyInfo.add(encryptedKey);
```

Now, we add the keyInfo itself to the cipher. This is done by obtaining a reference to its EncryptedData object and setting the KeyInfo on it:

```
// Add the key information to cipher
EncryptedData encryptedData = xmlCipher.getEncryptedData();
encryptedData.setKeyInfo(keyInfo);
```

In the next step, when we perform the actual encryption, this encryptedData element will contain the ciphertext corresponding to the plaintext from our document.

We perform the actual encryption by calling the doFinal method on the cipher object:

```
// This is where actual encryption takes place
xmlCipher.doFinal(document, rootElement, true);
```

The first parameter to the doFinal method refers to the context document to be encrypted; in our case, it is the program-generated PO document. The second parameter indicates the node whose contents are to be encrypted, and the third parameter indicates that we want to encrypt the contents of the node and not the node itself.

After successful execution, the doFinal method replaces the contents of the EncryptedData element with the generated ciphertext. At this stage, you have an in-memory encrypted document corresponding to our PO. We will serialize this to a physical file for transporting it to an intended receiver. The rest of the code in the main function does the job of serialization of the in-memory DOM structure by using XSLT transformations (discussed in Chapter 5).

Running the EncryptPO Application

Compile the EncryptPO.java file by using the following command line:

```
C:\<working folder>\ch08\src>javac -d . EncryptPO.java
```

Run the application by using the following command:

```
C:\<working folder>\ch08\src>java apress.ApacheXML.ch08.EncryptPO
```

The console output from running this application is as follows:

```
Key encryption key (KEK) stored in file:/C:/apress/ch08/src/SecretKEK
Wrote encrypted document to file:/C:/apress/ch08/src/encryptedPO.xml
```

The application has created two files, the SecretKEK that contains the key for decrypting the symmetric session key used for document encryption, and the encrypted document itself in the encryptedPO.xml file. The receiver must have access to both files to recover the original document contents.

Examining the Encrypted Document

If you open the generated encryptedPO.xml file in your browser, you will see output similar to the following:

```
<PurchaseOrder>
  <xenc:EncryptedData
    xmlns:xenc="http://www.w3.org/2001/04/xmlenc#"
    Type="http://www.w3.org/2001/04/xmlenc#Content">
    <xenc:EncryptionMethod
      Algorithm="http://www.w3.org/2001/04/xmlenc#aes128-cbc"
      xmlns:xenc="http://www.w3.org/2001/04/xmlenc#" />
    <ds:KeyInfo xmlns:ds="http://www.w3.org/2000/09/xmldsig#">
      <xenc:EncryptedKey
        xmlns:xenc="http://www.w3.org/2001/04/xmlenc#">
        <xenc:EncryptionMethod
          Algorithm="http://www.w3.org/2001/04/xmlenc#kw-tripledes"
          xmlns:xenc="http://www.w3.org/2001/04/xmlenc#" />
        <xenc:CipherData
          xmlns:xenc="http://www.w3.org/2001/04/xmlenc#">
          <xenc:CipherValue
```

```
            xmlns:xenc="http://www.w3.org/2001/04/xmlenc#">
            IgeLdkOmi9KOOq8bbsKAeImpXA8/FEnNKAE+SU3UOtQ=
            </xenc:CipherValue>
        </xenc:CipherData>
      </xenc:EncryptedKey>
    </ds:KeyInfo>
    <xenc:CipherData xmlns:xenc="http://www.w3.org/2001/04/xmlenc#">
      <xenc:CipherValue
        xmlns:xenc="http://www.w3.org/2001/04/xmlenc#">
2zqKbOKWiytZSOIwHQ5Zdb9o6stHPH8uhb2We9dQCo33a/r7JmQIe5TBdEFjl8N+ik1XZ6dTg8b7z1M
MVuN8kVZYrzQNcG/qpcuhGzbeDLYoEU7zjbMoJ1IX4fNaHltedLVJDVnPOk6ZzuFD8m6qj6ww9KtN7l
nBXGgqochuZngIBZiJV2TV41mk5SEL8HbcBHf4M3+/JJkDpgOFOtnQaA+FOX4cvd3GuIFpqy5elasGr
nVaS1DUuHfesBtPnaAJRx/CSeFD+l2+v6/vNLvbQERHIwL88hkSybTwSuXmG6B40QvwsAeS8cO6koDJ
DGWIWAF4+gzODc9nONemvjojyA==
      </xenc:CipherValue>
    </xenc:CipherData>
  </xenc:EncryptedData>
</PurchaseOrder>
```

Note the presence of the `CipherValue` and `CipherData` elements. These encapsulate the generated ciphertext. Our receiver will have to decrypt this data by using the procedures described in the next section to retrieve the original document contents. Any interceptor receiving this encrypted file will not gain any information about the contents in the original document.

Now, we will develop an application that decrypts the PO: `encryptedPO.xml`.

Developing an Application for Decrypting the PO

The application that decrypts our encrypted PO must have access to two files: the encrypted document file itself, and the file containing the KEK. The application will have to read the KEK, use it to decrypt the symmetric session key used for encryption, and then decrypt the encrypted document. This process is depicted in Figure 8-11.

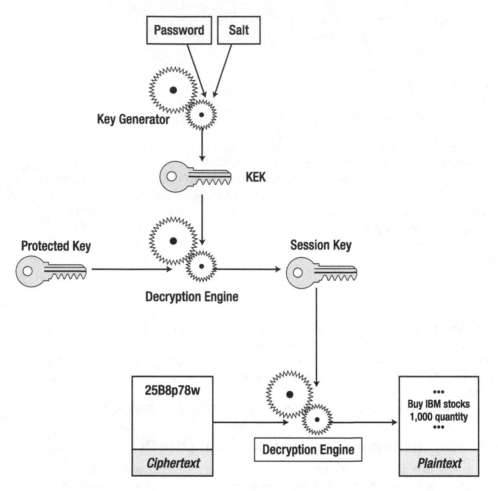

Figure 8-11. *Decryption based on both symmetric and asymmetric cryptography*

Listing 8-7 illustrates how the decryption is performed.

Listing 8-7. *Application for Decrypting Encrypted Purchase Order Document* (Ch08\src\ DecryptPO.java)

```
/*
 * DecryptPO.java
 */
package apress.ApacheXML.ch08;

// import required classes

public class DecryptPO {
```

```java
public static void main(String unused[]) throws Exception {
    org.apache.xml.security.Init.init();

    // Open the encrypted document and build a DOM tree from it
    File f = new File("encryptedPO.xml");
    javax.xml.parsers.DocumentBuilderFactory dbf =
            javax.xml.parsers.DocumentBuilderFactory.newInstance();
    dbf.setNamespaceAware(true);
    javax.xml.parsers.DocumentBuilder db = dbf.newDocumentBuilder();
    Document document = db.parse(f);
    System.out.println("Encrypted PO loaded from " +f.toURL().toString());

    // Read encrypted data element
    Element encryptedDataElement =(Element) document.getElementsByTagNameNS(
            EncryptionConstants.EncryptionSpecNS,
            EncryptionConstants._TAG_ENCRYPTEDDATA).item(0);

    // Load KEK
    String fileName = "SecretKEK";
    File kekFile = new File(fileName);

    // Construct the DES key specs from the file contents
    DESedeKeySpec keySpec = new DESedeKeySpec(
            JavaUtils.getBytesFromFile(fileName));

    // Create a key factory instance
    SecretKeyFactory skf = SecretKeyFactory.getInstance("DESede");

    // Generate the key from the specs
    Key kek = skf.generateSecret(keySpec);
    System.out.println("Key encryption key loaded from " +
            kekFile.toURL().toString());

    // Get cipher instance
    XMLCipher xmlCipher = XMLCipher.getInstance();

    // Initialize cipher for decryption
    xmlCipher.init(XMLCipher.DECRYPT_MODE, null);

    // Set the KEK that contains the key for decryption
    xmlCipher.setKEK(kek);

    // Perform the actual decryption
    xmlCipher.doFinal(document, encryptedDataElement);
```

```
        // Open file for writing in-memory decrypted document
        File decryptedFile = new File("decryptedPO.xml");
        FileOutputStream fo = new FileOutputStream(decryptedFile);

        // Serialize DOM to file using transformations
        TransformerFactory factory = TransformerFactory.newInstance();
        Transformer transformer = factory.newTransformer();
        transformer.setOutputProperty(OutputKeys.OMIT_XML_DECLARATION, "yes");
        DOMSource source = new DOMSource(document);
        StreamResult result = new StreamResult(fo);
        transformer.transform(source, result);

        fo.close();
        System.out.println("Wrote decrypted PO to " +
                decryptedFile.toURL().toString());
    }
}
```

After initializing the system, the main function loads the encrypted document and constructs an in-memory DOM for further processing. This code is similar to the code in Listing 8-4 that described how to decrypt a signed document.

The program then extracts the encrypted data element for the in-memory document:

```
// Read encrypted data element
Element encryptedDataElement =(Element) document.getElementsByTagNameNS(
        EncryptionConstants.EncryptionSpecNS,
        EncryptionConstants._TAG_ENCRYPTEDDATA).item(0);
```

Note that this encrypted data element contains the ciphertext and also a reference to the keys used for encryption. Before we decrypt the data, we must obtain the KEK and thus the symmetric key used for encryption. We construct the File object for reading the KEK:

```
// Load KEK
String fileName = "SecretKEK";
File kekFile = new File(fileName);
```

We construct the DES key specs from the data read from the KEK file:

```
// Construct the DES key specs from the file contents
DESedeKeySpec keySpec = new DESedeKeySpec(
        JavaUtils.getBytesFromFile(fileName));
```

We create an instance of the secret key factory:

```
// Create a key factory instance
SecretKeyFactory skf = SecretKeyFactory.getInstance("DESede");
```

We now generate the key itself by using the factory and the key specifications read from the KEK file:

```
// Generate the key from the specs
Key kek = skf.generateSecret(keySpec);
```

Now that we have obtained the encrypted data and the key used for encryption (in fact, only the KEK and not the symmetric key), we will proceed with the decryption. For this, we first construct the instance of the XMLCipher class. Remember, this class represents the ciphertext:

```
// Get cipher instance
XMLCipher xmlCipher = XMLCipher.getInstance();
```

We initialize the cipher for decrypt mode:

```
// Initialize cipher for decryption
xmlCipher.init(XMLCipher.DECRYPT_MODE, null);
```

We set the KEK on the cipher. Note that the KEK encapsulates the symmetric key:

```
// Set the KEK that contains the key for decryption
xmlCipher.setKEK(kek);
```

We now perform the actual decryption by calling the doFinal method on the cipher object:

```
// Perform the acutal decryption
xmlCipher.doFinal(document, encryptedDataElement);
```

At this stage, the content of the encrypted data element is replaced by the decrypted data, that is, the plaintext. We now simply need to serialize this in-memory DOM data to a file. The rest of the code in the main function does this. This uses transformations and is similar to the code described in earlier examples.

Running the DecryptPO Application

Compile the provided DecryptPO.java file by using the following command line:

```
C:\<working folder>\ch08\src>javac -d . DecryptPO.java
```

Run the application by using the following command:

```
C:\<working folder>\ch08\src>java apress.ApacheXML.ch08.DecryptPO
```

On a successful run of the application, you will find a file called decryptedPO.xml generated in your work folder. The content of this file is as follows:

```
<PurchaseOrder>
  <signedContents>
    We request that you EXECUTE the following trades
    <stock>GFW</stock>
    <quantity>50</quantity>
    <price>25.35</price>
    <type>B</type>
    <stock>ABNPRF</stock>
    <quantity>100</quantity>
    <price>24.83</price>
    <type>S</type>
  </signedContents>
</PurchaseOrder>
```

Note that this is the content generated by our sender.

Summary

In this chapter, you studied an important aspect of XML programming: how to implement security in your XML applications. XML is widely used for data transport, but if the data is not securely transported, these XML applications will find little use in practical life. The XML signature provides this security.

The chapter started by describing important security terms such as authentication, authorization, and nonrepudiation. Authentication signifies that you are allowed to use the application. Within the application, what you are allowed to do is decided by the authorization. Nonrepudiation guarantees that the parties involved in the secured communication cannot deny at a later time that they performed a particular operation during their secured communication. You were also introduced to other security terms such as message integrity and message confidentiality.

These requirements of security are implemented by using two cryptography techniques: symmetric and asymmetric. As their names suggest, symmetric cryptography is based on a single shared key used by both sender and receiver during their secured communication. Asymmetric cryptography uses a matching key pair consisting of a public and a private key. The public key is given to everybody, while the private key is held only by the person generating the key pair. The sender signs and/or encrypts the document by using her private key, and the receiver verifies and/or decrypts the document by using the public key supplied by the sender.

Asymmetric cryptography solves the problem of sharing and distributing the key. However, asymmetric cryptography is much slower than its counterpart. Thus, in practice we use a combination of both. We create a message digest on the input document by using a symmetric key, and encrypt this symmetric key by using asymmetric cryptography. The symmetric key is encrypted by using the private key of the sender. The receiver retrieves the symmetric key by using the sender's public key. The encrypted session key must itself be transported over a secured channel. This is what is done in HTTPS protocol, where the session key is transported after establishing the authentication. In HTTPS, the session key is also changed periodically to add further security against hackers who may intercept network traffic and perform a brute-force or any other attack on a session key.

The XML signature uses these cryptography techniques for implementing security in XML applications. Unlike other digital signatures, an XML signature allows you to sign only a part of the input document. This gives us an advantage of being able to pass the XML document through a series of approvers, where each approver can process the document and add some information to it. Note that when using a digital signature, because the entire document as a whole is signed, any changes made to the document invalidate its signature.

This chapter also described the three types of XML signatures: The signature can be included in a document that is signed, or the Signature element can include the document, or the signature can be totally detached from the document.

Because of XML's less-restrictive structuring, two XML documents may differ physically but carry the same logical content. Because digital signatures are sensitive to the physical content of a signed document, creating identical signatures for the two logically same documents is impossible. This problem is solved by creating canonical XML, whereby predefined transformation rules transform the input document to standard XML format.

This entire theory was explained further through examples. We considered a case of signing and verifying a purchase order by using both runtime-generated key pairs and the key pair taken from a digital certificate.

Signing the document helps in establishing the sender's identity and the integrity of the signed document's content. It does not solve the problem of hiding the content from the hacker's eyes. Encryption techniques solve this problem by converting the plaintext to gibberish that does not make any sense to the interceptor. The legitimate user of the data decrypts the data to look up the original content. The chapter described the Apache implementation of encryption/decryption techniques with the help of practical examples.

CHAPTER 9

■ ■ ■

XML Databases

We have been using XML documents throughout this book. Considering our brokerage house, imagine the number of XML documents that the brokerage would create and maintain over a period of time. These documents need to be organized properly so that they can be located on demand. Also, these documents may need to be queried to locate those containing a specified search string. Storing these documents in an XML database can greatly enhance your ability to effectively carry out these tasks and more.

An XML database stores the information in a hierarchical structure that enables users to quickly search by using keyword indexes. It stores the data (that is, the information) within XML format itself, foregoing the need to transform the data when performing inserts or retrievals. Because the documents do not need any transformation, storing documents that have complicated structures is easy. Compare this to storing data in a conventional relational database, where the data must often undergo complicated transformations to meet the storage requirements defined by that technology.

However, you must be wondering how you interact with the database. To query XML databases, we use XPath specifications. As you saw in earlier chapters, XPath provides a powerful syntax for locating nodes in an XML document. Thus, we use XPath expressions to locate documents containing the desired elements and attributes. You may also want to update documents stored in the database without extracting them from storage. We use the XML:DB XUpdate language for writing such update queries.

You will learn all these techniques of database creation, data retrieval, and data updates in this chapter. You will use command-line tools for creating, querying, and updating XML databases. You will also learn about the administration tasks for the database and managing the database through programmatic control. The XML:DB project provides the API for managing the XML databases. You will learn this API in this chapter.

Introducing Apache Xindice

The Apache Xindice (pronounced zeen-dee-chay) project, initially known as dbXML Core, defines the structure and programming API for XML databases. The dbXML source code was donated to the Apache Software Foundation in 2001. You will use Apache Xindice in this chapter to learn about XML databases.

Apache Xindice is a native XML database designed to store XML documents. Using Xindice, you store XML documents in their native format. Thus, there is no need to transform these documents into any other format. Contrast this to the data storage in a typical Indexed Sequential Access Method (ISAM) database or Relational Database Management System

(RDBMS). The database can be queried by using command-line tools or through programmatic control. Similarly, the data in XML documents stored in the database can be modified without the need for retrieving them.

Understanding the XML Database Structure

Xindice is structured in a hierarchical fashion, meaning there are no tables, rows, columns, nor relations. You can think of the database as consisting of a series of XML documents organized in a tree structure, much like you might organize files and folders in a directory structure on your hard drive. In fact, just like a directory structure, the database has a root folder. Under the root you create various subfolders in which to add your XML documents. Figure 9-1 shows a typical database structure.

```
C:\xindice
+---db
    +---addressbook
    |       addressbook.tbl
    +---mycollection
    |       mycollection.tbl
    +---StockBrokerage
    |   |   StockBrokerage.tbl
    |   +---DailyOrders
    |   |       DailyOrders.tbl
    |   \---DailyQuotes
    |           DailyQuotes.tbl
    \---system
        +---SysAccess
        |       SysAccess.tbl
        +---SysConfig
        |       SysConfig.tbl
        +---SysGroups
        |       SysGroups.tbl
        +---SysObjects
        |       SysObjects.tbl
        +---SysSymbols
        |       SysSymbols.tbl
        \---SysUsers
                SysUsers.tbl
```

Figure 9-1. *Xindice database structure*

In Figure 9-1, db is the root folder of the database. Under this folder are four collections called addressbook, mycollection, StockBrokerage, and system. Under StockBrokerage are two subcollections called DailyOrders and DailyQuotes.

Each collection can store any number of XML document instances. Each collection can have additional subcollections. After a database is built, you can query these document instances by using XPath queries. You can also use XUpdate to update these documents without first retrieving them.

Installing Xindice

Before you try creating a database, you must install the necessary software. In this section, you'll download Xindice and then start the Xindice server.

Downloading the Software

You can download Xindice binaries from the Apache site:

http://xml.apache.org/xindice/download.cgi

The stable version as of this writing for the Windows platform is xml-xindice-1.0.zip. Download this file and unzip it to your local drive. Next perform the following tasks:

1. Set the XINDICE_HOME environment variable to <installation folder>.

2. Add the several JAR files from %XINDICE_HOME%\java\lib to your classpath.

3. Add the path %XINDICE_HOME%\bin to your environment PATH.

After you complete these steps, you are ready to test your installation.

Starting the Xindice Server

After installing the software, you need to start the Xindice database server. You do so by running the startup command in your Xindice installation folder. When you run this script, you will see screen output similar to the following:

```
C:\xindice>startup
java -classpath ".;C:\xindice\java\lib\xindice.jar;C:\soap-2_3_1\lib\soap.jar;C:
\Sun\AppServer\lib\activation.jar;C:\Sun\AppServer\lib\mail.jar;c:\ApacheAnt162\
config;C:\xindice\java\lib\ant-1.4.1.jar;C:\xindice\java\lib\examples.jar;C:\xin
dice\java\lib\infozone-tools.jar;C:\xindice\java\lib\openorb-1.2.0.jar;C:\xindic
e\java\lib\openorb_tools-1.2.0.jar;C:\xindice\java\lib\xalan-2.0.1.jar;C:\xindic
e\java\lib\xerces-1.4.3.jar;C:\xindice\java\lib\xindice.jar;C:\xindice\java\lib\
xml-apis-1.0.jar;C:\xindice\java\lib\xmldb-sdk.jar;C:\xindice\java\lib\xmldb-xup
date.jar;C:\xindice\java\lib\xmldb.jar;C:\Java\jdk1.5.0\lib\tools.jar" -noverify
org.apache.xindice.core.server.Xindice C:\xindice\config\system.xml

Xindice 1.0 (Birthday)

Database: 'db' initializing
Script: 'GET' added to script storage
Service: 'db' started
Service: 'HTTPServer' started @ http://DrSarang:4080/
Service: 'APIService' started

Server Running
```

After the server starts running, you can open the server URL (http://localhost:4080) in your browser. When you do so, you will see the Xindice server's home page, as shown in Figure 9-2.

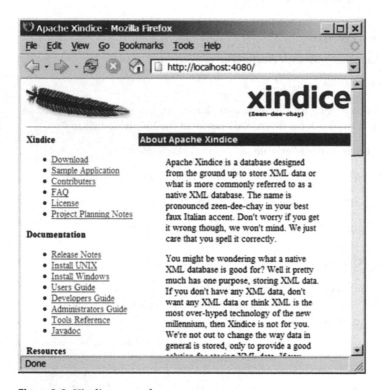

Figure 9-2. *Xindice server home page*

You are now ready to create a database.

Creating an XML Database

We will create a database used to store documents for the stock brokerage discussed in Chapter 2. The stock brokerage regularly creates several XML documents such as purchase orders, end-of-day quotes, and more. We will organize this data in a hierarchy of collections in the default db database.

To create and manage a Xindice database, Apache provides a command-line administrator utility called xindiceadmin. This utility allows you to create collections and subcollections in an existing database. A collection and a subcollection are the equivalent of a folder and a subfolder, respectively, in your directory hierarchy. A collection can contain a subcollection just as a folder can contain a subfolder.

It is also possible to create collections and subcollections through application code. This is explained later, in the "XML:DB API" section. For now, we will create collections for our stock brokerage by using the xindiceadmin utility.

Creating a Collection

Open a command prompt and change your working folder to your Xindice installation folder. You will create a collection called StockBrokerage under db.

To add a StockBrokerage collection to the db database, you use the add_collection (abbreviated ac) command switch on the xindiceadmin utility. Create the collection with the command line shown in the following screen output:

```
C:\xindice>xindiceadmin ac -c /db -n StockBrokerage
Created : /db/StockBrokerage
```

The -c switch specifies the context (/db in this case) under which the collection is to be added, and the -n switch specifies the name for the new collection. The full syntax for the add_collection command is as follows:

```
xindiceadmin add_collection {-c context} {-n name} [-v ]
```

The -v switch specifies verbose output.

If you examine the folder structure on your hard drive after running the command, you will notice that a subfolder called StockBrokerage has been created under the <xindice installation folder>\db folder. Also, note the creation of a TBL file called StockBrokerage.tbl in the created folder. This is used internally by the Xindice database server to save and track the documents added to this collection.

Creating Subcollections

You will now create two subcollections for our stock brokerage. The first collection, which we will call DailyOrders, will hold the XML document instances of the daily orders. The second collection, DailyQuotes, holds the documents containing the daily end-of-day prices of the various stocks traded on the exchange.

You add the DailyOrders subcollection by using the command line shown in the following screen output:

```
C:\xindice>xindiceadmin ac -c /db/StockBrokerage -n DailyOrders
Created : /db/StockBrokerage/DailyOrders
```

Note that, in this case, we specify the context as /db/StockBrokerage. The DailyOrders folder is now created under this context (folder). If you examine the folder structure after running the command, you will notice that a file called DailyOrders.tbl is added under the DailyOrders folder. Likewise, add a subcollection called DailyQuotes under StockBrokerage with the following command line:

```
C:\xindice>xindiceadmin ac -c /db/StockBrokerage -n DailyQuotes
```

Adding Documents

You will now add the daily orders documents and end-of-day quote files to the respective collections created in the previous sections. To add a document to a collection, you use another command-line utility called xindice with the add_document (abbreviated ad) switch.

Assume that our brokerage stores the daily orders files under the name OrderMMDDYYYY.xml, where MMDDYYYY specifies the date. Likewise, assume that it stores the daily quotation files under the name EODMMDDYYYY.xml.

Note The sample document files are available in the Ch09\XMLDocs folder of the code downloaded from the Source Code area of the Apress website (http://www.apress.com).

First, you will add the orders to our DailyOrders collection. The following screen output shows how to add an orders document:

```
C:\xindice>xindice ad -c /db/StockBrokerage/DailyOrders -f Ch09\X
MLDocs\Orders\Order01022006.xml -n Order01022006
Added document /db/StockBrokerage/DailyOrders/Order01022006
```

As in the case of xindiceadmin, the -c switch specifies the context (the collection) in which the document is to be added. The -f switch specifies the full path of the document on your local drive, and -n specifies the key to be assigned to the document. The key uniquely identifies the given document in the current context. If the -n switch is not specified, xindice will autogenerate the key. You will need this key to access this document in the database. To delete a document from the database, for example, you need to specify its key.

Adding Multiple Documents

You may occasionally want to add multiple documents to the database collection by using a single command. To do so, you use add_multiple_documents (alias addmultiple) on the xindice utility. The following screen output shows how the rest of the orders documents are added to the DailyOrders collection:

```
C:\xindice>xindice addmultiple -c /db/StockBrokerage/DailyOrders -f Ch
09\XMLDocs\Orders -e xml -v
Reading files from: XMLDocs
Added document /db/StockBrokerage/DailyOrders/Order01022006.xml
Added document /db/StockBrokerage/DailyOrders/Order01032006.xml
Added document /db/StockBrokerage/DailyOrders/Order01042006.xml
Added document /db/StockBrokerage/DailyOrders/Order01052006.xml
Added document /db/StockBrokerage/DailyOrders/Order01062006.xml
Added document /db/StockBrokerage/DailyOrders/Order01092006.xml
Added document /db/StockBrokerage/DailyOrders/Order01102006.xml
```

```
Added document /db/StockBrokerage/DailyOrders/Order01112006.xml
Added document /db/StockBrokerage/DailyOrders/Order01122006.xml
Added document /db/StockBrokerage/DailyOrders/Order01132006.xml
```

When you add multiple documents in this manner, xindice creates a unique key for each added document. This key has a value that is the same as its filename. Thus, the key for the Order01132006.xml file is Order01132006.xml. Note that even the file extension is used in the key value.

Likewise, add the provided EOD files to the DailyQuotes collection. The following screen output shows how to do this:

```
C:\xindice>xindice addmultiple -c /db/StockBrokerage/DailyQuotes -f Ch09\XMLDocs ➡
\Quotes -e xml -v
Reading files from: EOD
Added document /db/StockBrokerage/DailyQuotes/EOD01022006.xml
Added document /db/StockBrokerage/DailyQuotes/EOD01032006.xml
Added document /db/StockBrokerage/DailyQuotes/EOD01042006.xml
Added document /db/StockBrokerage/DailyQuotes/EOD01052006.xml
Added document /db/StockBrokerage/DailyQuotes/EOD01062006.xml
Added document /db/StockBrokerage/DailyQuotes/EOD01092006.xml
Added document /db/StockBrokerage/DailyQuotes/EOD01102006.xml
Added document /db/StockBrokerage/DailyQuotes/EOD01112006.xml
Added document /db/StockBrokerage/DailyQuotes/EOD01122006.xml
Added document /db/StockBrokerage/DailyQuotes/EOD01132006.xml
```

Now your database is ready for some real use.

Querying the Database

After a database is created, it can be queried to get a list of documents in the database, to retrieve a specified document from the database, to retrieve all the documents matching a specified search criterion, and more. In this section, I will introduce several commands to demonstrate these techniques.

Listing Documents in the Database

Imagine that our stock brokerage will retrieve a list of orders documents stored in the database. You use the xindice utility for this with the command list_documents (abbreviated ld). The screen output that results when you run the list query on your DailyOrders collection is as follows:

```
C:\xindice>xindice ld -c /db/StockBrokerage/DailyOrders

        Order01022006.xml
        Order01032006.xml
        Order01042006.xml
        Order01052006.xml
        Order01062006.xml
        Order01092006.xml
        Order01102006.xml
        Order01112006.xml
        Order01122006.xml
        Order01132006.xml


Total documents: 10
```

The -c switch specifies the context to search.

Retrieving a Document

Consider that the brokerage wants to retrieve the orders document for the date January 5, 2006 from the database. The following screen output shows how to perform this operation:

```
C:\xindice>xindice rd -c /db/StockBrokerage/DailyOrders -f c:\TempOrder.xml -n ➡
Order01052006.xml
Writing...
Wrote file c:\TempOrder.xml
```

The command switch used for retrieving documents is rd (retrieve_document). The -n switch specifies the document key. Note the use of the file extension in the key name. You specify the name of the output file with the switch -f. You can check the presence of the TempOrder.xml file in your root folder of drive C after running the preceding command. Check the file's contents to verify that it matches the original orders document for the said date.

Selecting Records Based on a Selection Criterion

You will now create a few queries that will select the records from our database based on the user-specified selection criterion. We specify the criterion with the help of an appropriate XPath[1] query. You will create a few such XPath queries to query our database.

Retrieving a Specific Order

Suppose the broker wants to retrieve an order for a specific customer on a specific date from the database. This can be achieved by using an XPath expression such as "/customers[@date='01022006']/customer[@ID=1]". This would select the orders placed

---

1. Refer to Chapter 5 for details on XPath syntax.

on January 2, 2006 by the customer whose ID is 1. You specify this XPath query as a value to the -q switch on the xindice command-line utility.

The command line to run the query and its output are shown here:

```
C:\xindice>xindice xpath -c /db/StockBrokerage/DailyOrders -q "/customers➥
[@date='01022006']/customer[@ID=1]"

<?xml version="1.0"?>
<customer ID="1" xmlns:src="http://xml.apache.org/xindice/Query" src:col="/
db/StockBrokerage/DailyOrders" src:key="Order01022006">
    <name>Pat Irwin</name>
    <order>MSFT</order>
    <quantity>50</quantity>
    <price>25.35</price>
  </customer>
```

Tip The Xindice release notes given in file:///C:/xml-xindice-1.0/docs/README state the following: "On Windows, command-line queries can have problems with the quote handling of the Windows shell. In general, you should put double quotes around the entire query string and use single quotes in your XPath." If you encounter problems while running some of these queries, try them on Linux. I have successfully run all the examples in this chapter on Windows 2000, but had a few problems running them on Windows XP.

Retrieving All Orders for a Specific Customer

Our broker may want to retrieve the history of all the orders placed by a certain customer. In this case, you would use an XPath expression such as /customers/customer[@ID=1]. The result of running this query on the sample database is as follows:

```
C:\xindice>xindice xpath -c /db/StockBrokerage/DailyOrders -q "/customers/➥
customer[@ID=1]"

<?xml version="1.0"?>
<customer ID="1" xmlns:src="http://xml.apache.org/xindice/Query" src:col="/
db/StockBrokerage/DailyOrders" src:key="Order01022006">
    <name>Pat Irwin</name>
    <order>MSFT</order>
    <quantity>50</quantity>
    <price>25.35</price>
  </customer>
<?xml version="1.0"?>
<customer ID="1" xmlns:src="http://xml.apache.org/xindice/Query" src:col="/
```

```
db/StockBrokerage/DailyOrders" src:key="Order01032006">
    <name>Pat Irwin</name>
    <order>MSFT</order>
    <quantity>70</quantity>
    <price>25.30</price>
  </customer>
<?xml version="1.0"?>
<customer ID="1" xmlns:src="http://xml.apache.org/xindice/Query" src:col="/
db/StockBrokerage/DailyOrders" src:key="Order01042006">
    <name>Pat Irwin</name>
    <order>MSFT</order>
    <quantity>20</quantity>
    <price>25.80</price>
  </customer>
C:\xindice
```

Retrieving Orders for a Specific Stock

Say you want to retrieve all the trade orders for IBM for a specified date. The XPath query for selecting this is /customers[@date='01022006']/customer[order='IBM']. Note that on the customers element you specify the date for selection of the orders, and for the customer element you specify the order element. The date is an attribute on the customers element and is thus preceded by an @ sign. The following is the result of running this query on our sample database:

```
C:\xindice>xindice xpath -c /db/StockBrokerage/DailyOrders -q ➥
"/customers[@date='01022006']/customer[order='IBM']"

<?xml version="1.0"?>
<customer ID="2" xmlns:src="http://xml.apache.org/xindice/Query" src:col="/
db/StockBrokerage/DailyOrders" src:key="Order01022006">
    <name>Nancy Scheffler</name>
    <order>IBM</order>
    <quantity>75</quantity>
    <price>25.30</price>
  </customer>
<?xml version="1.0"?>
<customer ID="3" xmlns:src="http://xml.apache.org/xindice/Query" src:col="/
db/StockBrokerage/DailyOrders" src:key="Order01022006">
    <name>Cheryl Zuckschwerdt</name>
    <order>IBM</order>
    <quantity>30</quantity>
    <price>25.50</price>
  </customer>
<?xml version="1.0"?>
```

```
<customer ID="4" xmlns:src="http://xml.apache.org/xindice/Query" src:col="/
db/StockBrokerage/DailyOrders" src:key="Order01022006">
    <name>Bennie Furlong</name>
    <order>IBM</order>
    <quantity>65</quantity>
    <price>25.55</price>
  </customer>
```

Determining Trades for a Specific Stock by a Specified Customer

You might want to retrieve a history of all the trades performed by a specified customer on a specified stock. The XPath query for this is given by /customers/customer[@ID=4] [order='IBM'].

The output after running this query on a sample database is as follows:

```
C:\xindice>xindice xpath -c /db/StockBrokerage/DailyOrders -q "/customers/➥
customer[@ID=4][order='IBM']"

<?xml version="1.0"?>
<customer ID="4" xmlns:src="http://xml.apache.org/xindice/Query" src:col="/
db/StockBrokerage/DailyOrders" src:key="Order01022006">
    <name>Bennie Furlong</name>
    <order>IBM</order>
    <quantity>65</quantity>
    <price>25.55</price>
  </customer>
<?xml version="1.0"?>
<customer ID="4" xmlns:src="http://xml.apache.org/xindice/Query" src:col="/
db/StockBrokerage/DailyOrders" src:key="Order01032006">
    <name>Bennie Furlong</name>
    <order>IBM</order>
    <quantity>60</quantity>
    <price>25.25</price>
  </customer>
<?xml version="1.0"?>
<customer ID="4" xmlns:src="http://xml.apache.org/xindice/Query" src:col="/
db/StockBrokerage/DailyOrders" src:key="Order01042006">
    <name>Bennie Furlong</name>
    <order>IBM</order>
    <quantity>70</quantity>
    <price>25.20</price>
  </customer>
```

Determining Orders for a Specified Stock at a Specified Price

A broker may want to consolidate all the orders by different customers placed on a particular stock at a particular requested price, before the order is finally placed on the stock exchange. The XPath query to select such records is given by /customers[@date='01032006']/ customer[price='$25.25']. The following is the result of running this query on the sample database:

```
C:\xindice>xindice xpath -c /db/StockBrokerage/DailyOrders -q "/customers➡
[@date='01032006']/customer[price='$25.25']"

<?xml version="1.0"?>
<customer ID="3" xmlns:src="http://xml.apache.org/xindice/Query" src:col="/
db/StockBrokerage/DailyOrders" src:key="Order01032006">
    <name>Cheryl Zuckschwerdt</name>
    <order>IBM</order>
    <quantity>100</quantity>
    <price>25.25</price>
  </customer>
<?xml version="1.0"?>
<customer ID="4" xmlns:src="http://xml.apache.org/xindice/Query" src:col="/
db/StockBrokerage/DailyOrders" src:key="Order01032006">
    <name>Bennie Furlong</name>
    <order>IBM</order>
    <quantity>60</quantity>
    <price>25.25</price>
  </customer>
```

Using the XML:DB API

So far you have learned how to create, maintain, and query the XML database through command-line utilities. Now you will learn to do the same through a programmatic interface.

The XML:DB Working Group has developed the API for XML databases. This API can be implemented in multiple languages. A CORBA API is designed to access the database. The Xindice libraries provide a Java-based API that uses this CORBA API for the following:

- Creating and maintaining the database collections

- Querying the database

- Deleting the data

- Updating the database

In this section, you will learn all these techniques. First, you will learn to create and maintain a collection of XML documents in a database. You will use the database structure described earlier in this chapter for the command-line interface.

Creating Collections

You will write an application that creates a collection called Brokerage in the default database db. You will use a different name than the earlier case. Earlier in this chapter you used the name StockBrokerage while creating the database by using a command-line tool. If you try to create a collection with an existing name, the program will throw an application exception. Thus, the change in name!

Under the Brokerage collection, you will create two subcollections called DailyQuotes and DailyOrders. You will use the same names for the subcollections as in the earlier case. Note that the fully qualified path for these two subcollections would be different from the path for the subcollections created earlier.

The program that creates this database is presented in Listing 9-1.

Listing 9-1. *Program to Add Collections and Subcollections to a Xindice Database* (Ch09\src\ BrokerDatabase.java)

```java
package database;

import org.xmldb.api.base.*;
import org.xmldb.api.modules.*;
import org.xmldb.api.*;
import org.apache.xindice.client.xmldb.services.*;
import org.apache.xindice.xml.dom.*;

public class BrokerDatabase {
  public static void main(String[] args) throws Exception {
    Collection col = null;
    try {
      // Load the database driver
      String driver = "org.apache.xindice.client.xmldb.DatabaseImpl";
      Class c = Class.forName(driver);

      // Create a Database instance and register it to the DatabaseManager
      Database database = (Database) c.newInstance();
      DatabaseManager.registerDatabase(database);

      // Get the reference to the root collection
      col = DatabaseManager.getCollection("xmldb:xindice:///db");

      // Set up name for the new collection
      String collectionName = "Brokerage";

      // Obtain an instance
      CollectionManager service = (CollectionManager)
      col.getService("CollectionManager", "1.0");
```

```
// Build up the Collection XML configuration.
String collectionConfig =
    "<collection compressed=\"true\" name=\"" +
    collectionName + "\">" +
    " <filer class=" +
    "\"org.apache.xindice.core.filer.BTreeFiler\" " +
    "gzip=\"true\"/>" +
    "</collection>";

service.createCollection(collectionName,
    DOMParser.toDocument(collectionConfig));

System.out.println("Collection " + collectionName + " created.");

col = DatabaseManager.getCollection("xmldb:xindice:///db/Brokerage");
collectionName = "DailyQuotes";
service = (CollectionManager)
col.getService("CollectionManager", "1.0");

// Build up the Collection XML configuration.
collectionConfig =
    "<collection compressed=\"true\" name=\"" +
    collectionName + "\">" +
    " <filer class=" +
    "\"org.apache.xindice.core.filer.BTreeFiler\" " +
    "gzip=\"true\"/>" +
    "</collection>";

service.createCollection(collectionName,
    DOMParser.toDocument(collectionConfig));

System.out.println("Collection " + collectionName + " created.");

collectionName = "DailyOrders";
// Build up the Collection XML configuration.
collectionConfig =
    "<collection compressed=\"true\" name=\"" +
    collectionName + "\">" +
    " <filer class=" +
    "\"org.apache.xindice.core.filer.BTreeFiler\" " +
    "gzip=\"true\"/>" +
    "</collection>";

service.createCollection(collectionName,
    DOMParser.toDocument(collectionConfig));
```

```
      System.out.println("Collection " + collectionName + " created.");
    } catch (XMLDBException e) {
      System.err.println("XML:DB Exception occured " +
        e.getLocalizedMessage());
    } finally {
      if (col != null) {
        col.close();
      }
    }
  }
}
```

Let's examine the program in detail. To begin, the main function first loads the database driver:

```
// Load the database driver
String driver = "org.apache.xindice.client.xmldb.DatabaseImpl";
Class c = Class.forName(driver);
```

The database driver is implemented in the org.apache.xindice.client.xmldb. DatabaseImpl class. The forName method of the class Class loads this driver file in memory.

Next, the program obtains an instance of the Database class and registers it with the DatabaseManager by calling its registerDatabase static method:

```
// Create a Database instance and register it to the DatabaseManager
Database database = (Database) c.newInstance();
DatabaseManager.registerDatabase(database);
```

You now obtain a reference to the root collection as follows:

```
// Get the reference to the root collection
col = DatabaseManager.getCollection("xmldb:xindice:///db");
```

The /db specifies the XPath to the root collection, and xmldb:xindice specifies the protocol used for accessing the database collections.

At this point, you are ready to add a collection to the root you have obtained. First, you create a name for the collection to be added:

```
// Set up name for the new collection
String collectionName = "Brokerage";
```

Next, you obtain a reference to the CollectionManager object:

```
// Obtain an instance
CollectionManager service = (CollectionManager)
col.getService("CollectionManager", "1.0");
```

The getService method of the Collection class returns a reference to the CollectionManager. The CollectionManager class, as the name suggests, is responsible for managing collections.

Next, you need to set up the collection configuration XML fragment as follows:

```
<collection compressed="true" name="Brokerage">
  <filer class="org.apache.xindice.core.filer.BTreeFiler" gzip="true"/>
</collection>
```

While creating the collection, the CollectionManager will use this configuration, which specifies that the collection should be stored in compressed form and that the name of the collection is Brokerage. It also specifies the class that is used for filing the document instances. The BTreeFiler is a Xindice-provided class that files (arranges) the documents in a binary tree.

You construct this XML document fragment by creating a String object as follows:

```
// Build up the Collection XML configuration.
String collectionConfig =
    "<collection compressed=\"true\" name=\"" +
    collectionName + "\">" +
    " <filer class=" +
    "\"org.apache.xindice.core.filer.BTreeFiler\" " +
    "gzip=\"true\"/>" +
    "</collection>";
```

Now, you will add the collection to the root by calling the createCollection method on the service manager. The method takes the collection name and the instance of the DOM[2] tree representing the configuration:

```
service.createCollection(collectionName,
    DOMParser.toDocument(collectionConfig));
```

On success, the collection is added to the desired path in the database. Next, you will add a subcollection to the newly created collection. The procedure for adding a subcollection is similar to that of adding a collection, except that you need to set the appropriate root path for adding the subcollection. This is done by obtaining the reference to the new desired root as follows:

```
col = DatabaseManager.getCollection("xmldb:xindice:///db/Brokerage");
```

Note that you specify the path as /db/Brokerage. The collections will now be added to this path. As in the earlier case, you set the name for the new collection:

```
collectionName = "DailyQuotes";
```

Next, you will add this collection by using the steps as outlined earlier. Likewise, you add another subcollection called DailyOrders to the Brokerage collection.

Running the Application

Compile the preceding program by using the following command line:

```
C:\{working folder}>javac -d . BrokerDatabase.java
```

---

2. Refer to Chapter 2 for DOM details.

Run the application by using the following command line:

```
C:\{working folder}>java database.BrokerDatabase
```

If the program succeeds, you will find that collections are created in the specified database. You can verify this by using the list_collection method on the xindice command-line utility and specifying the context as /db and /db/Brokerage, respectively. The output of these commands is shown here:

```
C:\xindice>xindice lc -c /db

        Brokerage
        system
        StockBrokerage

Total collections: 3
```

```
C:\xindice>xindice lc -c /db/Brokerage

        DailyOrders
        DailyQuotes
Total collections: 2
```

Note The list of collections may be different on your machine, depending on the existing collections in your database.

If you run the application a second time, you will get a duplicate collection exception. To avoid the exception, you'll first need to delete the created collections. You can do this by using the delete_collection (abbreviated dc) command on the xindice utility. The screen output when deleting the collection is shown here:

```
C:\xindice>xindiceadmin dc -c /db -n Brokerage
Are you sure you want to delete the collection Brokerage ? (y/n)
y
Deleted: /db/Brokerage
```

Alternatively, you can delete the collections through your application program by calling the removeCollection method on the service manager.

Note The program for removing the Brokerage collection is available in the file Ch09\src\
DeleteCollection.java in the source downloaded from the Source Code area of the Apress website
(http://www.apress.com).

Adding Documents to Collections

Previously you learned how to create collections and subcollections in your XML database.
Now you will learn to add XML documents to the created collection. An XML document is
added to the collection as its resource object. For this purpose, the XML:DB API provides a
class called XMLResource. You will create an instance of this class, initialize its contents with
the contents from the XML file resource, and then add it to the desired collection. The program that does all this is given in Listing 9-2.

Listing 9-2. *Application for Adding Documents to a Database Collection* (Ch09\src\
AddDocument.java)

```
package database;

// import required packages

public class AddDocument {
  static AddDocument doc;
  Collection col = null;
  public static void main(String[] args) throws Exception {
    if (args.length != 2)
    {
      System.out.println("Usage: java AddDocument path extension");
      System.exit(1);
    }
    // Copy the command line arguments
    String path = args[0];
    String ext = args[1];
    try {
      // Create the class instance
      doc = new AddDocument();
      // Obtain the database collection reference
      doc.col = doc.getDatabaseRoot();
      // Add documents to the database
      doc.addFiles(doc.col, path, ext);
    } catch (XMLDBException e) {
      System.err.println("XML:DB Exception occured " + e.errorCode);
    } catch (Exception e) {
        e.printStackTrace();
    } finally {
```

```
      // Close the collection
      if (doc.col != null) {
         doc.col.close();
      }
   }
}

/*
 * getDatabaseRoot makes a database connection and returns a reference
 * to the collection given by an XPath expression.
 */
private Collection getDatabaseRoot() throws XMLDBException, Exception {
   Collection coll;
   // Load the database driver
   String driver = "org.apache.xindice.client.xmldb.DatabaseImpl";
   Class c = Class.forName(driver);
   // Create a database instance
   Database database = (Database) c.newInstance();
   // Register the database instance with the Manager
   DatabaseManager.registerDatabase(database);
   // Obtain a reference to the predefined collection
   coll = DatabaseManager.getCollection
          ("xmldb:xindice:///db/StockBrokerage/DailyOrders");
   // Return the collection reference to the caller
   return coll;
}

/*
 * addFiles adds the files to the specified collection from the
 * specified folder and having a specified extension
 */
private void addFiles(Collection c, String path, String ext)
   throws IOException, Exception {
   // Create a directory object
   File f = new File(path);
   // Get the list of files having the specified extension
   File[] list = f.listFiles(new ExtensionFilter(ext));
   // Iterate through the file collection
   for (int i=0; i<list.length;i++) {
      // Read the file contents into a string buffer
      String data = readFileFromDisk(list[i]);
      // Create a new resource on the specified collection
      XMLResource document =
                  (XMLResource) col.createResource(null,"XMLResource");
      // Set the contents of the created resource
      document.setContent(data);
```

```java
            // Add the resource to the collection
            col.storeResource(document);
            // Print a message to the user
            System.out.println
                    ("Document " + list[i].getCanonicalFile() + " inserted");
        }
    }


    /*
     * readFromDiskFile reads the contents of the specified File object
     * into a string buffer and returns it to the caller
     */
    public String readFileFromDisk(File fileName) throws IOException {
        // Open an input stream on the given File
        FileInputStream in = new FileInputStream(fileName);
        // Create a buffer for reading file contents
        byte[] fileBuffer = new byte[(int)fileName.length()];
        // Read the file contents into the created buffer
        in.read(fileBuffer);
        // Close the file object
        in.close();
        // Return the buffer to the caller
        return new String(fileBuffer);
    }


    /*
     * ExtensionFilter creates a filter class for selecting the files
     * with the specified extension from a folder. The class implements the
     * accept method of the FilenameFilter interface that filters the files
     * using the specified extension.
     */
    public class ExtensionFilter implements FilenameFilter {
        private String extension ;

            // Constructor that initializes the extension filter
        public ExtensionFilter(String ext) {
            extension="." + ext;
        }
        // The accept method returns files matching the specified extension
        public boolean accept(File dir, String name) {
            return name.endsWith(extension);
        }
    }
}
```

The program accepts two command-line parameters. The first parameter specifies the folder name in which the documents are stored, and the second parameter specifies the filename extension on which the files from this folder will be filtered out. You copy the command-line arguments into local variables:

```
// Copy the command line arguments
String path = args[0];
String ext = args[1];
```

You create a class instance so that you can call its nonstatic methods:

```
doc = new AddDocument();
```

You obtain the reference to a predefined database collection in which you will add the documents:

```
// Obtain the database collection reference
doc.col = doc.getDatabaseRoot();
```

You add the documents by calling the addFiles method (discussed later) of our class:

```
// Add documents to the database
doc.addFiles(doc.col, path, ext);
```

You provide the exception processing for the entire application in the main method and finally close the database collection:

```
} catch (XMLDBException e) {
  System.err.println("XML:DB Exception occured " + e.errorCode);
} catch (Exception e) {
  e.printStackTrace();
} finally {
// Close the collection
if (doc.col != null) {
    doc.col.close();
}
}
```

You will now look at the implementation of the getDatabaseRoot method:

```
private Collection getDatabaseRoot() throws XMLDBException, Exception {
```

The method throws two types of exceptions that are then processed by the caller (this is the main method in our case).
The method first loads the database driver into the system:

```
// Load the database driver
String driver = "org.apache.xindice.client.xmldb.DatabaseImpl";
Class c = Class.forName(driver);
```

You then create a Database instance and register it with the database manager:

```
// Create a database instance
Database database = (Database) c.newInstance();
// Register the database instance with the Manager
DatabaseManager.registerDatabase(database);
```

You obtain a reference to the predefined collection in the database. Remember that you created the StockBrokerage/DailyOrders collection in the previous example. If you have not run this program (Listing 9-1) earlier, you may do so now or you may create this collection by using the command tool xindiceadmin described earlier:

```
// Obtain a reference to the predefined collection
coll = DatabaseManager.getCollection
("xmldb:xindice:///db/StockBrokerage/DailyOrders");
```

The method returns a reference to the obtained Collection object:

```
// Return the collection reference to the caller
return coll;
```

You will now learn about the implementation of the addFiles method. The addFiles method accepts the reference to the collection object obtained in the previous method (getDatabaseRoot) call, the folder path in which the documents are stored, and the extension that is used as a filter string:

```
  private void addFiles(Collection c, String path, String ext)
      throws IOException, Exception {
```

You first construct a File object by using the specified path as its argument:

```
// Create a directory object
File f = new File(path);
```

This opens the folder with the specified path. You call the listFiles method on this folder object to obtain a list of files from this folder:

```
// Get the list of files having the specified extension
File[] list = f.listFiles(new ExtensionFilter(ext));
```

While obtaining the list of files, you specify the filter by instantiating the custom class ExtensionFilter (discussed later) that accepts the filter string to be used as an argument to its constructor.

You now iterate through the list of retrieved files:

```
// Iterate through the file collection
for (int i=0; i<list.length;i++) {
```

For each File object, you read its contents by calling the readFileFromDisk method (discussed later) that returns the file contents into a string buffer:

```
// Read the file contents into a string buffer
String data = readFileFromDisk(list[i]);
```

You create an XMLResource object for adding it to the collection:

```
// Create a new resource on the specified collection
XMLResource document =
            (XMLResource) col.createResource(null,"XMLResource");
```

You set the contents of the resource to the string data returned by the readFileFromDisk method:

```
// Set the contents of the created resource
document.setContent(data);
```

You add the resource to the collection by calling its storeResource method:

```
// Add the resource to the collection
col.storeResource(document);
```

You print a confirmation message to the user and go into another iteration of the file list:

```
// Print a message to the user
System.out.println
            ("Document " + list[i].getCanonicalFile() + " inserted");
```

You will now look at the implementation of the readFromDiskFile method. The method takes a File object as its argument and returns a string containing the file contents:

```
public String readFileFromDisk(File fileName) throws IOException {
```

You open an input stream on the specified file:

```
// Open an input stream on the given File
FileInputStream in = new FileInputStream(fileName);
```

You create a buffer equal to the length of the file for storing the file contents:

```
// Create a buffer for reading file contents
byte[] fileBuffer = new byte[(int)fileName.length()];
```

You read the file contents into the created buffer and then close the file:

```
    in.read(fileBuffer);
    in.close();
```

You construct a String object from the byte buffer and return it to the caller:

```
    return new String(fileBuffer);
```

You will now learn about the implementation of the ExtensionFilter class that is declared interior to our AddDocument class:

```
public class ExtensionFilter implements FilenameFilter {
```

The ExtensionFilter class implements the FilenameFilter interface. The object of this class is used in the listFiles method of the File class to filter the file selection. The FilenameFilter provides a method called accept that you need to implement in this class.

The class constructor accepts a string argument that represents the file extension to be used for filtering and initializes a private string variable by using this extension string:

```
// Constructor that initializes the extension filter
public ExtensionFilter(String ext) {
    extension="." + ext;
}
```

The accept method returns a boolean depending on whether the given name ends with the specified extension:

```
// The accept method returns files matching the specified extension
public boolean accept(File dir, String name) {
  return name.endsWith(extension);
}
```

Running the Application

Compile the application by using the following command line:

```
C:\{working folder}>javac -d . AddDocument.java
```

Run the application by using the following command:

```
C:\{working folder }>java database.AddDocument ..\XMLDocs\Demo xml
```

The first command-line argument (..\XMLDocs\Demo) specifies the folder in which the desired documents are stored, and the second argument (xml) specifies the file extension for filtering. On successful run of the application, you will see output similar to the following:

```
Document C:\apress\Ch09\XMLDocs\Demo\Order01162006.xml inserted
Document C:\apress\Ch09\XMLDocs\Demo\Order01172006.xml inserted
```

Next, you will write an application to list all the documents stored in our database starting from a specified collection path.

Listing All Documents in the Specified XPath

The XML database is arranged in a binary tree hierarchy. To visit every node of the tree, you need to write a recursive function. The program in Listing 9-3 illustrates how to traverse the tree recursively and list all the documents in each visited subcollection.

Listing 9-3. *Application to List All the Documents Under a Given Node* (Ch09\src\ListDocs.java*)*

```java
package database;

// import required packages

public class ListDocs {
  public static void main(String[] args) throws Exception {
    if (args.length != 1) {
      System.out.println("Usage: java ListDocs XPathtoDesiredCollection");
      System.exit(1);
    }
    try {
      // Load the database driver
      String driver = "org.apache.xindice.client.xmldb.DatabaseImpl";
      Class c = Class.forName(driver);
      // Create a database instance
      Database database = (Database) c.newInstance();
       // Register the database instance with the Manager
      DatabaseManager.registerDatabase(database);
      // Construct the XPath starting from the root
      String strPath = "xmldb:xindice:///db" + args[0];
      System.out.println("Printing the list of resources at " + strPath);
      // Get the reference to the desired collection
      Collection coll = DatabaseManager.getCollection(strPath);
      // Recursively get a list of subcollections and documents therein
      ListAllDocuments(coll);
    } catch (XMLDBException e) {
      System.err.println("XML:DB Exception occured " + e.errorCode);
    } catch (Exception e) {
       e.printStackTrace();
    }
  }

  /*
   * ListAllDocuments accepts a Collection object as an argument and
   * traverses the tree recursively listing all the sub-collections and
   * documents therein.
   */
  private static void ListAllDocuments(Collection coll) throws XMLDBException {
    // Get string names of all child collections
    String [] str = coll.listChildCollections();
    // Iterate through the list of subcollections
    for (int i=0; i<str.length; i++) {
      // Print the subcollection name
      System.out.println("Collection: " + str[i]);
```

```
    // Get a list of resources within each subcollection
    String [] docs = (coll.getChildCollection(str[i])).listResources();
    // Print the names of document resources within a subcollection
    for (int j=0; j<docs.length; j++) {
      System.out.println(docs[j]);
    }
    // Revisit the function using the subcollection
    ListAllDocuments(coll.getChildCollection(str[i]));
  }
 }
}
```

The application accepts the XPath expression to the desired collection as an argument. In the main method, you construct the reference to this collection. To do this, you first load the database driver in memory:

```
// Load the database driver
String driver = "org.apache.xindice.client.xmldb.DatabaseImpl";
Class c = Class.forName(driver);
```

You create a database instance and register it with the database manager:

```
// Create a database instance
Database database = (Database) c.newInstance();
 // Register the database instance with the Manager
DatabaseManager.registerDatabase(database);
```

You construct the path to the desired collection starting from the database root and using the xmldb:xindice protocol:

```
String strPath = "xmldb:xindice:///db" + args[0];
```

You now obtain a reference to the desired collection by calling the getCollection method on the database manager:

```
// Get the reference to the desired collection
Collection coll = DatabaseManager.getCollection(strPath);
```

Now you are ready to traverse the tree with this collection as the root element. You do so by calling the ListAllDocuments method of our class:

```
// Recursively get a list of sub-collections and documents therein
ListAllDocuments(coll);
```

You will now learn about the implementation of the ListAllDocuments method. This method accepts the reference to the root collection, from where the search to subcollections begins. It throws an XMLDBException to the caller:

```
private static void ListAllDocuments(Collection coll) throws XMLDBException {
```

First, you obtain the list of child collections by calling the listChildCollections method on the collection object:

```
// Get string names of all child collections
String [] str = coll.listChildCollections();
```

You iterate through the list of subcollections and print the name of each subcollection on the user console as you visit it:

```
// Iterate through the list of subcollections
for (int i=0; i<str.length; i++) {
  // Print the subcollection name
  System.out.println("Collection: " + str[i]);
```

You get the list of document resources within each subcollection by calling the listResources method on the Collection object:

```
// Get a list of resources within each sub-collection
String [] docs = (coll.getChildCollection(str[i])).listResources();
```

You print the name of each document by iterating through the entire list of documents:

```
// Print the names of document resources within a sub-collection
for (int j=0; j<docs.length; j++) {
  System.out.println(docs[j]);
}
```

You revisit the ListAllDocuments method by passing the new Collection reference to it. The reference to the subcollection is obtained by calling the getChildCollection method on the Collection object. The method takes the name of the desired collection as an argument and returns a Collection object having this name:

```
// Revisit the function using the subcollection
ListAllDocuments(coll.getChildCollection(str[i]));
```

Running the Application

Compile the code in Listing 9-3 by using the following command line:

```
C:\{working folder}>javac -d . ListDocs.java
```

Run the application by using the following command line:

```
C:\{working folder}>java database.ListDocs /StockBrokerage
```

If you have followed the instructions in this chapter and created the suggested sample database, you will see output similar to the following when you run the preceding program:

```
Printing the list of resources at xmldb:xindice:///db/StockBrokerage
Collection: DailyOrders
Order01022006.xml
Order01032006.xml
Order01042006.xml
Order01052006.xml
Order01062006.xml
Order01092006.xml
Order01102006.xml
Order01112006.xml
Order01122006.xml
Order01132006.xml
Collection: DailyQuotes
EOD01022006.xml
EOD01032006.xml
EOD01042006.xml
EOD01052006.xml
EOD01062006.xml
EOD01092006.xml
EOD01102006.xml
EOD01112006.xml
EOD01122006.xml
EOD01132006.xml
```

Deleting Documents

You will now write an application to remove all the documents recursively, starting from a specified node. Listing 9-4 provides the recursive function that does this. The rest of the code is similar to the code in Listing 9-3.

Tip The full source of this application is available at Ch09\src\RemoveDocs.java in the source download.

Listing 9-4. *Method to Remove All Documents from a Given Collection*

```java
private static void RemoveAllDocuments(Collection coll) throws XMLDBException
  {
     // Get string names of all child collections
     String [] str = coll.listChildCollections();
     // Iterate through the list of sub-collections
     for (int i=0; i<str.length; i++) {
```

```
      // Print the subcollection name
      System.out.println("Collection: " + str[i]);
      // Get a list of resources within each subcollection
      String [] docs = (coll.getChildCollection(str[i])).listResources();
      for (int j=0; j<docs.length; j++) {
        // Obtain the resource reference
          Resource resource =
              coll.getChildCollection(str[i]).getResource(docs[j]);
        // Remove the resource
        coll.getChildCollection(str[i]).removeResource(resource);
          System.out.println("Resource " + resource.getId() + "removed");
      }
      // Revisit the function using the subcollection
      RemoveAllDocuments(coll.getChildCollection(str[i]));
    }
  }
```

The RemoveAllDocuments method accepts the Collection reference under which the documents are to be deleted. This is a recursive method similar to the ListAllDocuments method discussed earlier:

```
private static void RemoveAllDocuments(Collection coll) throws XMLDBException {
```

We first obtain the list of child collections:

```
// Get string names of all child collections
String [] str = coll.listChildCollections();
```

We iterate through the list and print the name of each subcollection as we visit it:

```
// Iterate through the list of subcollections
for (int i=0; i<str.length; i++) {
  // Print the subcollection name
  System.out.println("Collection: " + str[i]);
```

We obtain the list of resources within each subcollection by calling the listResources method on the Collection object:

```
// Get a list of resources within each subcollection
String [] docs = (coll.getChildCollection(str[i])).listResources();
```

For each listed resource, we obtain its Resource object reference by calling the getResource method on the Collection object. The getResource method accepts the resource name as its argument and returns a reference to the Resource object:

```
for (int j=0; j<docs.length; j++) {
  // Obtain the resource reference
    Resource resource =
        coll.getChildCollection(str[i]).getResource(docs[j]);
```

The resource is removed by calling the `removeResource` method on the `Collection` object. The method accepts the reference to the resource that is to be removed as a parameter.

```
// Remove the resource
coll.getChildCollection(str[i]).removeResource(resource);
    System.out.println("Resource " + resource.getId() + "removed");
```

We revisit the method for a recursive call:

```
// Revisit the function using the sub-collection
RemoveAllDocuments(coll.getChildCollection(str[i]));
```

So far, you have learned how to create collections and subcollections, and how to manage the database hierarchy of collections. You have also learned how to add documents to a collection, how to list documents in a given collection, and how to remove documents from a collection. Next, you will learn how to use XUpdate to modify the content of a document without removing it from the database.

Using the XUpdate Language

XUpdate is a language for updating XML documents and is the result of the work done as a part of the XML:DB project. To update a document, you create an XUpdate query and then run it by using the provided update query service. The query itself is written as a well-formed XML document fragment.

A typical XUpdate query is shown here:

```
<xu:modifications version="1.0" xmlns:xu="http://www.xmldb.org/xupdate">
    <xu:remove select="/customers[@date='01022006']/customer[@ID=5]"/>
</xu:modifications>
```

The query is specified in the `modifications` element, which is defined in the `http://www.xmldb.org/xupdate` namespace. The `remove` subelement is a subelement to `modifications` and indicates that we are interested in removing something (obviously an element). An element to be removed is located by using an XPath query. This is specified as a value to the `select` attribute. This query is explained further in the "Updating a Node in the Orders Collection" section. Let's first look at the full syntax of the XUpdate query.

Creating the XUpdate Query

As I said, the XUpdate query is defined by using the `modifications` element. The modifications that are allowed consist of Insert/Update/Delete operations. Thus, it is possible to insert a node in an existing document by using the XUpdate query. For this, the XUpdate specifications define the following three subelements:

- `xupdate:insert-before`: Inserts a node before the specified record (given by an XPath expression)

- `xupdate:insert-after`: Inserts a node after the specified record

- `xupdate:append`: Adds a node to the end of the document

A record position is specified by using an XPath expression assigned to the select attribute of the appropriate child element.

To insert a record, you must first construct it. The record is constructed with the help of the following subelements:

- xupdate:element

- xupdate:attribute

- xupdate:text

- xupdate:processing-instruction

- xupdate:comment

You will learn to construct a record and add it to an existing document in the programming section that follows shortly.

To modify an existing record, you use the update subelement of the modifications element. Similarly, to remove a record, you use the remove subelement.

Let's now look at some coding examples so you can understand how to perform database updates by using an XUpdate query.

Removing a Node

Suppose you want to remove an order placed by a customer from the orders document. You will use an XUpdate query to do this. Listing 9-5 shows the program that removes a record from the specified orders document for a specified customer ID.

Listing 9-5. *Application to Remove a Node* (Ch09\src\DeleteNode.java)

```java
package database;

import org.xmldb.api.base.*;
import org.xmldb.api.modules.*;
import org.xmldb.api.*;
import java.io.*;

public class DeleteNode {
  public static void main(String[] args) throws Exception {
    Collection col = null;
    // Check arguments
    if (args.length != 2) {
      System.out.println("Usage: java DeleteNode CustomerID");
      System.exit(1);
    }
    try {
      // Load driver class
      String driver = "org.apache.xindice.client.xmldb.DatabaseImpl";
      Class c = Class.forName(driver);
```

```
        // Create and register database instance
        Database database = (Database) c.newInstance();
        DatabaseManager.registerDatabase(database);
        // Retrieve a reference to DailyOrders collection
        col = DatabaseManager.getCollection
            ("xmldb:xindice:///db/StockBrokerage/DailyOrders");
         // Construct a Remove query
        String xupdate =
          "<xu:modifications version=\"1.0\"" +
          "xmlns:xu=\"http://www.xmldb.org/xupdate\">\n" +
          "xu:remove " +
          "select=\"/customers[@date='" +
          args[0] +
          "']/customer[@ID=" +
          args[1] +
          "]\"/>"
          + "\n</xu:modifications>";
        // Obtain a reference to the update query service
        XUpdateQueryService service =
            (XUpdateQueryService)col.getService
            ("XUpdateQueryService", "1.0");
        // Run the query using the service
        System.out.println("Running Remove Query: ");
        System.out.println(xupdate);
        service.update(xupdate);
    } catch (XMLDBException e) {
        System.err.println("XML:DB Exception occured " + e.errorCode + " " +
            e.getMessage());
    } finally {
        // Close the collection
        if (col != null) {
            col.close();
        }
    }
  }
}
```

The program accepts the two command-line parameters. The first parameter specifies the date for the orders document in our DailyOrders collection. The date is specified in MMDDYYYY format. The second argument specifies the customer ID as a string. The record matching this customer ID will be removed from the specified document.

The main function first loads the driver:

```
// Load driver class
String driver = "org.apache.xindice.client.xmldb.DatabaseImpl";
Class c = Class.forName(driver);
```

As in the earlier examples, you create an instance of the database and register it with the database manager:

```
// Create and register database instance
Database database = (Database) c.newInstance();
DatabaseManager.registerDatabase(database);
```

Next, you obtain a reference to the DailyOrders collection:

```
// Retrieve a reference to DailyOrders collection
col = DatabaseManager.getCollection
    ("xmldb:xindice:///db/StockBrokerage/DailyOrders");
```

You now construct the XML document fragment to create a remove query by using the XUpdate language syntax:

```
// Construct a Remove query
String xupdate =
  "<xu:modifications version=\"1.0\"" +
  "xmlns:xu=\"http://www.xmldb.org/xupdate\">\n" +
  "xu:remove " +
  "select=\"/customers[@date='" +
  args[0] +
  "']/customer[@ID=" +
  args[1] +
  "]\"/>"
  + "\n</xu:modifications>";
```

The XML document fragment that is generated by the preceding statement for the command-line arguments 01022006 and 8 is given here:

```
<xu:modifications version="1.0" xmlns:xu="http://www.xmldb.org/xupdate">
  <xu:remove select="/customers[@date='01022006']/customer[@ID=8]"/>
</xu:modifications>
```

Note the use of the date attribute to select the orders document and the use of the ID attribute to select a particular customer.

To run the query, you need to obtain a reference to the provided query service. You do this by calling the getService method of the Collection class:

```
// Obtain a reference to the update query service
XUpdateQueryService service =
    (XUpdateQueryService)col.getService
    ("XUpdateQueryService", "1.0");
```

Finally, you run the query itself by calling the update method on the service object obtained in the previous step:

```
// Run the query using the service
System.out.println("Running Remove Query: ");
System.out.println(xupdate);
service.update(xupdate);
```

If the query runs successfully, the specified record will be deleted from the selected document.

Running the Application

Compile the preceding source (Listing 9-5) by using the following command line:

```
C:\{working folder}>javac -d . DeleteNode.java
```

Run the application by using the following command:

```
C:\{working folder}>java database.DeleteNode 01022006 8
```

This will delete the record for the customer with an ID equal to 8 from the
Order01022006.xml document in our database. Before you run the application, you may want
to list the document content. You can do so by running the following XPath query on your
xindice command line:

```
C:\xindice>xindice rd -c /db/StockBrokerage/DailyOrders -n Order01022006.xml
```

You will see the following output on your screen:

```
<?xml version="1.0"?>
<customers date="01022006">
...
  <customer ID="7">
      <name>John-Weigert</name>
      <order>IKJ</order>
      <quantity>20</quantity>
      <price>25.50</price>
  </customer>

  <customer ID="8">
    <name>Marilia-Oliver</name>
    <order>IKL</order>
    <quantity>87</quantity>
    <price>26.00</price>
  </customer>

  <customer ID="9">
    <name>Marilia-Oliver</name>
    <order>IKM</order>
    <quantity>90</quantity>
    <price>25.20</price>
  </customer>
...
</customers>
```

Now run the application. When the application runs successfully, you will see the following screen output:

```
Running Remove Query:
<xu:modifications version="1.0" xmlns:xu="http://www.xmldb.org/xupdate">
   <xu:remove select="/customers[@date='01022006']/customer[@ID=8]"/>
</xu:modifications>
```

Now, if you list the document content again by using the previous command line, you will notice that the record for the customer with ID equal to 8 has been removed from the document.

Next, you will study how to insert a record in the orders database.

Inserting a Node in the Orders Collection

You can insert a record in your document by constructing an insert XUpdate query. You will now insert an order record in our orders document. The XUpdate query for doing this is given here:

```
String xupdate = "<xu:modifications version=\"1.0\"" +
    "     xmlns:xu=\"http://www.xmldb.org/xupdate\">\n" +
    "   <xu:insert-after select=\"/customers/customer[@ID=17]\">\n" +
    "      <xu:element name=\"customer\">\n"+
    "         <xu:attribute name=\"id\">2</xu:attribute>\n"+
    "         <name>pradeep</name>\n"+
    "         <order>IBM</order>\n"+
    "         <quantity>50</quantity>\n"+
    "         <price>25.22</price>\n"+
    "      </xu:element>\n" +
    "   </xu:insert-after>\n"+
    "</xu:modifications>";
```

■**Tip** The full source for the update node application is available in the file Ch09\src\InsertNode.java in the source download.

The XML document fragment generated by the preceding statement is as follows:

```
<xu:modifications version="1.0"       xmlns:xu="http://www.xmldb.org/xupdate">
  <xu:insert-after select="/customers/customer[@ID=17]">
    <xu:element name="customer">
      <xu:attribute name="id">2</xu:attribute>
      <name>pradeep</name>
      <order>IBM</order>
      <quantity>50</quantity>
      <price>25.22</price>
    </xu:element>
  </xu:insert-after>
</xu:modifications>
```

When you run the query by calling the update method on the query service object, the following XML fragment will be added after the record with the customer ID 17.

```
...
<customer id="2">
        <name>pradeep</name>
        <order>IBM</order>
        <quantity>50</quantity>
        <price>25.22</price>
</customer>
...
```

Note that the position for inserting the record is specified by the XPath expression /customers/customer[@ID=17] as a value of the select attribute.

Updating a Node in the Orders Collection

I will now discuss the construction of an XUpdate query for updating a specified record in our database. Imagine that we want to modify the order placed by the customer with ID equal to 1 on January 2, 2006. We will modify the stock code from an existing value of MSFT to a new value of IKJ. The code that constructs the XUpdate query is shown here:

```
// Construct an update query
String xupdate = "<xu:modifications version=\"1.0\"" +
        " xmlns:xu=\"http://www.xmldb.org/xupdate\">\n" +
        "     <xu:update select=" +
        "\"/customers[@date='01022006']/customer[@ID=1]/order\">\n"
        + "          IKJ" +
        "\n     </xu:update>\n" +
        "</xu:modifications>";
```

■**Tip** The full source for the update node application is available in the file Ch09\src\UpdateNode.java in the source download.

The following XML document fragment is generated by the preceding code:

```
<xu:modifications version="1.0" xmlns:xu="http://www.xmldb.org/xupdate">
    <xu:update select="/customers[@date='01022006']/customer[@ID=1]/order">
        IKJ
    </xu:update>
</xu:modifications>
```

Note how the XPath expression selects the order element of customer ID equal to 1 from the January 2, 2006 document. The new value for the order node is set to IKJ.

As in the earlier cases, after constructing the query, we will execute it by calling the update method of the query service.

Performing Database Administration

Every database requires some sort of administration to keep it efficient while it is being accessed. This administration consists of organizing the database collection structure, adding/removing resources, creating indexes for faster access, backing up the data, and so on. In this section, you will learn about the various facilities available for a Xindice database administrator.

You use the `xindiceadmin` utility for administering the Xindice database. You have used this utility previously for adding/removing collections and more. In this section, I will summarize the functionalities provided by the `xindiceadmin` utility. The functionalities can be classified as management commands and actions, as listed here:

- Management commands

    - Collection management

    - Document management

- Actions

    - Indexer actions

    - XPath query actions

    - Miscellaneous actions

Most of the management commands have been discussed earlier and I will not repeat them here. I will discuss whatever I have not yet covered.

Tip You can refer to the Command Line Tools Reference guide for full details on the command syntax (`C:\<xindice installation folder>\docs\ToolsReference.html`).

Creating/Managing Indexes

An index improves database access performance. To create an index, you use the `add_indexer` command on the `xindiceadmin` utility. To illustrate how to add an index, you will create an index on the `order` element of our `DailyOrders` collection. The command to add such an index is as follows:

```
C:\xindice>xindiceadmin add_indexer -c /db/StockBrokerage/DailyOrders -n ➥
orderindex -p order
CREATED : orderindex
```

The `-c` switch specifies the collection context (which in this case is the `DailyOrders` subcollection in our `StockBrokerage` collection). The `-n` switch specifies the name of the index, and the `-p` switch specifies the pattern used to create an index.

You can also create indexes on the element attributes. For example, if you want to create an index on the ID attribute of the customer element, you would use a command as follows:

```
C:\xindice>xindiceadmin add_indexer -c /db/StockBrokerage/DailyOrders ➡
-n IDindex -p customer@ID
```

In this case, the pattern used is customer@ID.

Listing Indexes

You use the list_indexers (abbreviated li) command on the xindiceadmin to list the available indexes. The following screen output shows how to list the indexes in our DailyOrders collection:

```
C:\xindice>xindiceadmin li -c /db/StockBrokerage/DailyOrders
Indexes:

IDindex
orderindex

Total Indexes: 2
```

Deleting an Index

You delete an index by using the delete_indexer (abbreviated di) command on the xindiceadmin utility. To delete the ID index you just created, use the command shown in the following screen output:

```
C:\xindice>xindiceadmin di -c /db/StockBrokerage/DailyOrders -n IDindex
Continue deletion process? (y/n)
y
DELETED: IDindex
```

Backing Up Your Data

Every database administrator is concerned with the periodic backups of the database. The process of backing up the Xindice database is straightforward and simple. Simply copy the db folder along with its subfolders to any other storage device. Restoring the database requires the reverse process of copying from the backup folders to the db folder.

Exporting Data

Sometimes you may want to export the database contents to its native format. You do this by using the export command on the xindiceadmin utility. The screen output from running this command is shown here:

```
C:\xindice>xindiceadmin export -c /db/StockBrokerage -f c:\apress\Ch09\backup

Creating directory c:\apress\Ch09\backup\StockBrokerage
Extracting 0 files from /db/StockBrokerage
Creating directory c:\apress\Ch09\backup\StockBrokerage\DailyOrders
Extracting 10 files from /db/StockBrokerage/DailyOrders
Creating directory c:\apress\Ch09\backup\StockBrokerage\DailyQuotes
Extracting 0 files from /db/StockBrokerage/DailyQuotes
```

Here we export the contents of the StockBrokerage collection to the backup folder on the
C drive. The utility creates an appropriate folder structure under the backup folder and copies
all the documents in the subcollections to the appropriate subfolders. Each document is
copied in its native format.

Importing Data

The data that you have exported earlier can be imported into the database by using the import
command of xindiceadmin. You use the import command as follows:

```
C:\{xindice installation folder}>xindiceadmin import -c /db -f c:\apress\Ch09\import
```

This imports the data from the import folder and its subfolders into the db database.
During the imports, the folder hierarchy is maintained in the database.

Shutting Down the Server

To shut down the Xindice server, you use the shutdown command shown here:

```
c:\xindice>xindiceadmin shutdown -c /db
```

Summary

XML databases provide an easy and powerful way to store your XML documents so they can
be quickly searched later. The XML database follows a hierarchical storage structure analo-
gous to the folder structures in your file system.

The XML documents stored in the database are organized into collections. You learned
how to create collections, how to create subcollections, and how to delete collections and
subcollections by using command-line utilities. You also learned how to add and remove
documents to the collections by using command-line utilities.

In addition, you learned to perform all these activities through a program interface. You
learned the XUpdate language syntax that allows you to write queries for updating the contents of the XML database.

Finally, you learned about database administration used to manage the database and its
contents. You learned the techniques of backing up and restoring the database. You also
learned to export the database content into its native format and to import the earlier
exported content into the database again.

■ ■ ■

## CHAPTER 10

Apache Forrest

You have studied several Apache XML projects in this book. Now comes the time for a grand finale. In this chapter, you will put together the various techniques you have learned so far to create a website for our stock brokerage case study of Chapter 2. Apache Forrest is the project that helps us achieve this. It uses several APIs discussed in the previous chapters.

Apache Forrest is a publishing framework that allows you to generate a unified presentation from various input sources. You might recall the Cocoon framework introduced in Chapter 7. Cocoon uses the pipeline architecture and can generate static and dynamic content for presentation in various formats. Forrest uses Cocoon for document generation and presentation. Thus, Forrest derives its benefits from the extensible and modular architecture of Cocoon, which provides a separation between presentation and content. Because Cocoon can generate content dynamically, so does Forrest. Thus, you can easily create both static and dynamic websites when using Forrest.

In this chapter, you will learn about many of Forrest's features by creating a website for our stock brokerage. You will customize the website by adding tabs and menus to it. You will learn to incorporate new content and your existing web pages into the new site. You will facilitate rendering the web pages to various output formats. Finally, you will learn to integrate external RSS feeds in your web pages.

Before you create the brokerage site by using Forrest, let's briefly look at its history.

The History of Forrest

The Apache Forrest project was founded to create consistent documentation for all Apache projects and to provide efficient and easy management of these projects. Established in January 2002, its initial goal was to create uniform, lightweight, easily navigable project websites. It was also expected to provide built-in project management tools. However, soon the focus changed to creating a generic documentation tool.

Today Forrest can be used for various purposes, such as the following:

- Creating project documentation sites, especially quite useful for creating documentation for software projects

- Creating and maintaining both small and large static and dynamic websites

The Apache Software Foundation itself has used Forrest for some of its project sites. Besides Apache's own sites, several third-party sites have been created by using Apache Forrest, including the Krysalis Community Project site (`http://www.krysalis.org/index.shtml`), the Learn Linux site (`http://learnlinux.tsf.org.za/`), and the j2world—Smart Solutions for a Mobile World site (`http://www.j2world.net/`). The last example is not an English language site; I selected this example to show that international sites are created by using Forrest. There are many more sites created by using Forrest. For a more comprehensive list, refer to `http://forrest.apache.org/live-sites.html`.

Using Forrest, you can easily create websites that provide a unified presentation of data from various input sources. You need not learn HTML to create a website. Instead, Forrest uses XML for creating web pages. The website can then be easily customized by modifying the XML configuration files. Furthermore, the pages can be rendered in various formats by using Cocoon's serializers discussed in Chapter 7.

You will focus on learning all these features by creating a brokerage site rather than learning to use Forrest merely to create documentation for a website.

Forrest Features

To a website developer or a document creator, Forrest offers several benefits:

- *User-friendly*: Forrest allows you to easily generate a new website. The process of creating a new site has been greatly simplified as you will soon see in the following sections.

- *Low "start-up cost"*: If you want to create a small website, Forrest provides a quick, although not constraining, solution because the powerful features of Forrest allow for the easy expansion of the site.

- *Rapid development*: Forrest quickly creates a skeleton website for you that later can scale up to large projects. The rapid development helps in overcoming any time and budget constraints.

- *No learning curve*: To use Forrest, you need not know Java or HTML. You can simply focus on content and site design.

- *Configurable*: After a site is created, it can be easily configured by using content templates and prewritten skins (stylesheets) to change the site's look and feel. Because these configuration changes are XML based, they are easy to implement.

- *Flexible*: Forrest can be used for a wide variety of applications.

- *Platform independent*: Because Forrest is based on Java and XML, it is platform independent.

As mentioned earlier, Forrest derives several benefits from the Apache Cocoon framework on which it is based. If you are an advanced user who understands Cocoon, you know you have the following additional benefits at your disposal:

- *Multiple input source formats*: You can derive your input source documents from various sources, such as XML, plain HTML, Text, Wiki,[1] and more.

- *Multiple output formats*: Because Cocoon allows you to produce output content in a wide variety of formats by providing configurable serializers[2] in its pipeline, Forrest too can produce output in different formats such as PDF, HTML, Text, XML, and so on.

- *SVG (Scalable Vector Graphics) to PNG[3] (Portable Network Graphics) rendering*: The underlying Cocoon engine transforms SVG files to PNG at runtime. Thus, you can freely include SVG documents in your site without worrying about how to render them.

- *External content*: Content from an external source such as an RSS[4] feed can be included in the content provided internally. This is possible due to the pluggable transformers in the Cocoon pipeline. The content from the various sources can be aggregated by using the aggregator component of the Cocoon framework.

- *Integration with external systems*: It is possible to integrate the content from external systems such as web services or database queries in the internal content to produce aggregate output to the user.

Installing Forrest

Before you use Forrest to create a website, you need to download and install the Forrest software. After downloading it, you will test the installation.

Downloading the Software

Like the Apache software installations discussed in earlier chapters, the installation of Forrest is quite easy.

Download the Forrest software (`apache-forrest-0.7.tar.gz` for Unix and `apache-forrest-0.7.zip` for Windows) from the Apache site:

```
http://www.apache.org
```

Unzip the file to a desired folder. After this, you need to set up the environment variables. Create a new environment variable called `FORREST_HOME` and set its value to your Forrest installation folder. Add the path `%FORREST_HOME%\bin` (for Windows) or `$FORREST_HOME/bin` (for Unix, Linux) to your `PATH` environment variable.

That's all that is required for the installation.

---

1. Wiki is an online resource that allows users to add and edit content collectively. *Wiki* means *rapid* in Hawaiian.

2. Refer to Chapter 7 for information on Cocoon pipelines.

3. Refer to the official PNG home page (`http://www.libpng.org/pub/png/`) for details.

4. RSS is an acronym for Rich Site Summary or Really Simple Syndication.

Testing the Installation

You can test the installation with the forrest command-line utility provided in the bin folder of your Forrest installation. Change the working directory to your Forrest installation folder and type the forrest -projecthelp command at the command prompt. The result of running this command is shown in the following screen output:

```
C:\apache-forrest-0.7>forrest -projecthelp

Apache Forrest.  Run 'forrest -projecthelp' to list options


Buildfile: C:\apache-forrest-0.7\main\forrest.build.xml

    *=========================================================*
    |                 Forrest Site Builder                    |
    |                      0.7                                 |
    *=========================================================*

            Call this through the 'forrest' command

Main targets:

  available-plugins    What plugins are available?
  available-skins      What skins are available?
  clean                * Clean all directories and files generated during the build
  init-plugins         Ensure the required plugins are available locally, if any
are not, download them automatically
  install-skin         Install the needed skin from the remote repository
  package-skin         Make a package of an existing skin
  run                  * Run Jetty (instant live webapp)
  run_custom_jetty     Run Jetty with configuration file found in the project
  run_default_jetty    Run Jetty with configuration file found in Forrest
  seed                 * Seeds a directory with a template project doc structure

  site                 * Generates a static HTML website for this project
  validate             Validate all: xdocs, skins, sitemap, etc
  validate-sitemap     Validate the project sitemap
  validate-skinchoice  Validate skin choice
  validate-skinconf    Validate skinconf
  validate-skins       Validate skins
  validate-stylesheets Validate XSL files
  validate-xdocs       Validate the project xdocs
  war       * Generates a dynamic servlet-based website (a packaged war file)
  webapp    Generates a dynamic servlet-based website (an unpackaged webapp).
  webapp-local         Generates a dynamic servlet-based website (an unpackaged
webapp).  Note this webapp is suitable for local execution only, use the 'war' or
'webapp' target if you wish to deploy remotely.
Default target: site
```

The commands marked with an asterisk (*) are the most commonly used commands. For example, you use the `seed` option to create a new project based on a predefined template. You will use this switch while creating a new site in the next section. You use the `clean` option to clear the project content. You use the `site` option to generate a static HTML website for the project, and you use the `war` option to generate a WAR file that can be deployed on your web server for generating a servlet-based website for your project. To test your dynamic website, you run `forrest` with the `run` option; this deploys the project and starts a default Jetty web server.

Note The Jetty web server gets installed on your machine as a part of the Forrest installation. Jetty is a 100 percent Java HTTP server and servlet container developed under the guidance of Mort Bay Consulting and released under the Apache 2.0 license. It is free for commercial use and distribution with few restrictions on its usage.

We will use this default web server while developing the brokerage site. It is easier to redeploy the site on this web server after modifications are made to it.

You can use the Tomcat web server or any other commercial web server for production use. In this case, you will need to create a WAR file for the project and deploy it on the web server of your choice following the instructions thereupon.

You are now ready to create the stock brokerage website.

Creating the Brokerage Site

Creating a new site by using Forrest is easy. You simply need to run the provided `forrest` command-line utility with the appropriate parameters. Create a folder called `Brokerage` in the root of your hard drive. (You can use any other name for the folder, but for the examples in this chapter I have created the Forrest project in this folder.) Change the directory to the `Brokerage` folder and execute `forrest seed` on the command line. The result of running this command is shown in the following screen output:

```
C:\Brokerage>forrest seed

Apache Forrest.  Run 'forrest -projecthelp' to list options


Buildfile: C:\apache-forrest-0.7\main\forrest.build.xml

init-props:
Created dir: C:\Brokerage\build\tmp

seed:
Copying 49 files to C:\Brokerage
```

```
-------------------------------
~~ Template project created! ~~

Here is an outline of the generated files:

/                        # C:\Brokerage
/status.xml              # List of project developers, todo list and change log
/forrest.properties      # Optional file describing your site layout
/src/documentation/      # Doc-specific files
/src/documentation/skinconf.xml    # Info about your project used by the skin
/src/documentation/content         # Site content.
/src/documentation/content/xdocs   # XML content.
/src/documentation/content/xdocs/index.xml # Home page
/src/documentation/content/xdocs/site.xml  # Navigation file for site structure
/src/documentation/content/xdocs/tabs.xml  # Skin-specific 'tabs' file.
/src/documentation/content/xdocs/*.html,pdf # Static content files, may have sub
dirs
/src/documentation/resources/images    # Project images (logos, etc)
# you can create other directories as needed (see forrest.properties)


What to do now?

- Render this template to static HTML by typing 'forrest'.
  View the generated HTML in a browser to make sure everything works.
- Alternatively 'forrest run' and browse to http://localhost:8888/ live demo.
- Edit status.xml and src/documentation/skinconf.xml
  to customize for your project.
- Start adding content in xdocs/ remembering to declare new files in site.xml
- Follow the document http://forrest.apache.org/docs/your-project.html
- Provide any feedback to dev@forrest.apache.org

Thanks for using Apache Forrest
-------------------------------


BUILD SUCCESSFUL
Total time: 2 seconds
```

Deploying the Brokerage Project

After the project is created, you need to create a WAR file and deploy it on the web server to make it available to users. You deploy the project created in the preceding step by running the forrest command with the run command-line switch. This starts the default Jetty server and deploys the site on this server.

Jetty, being fully Java-based, can be easily integrated with your application distribution and deployment. Jetty runs in the same process as your application, thereby reducing the overhead of interconnection and improving the application performance. If you prefer using another web server, you will need to deploy the WAR file on that web server by following the instructions thereupon.

The output produced after running this command is given in the following screen output:

```
C:\Brokerage>forrest run

Apache Forrest.  Run 'forrest -projecthelp' to list options


Buildfile: C:\apache-forrest-0.7\main\forrest.build.xml

check-java-version:
This is apache-forrest-0.7
Using Java 1.5 from C:\Java\jdk1.5.0\jre

init-plugins:
Copying 1 file to C:\Brokerage\build\tmp
Copying 1 file to C:\Brokerage\build\tmp
Copying 1 file to C:\Brokerage\build\tmp
Copying 1 file to C:\Brokerage\build\tmp
Installing plugin: org.apache.forrest.plugin.output.pdf

check-plugin:
org.apache.forrest.plugin.output.pdf is available in the build dir

configure-output-plugin:
Mounting output plugin: org.apache.forrest.plugin.output.pdf
Processing C:\Brokerage\build\tmp\output.xmap to C:\Brokerage\build\tmp\output.x
map.new
Loading stylesheet C:\apache-forrest-0.7\main\var\pluginMountSnippet.xsl
Moving 1 files to C:\Brokerage\build\tmp

run_default_jetty:

  Note: Use Ctrl-C to stop the Jetty server


        ... and reply 'n' and press [Enter]
            when asked about aborting the batch!

14:06:34.841 EVENT  Checking Resource aliases
14:06:35.912 EVENT  Starting Jetty/4.2.19
14:06:36.072 EVENT  Started WebApplicationContext[/,Apache Forrest]
14:06:36.213 WARN!! Delete existing temp dir C:\DOCUME~1\DRA762~1.SAR\LOCALS~1\T
emp\Jetty__8888__ for WebApplicationContext[/,Apache Forrest]
Lazy mode: false
14:06:38.646 EVENT  Started SocketListener on 0.0.0.0:8888
14:06:38.646 EVENT  Started org.mortbay.jetty.Server@30e280
```

As you can see from the screen output, the Forrest utility starts the Jetty web server and deploys our brokerage project on it.

■**Tip** If you are running Forrest for the first time, you must be connected to the Internet when you use the `run` switch. Forrest requires a few plugins that are automatically downloaded as a part of running Forrest with the `run` switch.

You can now open the home page for the project by opening the URL `http://localhost:8888` in your browser. Figure 10-1 shows the output produced in the browser.

Figure 10-1. *Home page for the newly created Forrest project*

You can stop the Jetty server at any time by pressing Ctrl+C in the server console window. When prompted for terminating the batch, reply **n** and press Enter. If you terminate the batch by replying **y**, the values of ANT_HOME and CLASSPATH variables are not restored. If you rerun Forrest in the same shell, the new classpath would be appended to the existing classpath, making it unnecessarily long.

Though we have run the project by deploying it as a servlet, you can create a static site for your project by using the `site` switch on the `forrest` command. This creates all the required files in the various folders under the build folder of your site installation. You can examine the various created folders in the generated screen output or examine the folder hierarchy in Windows Explorer.

After creating the static site, open the home page by opening the file file://c:/ Brokerage/build/site/index.html in your browser. You will see a page similar to the one shown in Figure 10-1.

Examining the Project

When you create a default project, Forrest creates several files neatly organized in a tree structure. The created folder hierarchy is shown in Figure 10-2.

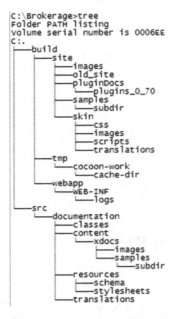

```
C:\Brokerage>tree
Folder PATH listing
Volume serial number is 0006EE
C:.
├───build
│   ├───site
│   │   ├───images
│   │   ├───old_site
│   │   ├───pluginDocs
│   │   │   └───plugins_0_70
│   │   ├───samples
│   │   │   └───subdir
│   │   └───skin
│   │       ├───css
│   │       ├───images
│   │       ├───scripts
│   │       └───translations
│   ├───tmp
│   │   └───cocoon-work
│   │       └───cache-dir
│   └───webapp
│       └───WEB-INF
│           └───logs
└───src
    └───documentation
        ├───classes
        ├───content
        │   └───xdocs
        │       ├───images
        │       └───samples
        │           └───subdir
        ├───resources
        │   ├───schema
        │   └───stylesheets
        └───translations
```

Figure 10-2. *Default file hierarchy*

To customize the site, you will modify these generated files. This process is introduced next.

Customizing the Default Site's Content

As you can see from the preceding output, Forrest creates the skeleton code and layout for the new site. Because Forrest is XML based and provides several templates, customizing the site is easy. You need to know only XML for customization and you can simply concentrate on the site content and presentation.

In this section, you will carry out several customizations in the default site. You will modify the home page content, create your own tabs, incorporate images, and add menus.

Modifying the Home Page Content

Let's first modify the home page of the default site. To modify the content of the home page, you do not have to write any HTML code. Instead you will write the content in an XML document. Create an XML document called index.xml, as shown in Listing 10-1.

Listing 10-1. *The* index.xml *Page for the StockBrokerage Site*

```
<?xml version="1.0" encoding="UTF-8"?>

<!DOCTYPE document PUBLIC "-//APACHE//DTD Documentation V2.0//EN"
"http://forrest.apache.org/dtd/document-v20.dtd">
<document>
  <header>
    <title>Welcome to StockBrokerage</title>
  </header>
  <body>
    <section id="intro">
      <title>Introduction</title>
      <p>You have logged on to the StockBrokerage Website.
          We provide the latest updates on the stocks.
      </p>
    </section>

    <section id="quote">
      <title>Technical Charting</title>
      <p>
        You can now obtain the technical charts of the traded stocks.
      </p>
    </section>

    <section id="order">
      <title>trade</title>
        <p>
         You may buy/sell stocks online using our user-friendly interface.
        </p>
    </section>
    <p>
      <a href="docs/rules.txt">click here</a>to read about rules and regulations
    </p>

  </body>
</document>
```

Replace the <your site root folder>\src\documents\contents\xdocs\index.xml file with the index.xml file of Listing 10-1. Run the forrest run command at the command prompt to deploy the site and start the Jetty server. Now, if you reopen the site in your browser, you will get the output shown in Figure 10-3.

Figure 10-3. *Modified home page of the StockBrokerage site*

Note how various XML tags are transformed into HTML code for generating the home page. These transformations are done by using the transformer defined in the Forrest libraries.

The root element of the XML document shown in Listing 10-1 is document. Within the document element, you have header and body elements. As their names suggest, the header element defines the page header, and the body element defines the body content. The header element contains a subelement called title that defines the title for the page:

```
<header>
  <title>Welcome to StockBrokerage</title>
</header>
```

You can change the text content of the title tag to display a different heading than shown in this example.

The body element defines one or more sections with the help of the section subelement. Each section has a unique ID associated with it. Each section contains its own title defined by the title subelement and some text information defined by the p tag:

```
<body>
  <section id="Unique ID">
    <title>Title Text goes here</title>
    <p>Some Information on the current section</p>
  </section>
```

```
<section id="Unique ID">
  <title>Title Text goes here</title>
  <p>Some Information on the current section</p>
</section>

<!-- more sections follow here -->

</body>
```

You can add any number of sections in the page body. Each section appears under the page title in the order it is defined. The section descriptions follow the section titles. The appearance of section titles and their descriptions can be seen in Figure 10-3.

Creating Your Own Tabs

By default, the generated site contains four tabs: Home, Samples, Apache XML Projects, and Plugins. You will now replace these tabs with three tabs specific to the brokerage site: Home, Trades, and Technical Charting. The tabs for the page are defined in the tabs.xml document. This document is available in the folder <brokerage site folder>\src\documentation\ content\xdocs. You will replace this document with our version of the tabs.xml file shown in Listing 10-2.

Note The source for tabs.xml and all subsequent modifications that we perform on the site are available under the Brokerage folder of the code downloaded from the Apress website (http:// www.apress.com). This folder name is the same as the name of the <brokerage site folder> that you created earlier. You need to copy the suggested files from the source Brokerage folder to the <brokerage site folder>.

Listing 10-2. *Defining Tabs for the Home Page*
(\Brokerage\src\documentation\content\xdocs\tabs.xml)

```
<?xml version="1.0" encoding="UTF-8"?>

<!DOCTYPE tabs PUBLIC "-//APACHE//DTD Cocoon Documentation Tab V1.1//EN"
"http://forrest.apache.org/dtd/tab-cocoon-v11.dtd">

<tabs xmlns:xlink="http://www.w3.org/1999/xlink">

 <tab id="" label="Home" dir="" indexfile="index.html"/>
 <tab id="trades" label="Trades" dir="docs" indexfile="trades.html"/>
 <tab id="quotes" label="Technical Charting" dir="docs" indexfile="chart.html"/>

</tabs>
```

You create tabs for your home page by creating a tabs.xml document having the root element tabs. Within the tabs element, you define several tab elements. Each tab element has an id associated with it that uniquely identifies a tab on the page. A tab has a label attribute that defines the text for the tab. It also contains an attribute called indexfile that points to the document that will be opened whenever the user selects this particular tab. The location of this document is specified in the dir attribute. The following statement defines the Home tab:

```
<tab id="" label="Home" dir="" indexfile="index.html"/>
```

The tab label is Home. The file opened when the user selects this tab is index.html, and this file is located in the current folder.

After copying the tabs.xml file of Listing 10-2 into the xdocs folder of our brokerage site, you will see the output shown in Figure 10-4 when you reopen the site.

Tip Reopening the site requires running the forrest run command and opening the URL http://localhost:8888 in your browser. If you are creating a static site, you will need to run the forrest site command and use the URL file:///<brokerage site folder>/build/site/index.html in your browser.

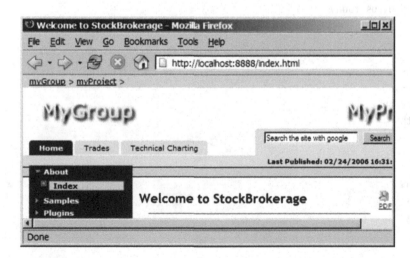

Figure 10-4. *Setting tabs for the StockBrokerage site*

Note the presence of new tabs in the screen output of Figure 10-4. When the user clicks one of the tabs, the page defined in the corresponding tab element will be shown to the user. For example, the Trades tab uses the trades.html file found in the docs folder as defined here:

```
<tab id="trades" label="Trades" dir="docs" indexfile="trades.html"/>
```

■Note The underlying Cocoon architecture maps the URL pattern .html to an input source document of type .xml. Thus, you will not be required to create HTML files; rather you will work only on XML documents.

Thus, you will need to create an appropriate document and store it in the docs folder. The path is specified with respect to the <brokerage site folder>\src\documentation\ content\xdocs folder. Create a docs folder as a subfolder to the xdocs folder. Create the trades.xml file shown in Listing 10-3 in this folder.

Listing 10-3. *XML Document That Displays Today's Trades* (\Brokerage\src\documentation\ content\xdocs\docs\trades.xml)

```xml
<?xml version="1.0" encoding="utf-8"?>
<!DOCTYPE document PUBLIC "-//APACHE//DTD Documentation V2.0//EN"
"http://forrest.apache.org/dtd/document-v20.dtd">
<document>
  <header>
    <title>Order Book</title>
  </header>
  <body>
    <p>
      Orders executed by us today
    </p>
    <table>
      <tr>
        <th>Type</th>
        <th>Order</th>
        <th>quantity</th>
        <th>price</th>
      </tr>
        ...
      <tr>
        <td>sell</td>
        <td>IBM</td>
        <td>200</td>
        <td>90</td>
      </tr>

    </table>
  </body>
</document >
```

■Note The complete listing of trades.xml is available in the <code download folder>\brokerage\ src\documentation\content\xdocs\docs\trades.xml file.

The source document name that is mentioned in the trades tag is trades.html. However, we have created an XML document called trades.xml. The default Cocoon pipeline defined in Forrest's sitemap (discussed later) uses the .html pattern for page match, takes the input .xml file as a document source, transforms it to .html, and renders it as an HTML document. This pipeline processing was explained in Chapter 7.

The page designer does not have to work with HTML coding; rather she works on an XML document to develop the page. The XML document has header and body elements, as in the index.xml (Listing 10-1) document discussed earlier. Within the body, we create a table by using the table element. The tr subelement defines the rows, and the td element defines the column content.

Figure 10-5 shows the output rendered from trades.xml.

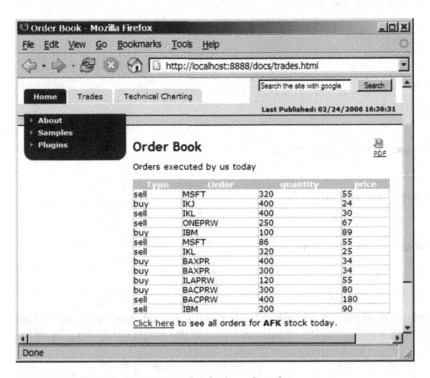

Figure 10-5. *The tabular output of today's trade orders*

■**Note** The trades.xml file rendered in Figure 10-5 is a static file and does not generate its content dynamically as may be the case in a real-life situation.

Incorporating Images

Now you're ready to incorporate a few images in our brokerage site. When the user selects the Technical Charting tab, we will present a few technical charts to the user. For this, create a charts.xml document as shown in Listing 10-4 and copy it to the xdocs\docs folder.

Listing 10-4. *The XML Document That Incorporates Images in the Final Output* (\Brokerage\ src\documentation\content\xdocs\docs\charts.xml)

```
<?xml version="1.0" encoding="utf-8"?>
  <document>
    <header>
      <title>Technical Charting</title>
    </header>
    <body>
      <section>
      <title>
      Single Stock Charts
    </title>
    </section>
      <li>
      <a href="/images/infosys.jpg">Infosys</a>
      </li>
      <li>
      <a href="/images/tcs.jpg">TCS</a>
      </li>
      <li>
      <a href="/images/wipro.jpg">Wipro</a>
      </li>
    </body >
  </document>
```

Listing 10-4 defines three list index items and specifies the desired chart on each list index item by specifying the link reference. The images are stored in the images subfolder relative to the xdocs folder.

■**Note** These images are provided in the source download. You will need to copy them to the <brokerage site folder>\src\documentation\content\xdocs\images folder.

If you open the brokerage site and click on the Technical Charting tab, you will see the output shown in Figure 10-6.

Clicking one of the links will bring the corresponding image to the front. For example, clicking the TCS link brings the tcs.jpg file in front, and clicking the Wipro link brings the wipro.jpg file in front. This image source is specified by the href element. A typical image for Infosys stock is shown in Figure 10-7.

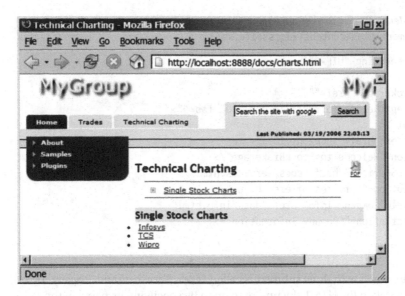

Figure 10-6. *Incorporating images in the document*

Figure 10-7. *Technical charting for Infosys* (infosys.jpg)

Adding Menus

Now you will add a few menus to our brokerage site. The menus are defined in a file called
site.xml that is situated in the xdocs folder. Replace the existing site.xml file with the new
content shown in Listing 10-5.

Listing 10-5. *Defining Menus for the Brokerage Site*
(\Brokerage\src\documentation\content\xdocs\site.xml)

```xml
<?xml version="1.0" encoding="UTF-8"?>

<site label="StockBrokerage" href=""
     xmlns="http://apache.org/forrest/linkmap/1.0" tab="">
  <About label="About">
    <index label="Index" href="index.html"
          description="Welcome to StockBrokerage"/>
    <services label="Services" href="docs/services.html"
             description="Services offered by us"/>
    <companyinfo label="Company Info" href="docs/info.html"
                description="Company Information"/>
  </About >
</site>
```

You create an About menu with three submenus called Index, Services, and Company Info. For each submenu, you define the HTML document to open by specifying its name in the value of the href attribute:

```xml
<services label="Services" href="docs/services.html"
         description="Services offered by us"/>
```

The label attribute defines the menu text, and the description attribute defines the ToolTip text that is displayed when the mouse hovers over the menu item.

As in earlier examples, you need not create an HTML document for the menus; instead you will create XML documents that will be transformed by the Forrest runtime into the HTML code for rendering on the browser. You will create three XML documents: index.xml, services.xml, and info.xml. We have already discussed the construction of index.xml under Listing 10-1. The services.xml and info.xml files should be created in the docs folder because the href path in site.xml specifies this location. These files are provided in the code download. Clicking on the corresponding submenus results in opening these files.

The screen output after adding the site.xml file of Listing 10-5 and copying the services.xml and info.xml files in the xdocs\docs folder is shown in Figure 10-8.

Figure 10-8. *Adding customized menus to the brokerage site*

Modifying the Site's Appearance

Forrest allows you to modify the site looks easily by using one of the provided skins. A *skin* is a sort of stylesheet that defines the page layout and its looks for your web page. Forrest provides several skins that you must first install on your machine before you use them on your site. You can also download skins developed by third parties and install them on your machine.

Installing Provided Skins

As I said, Forrest comes with several predefined skins. When you build Forrest, these skins are installed in your project. Examine the contents of the `<forrest installation folder>\main\webapp\skins` folder. You will notice the presence of several files and folders, as shown in Figure 10-9.

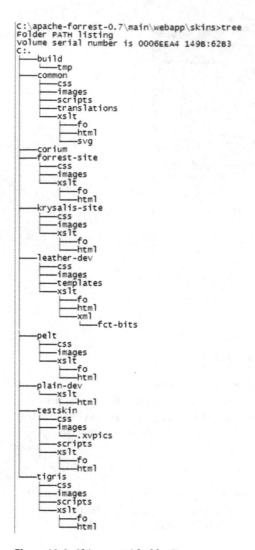

```
C:\apache-forrest-0.7\main\webapp\skins>tree
Folder PATH listing
Volume serial number is 0006EEA4 149B:62B3
C:.
├───build
│   └───tmp
├───common
│   ├───css
│   ├───images
│   ├───scripts
│   ├───translations
│   └───xslt
│       ├───fo
│       ├───html
│       └───svg
├───corium
├───forrest-site
│   ├───css
│   ├───images
│   └───xslt
│       ├───fo
│       └───html
├───krysalis-site
│   ├───css
│   ├───images
│   └───xslt
│       ├───fo
│       └───html
├───leather-dev
│   ├───css
│   ├───images
│   ├───templates
│   └───xslt
│       ├───fo
│       ├───html
│       └───xml
│           └───fct-bits
├───pelt
│   ├───css
│   ├───images
│   └───xslt
│       ├───fo
│       └───html
├───plain-dev
│   └───xslt
│       └───html
├───testskin
│   ├───css
│   ├───images
│   │   └───.xvpics
│   ├───scripts
│   └───xslt
│       ├───fo
│       └───html
└───tigris
    ├───css
    ├───images
    ├───scripts
    └───xslt
        ├───fo
        └───html
```

Figure 10-9. *Skins provided by Forrest*

Each skin uses its own folder name. Thus, `pelt` and `tigris` are two such skins, as seen in the preceding output. The names ending with -dev, such as `plain-dev`, indicate that these skins are still under development.

You will use these folder names as skin names in your properties file to modify the site's looks. You set the desired skin for your site by modifying the `forrest.properties` file in your brokerage site folder. If you open this file in your text editor, you will notice that it defines several property settings for your project. By default, all these settings are commented. To set the site looks, you will need to uncomment the `project.skin` property and set its value to a certain predefined value as shown here:

```
# Specifies name of Forrest skin to use
# See list at http://forrest.apache.org/docs/skins.html
project.skin=tigris
```

The skin is now set to `tigris`. If you set the skin to `tigris` and open the site, you will see the output shown in Figure 10-10.

■**Note** You will need to restart the Jetty server each time you modify the properties file to see the effects of the modifications.

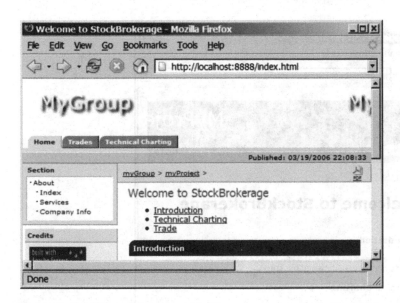

Figure 10-10. *Effect of changing the skin*

Installing Third-Party Skins

You can also develop your own skins. Nicola Barozzi has created skins and made them available on his site (http://people.apache.org/~nicolaken/). These skins can be downloaded from the following URL:

```
http://people.apache.org/~nicolaken/whiteboard/forrestskins/
```

Two skins are listed at this URL, and both are available in downloadable zip format. These skins are named testskin and testskin2-0.5. Download these archives and unzip them into the C:\<forrest installation folder>\main\webapp\skins folder. Now install them by using the following command:

```
C:\<forrest installation folder>\forrest package-skin
```

This command asks you to enter the name of the skin that you want to install. Specify the skin name at the command prompt when asked.

Now the skins are ready for your use. Edit the forrest.properties file and change the skin definition to testskin as shown here:

```
# Specifies name of Forrest skin to use
# See list at http://forrest.apache.org/docs/skins.html
project.skin=testskin
```

Reopen the site and you will see the output shown in Figure 10-11.

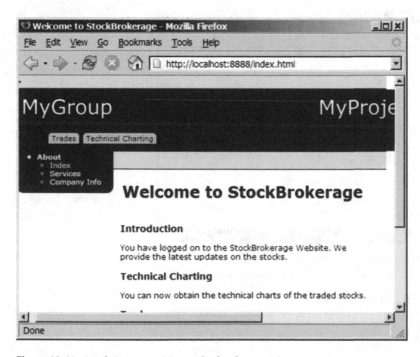

Figure 10-11. *Applying* testskin *to the brokerage site*

Customizing Skins

In the previous section, you changed the skin in the `forrest.properties` file to change the site looks. You can further customize the site's appearance by modifying the default values defined for the selected skin in the `skinconf.xml` file. The `skinconf.xml` document is located in `<site installation folder>\src\documentation`. You will modify this file to alter the site looks further.

Setting Your Company Logo

We will first replace the default logo with our company's logo. The default page contains two logos, one for your company's group and the second one for the current project. The company logo is defined by setting the value of the `group-logo` element. Change this value to the name of our company's logo file as shown:

```
<group-logo>images/ais.jpg</group-logo>
```

We will not display any project logo. For this, comment the statement containing the `project-logo` element as follows:

```
<!-- <project-logo>images/project.png</project-logo> -->
```

Copy the supplied `ais.jpg` file to the site's `images` folder and reopen the site. You will see the output shown in Figure 10-12.

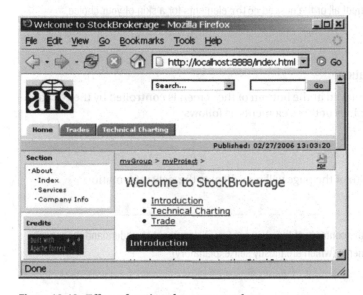

Figure 10-12. *Effect of setting the company logo*

Setting Colors

Now we will set colors for different regions of the page. You set the colors by setting the value of the `color` element in the `skinconf.xml` file. The `skinconf.xml` file contains a `colors` element that in turn defines a `color` subelement. A `color` subelement contains an attribute called `name` that defines the page region, and another attribute called value that defines the color for the selected region. The following example shows how to set the color for the page header to cyan:

```
<colors>
  <color name="header"    value="#00FFFF"/>
</colors>
```

To change the footer color, you use the following declaration:

```
<color name="footer" value="#FF00FF"/>
```

Note The screen output of the color changes is not shown here because the changes may not be properly visible in black-and-white print.

The color values are set as RGB values, where each color value is written as a hexadecimal number between 0 (hex) and FF (hex).

Tip The skinconf.xml file contains color schemes for the various skins. These are originally commented in the file. You can uncomment all or the desired color elements for a skin of your choice.

Setting the Copyright Information

The copyright information displayed at the bottom of the screen is controlled by the year and vendor elements. Modify the values of these elements as follows:

```
<year>2006</year>
<vendor>The Stock Brokerage</vendor>
```

The copyright at the bottom of the page will now display the new information.

Note I encourage you to study the contents of the skinconf.xml document to understand the purpose of the remaining configuration elements (which are mostly self-explanatory).

Customizing Forrest Properties

When you create a new Forrest site, the contents are organized in a predefined folder hierarchy. You might want to customize the folder hierarchy for your own purposes. You do this by setting certain properties discussed in this section.

Your site may be running behind a firewall. In such cases, you may need to configure the proxy to access the site. Again, you will need to set a few properties for configuring the proxy. This is discussed in the next section.

Changing the Folder Hierarchy

When you seed a project, Forrest creates a default folder hierarchy as shown in Figure 10-13.

```
c:\Brokerage>tree
Folder PATH listing
Volume serial number is 0006EEA4 149B:62B3
C:.
├──build
└──src
    └──documentation
        ├──classes
        ├──content
        │   └──xdocs
        │       ├──images
        │       └──samples
        │           └──subdir
        ├──resources
        │   ├──schema
        │   └──stylesheets
        └──translations
```

Figure 10-13. *Forrest's default folder hierarchy*

Forrest organizes various documents under these folders. You might want to set up your own folder hierarchy for organizing the documents. This can be easily configured by modifying a few elements in the forrest.properties file. The forrest.properties file contains declarations shown in Listing 10-6 that define the directory structure for your site.

Listing 10-6. *Properties That Define the Directory Structure for the Site*

```
#project.content-dir=src/documentation
#project.raw-content-dir=${project.content-dir}/content
#project.conf-dir=${project.content-dir}/conf
#project.sitemap-dir=${project.content-dir}
#project.xdocs-dir=${project.content-dir}/content/xdocs
#project.resources-dir=${project.content-dir}/resources
#project.stylesheets-dir=${project.resources-dir}/stylesheets
#project.images-dir=${project.resources-dir}/images
#project.schema-dir=${project.resources-dir}/schema
#project.skins-dir=${project.content-dir}/skins
#project.skinconf=${project.content-dir}/skinconf.xml
#project.lib-dir=${project.content-dir}/lib
#project.classes-dir=${project.content-dir}/classes
#project.translations-dir=${project.content-dir}/translations
```

By default, these properties are commented. Uncomment the desired properties and set their values to the appropriate desired values to change the directory structure.

Configuring Proxy Settings

Another important property that you will be required to set if you are behind the firewall is the proxy setting. The proxy settings are configured by uncommenting the host and the port settings and setting their appropriate values as follows:

```
# Proxy configuration
# proxy.host=
# proxy.port=
```

Adding External Documents

You may have several documents created in different formats such as HTML, PDF, or even Text. You might not be able to convert these into the XML format required by Forrest because of a lack of time or permissions to modify them. For example, a stock exchange may publish its rules and regulations to do business on the stock exchange as a Text or a PDF document. Obviously, you would not want to convert this into XML format. Forrest allows you to include such documents directly in your Forrest site. To include a document, you need to simply create an HTML link in your source document and ensure that the target document is available in the specified path.

Including a Text Document

We will now create a link to the rules and regulations page provided by the stock exchange. Let's assume that this page is available only in Text format. We will store this page in the docs folder of our brokerage site. The file called rules.txt is supplied in the code download. You will create a link to this page by adding the following lines of code in the index.xml file before the closing body tag:

```
    ...
    <p>
      <a href="docs/rules.txt">Click here</a> to read about rules and regulations
    </p>
  </body>
```

After making these modifications, reopen the index page and click the created link. This opens the rules.txt file, as displayed in Figure 10-14.

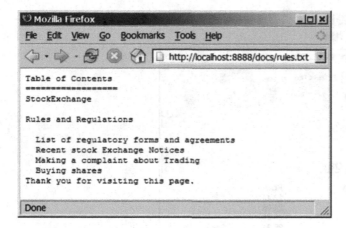

Figure 10-14. *Opening an external Text document*

Including PDF Documents

In Chapter 7, you looked at the construction of a few PDF documents while developing the application for the stock brokerage. One such PDF document listed all orders placed today for a particular stock. Because this PDF file is already created by another application running at the stock brokerage, we will provide a link on our page to directly open this PDF document. We will create a link in our `trades.xml` file. Add the following lines of code in the body element after the closing `table` tag in the `trades.xml` document:

```
...
  </table>
  <p>
      <a href ="AFKOrders.pdf">Click here</a> to see all orders for
              <strong>AFK</strong> stock today.
  </p>
</body>
```

Now, if you reopen the trades page by clicking the Trades tab, you will see the preceding line appear below the trades table. Clicking the displayed link will open the PDF document, as shown in Figure 10-15.

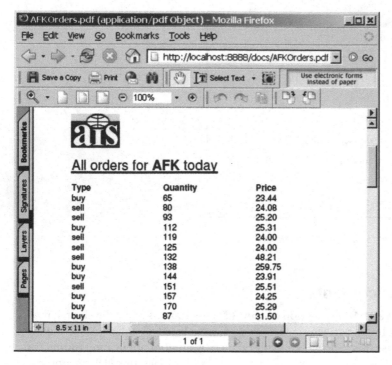

Figure 10-15. *Opening an external PDF*

Further Enhancing the Page's Appearance

Forrest allows you to easily improve the page's looks by providing a few elements such as
note, figure, and icon. The note element inserts a nicely formatted note on the web page.
To see its effect, enclose the previous rules and regulations link on the index page in the
note tag as shown here:

```
<note>
  <a href="docs/rules.txt">Click here</a> to read about rules and regulations
</note>
```

If you now reopen the index page, you will see the screen shown in Figure 10-16.

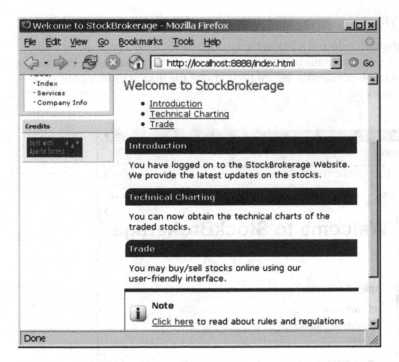

Figure 10-16. *Effect of using a* note *element*

Likewise, you can insert an image or an icon anywhere in your XML document by using the img or icon elements as shown here:

```
<p>
  <img src="docs/myimage.png"/>
</p>
<p>
  <icon height="22" width="26" src="../images/icon.png" alt="feather"/>
</p>
```

The inclusion of the img element results in displaying the image document specified by the src attribute at the current location on the page. The inclusion of the icon element results in displaying the icon specified by the src attribute at the current location.

Rendering Web Page Content

Because Forrest uses Cocoon architecture, it is easy to render the web page content into various output formats, such as PDF, Text, XML, and so on. Forrest uses the Cocoon-provided transformers to transform the page content. Thus, if a new transformer is made available by Cocoon or if you develop your own transformer and a serializer,[5] you will be able to render the web pages of your Forrest site into these new formats.

---

5. Refer to Chapter 7 for a discussion on transformers and serializers in the Cocoon pipeline.

Rendering to PDF

You may have noticed the PDF icon and a link at the top-right side of each page of our brokerage site. Clicking this link transforms the page content into a PDF and opens it in a PDF reader if you have one installed on your machine. Figure 10-17 shows the output produced by clicking the PDF link on the index page.

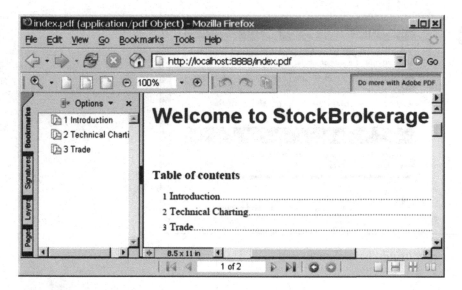

Figure 10-17. *PDF output of the index page*

The presence of this link is controlled by the value of the `disable-pdf-link` element in the `skinconf.xml` document discussed earlier. The default value for this element is set to `false` as shown here:

```
<!-- Disable the PDF link? -->
<disable-pdf-link>false</disable-pdf-link>
```

If you set this value to `true`, the PDF icon will disappear from your web pages.

Adding Support for Other Formats

As mentioned earlier, you can add support for other output formats such as Text, XML and so on. To add support for Text format, set the value of the `disable-txt-link` element to `false` as shown here:

```
<disable-txt-link>false</disable-txt-link>
```

Now, if you reopen the page, you will see a link for the text output next to the PDF link, as shown in Figure 10-18.

Clicking the displayed link produces the output shown in Figure 10-19.

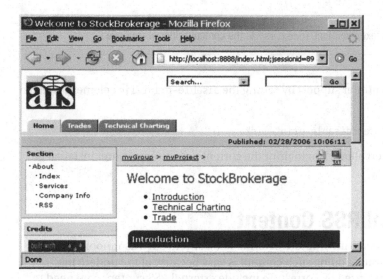

Figure 10-18. *Home page displaying the Text link*

Figure 10-19. *Text output of the index page*

You can enable the XML output by setting the `disable-xml-link` element value to `false` as shown here:

```
<disable-xml-link>false</disable-xml-link>
```

Now you will be able to render the page content in Text format.

> **Note** You must provide the Text document `index.txt` in the content folder of your site.

Similarly, you can add printer support by setting the `disable-print-link` element value to `false` as shown here:

```
<disable-print-link>false</disable-print-link>
```

Enabling printer support allows you to print the current page to any printer installed on your machine.

Adding External RSS Content

Suppose our brokerage wants to incorporate external RSS content such as Yahoo! Stock Markets News on their website. Adding such content is easy because of the underlying Cocoon pipeline architecture used by Forrest. To include external RSS content, you need to add a new `match pattern` element to the Cocoon pipeline defined in the `sitemap.xmap` document of the brokerage site. Add the lines shown in boldface to the `sitemap.xmap` file:

```
  <map:match pattern="**.xml">
   <map:call resource="transform-to-document">
     <map:parameter name="src" value="{project:content.xdocs}{1}.xml" />
   </map:call>
  </map:match>
  <map:match pattern="**news.xml">
    <map:generate src="http://rss.news.yahoo.com/rss/stocks"/>
    <map:serialize type="xml"/>
  </map:match>
 </map:pipeline>
```

The match pattern used is `news.xml`. Thus, if the brokerage site opens a URL that ends with `news.xml`, the RSS feed from Yahoo! will be displayed on the screen. For example, you can try the URL `http://localhost:8888/news.xml` in your browser. The screen output in this case is shown in Figure 10-20.

The pipeline takes the content of the RSS feed as a source and renders it as an XML document on the browser. Note that you could add a transformation in the pipeline to transform the input document into any desired format by adding the `transform` element in the pipeline.

Figure 10-20. *Integrating external RSS content*

Creating Short Names to External Links

When you integrate external content, you need to specify the URI for the external content source on your web page. You can include this URI at several places on your site. If the URI changes in the future, you will need to modify all its occurrences on the site. This can be time-consuming and sometimes unmanageable.

Forrest allows you to create a shorter name for such URIs and use this short name any-where you want on the site. Because the definition of the short name is stored in a centralized place, managing changes to it becomes easy if the URI changes anytime. For example, you can create an external reference called market by adding the following lines of code in your site.xml document:

```
...
<external-refs>
  <market href="http://www.nyse.com/"/>
</external-refs>
</site>
```

You can now use this reference name anywhere on your site page as follows:

```
<a href="ext:market">Click here</a> to visit NYSE site.
```

When the user clicks on the displayed link, the NYSE home page will open. Should the NYSE site change its URL in the future, you would simply need to modify the href attribute value in the market definition.

Deploying the Forrest Site on Other Web Servers

You have created and tested Forrest sites on the provided default Jetty web server. If you prefer to deploy the created site to any other server of your choice, it is a simple task. Simply run the following command from your site folder:

```
{site folder}>forrest site
```

This creates all the required files under the build\site folder of your site folder. After this is done, copy the site folder under the public folder of your web server. Restart the web server if your web server requires it to make the changes visible. Now, open the URL http://localhost:port/<site folder>/build/site/index.html in your browser to see the site.

Summary

In this chapter, you studied one of the important Apache projects that can help you create a website or the documentation for an existing site. This project is called Apache Forrest. Forrest uses several other Apache projects discussed in this book. It is mainly based on Cocoon, which defines a pluggable, easily configurable component architecture for creating static and dynamic web pages and for rendering web page output in several different formats. The Cocoon architecture in turn uses several other Apache XML APIs such as XSLT, parsing, and so on.

This chapter took the approach of using Forrest to create a new website rather than to create documentation for the existing site. You created a new site for the brokerage case study of Chapter 2. Forrest allows the easy creation of a new site that is customized later to suit one's purpose. The customization involves modifications to the XML-based configuration files. To use Forrest, you need not know anything other than XML. You can create fancy sites that are easy to navigate and customize, and you don't need to possess the knowledge of Java programming or HTML coding. The Forrest-created site can be customized for its content, its appearance, and its navigation. You learned the techniques of achieving such customizations in this chapter.

Forrest allows you to include both static and dynamic content on the site. It allows you to link documents in different formats and even take inputs from different sources such as RSS feeds.

Basically, this chapter served the purpose of consolidating the use of several Apache XML projects for real practical use.

APPENDIX A

■ ■ ■

Linux Installations

This appendix provides comprehensive instructions for installing on Linux- and Unix-like operating systems all the software that is required for running applications discussed in the book. The JDK installation is common and is required by all the examples in this book. Thus, it is listed first. Following that section, the installation procedures are listed by chapter for your convenience. Also, any installation instructions presented in earlier chapters are not repeated here.

JDK 1.5.0

You can download the jdk-1_5_0_06-linux-i586.rpm archive from the following URL:

http://java.sun.com/j2se

Double-clicking on this installer guides you through the various steps of installation. These steps are not exhaustive; they simply ask you to accept the license agreement and specify the folder where you would like to install the software.

After installing the software, you need to set the JAVA_HOME environment variable, which you do by using the following command:

export JAVA_HOME=/usr/java/jdk1.5.0

Add the bin folder to your PATH environment variable as follows:

export PATH=$PATH:$JAVA_HOME/bin

Note The environment variables can be set permanently by adding the given commands to the \etc\profile file. To make the changes visible, use the source command.

Chapter 2

You need to install Apache Xerces, XMLBeans, and Ant to run the applications found in Chapter 2.

Apache Xerces

You can download Apache Xerces project code from one of the following URLs:

http://xml.apache.org/xerces2-j/

or

http://archive.apache.org/dist/xml/xerces-j/

    The Apache Xerces project is available in binary and source distribution. You can download the Xerces-J-bin.2.7.1.tar archive and unzip it to the desired folder. After installing software, add the xml-apis.jar file to your classpath as follows:

```
export CLASSPATH=$CLASSPATH:/usr/xerces/xml-apis.jar
```

Apache XMLBeans

You can download Apache XMLBeans project code from the following URL:

http://xmlbeans.apache.org/

    Download the xmlbeans-current.tgz archive and unzip it to the desired folder. Update your environment by using the following commands:

```
export XMLBEANS_HOME=/usr/xmlbeans
export PATH=$PATH:$XMLBEANS_HOME/bin
```

Apache Ant

The Apache Ant project is available in binary and source distribution. You can download the binary distribution from the following URL:

http://ant.apache.org/bindownload.cgi

    Unzip the archive to the desired folder and update your environment as follows:

```
export ANT_HOME=/usr/ant
export PATH=$PATH:$ANT_HOME/bin
```

Chapter 4

Running applications from Chapter 4 requires you to install the Tomcat web server and Apache SOAP toolkit.

Apache Tomcat

You have to download `apache-tomcat-5.5.9.tar.gz` from the following URL:

`http://archive.apache.org/dist/jakarta/tomcat-5/`

Unzip the archive to the desired folder. Set the environment by using the following commands:

```
export CATALINA_HOME=/usr/tomcat
export PATH=$PATH:/$CATALINA_HOME/bin
```

You can run the Tomcat server by using the following command:

```
./startup.sh
```

The command to shut down the server is as follows:

```
./shutdown.sh
```

You can test the Tomcat installation by opening the following URL in the browser:

`http://localhost:8080`

Apache SOAP

You can download the Apache SOAP toolkit from the following URL:

`http://mirrors.isc.org/pub/apache/ws/soap/version-2.3.1/`

Apache SOAP is available in binary and source distribution. If you are using the binary distribution, simply unzip the downloaded archive. Copy the `soap.war` file to the `webapps` folder of the Tomcat installation and restart the Tomcat server if you are running it. Make sure that you have the `mail.jar` and `activation.jar` files in the `shared\lib` folder of the Tomcat installation. Now you can test the installation by opening the following URL in the browser:

`http://localhost:8080/soap`

Chapter 5

Running applications from Chapter 5 requires you to install code for the Apache Xalan project.

Apache Xalan

The Apache Xalan project code is available in binary and source distribution. You can download it from the following URL:

```
http://xalan.apache.org/
```

Unzip the downloaded binary archive to the desired folder. Add the required JAR files to your classpath as follows:

```
export CLASSPATH=$CLASSPATH:/usr/xalan/xalan.jar:/usr/xalan/xsltc.jar
```

Chapter 6

Running examples from this chapter requires you to install the Apache FOP project code.

Apache FOP

The Apache FOP project code is available in binary and source distribution. You can download it from the following URL:

```
http://xmlgraphics.apache.org/fop/download.html
```

Download the `fop-current-bin.tar.gz` archive and unzip it to the desired folder. Add the required JAR file to your classpath as follows:

```
export CLASSPATH=$CLASSPATH:/usr/fop/xml-apis.jar
```

Chapter 7

This chapter requires you to install Cocoon on your machine.

Apache Cocoon

Download the `cocoon-2.1.8-src.tar` archive from the following URL:

```
http://cocoon.apache.org/
```

Unzip the downloaded archive file to the desired folder. You have to build Cocoon to create a WAR file. You can do this by running the `build.sh` file as follows:

```
./build.sh war
```

This will create a `cocoon.war` file in the `\build\cocoon` directory of the Cocoon installation folder. Copy this WAR file to the `webapps` folder of your Tomcat installation and restart Tomcat if it is already running. Test your installation by opening the following URL in the browser:

```
http://localhost:8080/cocoon
```

Chapter 8

Running applications from this chapter requires you to install XML-Security project code on your machine.

Apache XML-Security

Download the distribution archive from the following URL:

```
http://xml.apache.org/security/dist/java-library/
```

Unzip the archive to the desired folder. Modify the classpath by using the following command:

```
export CLASSPATH=$CLASSPATH:/usr/xml-security/libs/xmlsec-1.3.0.jar
```

Chapter 9

Running applications from this chapter requires you to install Apache Xindice project code on your machine.

Apache Xindice

Download the xml-xindice-1.0.tar.gz archive from the following URL:

```
http://xml.apache.org/xindice/download.cgi
```

Unzip the archive to the desired folder. You have to set the XINDICE_HOME environment variable to the Xindice installation folder. You have to add $XINDICE_HOME\bin to your path so that you can use xindice and xindiceadmin commands from anywhere. Modify the environment by using the following commands:

```
export XINDICE_HOME=/usr/xindice
export PATH=$PATH:$XINDICE_HOME/bin
```

You should have the JAVA_HOME variable set to the Java installation folder to run the Xindice server. The classpath has to be modified to include the xindice.jar file:

```
export CLASSPATH=$CLASSPATH:/$XINDICE_HOME/java/lib/xindice.jar
```

You can run the Xindice server by using the following command:

```
cd $XINDICE_HOME
./start
```

Chapter 10

Running applications from this chapter requires you to install Apache Forrest project code on your machine.

Apache Forrest

You can download Apache Forrest code from the following URL:

```
http://www.apache.org
```

Unzip the downloaded `apache-forrest-0.7.tar.gz` file to the desired folder. Create a new environment variable called `FORREST_HOME` and set its value to your installation folder of `Forrest`. Also add `FORREST_HOME` to your path. This can be done as follows:

```
export FORREST_HOME=/usr/forrest
export PATH=$PATH:$FORREST_HOME/bin
```

Index

You Need the Companion eBook

Your purchase of this book entitles you to buy the companion PDF-version eBook for only $10. Take the weightless companion with you anywhere.

We believe this Apress title will prove so indispensable that you'll want to carry it with you everywhere, which is why we are offering the companion eBook (in PDF format) for $10 to customers who purchase this book now. Convenient and fully searchable, the PDF version of any content-rich, page-heavy Apress book makes a valuable addition to your programming library. You can easily find and copy code—or perform examples by quickly toggling between instructions and the application. Even simultaneously tackling a donut, diet soda, and complex code becomes simplified with hands-free eBooks!

Once you purchase your book, getting the $10 companion eBook is simple:

❶ Visit **www.apress.com/promo/tendollars/**.

❷ Complete a basic registration form to receive a randomly generated question about this title.

❸ Answer the question correctly in 60 seconds, and you will receive a promotional code to redeem for the $10.00 eBook.

2560 Ninth Street • Suite 219 • Berkeley, CA 94710

eBookshop

Offer valid through 11/15/2006.